Art, Life and UFOs

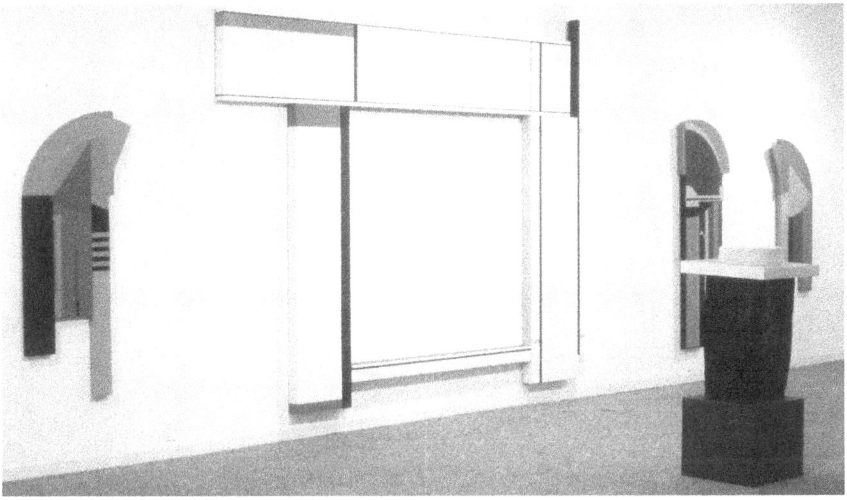

Other books by Budd Hopkins

Sight Unseen: Science, UFO Invisibility and Transgenic Beings
(with Carol Rainey)

Witnessed: The True Story of the Brooklyn Bridge UFO Abductions

Intruders: The Incredible Visitations at Copley Woods

Missing Time: A Documented Study of UFO Abductions

Art, Life and UFOs

By Budd Hopkins

Anomalist Books
San Antonio * New York

An Original Publication of ANOMALIST BOOKS

Art, Life and UFOs

ISBN: 1933665416

Cover: Budd Hopkins, *Guardian*, collage, 1999, 11 3/8" x 4½"
Frontpiece: Budd Hopkins, *Hera's Wall*, installation, 1978, Lerner-Heller Gallery, New York

Book design by Seale Studios

For information, go to anomalistbooks.com or write to:
Anomalist Books, 5150 Broadway #108, San Antonio, TX 78209

Contents

This book is dedicated to the many hundreds of people who have made my life incomparably richer:

To Grace, Andrew, and GiGi, my beautiful new grandchild,

To my fellow artists and especially my life-long companions, Nora Speyer and Sideo Fromboluti,

To David Jacobs, my colleague and irreplaceable friend for so many years,

To Joan Baer, Dan and Judyth Katz, Diana Graves, Robert Bigelow, Phyllis Wender, and the many other loyal and generous supporters of my work,

And finally, to Leslie Kean, a sun whose rays have warmed my life and renewed my hopes.

"When we are young, the words are scattered all around us. As they are assembled by experience, so also are we, sentence by sentence, until the story takes shape."

– Louise Erdrich

"Memory likes to play hide-and-seek, to crawl away. It tends to hold forth, to dress up, often needlessly. Memory contradicts itself; pedant that it is, it will have its way."

– Gunter Grass

"When I was fifteen I loved volumes of letters, intimate journals, books that attempted to make time stand still. I dreaded night and oblivion; it was agony to condemn to silence all that I had seen, felt, and liked."

– Simone de Beauvoir

Part One: Beginnings

Wheeling, West Virginia

IN 1931, THE YEAR I WAS BORN, automobiles were boxy, upright, and graceless, and my father, a Dodge and Plymouth dealer, struggled to sell them, not because of their stodgy appearance but because of the ongoing Great Depression. A new Plymouth, costing up into the high three figures, was an expensive item. We lived in Wheeling, West Virginia, where the lawns were broad, the elm trees shady, and society, under the clueless Hoover administration, happily asleep. Controversy was as distant as Peru. No African-American man, woman, or child, other than a menial employee or servant, ever crossed our threshold. The country club to which my parents belonged was "restricted," a euphemism meaning No Jews Allowed, and almost no one I was to know for the next ten years of my life felt anything but hatred for President and Mrs. Roosevelt. In short, I was born into the antediluvian Middle West.

Looking back, 1931 holds resonance for two major aspects of my life. In Paris, Pablo Picasso, one of my icons, turned 50, fell in love with the pneumatic teenager Marie-Therese Walter, and began a series of voluptuous paintings of her, culminating the next year in one of his greatest masterpieces, *Girl Before A Mirror*. On June 10, five days before I came wailing into the world, Sir Francis Chichester, the famous aviator, sailor, and author, looked out of the cockpit of his Gypsy Moth aircraft and sighted a dull, gray-white UFO, which seemed to play a dangerous game

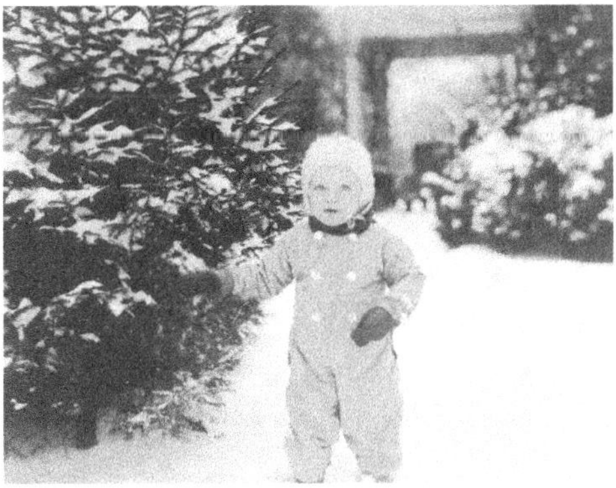

Nearly two years old, I bravely face the snow and all the world.

of hide-and-seek with his tiny plane. At the time, neither he nor anyone else had any idea what this strange craft might be, but 33 years later, to my complete surprise, I saw one myself and began a second avocation.

In 1931, Adolf Hitler was a threatening cloud over Germany, but it would be two more years before he seized power and unleashed his murderous storm. In Wheeling, my apolitical parents listened to Rudy Vallee and Bing Crosby, went to the movies, visited with friends, and lived a quiet, uneventful life, knowing that Europe and Japan were far away and we were safe behind our broad, protective oceans. Up until the morning of December 7th, my father insisted that the Axis powers would never dare attack us. Eventually, World War II would be a galvanizing force in my life as I watched newsreels of panicked refugees and pored over photos of burning tanks and planes in *Life* magazine, always worrying about the fate of my father, then a colonel in the army somewhere in Europe.

The home I was brought to as a newborn infant was a large, comfortable Victorian structure with wooden Ionic columns around its

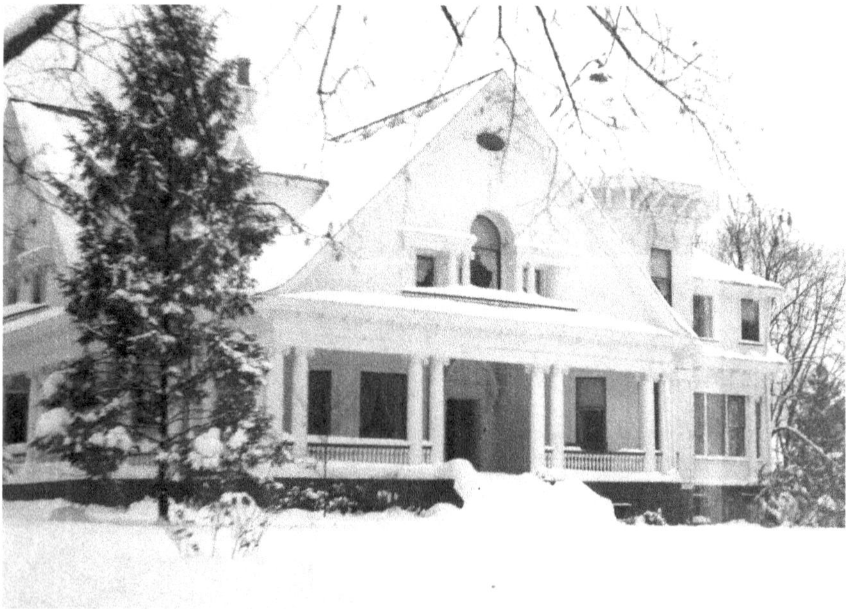

The house where I grew up. Built in 1899, razed in 1968.

wide porch and a grandiose staircase at its center. My tiny, squalling self was the building's fifth resident. I was preceded by my parents, my eight-year-old brother, Stewart, and my mother's mother, whom Stewart had labeled "Danomer," a vaguely humorous mispronunciation of "grandmother" that unfortunately took. I have virtually no surviving memories until my third year, when my right leg was paralyzed by polio and strapped into an inflexible metal brace.

My earliest specific memory is not a happy one. I was about three years old, sitting on the flat platform of a kind of homemade gurney, being wheeled down the back hall of our house. I was unable to walk. At the age of two and a half I had contracted what was then called Infantile Paralysis, and for the next year or two, I had to be carried or wheeled everywhere. The device on which I was being transported was something my father had improvised to solve the problem; it was an old baby carriage from which he had removed the sides and the bonnet, leaving a simple, flat surface on which I could sit or lie to be easily moved from one part of the house to another. At three years of age, with a heavy metal brace adding to my weight, I was evidently an awkward bundle for anyone to carry, and to make matters worse my mother had just given birth to my sister, Ellie. My father, ever the inventor, made this lightweight gurney so that I could be rolled along with my legs – the good one and the useless one – dangling over the side.

Though I don't recall who was pushing me that day, I was being wheeled from the front of the house back towards the kitchen, perhaps for a meal. I remember the distinctive odor of the back hall as I rode along, an aroma that emanated from the furniture polish used on the oak moldings, or perhaps from the thin woolen carpet. It was a permanent and not distasteful odor, sweet and oily, which I associated only with that part of the house. Rolling past the back stairs and the door to the room where our toys were kept, I remember feeling profound humiliation and anger at my helpless state. Everyone could walk but me.

Poliomyelitis was one of the major scourges of society in the 1930s, akin in some ways to the AIDS epidemic of the present. Throughout the country, parents were filled with dread, lest their children be infected by this mysterious, unpredictable, and virtually untreatable disease. Images of iron lungs, crutches, wheelchairs, and worse – dying infants – filled the nightmares of anyone with young children. It was everyone's fear, and it happened to our family one sunny, otherwise normal morning when my mother awakened me. Years later she told me about the horror she felt as I sleepily pulled myself out of bed and toppled over. I could not stand up.

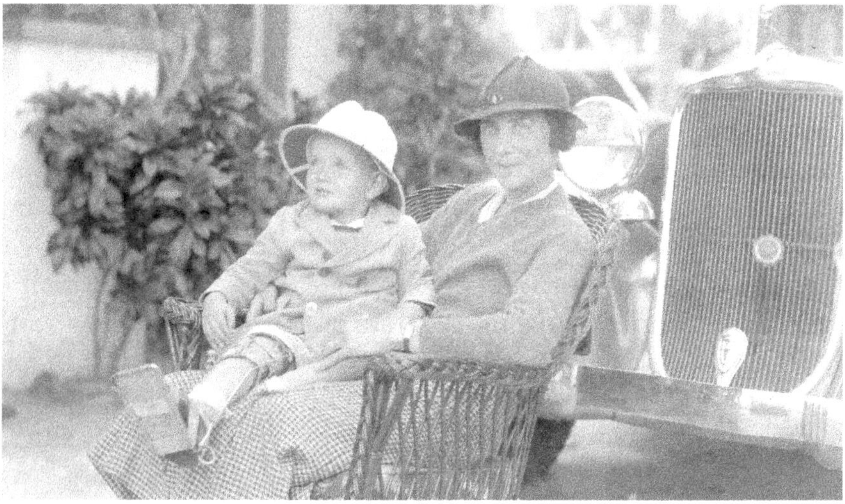

Seated in my mother's lap, my leg in its brace and my head in what looks like a safari helmet. Florida, 1933.

When I first contracted polio, the Board of Health formally quarantined our home. Visits from family friends tapered off, nervous deliverymen deposited groceries at some distance from the house, and my pregnant mother was not allowed in the hospital to give birth lest she contaminate the new babies. Because of this, on September 8, 1933, my sister came into the world at home, in the downstairs bedroom, with a brave but jittery obstetrician presiding at her birth. Ellie – officially Eleanor after my mother, but called "Sister" by just about everybody – completed the family, the third and final child.

My disease set in motion a chain of after-effects, physical, emotional, and psychological, which took a heavy toll. In a very real sense conscious life began for me under the shadow of my disease and its consequences. I grew up overprotected by my perpetually worried mother who at once feared, with reason, that I might die, or at least never walk again. Her anxiety must have communicated itself to me, because for years I felt that I possessed a body so fragile that it could not be relied upon for any sports or other strenuous activities. Yet from this perception of my physical limitations there arose a raft of unexpected benefits. In order to compensate, I began to rely more and more upon the inventive richness of my inner life, if such can be said of the mind of a three- or four-year-old. I exercised my creativity the way other children exercised their arms and legs, learning to use my developing imagination to build a complex and reassuring world around me, an environment which required neither physical mobility nor even the presence of playmates. Put simply, the depredations of polio led me to become an artist.

After about a year my leg brace was finally taken off, and I was forced to undergo a series of what surely must have been innocuous physical therapy sessions. However, to the fearful child I had become, they were a nightmare. In the ominous context of an echoing, medicinal hospital room, I was stripped of my clothes by a pair of bored strangers, thick-waisted nurses who plopped me into a zinc tub of rushing water and ordered me to kick and wiggle my legs. I wept and pleaded to be taken out, a response that naturally strengthened their determination to make me work my weakened limb. It was a battle every time I had to undergo this treatment, and together these sessions comprise one of the most terrifying and humiliating memories from my earliest years. Freud, I'm sure, could have come up with several cogent and fascinating reasons why they were so upsetting.

At the outset of my disease, my parents had taken me to Florida – then a virtual panacea for whatever ailed you – in the hope that voluntarily paddling about in the ocean might return some strength to my stricken leg. Though the Chamber of Commerce shouldn't brag, it was this Florida experience that effectively countered the trauma of my hospital therapy and gave me a new self-confidence. There, under a tropical sun, I could play in the shallows of the warm Atlantic, splashing around while wearing a bathing suit like other self-conscious children. I had a wonderful time. Little by little, the sweet, frothy surf established in me a natural trust of water so powerful that swimming eventually became my favorite sport – the only sport, in fact, in which I ever excelled.

Our first of several trips to Florida occurred in 1933, one of the worst years of the Great Depression, when I was still in my brace and had to be carried everywhere. Money was short, my sister was only a few months old, and under these difficult circumstances my parents moved the entire family, a teenage au pair girl, all of Ellie's baby paraphernalia, and Spot, our huge Great Dane, to a small rented house in West Palm Beach. And here I remember the dawning of what can only be called an incipient esthetic sensation. Our house was a cramped, tacky-looking stucco bungalow, a product of the real-estate boom of a few years before and one of the thousands of similar shoddily-built, one-family structures put up by speculators all over eastern Florida in the hopes of turning a quick profit. In front was a tiny yard, perhaps twenty feet deep, bisected by a cement walk leading down its center to the street and bordered on each side by a row of tropical plants. It was extremely neat and precise, like the yard in front of every other virtually identical stucco bungalow up and down our street. When I wasn't dragging myself around in the ocean or crawling on the sand, my mother would put me down in this sunny space to play with my toy trucks and cars.

I loved the order of my miniature domain, the way all of its boundaries, even the planted ones, were almost knife sharp. In my imagination, everything clearly became roads and walls and fields, and I could maneuver my toys around with utter precision. I formed a strange attachment to these boundaries, to the idea that one thing stopped cleanly, and then something else started. The short, dry, weedy grass of the yard ended abruptly at the hot, rough cement of the sidewalk, and I liked to mark the edge by pushing a little car along the place where the two worlds met. Without knowing why, I grew to dislike areas that were edgeless and unclear. Perhaps I felt safer in ordered places, where I could see the boundaries between everything, but essentially I think I just liked the look of such precision.

John Coplans, one of the *Artforum* editors who in the 1970s commissioned me to write several critical pieces for that famously jargon-ridden magazine, once told me that he liked my writing because "unlike some, you have a need to make everything absolutely clear." It's true. Clarity – the explainer's curse – has been as much a moral imperative in the way I've led my life, as it has been an esthetic necessity. In some way I feel that it originated in that hot little yard in Florida, where I drove my toy trucks around on their neat little roads and could see exactly where each thing ended and the next began.

My polio experience has remained with me ever since, most noticeably in a slight limp which, I am happy to say, was just pronounced enough to keep me out of the army when I had my physical at the end of the Korean war. But when I was a little boy, perhaps eight or ten, I remember opening the door of a rarely-used downstairs closet and seeing, hanging from a high hook, my metal leg brace, ostensibly preserved as a bizarre memento. I assumed my mother kept it there to remind herself of her trauma and my eventual recovery. That closet must have been her grotto at Lourdes, lined not by thousands of crutches and canes and wheelchairs, but with one lone, child's leg brace. Though it hung there for years, I never took it down to examine it more closely. It was familiar enough.

There was to be an odd and touching coda to the story of my experience with polio. In December 1993, my daughter Grace, then twenty years old, was about to fly to Wheeling to spend Christmas with my brother's family. A car service was hired to take her from our New York house to LaGuardia Airport, and the driver picked up a second passenger in another part of the city, a chatty, quite elderly woman. As she and Grace continued on to the airport, they found they were both headed for the USAir terminal, and, coincidentally, were taking the same flight to Pittsburgh. The older woman explained that she was going on from Pittsburgh by car to visit a small city in West Virginia – Wheeling – where she had been born more than 80 years before, though she hadn't lived there for a very long time. "I'm going to Wheeling, too," Grace said to her with genuine surprise. New York is, of course, a gigantic city with a population of millions, and Wheeling is a tiny place with a population of some 40,000, so the odds that both of them would both be heading there seemed astronomical.

Pursuing this coincidence, Grace asked her fellow passenger if, when she had lived there years ago, she had known anyone by the name of Hopkins. "Yes," the woman responded, "as a matter of fact I did. There was a Hopkins family I knew when I was a young girl. They had a little boy who had polio and they were taking him to Florida so that he could swim and try to regain the use of his leg. They hired me to go along with them on that trip to help take care of him."

"That little boy was my Dad," said Grace, stunned by the smallness of the world and the lightning passage of time.

I CAN'T REMEMBER A PERIOD IN MY CHILDHOOD when I wasn't drawing or coloring or making things out of clay or paper or cardboard. These were daily pleasures, and even when I was very little I could work alone by the hour with complete contentment. This creative drive, as I've said, had its source in a need to invent my own private, symbolic world because from my earliest years I'd been neither mobile enough, nor adventurous enough, to deal with the real world outside.

As might be expected, my parents loyally applauded my scrawly efforts, but it was in kindergarten and elementary school that I first remember someone outside the family giving me real encouragement. Along with about ten other children, I attended a small preschool class in the home of a woman named Mrs. Hogue, for whom education was a cottage industry. Each day, Monday through Friday, we entered her house from a high front porch, turned right into a dark, forbidding parlor, and then passed into a pleasantly sunny room furnished with an array of tiny desks and chairs. Just like in a fairy tale, it was as if we'd gone through the wicked witch's den and arrived at the seven dwarfs' cozy little home. When my mother first brought me there at the age of four, I was terrified, but eventually I came to love Mrs. Hogue's art-centered school because we were given paper and paints and allowed to work on our own.

My cloudy memories of this school include a young woman who, I believe, did the actual instruction. I recall nothing about our daily activities over the three years I was there except the painting I was allowed to do. At some point we were shown color photographs of brilliantly-hued tropical fish, and I was instantly mesmerized. I want to say that Mrs. Hogue's school had a real aquarium with real tropical fish, but I'm not sure if that's true. I tend to think that it's because of the vividness of the pictures we were shown that I remember these dazzling fish as being alive and actually swimming around. We were told to copy them with watercolor or poster paint and to make the little creatures big and bold.

My reactions were indelible. Even now, some 70 years later, I can't visit a city that has an aquarium, or pass a pet store on the street, without going in to gaze at the tropical fish tanks. I've snorkeled at Cancun and in the waters off the Florida Keys, and I've visited dozens of aquariums in various countries, yet I'm still utterly captivated by sea creatures of any kind. It's struck me that there are three major areas where nature bestows luscious color with such generosity: onto flowers, tropical fish, and birds, particularly tropical birds. It's as if the simmering heat and moisture in the equatorial air and sea have together forced all the color up to the surface, until the petals, the scales, and the feathers are permeated with gorgeousness. Vivid color aside, tropical birds, fish, and flowers also somewhat resemble one another, even down to their complex silhouettes and modest sizes.

And so at Mrs. Hogue's I looked, and painted, and fell in love with color. The kindly young teacher praised my work and encouraged me, and, as it turned out, I was hooked for life. One day, I remember, she brought sprigs of dogwood into class for us to paint, and I found blossoms almost as seductive and dazzling as tropical fish. But above everything, she confirmed me in my infatuation, telling me that my work was good, that I was talented, and that I should be an artist one day.

Though I had a great deal of freedom to produce childish art on my own, no one told me in those early years about Art with a capital

"A." I had no knowledge – none – of art history until I was nineteen years old and heard for the first time, while at Oberlin College, the names Van Gogh, Cezanne, and Picasso. As a child, I drew the faces of my family – my grandmother in particular, since she was usually more inert than the others – and when the war came, I drew Stukas and Spitfires and Flying Fortresses. I made meticulous pencil copies of the portraits of wartime leaders that appeared on the cover of *Time* magazine, and sent them on V-mail to my father in Europe. I drew and drew, but no one ever told me about Impressionism or the Renaissance; I never heard of Vermeer or Corot, and never visited a museum, until I entered college. And then, as I'll describe later, when I saw Art for the first time, capital-A Art, I fell in love. There is no other word for it. Until that time, I had been entirely on my own, innocent of any idea of "Art" or its great earlier practitioners. As a child, I looked around, seized what I could find, and created completely from within.

The things that interested me were everywhere. In 1940, my father took the family to the New York World's Fair, and the glamour of the modernistic buildings and the beautifully landscaped paths and lakes and grounds was utterly ravishing. I came back to Wheeling, drawing the spirals of the Ford building, the clean, geometrical contours of the Trylon and Perisphere, the ribs and bars of the parachute jump, and the glistening pool and curved stadium at Billy Rose's Aquacade. To make it all as real as possible, I secured a two-square-foot piece of mirror, and with brightly-colored modeling clay, covered it with a miniature version of the Fair. I used thin slabs of green clay to mark out the grassy places, but I left the pond areas bare so that the gleaming mirror stood in for the water. I worked each little building from the photographs and the illustrated programs we'd brought home. Today, I'm certain that some of the lines and curves and points of those late-1930s buildings have reappeared in my later paintings and sculptures. Like the color of tropical fish, it has all stayed somewhere in my head. One of the basic characteristics of art is its power to conserve; no matter how much life is lived by the artist, so little is ever really lost.

The Night of the Martians

I WAS ALONE AS USUAL that evening in late October, when my mother announced that it was time for bed. I don't remember whether initially I'd actually fallen asleep or was just heading that way, but I do recall that over a ten or fifteen minute period the telephone in my parents' bedroom rang several times, an unusual fact in itself. Apart from leaving me wide awake, the calls elicited from them what seemed to be hushed but noticeably nervous conversations.

My hexagonal room was separated from their more conventional space by a connecting bathroom, which served as a kind of hallway. With the doors partly ajar, sound traveled easily and I noticed that after the first phone call my parents switched on their radio. The next thing I sensed was alarming: my mother was crying and I could tell by her whispered speech that she was very frightened. Dad's voice in response was firm and reassuring, but with an edge of forced certainty.

Like most children dependent on their parents' changeable moods, I was acutely sensitive to any disturbing variations, no matter how subtle, in the way they spoke. As I lay in bed in my darkened room, I felt that whatever was upsetting my mother was also affecting my dad; he sounded as if he was uneasy, too, but was trying by sheer tone of voice to make the scary thing go away.

As my mother's crying became more audible, I heard broken snatches of words implying that some kind of horrible catastrophe was about to overtake us all. Now it was my turn to be terrified, and for a moment I pulled the covers over my head. "It's only a radio program," my father was saying rather loudly, turning the dial from station to station. "See, there's nothing about it on other programs." This observation had no effect on my mother. "They just haven't heard about it yet," she wailed. "We're all going to be killed." I heard her use the word "Martians."

"There's nothing out the window," Dad said. "Everything looks normal. It's just a radio program." The phone rang again, but when he spoke to the caller, he made no attempt to keep his voice down. "No, we'll wait and see. I'll call you back if we plan to do anything." He hung up and told my mother that he was going to go into my room to see if he could see anything unusual out of my windows, which faced in a different direction. As his assurances about our safety grew more tentative, I became even more petrified. I had no idea what was going on, but I heard my mother say something, between sobs, about the world coming to an end.

"What's happening?" I asked my father in a small, quavering voice when he came into the room. "Are we going to die?" My mother was only a step behind him, and when she heard my questions, she resumed her despondent crying. She knelt down beside my bed and hugged me, pressing her face to mine so that our tears mingled. Dad was at the window looking up into the night sky, peering quickly around as if he were about to see something unspeakable. "There's nothing to it," he said once more with barely a trace of certainty. "It's only a radio program." My mother, for a moment relieved that he hadn't spotted anything, managed to ask him who had just phoned.

"It was Buck," he said, naming one of his employees. "He told me he was putting his wife and kids in the car and loading it with rifles and a box of ammunition and some food and water and heading up to the top of Bethlehem Hill to make a stand. He wanted us to go with him. I told him I wouldn't do it yet, that I would wait and see what happens, because I don't think there's anything to it." Dad's answer fueled more tears and another outburst, this time from my mother and me in tandem.

He switched on my brother's little radio and tuned in the program that was causing Mom's terror. A tense, official-sounding voice was communicating with the pilot of an army bomber approaching the landed enemy. I've since listened to a tape of the original program, and it goes something like this: "8XCR calling. Where are you?" The pilot gives his position and reports a green flash from the enemy ships. Then, with panic in his voice, he says that his engines are failing. This brings an immediate response: "8XCR calling! 8XCR calling! What's the matter? Where are you?" A long period of silence follows, something that never happened on regular radio programs. I read it as death.

Another voice came on the air, stating that the Martians are invading northeastern New Jersey. They came to Earth in rocket ships and are now moving towards New York City. Many people are dying. At one point the announcer loses contact with some policemen at the scene; evidently the Martians killed them while they were trying to relay what was happening. It was utterly real.

My mother then went to my father, wrapping her arms around him and leaning her head against his shoulder. While the radio passed on the latest details of the invasion, Dad gazed over her toward the window, scanning the skies, awaiting the first ominous warning signs.

I had never seen my father afraid before. I knew that as a young man he had been in the World War and apparently never suffered fear. He seemed always calm in the face of danger, a rock of stability and protection for us all. I was, however, used to seeing my mother frightened by many trivial things, so her panic this time – and that is the only term for what she was feeling – was not nearly as unusual to me as Dad's disturbing lack of certainty.

I wept and shivered and buried myself under the covers and tried to listen to the radio announcer. I had to know how much time was left before the world ended. But in truth, the end of the world was a kind of abstraction. Martians meant nothing to my seven-year-old mind, and the only sort of invasion I'd heard about was the Japanese attack on China. For me, it was far more terrifying to see both of my parents frightened: my mother in tears and my father appearing to be so helpless and uncertain. When my mother came over to comfort me, Dad continued to pace from window to window, staring up into the star-filled sky and insisting – weakly – that we shouldn't worry; everything would be fine.

Describing the mounting carnage and panic in New York City, the announcer said, "This is 2X29 calling State HQ, New York." With growing tension he repeated it once, twice, with no response.

"State HQ, New York – is there anyone on the air?" Another disturbingly long silence followed. "Is there anyone on the air?" Another, even longer pause. Then one final time: "Is there anyone… on the air?"

A horrifying period of silence ensued, which could only mean the death of practically everybody. Then, suddenly, there was an announcement that the program would resume after a commercial. There was an ad, a concluding monologue, and it was over. It had been just a radio play after all. A *play*, a kind of trick, had brought almost unbearable fear into our lives. It had sounded so real. How could I, or my mother, or even my dad have known that it was only make-believe?

At last he was smiling and hugging my mother. She was no longer crying, but she still clung to him. Things were returning to… something, but it surely wasn't to normal. I thought for a moment of Mr. Buck heading up to the top of Bethlehem Hill with his car full of guns and terrified people, and wondered if he knew now that it was all right to come back home. As Dad wiped away a nervous tear, he cursed Orson Welles, the man who, he said, wrote the radio play. I lay back absolutely overcome with relief.

Since all childhood traumas leave psychic scars, Welles' radio program marked me in several ways. I learned the sad but valuable truth that, like my mother, my father was also capable of experiencing fear. Like me, he also dreaded the idea of the end of the world, the end of life. And it was also obvious that he didn't necessarily know what to do in such a dire emergency to protect his family.

Unlike my father, Mr. Buck took action. He packed his undoubtedly weeping wife and children into his car and headed for the hills, as if he believed that movement alone, no matter how foolish and precipitous, could delay the inevitable. Dad, by contrast, waited, fretted, denied what he was hearing, and nervously scanned the heavens. And yet in the end he surely felt less foolish than Mr. Buck. He had never given up the hopeful, rational idea that maybe – just maybe – this was not the end of the world.

I wish I could say that the *War of the Worlds* broadcast brought our family closer together; it didn't. Instead, I was left with the hard truth that the comfort we offered one another that night was not nearly enough to overcome the individual fright we each felt deep within the recesses of our separate and inviolable skulls.

WHEN I FIRST BEGAN TO WRITE about my 1938 experience with Orson Welles' infamous broadcast, I thought about any possible connection it may have with my research into the UFO phenomenon some 36 years later. The conclusions I came to about any cause and effect relationship are very clear.

Orson Welles' *War of the Worlds* broadcast, reduced to its essence, was a dramatic, theatrical *hoax*. A *fake*. Though undeniably powerful as a radio play, it was more important as an unprecedented assault on our cultural tranquility. Welles postponed commercial breaks during the broadcast and allowed an extraordinary amount of dead airtime in order to heighten the illusion that, rather than a play, what we were hearing was an improvised and very real emergency broadcast. I was only a child at the time, but when the program was over, I saw it as a devilish stunt that had deeply upset my parents and me, and so was eager to put it out of my mind.

Though I eventually became a devourer of newspapers, I have no memory of having read, nine years after the broadcast, anything about the beginning of the modern "flying saucer" wave in America. When the coverage began in the summer of 1947, I was too busy driving around Wheeling and chasing girls to pay attention, and by the fall of 1948 I was suffering at Lawrenceville, well away from daily papers. During my four years at Oberlin College (1949-1953), I was far too engrossed in art, more girls, and the struggle to graduate to have noticed such things as UFO reports, either. But the central reason I ignored whatever slivers of flying saucer information I might have been exposed to was this: I regarded such reports as nothing more than modern-day hoaxes, like the one that had scared me so badly as a child.

In 1947 I was not alone in my view that the hundreds of UFO accounts covered by the media, and the many reports that were officially made to the Air Force, were nothing more than clever, deceptive pranks like *The War of the Worlds*. At the end of 1947, a poll was conducted about the nature of the UFO wave, asking the public what they thought lay behind these bizarre accounts. The vast majority of respondents thought that flying saucers were either American or Russian experimental aircraft, misidentifications of natural phenomena, hoaxes, or unusual meteorological conditions. *Less than one percent thought that UFOs might be of extraterrestrial origin!* So instead of establishing the public acceptance of the UFO phenomenon as objectively real, Orson Welles' program led to exactly the opposite: *incredulity* and automatic dismissal. After all, no one wanted to be taken in twice.

In 1952, I was completely unaware of the widely reported series of radar-visual UFO sightings over Washington, D.C., though these dramatic flyovers in proscribed airspace were front-page news in virtually all the newspapers in America. In July, when these events were taking place and the Air Force was holding its most widely-attended press conference since World War II, I was in Europe, a young art student, traveling with my family and trying to locate every Mondrian, Vermeer, and Caravaggio I could find. The UFO reports of that historically important summer passed me by, and, in fact, it would not be until twelve years later, when I and two others had our daylight UFO sighting on Cape Cod, that the phenomenon first entered my consciousness. And now, 70 years after the infamous broadcast, UFO sighting reports have still not escaped from the suspicions engendered by Orson Welles' radio play. Until my experience in 1964, I was an illustration of that same knee-jerk rejection: until I saw one myself, UFOs were no more real to me than the fake Martian spaceships in *The War of the Worlds*. Like most Americans, Doctor Orson Welles had inoculated me against the disease of taking UFO reports seriously.

Washington, D.C., and the Coming War

My tenth birthday, June 15, 1941, was an important day in my life. I had no way of knowing it at the time, but this was to be my final birthday in the normal, peacetime childhood I had come to expect and understand. My father, who had fought in World War I and was now 52, had remained in the reserve army, spending two weeks every summer on active duty. By 1941 he had risen to the rank of full colonel, and as the war in Europe raged and President Roosevelt stepped up his re-armament program, Dad applied for full-time military service. It was not that he expected we would become involved in war – he insisted that would not happen – it was, I think, that he truly enjoyed army life and the deferential treatment a full colonel naturally received.

After writing a series of letters to the proper authorities, he was finally called up in the spring of 1941. Apparently anyone with command experience from World War I, 23 years earlier, was needed. So, by my birthday that year, Dad was already in uniform and was stationed in Washington, D.C.; after two years with the family in Memphis, he would not be home to live in Wheeling with us for nearly two more years. My brother, Stewart, would go off to school at Lawrenceville in September and a year and a half later would enlist in the army. We would see virtually nothing of him, either, until the war was over. Hovering over all of our personal concerns that summer was the massive specter of an impending war, a war that finally erupted at Pearl Harbor six months after my father went on active duty.

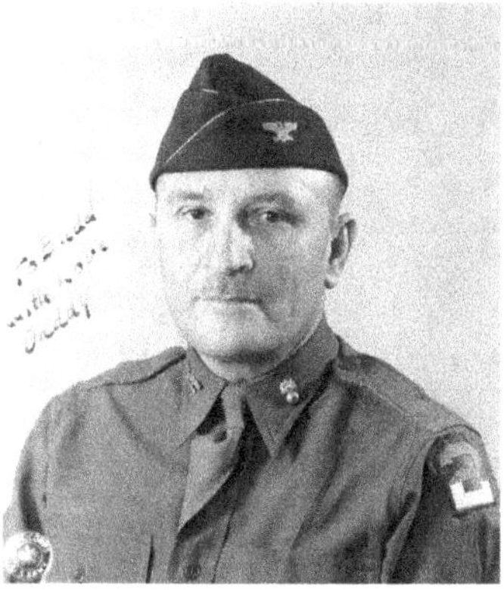

My father in the uniform he wore from the spring of 1941 until November 1945.

The tenth birthday party my mother organized for me back in Wheeling was a large one. Many children were herded together, and most of them, as I remember, were wearing white. It was a warm June afternoon and we were playing outside when one of those meaningless altercations developed between me and a little boy I didn't know very well. He was a year or so younger than I and had been invited largely because my mother and father were friendly with his parents. I have no idea now what caused our argument – perhaps a fight over who got to man the heavy German machine gun my father had smuggled home after World War I – but it soon escalated into a yelling and shoving match. The yelling definitely outdid the shoving; for the truth was that I was a cowardly child, afraid of things physical, and loath to get into an actual fight with anyone. I suppose my years of illness as well as my parents' chronic over-protectiveness had convinced me that I wouldn't do well in manly combat, so I generally slunk away from all confrontations. (The only exception, the only other child whom I bravely faced down and occasionally even attacked, was Ellie, my little sister.)

My mother and a second adult broke up the shoving match before it went very far, so I don't remember any actual blows being exchanged. Before it ended, however, both the other boy and I were angry, scared, and crying, and, to make things worse, there was a circle of children gawking at us as the women pulled us apart. The event stayed with me for years as a powerful and humiliating memory, partly because I had been too afraid of the other boy – someone actually smaller than I – to try to hit him.

A few weeks after my birthday, my mother, my sister, and I went to Washington, D.C., to visit Dad. In the first hectic months of the rearmament period, the capital was a madhouse. Military personnel and civilian officials were being summoned to the center of power from everywhere, but there were not enough places for all of these people to live. The housing shortage in the District of Columbia was so acute that anyone who had an extra bedroom in his house or apartment was urged to rent it. Luckily for us, Dad had somehow been able to reserve a hotel room for our three-day visit, but a few weeks before we arrived he had located and immediately sublet a bedroom for himself in the apartment of a young, newly married army officer. This landlord of Dad's was, I believe, a mere lieutenant, so he and his wife were both thrilled and intimidated at having a full colonel, a veteran of the First World War, as a tenant. They generously granted my father kitchen privileges, which included space in their small refrigerator and use of the stove and other appliances. So, despite these rather cramped living conditions and the lack of privacy for all three, Dad was quite comfortable.

These circumstances were to lead to a painful incident that was, unfortunately, the harbinger of a great deal of sadness yet to come. After my mother, my sister, and I arrived at our hotel, Dad's landlords, the young lieutenant and his wife, invited us to their apartment for drinks in the afternoon. It was an act of generosity on their part, and I'm certain they were tense about the idea of entertaining a full colonel and his family. Mindless social ceremonies such as this are far more important within the military – particularly during peacetime – than civilians may imagine.

We arrived about five o'clock, and after introductions, the young couple handed round drinks and plates of the hors d'oeuvres they'd carefully prepared. At first, conversation was rather stiff, with many formal "sirs" and "ma'ams" on their part, but time was passing pleasantly enough. Obviously, they were a friendly, attractive pair, and I knew that my parents were enjoying their company. At some point my mother alluded to the fact that I had recently turned ten, and a moment later I heard my father mention my birthday party. It was with a clear sense of paternal pride that he began to tell the young officer and his wife about my "fight" with the other little boy. I was horrified. Dad had not been there and could only have heard about it from my mother, but now the story was coming out differently. It was being embellished and the new version was violent. He went on about how I "stood up for my rights," and then, with a proud smile, said, "Budd really beat him up, the little Jew. He was asking for it, but Budd really beat him up."

I wanted to crawl under the table, not because of Dad's anti-Semitic remark, which I did not then understand, but because I knew he was trying to praise me and was not telling the truth. I hadn't beaten the boy; in fact, I'd been too afraid even to hit him. It hadn't happened the way Dad pretended it had. But before I could say anything, I noticed my mother's agitated expression, and then, suddenly, the same look of profound embarrassment on my father's face. He stood up in confusion, saying that it was time to leave, and almost helplessly repeated his last sentence: "Yes, he really beat him up, the little Jew." We said our hurried goodbyes, rushed out into the hallway, and the door closed behind us.

Before I could say anything to Dad, to deny the fight had happened that way, my mother was speaking to him in a strained and urgent whisper. "How could you say that?" she asked, as we hurried down the hall. "Didn't you know they were Jewish?"

My father was red-faced and seemed absolutely stupefied. "I knew, I knew, but I guess I forgot," he answered. I had never seen him so embarrassed, so bewildered, so obviously ashamed, but I didn't understand what they were talking about. All I knew was that Dad had made up a story about me to make me seem tougher, and it wasn't true. His tale had hurt me two ways: first, because he had told an untruth, and second, because it reminded me of my cowardice and the fact that my father wanted me to be different than I was – or ever could be. It would be several years before I understood the anti-Semitic meaning of his remarks, and was retroactively hurt in a third way, in what was the first memory I have of my father's intense bigotry.

For America, World War II began, of course, on December 7, 1941, with the Japanese bombing of the Pacific Fleet at Pearl Harbor, and I vividly remember my shock and disbelief. The next day my mother, my grandmother, my sister, and I gathered around the little radio that had been brought into the dining room, and together we listened to President Roosevelt's eloquent speech in which he announced that a state of war existed between the United States of America and the Empire of Japan. Not the least of my shock was the fact that my father had been so wrong about such an important matter, and that his future, as well as ours, was now so uncertain.

Things changed quickly. In the fall of 1942 Dad was transferred from Washington to Second Army Headquarters in Memphis, Tennessee, where his superiors had told him that he would be stationed for at least a year or so. As soon as he arrived, he began planning to move the family south so that we could remain together until the ominous moment when he would be sent overseas to join the battle. After scouting the Memphis real estate market, he rented a large, comfortable four-bedroom stone house, located, appropriately, on Stonewall Street, a residential area a few miles from the city's main business district and not far from a large junior high school. The house, probably built in the 1920s, had a wide front porch that faced a small, neatly kept yard. A *porte-cochere* was the only distinctive aspect of its plainspoken façade – a far cry from our ornate Victorian house in Wheeling.

We moved to Memphis en masse sometime in the late fall of 1942, a pack of West Virginia Oakies caught up in the swirling currents of a nation newly at war. I was eleven years old and in the seventh grade in Woodsdale, a public school in Wheeling, when our suddenly uprooted family left for the long drive south. We traveled, as I recall, in two cars. There were my parents, my sister, my grandmother, and Sally, our very large, fawn-colored Great Dane, along with piles of luggage. I don't remember much about the trip itself – only the powerful, mixed feelings of adventure and uneasiness at the prospect of a new life in a new place, and the dread of an unfamiliar school where I had no friends. As it turned out, I was right to be concerned.

We lived in Memphis during the war years from 1942 to the spring of 1944, when my father went overseas and the family returned to Wheeling. But while we were there, Memphis was a roiling inland sea of military activity, and uniforms were everywhere. Thousands of young trainees were passing through, on leave or on their way to new assignments, while thousands of others were stationed at various local army and navy bases, including the headquarters of the Second Army, the unit to which my father was attached.

Thoughts of war dominated everything, and for me, at the age of eleven, it was all endlessly glamorous. Every day I saw Dad impressively turned out in full uniform, his fierce colonel's eagles pinned to his tunic and his officer's cap firmly in place, seemingly invulnerable to any gunfire he might face. I had no concept of death, of course, and my view of warfare was largely shaped by the movies that Hollywood churned out to motivate the troops and mobilize the home front. I saw them all, and it was reassuring to know that the main good guys, like John Wayne and Errol Flynn, never got killed. Wounded maybe, usually in the arm or the shoulder, but they always managed to survive. By that token, Dad would be okay, too, because only the dirty Nazis or the dirty Japs always seemed to get it, often right between the eyes.

Apart from the excitement of wartime, my first year in Memphis was emotionally difficult. I knew no one, and the school I went to, Snowden, was a huge, impersonal junior high filled with boisterous kids who thought my Yankee accent was a hoot and told me so. Under the circumstances, it was not easy to make friends, but since I was already pretty much of a loner, I was used to it. Anyway, playing alone had usually been more fun than playing with other children, so I managed to get along.

Toy Guns and a Real Bomber

CENTRAL TO MY PLEASURES during the Memphis years were the solitary war games and elaborate battle scenarios I invented for my toy soldiers, a midget army and navy set up on the floor of a sunroom next to my bedroom. My forces included nearly a hundred soldiers, accumulated over the years, as well as tanks and artillery pieces, an entire fleet of Tootsietoy warships – destroyers, aircraft carriers and the like – and, of course, a small air force. But since these military toys came in a variety of sizes, the consequent scale disparity created a major problem. How could a jeep drive up next to a fighter plane only half its size? How could a miniature battleship be manned by a crew of toy sailors who towered over it?

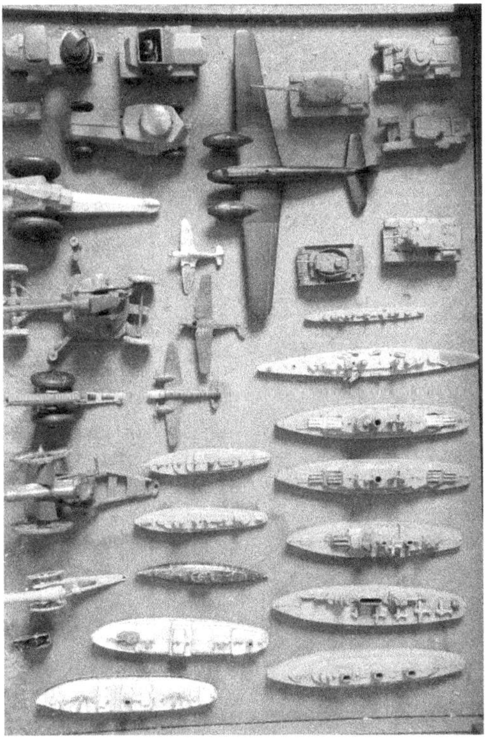

Though my play was childishly imaginative, derived as it was from movies and comic books, I was still old enough for esthetic logic to demand satisfaction. Therefore I was forced to segregate my toys into various groups of similar scale: the Tootsietoy ships together, the tanks and armored vehicles clustered elsewhere, the airplanes in yet another group, and so on. But some of the happier solu-

An aerial view of my battleships, tanks, and artillery. Photo: Charles Miller.

tions to the problem of harmonious scale were strictly homemade. One of these came about because of my father's purchase of a case of Scotch whiskey. Though he was a Bourbon drinker, he must have bought the Scotch for his military and civilian guests. The brand in question, White Horse, came with each bottle cradled in its own two-part cardboard container. This unusual British packaging was stiff and white, about an eighth of an inch thick and produced in a mold rather like very heavy hand-made paper. To my eye, the shape and silhouette of each discarded and up-ended container-top suggested a tank or armored personnel carrier. With a gun-slit here and a rear door there – easily cut into the soft cardboard – I soon had a fleet of vehicles, each of which held a three-man toy-soldier crew plus a small cannon, all consistent in size and scale.

The cast of my midget war was absolutely fixed. There were Nazis and Americans only – no Japanese or British or Russians or Italians – and most of the characters had names. The main Nazi, an evil, sadistic officer, was "Erik Von Streicher." I made him a colonel for two reasons: first, since Dad was a colonel, I felt I understood the power of that position better than others, and second, I liked saying "Oberst," the German name for that rank. One of the most common things my Nazi soldiers said was, "Ja, Herr Oberst," a bit of dialogue I'd remembered from a war film I'd seen at the Malco movie palace. Also about that time, I'd read and memorized a list of the German Army officer titles, so the dialogue often ran to "Ja, Herr Hauptman, Sieg Heil!" or "Ja, Herr Oberleuntnant." I don't remember that any of my German soldiers ever said "Nein" to anyone, because even at that age I had an intuitive sense of the nature of Nazism.

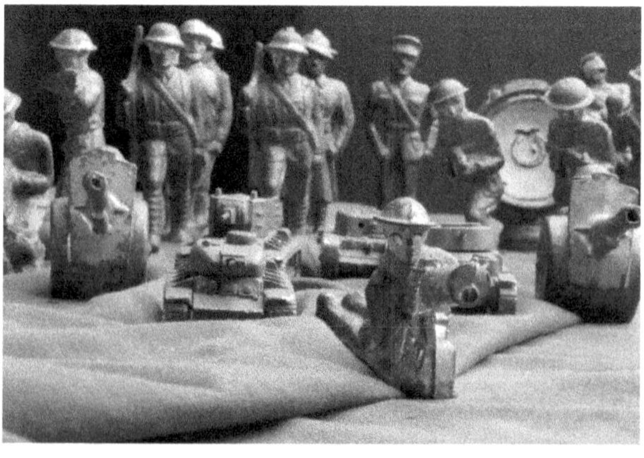

My embattled American troops in disarray. Photo: Charles Miller.

My American toy soldiers all had names, too, but most of them were first names. Unlike the Nazis, our side was informal, relaxed, and always the underdog. There was, for example, Geronimo, an Indian, and Joe, the tough guy, and Mac and Captain Davis and all the rest, a heterogeneous group whose names I'd partly adopted from the many bomber-crew movies I'd seen. In these quintessential propaganda films, the crew of a Flying Fortress would be made up of men from a range of stereotypical backgrounds who bickered and teased and argued ominously until they were over Hamburg; then they functioned as a marvelously efficient team, loyal to the death to one another and devastating in their effect on the targets below. An actor like Van Johnson, his battered officer's cap rakishly askew, would play the pilot, a breezy, moral man from the Midwest. He was, naturally, a Baptist who was good at defusing his crew's ongoing disagreements with simple homilies. His name would be something like "Joe Davis," while the bombardier, a Jewish officer of serious intellectual mien and great hatred for the Nazis, would be called "Specs" by crewmembers who never understood why he was always reading some book or other. The tail gunner, "Brooklyn," (John Garfield?) would be a kid of Italian parentage who always bragged about his mother's cooking and the great lasagna she served. His wise-guy way of talking usually got him into near fights with "Biff," the slightly dense but much bigger radioman who had been a high school football star. Or so these movies went.

In the subplot, a B-list actor like Don Defore or Gig Young would play the vaguer part of co-pilot. In order to keep the ethnic and religious balance, this flier would be a devout Catholic, and his role mainly involved talking to Van Johnson late at night about Elizabeth, his fiancée back home, and showing him her photograph. "If anything ever happens to me," he would say, "promise me you'll give her this." "This" was a lucky piece, a St. Christopher's medal or a Crucifix or something the co-pilot wore on a chain around his neck, and even as a kid I immediately knew he was the one who was going to get killed.

It was from this kind of heady filmic brew that I took my cues and lifted dialogue when I played with my toy soldiers. And as must be clear by now, these war scenarios were not silent. Far from it, they were filled with dialogue, the sounds of bombs falling, cannons firing, and the cries of the wounded, all produced by an eleven-year-old's uncertain vocal mimicry. Members of my family were alarmed from time to time when suddenly they heard through the closed bedroom door lines like, "Take that, you dirty Nazi!" followed by a ghastly scream and the sound of an explosion so loud as to wrench my uvula and sprain the soft palate. I could also produce realistic sirens, decent machine-gun fire, and an effective dive-bomber. The range of sounds naturally included periodic guttural "Heil Hitlers" and nervous Commando whispers as Mac, Geronimo, and Captain Davis sneaked up on the vile Von Streicher and his unsuspecting bodyguards.

The German I spoke mimicked the actors in the war movies I was devouring: "Ve vill conquer all uf Europe," Von Streicher might say to a pair of GI prisoners, adding a furious "Heil Hitler!" The Americans, though frequently captured and often tortured, always escaped, inevitably leaving a trail of dead Nazis behind. My plays went on and on for hours, their complex plots sometimes interrupted for dinner, but when I returned, I was always able to pick things up where they had been left, and once more the disgusting Von Streicher was in for it.

The toy soldier I used for the Oberst was a striding officer who had originally been wearing a shiny, World War I type of helmet fastened to his hollow head by a little internal clip. I had removed the helmet and fashioned a Nazi officers' cap, complete with insignia, from modeling clay. Though it was a tad large for his tiny head, to me the effect was powerful. Von Streicher *looked* cruel. Most of the other German soldiers were formed of a group of identical marching men loaded with equipment. On the other hand, the Americans were truly a motley bunch. Geronimo, for example, was not in uniform. He was a solid iron figure of a wild Indian in loincloth and full war bonnet. (In the pre-war years, some of the toy "soldiers" people gave me were actually cowboys and Indians, doctors and nurses, policemen and so on, but all of them found roles in my miniature wartime plays, as spies or saboteurs or FBI agents or what-not.) Somehow, it seemed fitting to have the embattled Americans – and we really were embattled in 1942 – appear as a collection of miscellaneous patriots, fighting the fanatic, organized, machine-like Nazis. That was, after all, pretty much the way our movies and our propaganda presented it. It was also largely true. So for me, Geronimo in his war bonnet fitted right in, manning the cannon next to Captain Davis as they charged the enemy in their armored White Horse Whiskey personnel carrier.

If it was fun playing up in the sunroom, it was the very best during warm weather when I could take Von Streicher and Captain Davis and all the Commandos and Nazis outside. In the front yard there was a huge oak tree whose thick roots had created a series of hollows and bulges around its trunk. There, in these deep valleys and atop the massive cliffs expertly camouflaged by grass and leaves, the GIs fought their battles against the Germans. Von Streicher's headquarters was always neat and orderly, until the Commandos in their cardboard attack vehicles struck without warning and the carnage commenced. Because of the neighbors, I had to hold back a bit on my usual vocal pyrotechnics – the machine-gun fire and the exploding shells – but the war was loud and violent nevertheless. I can still feel the excitement of setting up hidden gun emplacements beneath the fallen twigs and placing German sentries in exposed places where the Americans could easily pick them off. I crouched over my armies with the thrill of a real participant, a general, a GI, a Nazi – I was simultaneously all of them. I knew the limitations of armament, of position, and of military intelligence on each side, and from my controlling position as grand puppeteer, I knew everything that was fated to take place. It was truly heady stuff. And in the early autumn, the faint, musty odors of drying grass and crumbling, fallen leaves were as much a part of the texture of battle as the soldiers and tanks. Kneeling on the ground in my corduroy knickers, I felt the chill of the October breeze on my cheeks and the welcome late sunshine warming my back. Nothing diminished the excitement in front of me because, in the wild miniature landscape spread all around the yard, the battle raged and the Americans always won.

ANOTHER SPECIAL INTEREST OF MINE in that first year of the war was military aircraft, especially fighter planes like the Spitfire, the Mustang, and the Messerschmitt Me-109, which held for me a kind of lethal allure. I sketched them obsessively from photographs and drawings, but I also knew most of the world's warplanes by name and description, thanks to a small, well-indexed paperback book, the *Aeronautics Aircraft Spotters' Handbook*. Published by an organization called the National Aeronautics Council and edited by a mere ensign, I had no idea whether or not the spotter's guide was an official government publication, though I hoped it was. What I did know was that it had all the world's military aircraft methodically arranged by number of engines and position of wings, and that each plane was illustrated by a photograph and three silhouette drawings: front, side, and bottom views. At school and in the playground near my house I always kept the book by my side, hoping that its presence would lend me, in the eyes of my usually unfriendly classmates, the status of a semi-official military spotter. In the meantime I tried to memorize as many of the enemy silhouettes as possible, so that I would be prepared to sound the warning if one day a Junkers Ju-86 or a Mitsubishi OB-96 sneaked into the airspace over Memphis, Tennessee.

In addition to this handbook, I had yet another major source of information about warplanes, theirs and ours. Once a month there appeared on the newsstand a comic-book-style magazine entitled *Wings*. Each issue had several regular features: a continuing, adventure-type comic-strip about a heroic American fighter pilot; a section devoted to drawings and data about warplanes, including top speed, armament, etc. – things every boy needed to know; and re-creations of recent battles in the ongoing air wars in Europe and the Pacific. Fleets of outgunned Nazi and "Jap" aircraft went down in flames each month in the pages of *Wings*, victims of the unbeatable combination of Allied courage and our ostensibly faster, more powerful fighting machines.

A minor but very interesting brouhaha developed one day around a particular issue of the magazine. During dinner one evening, I told my father what I had just read about a new secret weapon developed by the British. *Wings* had presented a full and accurate account of the way RADAR worked, complete with drawings and diagrams. Dad had never heard of RADAR and looked upon *Wings* as a mere comic book, and therefore discounted my news with an air of condescension. However, it turned out that the detection system not only existed but at the time was still an officially classified military secret. Somehow an Air Corps officer, moonlighting as an adviser to *Wings*, assumed that information about RADAR was in the public domain – it very nearly was – so he unthinkingly handed to the publication's staff a simplified but faithful account of how it worked.

An article about this awkward comic-book breach of security appeared in newspapers shortly afterward, and, I'm almost certain, in *Time* magazine. With an air of smug satisfaction, I showed the articles to my shocked and incredulous father. I, a mere twelve-year-old civilian who carried around a semi-official spotter's guide, actually knew a military secret that my much older father, a full colonel, hadn't known. For a child my age, it was hard ever to be seen as a serious person, so the *Wings* article gave me a spurious but very temporary sense of adulthood. It made me happy for at least a week.

In 1943 the B-25 was one of my favorite warplanes. It was a twin-engine attack bomber made by North American, and it had become world famous because Jimmy Doolittle had used it for his daring, morale-building 1942 raid on Tokyo. A group of B-25 medium bombers had taken off from the reinforced deck of a specially prepared aircraft carrier on a virtual suicide attack against the Japanese homeland. Though they did little damage, they gave a tremendous boost to American self-esteem and helped to avenge the vast humiliation of Pearl Harbor.

But there were other reasons why I admired the B-25. Basically I liked its design, its clean, straightforward, undramatic lines. It looked very American. By contrast, the appearance of the German *Stuka* dive bomber, with its bent wings and voracious shark's-snout front, seemed to me positively depraved. It was a bit like the contrast between the comfortable, easy lines of our GI khaki fatigues and the cold field gray of the Germans' uniforms, the arrogant rake of their officers' caps, and the robotic brutality of their steel helmets. I believed that our side not only possessed basic virtue and moral right, but that in some almost mystical way our military uniforms and equipment demonstrated their appearance.

In 1943 Memphis was a hub of air activity. The municipal airport was host to an Air Transport Command wing, and at the nearby town of Millington there was a Naval Air Station. Military aircraft were constantly flying over the area, and I, as an alert spotter, was constantly looking up in case that one stray Focke-Wulf might slip in and strafe a strategically important bridge over the Mississippi River or drop one small, devastating bomb on Second Army Headquarters, where my father and the command staff worked. Though there was a vast distance between Tennessee and any German airbase, and I was aware of the limited range of all Luftwaffe planes, still, you could never be too sure. After all, look what happened at Pearl Harbor, just because no one – either official adult or alert child – was watching the sky.

B-25s flew over our house from time to time, as well as B-26s (another medium bomber, though not so physically appealing), many transport aircraft, and an occasional fighter plane or B-24 Liberator bomber. Since there was virtually no private or commercial air traffic, whenever I heard the sound of an approaching plane, I ran outside, book in hand, to identify it and do my bit to protect the community.

It was, as I remember, on a warm spring afternoon, perhaps a Saturday, when I heard the engines of an aircraft approaching unusually low. I dashed to the back yard, still unable to see anything, but aware, now, of the coughing, sputtering irregularity of failing engines. I called to my mother that a plane was in trouble and to hurry out. I was excited and curious, and yet at the same time extremely anxious. This was suddenly too real. The craft's engine – now I was hearing only one – was firing and missing, and in a moment I saw it: a B-25, only a few hundred feet above our yard. The pilot had evidently feathered one propeller, and the sole other engine was barely operating. The plane was losing altitude and I knew the pilot was in desperate trouble. And then I saw the man, a crewmember, crouching in the open rear doorway. I saw him for just a moment before the craft passed out of view. His knees were bent and he was holding on to the curved sides of the doorway. He was looking down. I was aware, as he surely must have been, that he was too low to use a parachute.

The bomber's engine went silent and it glided on, hidden from sight now by other houses. I knew the plane would crash. And I knew that the man crouching in the doorway was about to die. I stood in the yard paralyzed, having just seen a man a moment before his death, and from my position of safety I felt his terror. In some vivid, empathetic way I had participated in it. For a split second I had crouched helplessly in the plane's doorway and looked down at a little boy who gazed up from the ground I would never reach alive.

I don't know how long it was before I heard the first sirens. Four minutes, perhaps longer. From the front yard, I could see the column of smoke a mile or so away. The pilot had tried to land in a parking lot but was not successful. The plane had struck a house, and several people on the ground – five, as I remember – were killed, as well as the three men aboard the B-25. Including, of course, the poor, doomed man who clung to the doorway and looked down in my direction as the plane coasted to its death.

Whatever glamour I had felt about the war and its tanks and fighter planes and battleships – all of it died that afternoon in smoke and fire, only a mile or so away from my house.

Later that day, when my father came home from his office at Second Army Headquarters, I looked at him with different eyes. The thrill of his rank, his army uniform, his sense of authority, and his permanence in my life were now all in tatters. War meant death in a way that I, an inexperienced, well-protected twelve-year-old, had never allowed myself to imagine, despite the newsreels and bloody photographs in *Life*. I began to understand that the brave war movies I'd seen, the violent battle scenes and successful air raids, were essentially propaganda designed to conceal the actual messiness and tragedy of death. They were, I could see, a tidied up, deliberately misleading version of the real thing, and that the Hollywood actors who seemed invulnerable to the enemy could, at the end of the day, remove their makeup and go safely home to their families. But Dad, we all knew, was eventually headed for Europe, whenever the Allies were powerful enough to challenge Hitler's stronghold, and I saw for the first time that he might never come back.

We lived in Memphis until the spring of 1944, when Dad, like millions of others, was sent to England in preparation for the coming D-Day invasion. The four remaining family members drove back to Wheeling, but I would not see my father again until the fall of 1945, months after the long war had finally ended. During the time he was in Europe, I was by default the (adolescent) man of the house, tending the furnace, shoveling coal each morning, afternoon, and evening, and taking care of an assortment of chores in our aging home. But my most important job was helping my mother remain calm in the face of her profound worry over Dad's fate. Often, putting her arms around me and her head on my shoulder, she would weep while I tried to reassure her that Dad, as a full colonel on General Omar Bradley's staff, was unlikely to be in the front lines, and that I was certain he was safe. I later found out that, during the confused Battle of the Bulge, he had been in real danger, though I never let my mother see that I had been at all concerned.

My father returned to Wheeling in the fall of 1945 and my brother followed shortly thereafter. Things began to seem normal once more. It was the beginning of my second year in high school, and my interests had shifted from World War II to the mysteries of those delectable creatures W.C. Fields referred to as "those of the female persuasion." But there had been many emotional incidents in my life prior to the end of the war, and some of them had left psychological scars. A confrontation in Memphis in which Dad revealed his attitude toward black people was one such disturbing event.

Family Racism

LIVING IN A SOUTHERN CITY like Memphis had presented me with a host of unfamiliar new conditions, among which was a very large population of African-Americans. Or, as members of this underclass were then called, "colored people." Wheeling had had a very small black population, and the only African-American I'd ever known was a kindly, rail-thin man named Russell Hicks who worked for my father. In keeping with his caste in those benighted times, his job was that of washing cars, with little or no chance of either finding more challenging work or rising any higher in society. Russell, whose wife had lost her eyesight, was a very proud, thoughtful, and witty man, an autodidact with an elaborately florid vocabulary. And also, as one might guess from these melancholy circumstances, a man with a serious drinking problem.

Dad always liked Russell, an intensely loyal employee who seemed genuinely fond of my father. More than once, I remember Dad telling us, sometimes with a smile and sometimes a sad shrug, that he had had to go down to court to bail Russell Hicks out of jail; the poor man was often picked up by the police on drunk charges and locked up overnight. Dad told us he would lecture him on his responsibilities to his blind wife and family and then underline the point by threatening to fire him if it happened again. Russell, filled with gratitude, would weep and apologize, and life went on as before, the ritual repeating itself at predictable intervals.

Every summer my father's Dodge dealership held an annual picnic for its employees and their families, an event usually held at a campsite at Ogelbay Park. After the hotdog roasts and the games of softball and horseshoes but before the dancing, there would be a few brief speeches – brief except for Russell's, because once he had the floor, he was reluctant to relinquish it. With a vocabulary ornate enough to make William F. Buckley envious, Russell spoke about his friendship with "Mr. E.B.," as Dad was usually called, his pride at working at Hopkins Motor Company, his esteem for his fellow employees, and so on.

But as I was later to understand, Russell's elaborate, uplifting, polysyllabic oratory was essentially a delicate tightrope-walking enterprise in which he hoped to give himself some kind of importance and intellectual status without violating the pose of obsequiousness required of black men in such an environment. It didn't help that by the time he took to the soapbox Russell had usually over-fortified himself with beer or liquor, so his speeches always ended with tears of affection and gratitude and an inevitable confusion of syntax and pronunciation. His fellow employees, who probably didn't know the meaning of half the words he'd used or understand why a black car-washer had been compelled to teach himself to speak this way, restrained their mirth and indulged him with exaggerated applause. When I was ten or eleven years old, I thought Russell Hicks was funny, too. It was a few years later before I sensed the hopelessness and waste of mind that he must have experienced every day of his life. Not until I was a teenager did I understand that his sad eyes were as redolent of personal tragedy as they were of his need for the oblivion of alcohol.

Memphis represented a major step along the road that eventually let me see the injustice that one race – my own – was regularly inflicting upon another. Day by day, a mass of small, demeaning incidents demonstrated the immorality of the way we coldly and casually treated "colored people." There was, however, one major event that left me shaken and profoundly disillusioned about our behavior, and, sadly, it involved my father.

As I've suggested, Dad was, at heart, a man of the old school who rarely cursed, inveighed, or publicly lost his temper. Unlike many of his friends, he was not addicted to dirty jokes or coarse language of any sort. In fact, many years later, after I'd discovered the early movies of W.C. Fields and shared my enthusiasm with my father, assuming that he, too, must have been a fan, he surprised me by saying he never approved of W.C. Fields. The ribald old comedian did not, in my father's opinion, "present a good image for our

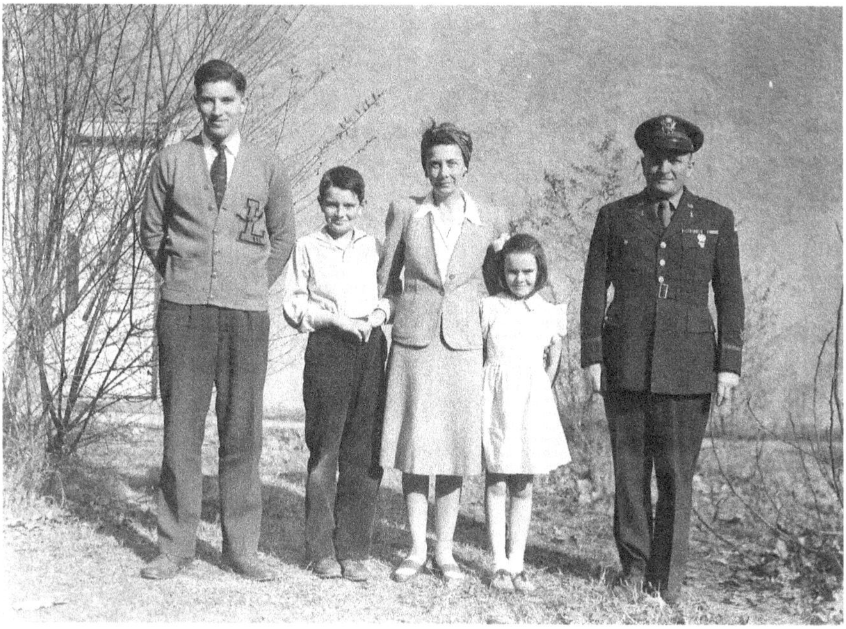

Memphis, 1942. From the left, my large brother Stewart; my awkward, rumpled self; my mother in her 1940s shoulder pads; my prim sister Ellie; and Dad, rigidly at attention.

country."

The kind of dignity that Fields routinely made fun of was a highly esteemed asset for my father and most of his contemporaries, middle-class men who had been born in the last decades of the nineteenth century. As a group, they cultivated a gentlemanly demeanor and made a conscious effort to maintain such an appearance before the world. Though he could be stern, my father possessed a natural politeness and sense of consideration for others, and to his family and friends he was invariably loving and generous. He rarely gave way to feelings of anger, and I don't ever remember seeing him darkened by a deep-seated rage. But accompanying these estimable qualities were all the prejudices and bigotries typical of many men born and bred before the First World War. As I've pointed out before, Dad was intolerant of Jews and "colored people," and yet his anti-Semitic and racist views seemed to be more ideological than personal. Though he held the group in contempt, occasionally he genuinely liked an individual member. He had always been kind to Russell Hicks, and he did have, in Wheeling, one or two Jewish friends, and though it may not be significant, the one Jew who was a frequent guest at our house had earlier married a Protestant woman and converted to her faith.

In keeping with his polite and generally pacific behavior, my father rarely used the racist language so common among his friends. I never once heard him use the word "nigger," a staple of supposedly polite Southern conversation, though a very few times (and usually fueled by anger) I heard him refer to someone as a "kike." In Memphis, repressive bigotry of every kind was a fact of everyday life, and Dad, though geographically a Northerner, acted as if these southern customs and forms of address were completely natural, even congenial. Older African-American men were routinely called "boy" by twenty-year-old white "men," and the black grandmothers who cooked and cleaned for young white matrons were always "girls." Virtually all public venues were strictly segregated. The colored-only section of the Malco Movie Theater was the top balcony, located well away from any white customers and far back from the screen as well. The large black ghetto centered on Beale Street was, as could be predicted by such enforced segregation, a hotbed of violent crime. Though more a relic of the past than a present reality, lynchings were occasionally mentioned as a legitimate available option if all else failed in keeping the colored population in line. I saw these racist facts of life with little comprehension and not much sense of outrage because never, even in my family or in a so-called Christian church, had I been taught a different morality.

Shortly after we arrived in the South, my father made friends with a local Chrysler dealer, a genial, well-to-do man named Bill Fisher. His wife, Daisy, was a charming woman who had two children, a son about my sister's age called, in typical southern fashion, John T., and a daughter closer to my age named Billie, who, to my eleven-year-old eyes, was ravishingly beautiful.

Fortunately for the Hopkins family, most southerners were extremely respectful of the military calling, a tradition that probably dates back to the Civil War and the glorification of Robert E. Lee.

But for whatever reason, this factor, in addition to the obvious business connection, served to cement the friendship between my father and Bill Fisher. My mother and Daisy Fisher, family-centered, modest, and naturally sociable, seemed in many ways to be counterparts of one another, northern and southern versions of the same kind of conservative woman, and we children also got on very well together.

Eventually we became so close to the Fishers that we visited one another virtually every weekend. And so it happened one Sunday afternoon that Dad told us we were going to drive out to the country and watch Bill Fisher drill with his unit. I knew that Mr. Fisher was a little too old to be in the army – he was probably in his late forties – so I had no idea why he might be drilling or what his unit might be. Dad explained that it was something called the Home Guard, so I didn't pursue the matter. The four of us drove to a remote wooded area surrounding a small open field that was now serving as a parade ground. We parked among a cluster of other cars to watch a fairly disheveled-looking group of perhaps 30 men marching back and forth, carrying old Enfield rifles, and wearing an irregular assortment of brown or olive shirts and trousers. Most of the men in this motley band seemed too old for the regular army, and none of them acted as if discipline or military bearing were very important issues.

My mother and sister lingered by the car, along with the members of a few other families who were also watching the drill, but I walked with Dad over to Mr. Fisher who was, as I recall, conducting the formation. I found it strange to see this eminently casual civilian dressed in khakis and an old-fashioned campaign hat. When the marchers halted for a spot of rest, he and Dad began an easy conversation, smiling with what I took to be a shared understanding of the purpose of this training operation. With my insatiable curiosity about all things military, I waited for an opening and then asked Mr. Fisher what kind of unit this was. It was the Home Guard, he replied, and, still confused, I asked if he meant the National Guard or the State Guard or what? No, he answered, it was the Home Guard, a kind of informal organization, and it only met during the weeks of voter registration and at election time.

Why did they meet then, I wanted to know. "To keep the niggers from trying to vote," Mr. Fisher explained with a patient smile. "We line up wearing our uniforms and carrying our rifles and guard the polling places so the niggers are too scared to try to register or to vote." I looked at Mr. Fisher and my father in helpless incomprehension. At school I'd been taught about the Constitution, and all the war movies I'd seen mentioned that we were fighting for democracy and the right to vote and against dictatorship and the rule of the few. I simply didn't understand.

"But isn't everyone supposed to vote?" I asked Mr. Fisher.

"The white people are supposed to," he replied, with the expression of someone wearily trying to explain the obvious to a simpleton. "The niggers aren't supposed to vote. It would be terrible if they did," he went on, glancing in my father's direction with an amused smile.

Dad smiled and nodded in casual agreement. What his friend had just said seemed to be his view, too. I was shocked and confused. Something was terribly wrong. Either what I'd learned about the right to vote was wrong, or what my father and Mr. Fisher and all those marching men believed was wrong. And if they were wrong, then they were not fully on the American side, the side that was fighting for democracy against Hitler and Tojo. Perhaps as a result of my bewildered questions and my obvious reluctance to accept the southern view of things, Dad seemed a bit uneasy. I was reminded of the way he looked the year before in Washington when he'd unthinkingly made that anti-Semitic remark to his friendly host and hostess, and a moment later realized they were Jewish.

Now, however, Dad was showing a common front with his racist friend. I went home saddened and deeply disillusioned. I felt abandoned by my father, but I also knew in my heart that he was wrong, not on a matter of fact but on an important moral issue. It was a bitter thought to have to live with. Outwardly, I let the matter drop, though down inside I knew that something very precious had been profoundly damaged.

Sex in the Boonies

My helpless fascination with women began in the early 1940s, in Memphis, when, at the age of twelve, I met Billie Fisher and was awed into terrified silence by her beauty and her strangeness. Though we were the same age, Billie was almost as tall as I, and as self-assured as I was withdrawn. She was slender and lithe, with marvelously wavy auburn hair and eyes that shone with a kind of adult awareness, the meaning of which I could only guess. Her strangeness lay primarily in the fact that she was a girl, an intimidating but suddenly captivating new breed that I'd only recently begun to take seriously. Until then the only young female I really knew anything about was my nagging and, at the time, supremely uninteresting little sister.

Like most children in that repressive wartime era, I knew almost nothing about sex, and whenever I asked my parents where babies came from I got the usual runaround. "We'll get you a book about it," they said, but the volume never materialized. (I assumed babies were born through the bellybutton, not knowing anything much about the vagina.) Nevertheless, I exchanged bits of salacious misinformation with other boys, looked up dirty words in the dictionary (breast, urine, intercourse, testicle, and other shocking terms), and gazed at photographs of women in bathing suits, trying to imagine exactly what lay beneath.

During the war, *Life* magazine was a great source for these images, providing quasi-innocent pinups – solo fantasy fodder for lonely boys in the service – but one day someone at *Life* either got careless or decided to give the GIs an extra treat. The magazine printed a full-page photograph of a pretty model named Chili Williams in a two-piece, polka-dot bathing suit. She was smiling and waving toward the camera in the standard, wholesome way, but when I, a sharp-eyed child, examined the photo closely, I had a welcome surprise. The fabric of Chili's bathing suit bottom was pulled up tight, and the effect at her crotch was to cause some of the large black polka dots to partially disappear in a vertical line at her cleft. Because of my avid curiosity, I knew where to look and thereby gained some specific new information about female anatomy. Apparently I was not alone in having noticed the seductively nestled polka dots; thousands upon thousands of servicemen wrote to *Life* asking for reprints of Chili's photograph. It was, according to the editors, the most popular picture the magazine printed during the entire Second World War.

My sexual education was extraordinarily slow and confused during that oppressive era, but a year or so later, when I was living back in Wheeling and beginning high school, I found another source of what passed for visual eroticism in those Comstockian days. At the south end of Market Street, there was a seedy little cigar and newspaper dealer who carried the nudist magazine *Sunshine and Health*. In its pages, naked people, mostly middle-aged and tending toward the portly, were shown cavorting in the lakeside mud of a place called Mays Landing, New Jersey. These amateur-looking photos showed them playing volleyball and wandering around the nudist colony, posing so that we young readers could get a good look at human anatomy in the rough. So far as it went, *Sunshine and Health* was fascinating and informative, but it had one enormous flaw: all the genitals had been airbrushed out. Breasts of all shapes, pendulous, perky, budding and gigantic were fully visible, and, of course, flat and bulging bellies, svelte and sagging bottoms, male and female, young and old. But in front, between the legs, nothing. Just blank, perfectly smooth areas exactly where I needed to know the truth.

No one alive in those years could have ever, in his wildest fantasies, imagined our present-day, porn-drenched society, or our casual and refreshing openness about human sexuality. Nevertheless, it's ironic that the 1940s' smothering secrecy and repression about all things physical only made sex sexier and more desirable.

High school was an idyllic time in my life, partly because of a new group of close friends, boys with names like Mac and Stubbs and Dave and Joe. Since I was only thirteen when I'd begun high school at Linsly, I was the youngest. Mac, my closest friend, was a year older and far more experienced with girls. He had a cousin named Virginia, an older woman of seventeen, who was not only beautiful but ripely voluptuous. She dazzled all of us, and on a camping trip one summer, Mac told a story about her which I'm sure none of us who were there has ever forgotten.

The setting for his tale was important. On a weekend camping and canoeing trip, four of us – Mac, Dave, Stubbs and I – had pitched our tent near the bank of Cheat Lake. We'd built our campfire and cooked a typical ghastly supper of canned Vienna sausages and Heinz baked beans. It was dark and the fire had burned down to glowing embers, so we decided to put it out and turn in. We'd each brought a sleeping bag, and as we settled down and lay there in the dark, our conversation turned to its usual subject.

Mac had obviously been holding his story for the proper occasion, and this was it. He began by explaining that recently Virginia and her parents had spent the weekend with his family. For about a year he'd been carrying on a kind of quiet flirtation with his older cousin, and she had begun reciprocating. "One night," he told us, "I walked past her bedroom door when everybody had gone to bed. She motioned me to come in. She was sitting on her bed in her bathrobe, wearing only her nightgown under it."

The silence was palpable from all of us. Virginia! The most desirable girl any of us knew. It was everyone's wildest fantasy to be invited, like Mac, into her bedroom. He went on to tell us that she whispered she wanted to kiss him goodnight. He described the kiss, and how it turned passionate: a French kiss, tongues entwined. And then, miracle of miracles, he said that he dared to put his hand on her marvelous breast through the fabric of her bathrobe. The three of us in his audience were now almost breathless with anticipation. This was like a dream coming true. To actually feel Virginia's full, very adult breasts, breasts I always gaped at whenever she wore anything even half revealing!

Mac paid out the delicious details of his story little by little, creating unbearable suspense. He described how, as their kiss became more passionate, he slipped his hand under the lapel of her robe so that now only the thin, lacy fabric of her nightgown lay between his exploring fingers and her bare, succulent flesh. Wild with impatience, we interrupted him with urgent questions: Did you ever get to feel her breast, naked? How far did you go? Did you do anything *below the waist*? What else happened? *Tell us, for God's sake!*

Mac continued his seductive tale, ignoring our interruptions. He slowly built up to what was, for him, the summit: he finally slipped his hand *inside* her nightgown and felt her naked breast.

"God," somebody whispered in awe. And after a long pause, "What did it feel like?"

"Well," Mac said, "it was full, and heavy, and it felt great to hold."

"But that doesn't tell us anything. What did it feel like exactly?"

"It was warm and soft," he explained, "but also firm. Firm, but somehow soft. It felt wonderful."

"That's still not enough. What did it feel like *exactly*?"

He pondered a moment and then answered. "Well," he said, "it kind of felt like the bottom part of your ass."

There was an immediate silence, and then sounds of twisting and turning within various sleeping bags. In the safety of the dark, each one of us, I later learned, reached down and took hold of his own nether cheek, squeezing, testing, checking. "Yeah," someone whispered after a few moments. "I see what you mean."

When I turned fifteen and my friends, sixteen, obtained drivers' licenses, we had wheels. The usual pattern – unbelievably innocent in retrospect – was that on the weekends three of us, usually Mac, Stubbs, and I, would triple date, with one or the other of them with his date in front, at the wheel, and the other two couples crowded in the rear. We would go to a movie and then drive around for an hour or so and, believe it or not, spend much of the time singing! We knew the usual trite campfire songs and all kinds of ancient, easy-to-handle chestnuts, from Jolson to Cohan: "Mammy," "I've Been Workin' On the Railroad," "Over There," "California,

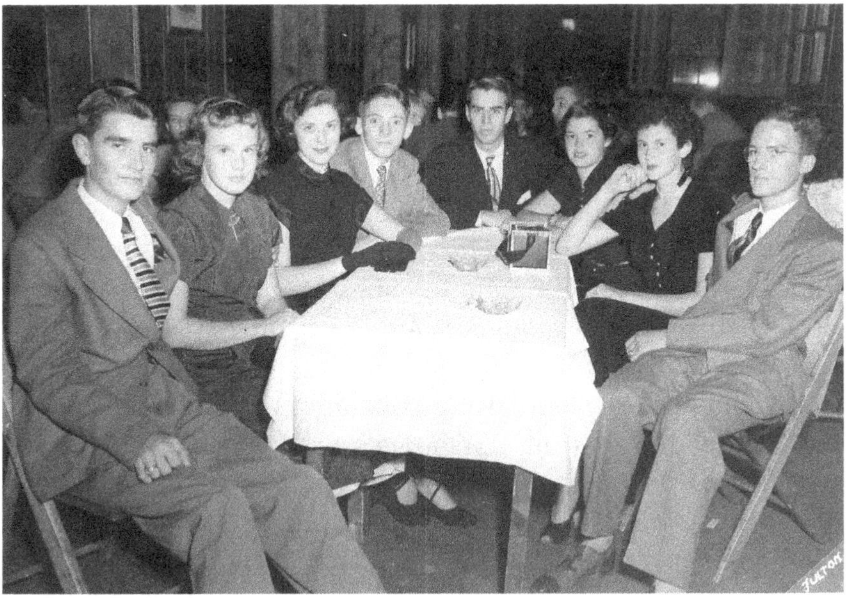

Prom night, 1948: I am on the left, hoping to grow into my suit; then my girlfriend Janie; Mac in the center; and Stubbs is far right. A typical party with no beer, no booze, no sex, and not much fun.

Here I Come," and so on. (I blush to report such naïveté.) Though there were no really decent voices among us, we sang as if we really could, straining our vocal chords severely on numbers with high notes, like "The Whiffenpoof Song." Inevitably our girlfriends also learned our cornball repertory and reluctantly joined in, sweetening the ensemble a bit. On many a Saturday night, Mac's '39 Oldsmobile rolled along the quiet back roads with a small, very loud, and slightly out-of-tune glee club belting away inside.

But then, at some point, the singing would stop and we'd park on a deserted country road to "neck" with our dates, as the saying had it then. "Making out," the present-day phrase for heavy kissing and caressing, to us meant having sexual intercourse, actually *doing it*, something we only dreamed about as a magical event that would occur only in the cloudy, very distant future. At the time, we only went so far as kissing passionately and trying to fondle our hesitant girlfriends' tender young breasts through layers and layers of protective clothing and dire maternal warnings.

Some months before the extensive triple dating began, I had my first truly passionate, adult-type kiss. The girl involved was named Phyllis – Phillie, for short. She had a plump, oval face, short brown hair with bangs cut straight across her forehead, and a somewhat chunky body. At fourteen and stumbling into puberty, she was just at the point of shedding both her baby fat and her tomboy image.

The event, which was momentous for me, took place on a warm June afternoon. A gentle summer rain was falling, and Phillie and I were sitting on the wide, roofed-in front porch at my house, lazing about, watching the rain, and rocking back and forth on the creaky old wicker porch swing. But then, for some reason, we started to wrestle playfully. Grabbing arms, laughing, straining, we soon landed on the floor, rolling over together on the dry, dusty, fibrous rug. Phillie's old tomboy persona kicked in and she began to wrestle more seriously, trying to force me under her in order to pin me. Obviously I couldn't let that happen, so I used more force and struggled back. Phillie was actually quite strong, and our fooling around had now become a serious, vigorous match. We rolled over each other several times, each trying to get the upper hand.

And then I found myself lying partly on top of her, finally pinning her arms and shoulders to the rug. Angry now, she struggled up against me, trying to break free while I strained to hold her in place. Then, in a split second, a flash, everything changed. Phillie stopped struggling, her body went limp, and she suddenly lifted her face and kissed me with a fierce passion. My own desire flared and I returned the kiss with even greater force. These amazing new feelings were simultaneously scary, sexual, and intense. I'd kissed girls before this – I'd kissed Phillie before – but this was something entirely different. We clung together in a ferocious embrace, tongues intertwined, arms clutching almost painfully. It was hard to understand exactly what had happened, but I knew that I'd just left a piece of childhood behind, for good.

It's almost impossible, now, after three marriages and a number of intimate relationships, to recall my crippling innocence in those early years, but innocent I was. When I turned sixteen and was finally able to drive, I made a date with a girl whom I knew mainly by reputation for being generous with her favors. After the requisite movie, I drove to a deserted area and parked. Though I was as nervous as a pickpocket, I had finally made up my mind to "do it," to learn firsthand what intercourse was all about. We embraced, and as my caresses slowly began to approach their target, the girl lay back, panting, and made herself available. But the closer I got to my goal, the more nervous I became. When my exploring fingertips moved between her thighs and finally slipped inside, I was suddenly shocked by her moisture and inner heat. This was not what I had expected, though I had no idea as to what I should have expected. In rapid succession I withdrew my hand, straightened my clothes, and announced that I was ready to take her home. I drove to her house, trembling with shame, with aborted desire, and with a profound uneasiness that was my companion through a sleepless night.

It would be another few years before desire overcame my shame and fear, and with a girl I loved, in ideal surroundings, I was finally able to "do it." But I've thought many times about that embarrassing night when, at the age of sixteen, I allowed a state of something like panic to rule, and so unchivalrously left that compliant young girl perplexed and sexually stranded.

In retrospect, I see that it has always taken me an inordinately long time to move ahead, to explore, to dare – or even, for that matter, to actually learn anything, no matter how much I desired the experience.

Elite Imprisonment

DESPITE THE MANY PLEASURES of those exploratory times, my junior and senior years in high school were shadowed by a major threat. My father was insistent that I transfer to Lawrenceville, a prestigious and tony prep school in New Jersey where he had sent my brother, Stewart, a few years earlier. Dad's obsession with Lawrenceville was based on his hope that once there, I might befriend boys from elite families who would later on be helpful in the business career he intended for me – a career that I had no desire, even at the age of sixteen, to follow. To my great relief, a compromise was reached when Dad agreed to let me finish all four years of senior high in Wheeling, if I would then attend Lawrenceville for one post-graduate year. Since I would graduate in Wheeling at the age of sixteen, a year ahead of most others, Dad argued that a post-grad high school year would bring me up to the proper age level for college. Thus I allowed myself to be dragooned off to boarding school and what was, by any reckoning, the unhappiest period of my life. But in a strange irony, those nine months also served to deepen my identification with the world's disadvantaged and moved me a few steps closer to the liberal political ethic that my conservative father detested.

My long sentence at boarding school had come about because one of Dad's friends, a Lawrenceville alumnus, had, years before, described the wealth and position of the students there. Since Dad's own early years had been financially and socially troubled, sending his sons to Lawrenceville must have seemed to him an ideal way to launch us into a privileged, upper-class world he had never known. (In fact, my brother hinted to me that Dad's father had once served time in prison for embezzlement.) So, in the fall of 1948, I arrived at the small village outside the ivied walls of Lawrenceville, feeling trapped and depressed. Though the campus itself appeared pleasantly tidy and solid, with conservative brick buildings and well-tended grounds, my initial feeling of gloom deepened when I found out what my life would be like for the next nine months. There was a policy of lights out at a certain hour, strict rules against leaving the school grounds, and an all-male student body largely made up of sad, adolescent boys from very wealthy families.

Few of the boys in the dormitory I was assigned to had ever experienced anything approaching a normal life. For most, there was no center, no real hometown or gang of regular friends. Many had been in boarding school since they were mere children. Christmas and spring vacations were spent in Bermuda or Nassau or Florida or some other expensive resort area, and naturally the friendships they managed to make here and there were constantly changing. The long summer vacations, of course, were spent at summer camp, away from their parents, with yet another group of temporary acquaintances. Under these circumstances, few of the boys felt close either to their parents or their siblings, and almost none were intimately familiar with a hometown. None had girlfriends because their rare encounters with the opposite sex were carefully controlled and chaperoned. And since sexual desire and the need for love demanded recognition no matter what, many of them, like frustrated adults in prison, had sex with each other.

As a post-grad, I was a fifth wheel in the system, and was assigned for some reason to a room in a dormitory for boys about fourteen or fifteen years old. Though I had just turned seventeen, I was regarded there as a worldly, experienced "older man" who had already done all of the things the younger boys only dreamed of one day doing themselves. I had a girlfriend. I knew how to talk to girls, and what it was like to kiss them. (I was asked to describe exactly what it felt like to fondle a girl's breasts, and used my friend Mac's practical analogy.) I had my own old car and could drive around at night in my own hometown, and I knew the names of all the streets. I'd had breakfast and supper with my family almost every day of my life. I had friends – close friends – whom I saw year after year. Each December I celebrated the Christmas holidays with relatives and family in my own home. I had gone on camping trips with a gang of old friends and had even helped to build a cabin hide-away in the country. In the envious eyes of these deprived boarding-school adolescents, I had enjoyed an ideal life vastly more desirable than their own.

Normal adolescents can be cruel, but the Lawrenceville students living such narrow lives under such hothouse conditions were capable of cruelty such as I'd never seen before. The classmates they disliked, the dormitory outcasts (and there were many), were not only snubbed but also frequently tormented by the dominant clique. A boy from South America was disliked because he "smelled" and didn't speak English fluently enough. I came into the bathroom once to find him being held, fully clothed, under a cold shower by a gang of taunting classmates, giggling and holding their noses. Other boys were teased because they were shy or "looked funny," or had some noticeable peculiarity such as a lisp or a speech impairment, or were Jewish. (Jews were a very small minority at this "exclusive" institution. I recall no African-Americans.) This rigid adolescent caste system ranged from a self-proclaimed aristocracy to a middle group that was simply ignored and all the way down to the ill-fated untouchables. It was apparent that the unhappy in-group boys had had to create a fragile sense of superiority and self-worth by lording it over the even more unhappy outcasts.

I began, one by one, to befriend some of these outcasts because I felt sorry for them. With my memories of having been an outsider as a child, I understood what they were enduring, though it was far more upsetting than anything I had known. Unlike my childhood situation, at boarding school these young boys had no nurturing mother or protective father to go to for support and reassurance. Though a faculty couple lived in an apartment within the dormitory building, few of the outcasts ever risked bringing further misery upon themselves by reporting their classmates' behavior. For me, watching the dominant clique bully the helpless became a haunting moral issue and led to a great deal of sorrowful introspection. Until then I had naively thought that life seemed, on balance, mostly fair, but the entire Lawrenceville situation was unfair, from top to bottom.

In the evenings and late afternoons, the young residents of the dormitory gathered in what was called the common room, a sitting area resembling a greatly expanded lobby of a Motel 6. It contained a number of institutional couches and easy chairs, upholstered, if memory serves, in some brownish, heavy-duty fabric, and a few insipid flower prints on the wall to cheer the place up. This fairly grim sitting room was home turf for the dominant clique, and when they were there, many of the outcasts stayed away.

For their part, the in-group members could never understand why I bothered to befriend the untouchables. Often, when I entered the common room with a couple of them accompanying me, someone would say for all to hear, "Here comes Hopkins and his cripples." It became a catch phrase – "Hopkins and his cripples" – and though my limp from polio was slight at the time, I wondered if their phrase might not be connected with my peculiarity. At no time, however, was I treated like an untouchable, even when I spent a great deal of time trying to cheer up one of their weeping victims. The ruling clique envied me too much and needed all the information they could get from me about life in the outside world to risk turning me against them.

In November of 1948, Harry Truman defeated the little man on the wedding cake, Thomas E. Dewey, whom I, a political naïf, always confused with Lowell Thomas. Breaking one of the rules about bedtime and radios (I broke many, many rules, deliberately and systematically), I listened to the late election results, and though ostensibly still a Republican like my family, I was oddly pleased and surprised when the honest, humble Harry Truman was pronounced the winner. I decided to tiptoe down the hall and listen to hear if anyone was still up so that I could pass on the surprising news. I heard whispering coming from the room of one of the leading in-group boys, and turning the knob, peeked in to present the election result. As the light from the hall shone into the room in a bright swath, there was a frantic scurrying and cursing. I had walked into a sex orgy involving about six boys. I lowered my eyes and backed away as they fumbled to cover up. "Truman beat Dewey," I whispered, and hurriedly retreated to my room. A few minutes later the incident began to seem very funny to me, though not, I'm sure, to them.

I felt no moralistic disapproval of their sexual shenanigans; under the prison-like circumstances of boarding school, this kind of behavior was quite understandable. Though some of these boys may have formed lifetime same-sex preferences as a result, I'm willing to bet that most of them grew up to be wealthy, ravenous heterosexuals whose glances lay more in the direction of the buxom flight attendant than toward the man standing at the next urinal. The patterns I objected to at Lawrenceville were not sexual, but rather those involving the snobbery and bullying behavior toward the weak, which sometimes led to devastating cruelty.

The sadness of life at Lawrenceville finally became so overpowering that I ended up visiting the school chaplain. Though the central issue was moral rather than religious, this conversation was the start of my brief and intermittent flirtation with religion, which waxed and waned during my first years at Oberlin. But as a young seventeen-year-old, I needed to talk to someone about the pain I was feeling and observing every day at my dormitory. I don't remember what the chaplain said – I don't even remember exactly what I said to him – but I know I received nothing that gave me much solace. I decided, finally, there was nothing to do but to hunker down and wait it out, focusing on the inevitable end of my nine-month sentence.

Meanwhile, the convoluted mini-dramas of repressed adolescence continued to unfold. I remember one fifteen-year-old who longed to be accepted by the dominant clique, so he occasionally tormented the younger boys to earn admittance to the inner circle. But one day he was caught stealing from one of the clique's leaders, someone he looked up to with near reverence. The word was passed and soon an angry group assembled in his room, tearing it apart and ultimately discovering a crudely installed false panel in the back of his desk drawer. Here the unfortunate boy had stashed away an initialed belt, a necktie, paperback books, and various small personal objects he'd stolen from those he admired and followed. Anyone familiar with adolescent psychology could have easily explained his fetishistic activities, but in any case the mental torture and social ostracism subsequently visited upon this troubled thief by his former friends were most unpleasant to see.

For me, it was imperative to make another life. Whenever I could, I sneaked away on weekends, taking the train to New York just to wander around the city and listen to jazz. These illegal excursions helped keep me alive. I remember hearing the great Sidney Bechet, Zutty Singleton, Hot Lips Page, and many others at the small, smoky jazz clubs on 52nd Street. Sometimes alone, but sometimes with another escapee or two, I would sit at a narrow table and sip a coke and lose myself in the music. Once I enticed Sidney Bechet to my table and bought him a drink, enabling me to study, through the haze of cigarette smoke, the melancholy dignity and resignation of his placid face. Though he was polite and reserved, I saw him as a giant, a veteran of humiliations and triumphs so powerful as to be inconceivable to me, an inexperienced white kid from Wheeling, West Virginia.

I developed other ways to keep myself separate from the hated institution. Near my dormitory, there was a man-made pond with a little footbridge leading to a tiny island in the center. Often, when we were all supposed to be in bed, I would escape to that little island and sit there in the dark, leaning against its single scrawny tree and feeling immensely sorry for myself. In those months, I raised self-pity to a high art. I would take out my girlfriend Janie's photograph and talk to it – to her – knowing that in her flirtatious, easily-distracted, sixteen-year-old heart, out-of-sight was truly out-of-mind. (I learned later that she'd been going steady with a football player.) I imagined that all of my old high school buddies, and all the rest who were now dispersed into various colleges, must by now have replaced me with interesting new friends and were absorbed by arcane new intellectual pursuits. I cried, I moaned and cursed this malevolent system of torture known as the boarding school. I don't know how the English, who invented the damned thing, ever survived and prospered.

But the nine-month sentence finally came to an end and I was sprung, so to speak. I tried to banish the experience from my mind and was very largely successful. Almost none of my later friends ever knew that I'd briefly attended a haughty prep school before I went on to Oberlin College, and I worked to keep it that way. However, years later, the comment of an artist friend made me think back to my days at Lawrenceville and remember "Hopkins and his cripples." This friend had always thought of me as a strong-willed, opinionated painter absorbed in his work, but one day he saw me dealing with a distraught, traumatized UFO witness, and remarked upon it in surprise. "I didn't know you were such a good listener," he said. "You were sympathetic with that poor guy you were interviewing, and I could tell that you really cared about his situation. Where did you learn how to do that?" The answer was simple: at Lawrenceville, during that dreadful year among America's tormented elite.

Part Two: Art

Art, Oberlin, and a New Life

I'VE NEVER REGRETTED IT for a moment, but my enrollment in Oberlin College was the result of a series of flukes, gaffes, and garbled information. Originally I had picked Oberlin, a highly-regarded Ohio liberal arts college, in order to be only a few hours drive from Wheeling, close to my family and old high school friends. During my temporary spring parole from penal servitude at Lawrenceville, Dad and I drove to Oberlin for a preliminary interview. Since my appointment with the Dean of Admissions was set for early the next morning, we spent the night at the Oberlin Inn. After we finished breakfast and arrived at the admissions office, I sensed an undertone of nervous confusion. The secretary told us, uneasily, that the Dean was unavoidably delayed, but that another professor would conduct the interview in his place. We waited a while until a rather flustered Professor Butler arrived and gingerly took the absent admission officer's desk. Dad began the conversation by asking Prof. Butler what business classes Oberlin offered, and did they include such things as typing, salesmanship, shorthand, and so on. Prof. Butler assured him that the college not only offered all of these courses, but that they were top flight, the best in the Middle West. The interview went on quickly, as if Prof. Butler was anxious to get it over with, but since he seemed satisfied with me, and Dad was satisfied by the roster of Oberlin's basic business classes, I regarded my enrollment as a *fait accompli*. We left, and I was later informed by mail that in the fall I would become a member of the class of 1953.

It was only when I came to Oberlin in September that I learned that the night before my peculiar spring interview, the Dean of Admissions had committed suicide and that Prof. Butler, the emergency replacement, was in fact the football coach and a professor of physical education. Half of the business classes he had reassured my father about did not exist, because, outside of sports, the good professor was evidently not well informed about the college curriculum.

For my part, I had entered Oberlin with no idea of what I might major in, or, for that matter, what I would do after graduation, though I knew my father expected me to follow him into the automobile business. I also knew at the time that I would never be a car dealer. I just assumed that sooner or later some prospective life work would turn up, but in the meantime I planned to explore the world and, after the ordeal of Lawrenceville, to enjoy myself. The erroneous information the football coach had given us turned out to be fortuitous, because I learned that Oberlin was not only the first college in America to become co-ed, it was also the first to admit black students. Thus, instead of a boring, buttoned-down business school as Dad had been led to believe, it was a virtual bastion of humanistic liberalism and, had he known, the last kind of place he would have chosen for me.

After Lawrenceville the freedom of Oberlin was exhilarating. I plunged into my first-year courses, formed close friendships with some of my classmates, and began dating several of the young women I met easily at our co-ed dining halls. At first I thought I might major in English – vanilla ice cream on the liberal arts menu – but I also considered a history major, though I wasn't really drawn to that, either. My lack of focus didn't bother me since many of my classmates were in the same holding pattern. It wasn't until the beginning of my sophomore year that lightning struck, thanks in part to my friend George Lubasz. One day, halfway through the first semester of my second year, he told me he was taking a class in art history, and that he found it very interesting and suggested I audit the course to see if I liked it. It was easy, he explained, because you just sat in the dark most of the time and looked at slides of paintings and no one bothered you. The teacher gave his lecture and you just enjoyed the pictures he was showing and took notes if you wanted to, but if you were asleep or bored no one would ever know.

It sounded like a good idea to me. I had absolutely no knowledge of art history, but since I had always loved to draw I thought it might be fun. The first lecture I attended was on Corot. The course was on nineteenth and twentieth century art, and though I had come in during a halfway point, I was ravished by what I saw. The Corot landscapes were beautiful beyond anything I'd ever seen, and there was something about the slides themselves – bright rectangles of brilliant color in a darkened room – that glamorized the images even more dramatically. And the lecturer, a young Rembrandt expert named Seymour Slive, pointed out things about an artist's intensely personal vision that I'd never even imagined. I sat in the dark and listened and looked and sketched from the slides on the screen, and slowly realized that art was not just something you did at home as a hobby, as I had been doing all my life, but that it was important, even one of the most significant things a person could do.

In a totally unforeseen hour with the work of Corot in a darkened room, Art for me had grown a capital "A." And I eventually discovered that I had an eye in the way that people at the Conservatory of Music were said to have an ear. I could remember the paintings I'd seen in class and sketch them from memory later on with some degree of accuracy. I had a sense of the individual styles of these nineteenth century artists almost from the start; I could tell a Corot from a Daubigny faster than anyone in the class. I began to draw and draw during the lectures, trying to capture the beautiful, luminous images I saw on the screen. There was only one way to describe it: it was as if I'd suddenly fallen in love with someone I'd known casually all my life.

If, for many people, French Impressionism is still the most seductive example of art as the ultimate visual feast, it was surely that for me when I first saw Monet's and Renoir's and Pissarro's sunlit skies, dappled trees, and lolling picnickers. Emotionally, these works created an achingly nostalgic world of "vacation culture," in Meyer Schapiro's memorable phrase, one free from anxiety and stress and populated by the relaxed, untroubled French. Apparently no one in these paintings held a job or needed to work; they merely sat or strolled, calmly observing the landscape and each other. Impressionist works were made up of easy, seemingly casual brushstrokes that to my eye paralleled in their very nature the clouds and grasses and sandy beaches they represented. By some alchemy they managed to depict objects while at the same time existing on their own as delectable, independent spots of colored paint.

I remember in particular a painting by Berthe Morisot of her sister in a brilliant white dress sitting in a grassy field and reading a book. Her unfurled parasol is lying upended on the ground to her right and an open fan rests on the grass to her left. Here and there small flecks of color interrupt the cool green of the grass around her, tiny, shapeless spots that one instantly translates into wildflowers. Those tiny spots, pale blue, pink, lavender, and white, seemed miraculous to me, being simultaneously raw paint and bits of living, accidental nature.

The Morisot was not a "great" Impressionist work, merely a respectable and typical one from the finest Impressionist moment, the years around 1870. But for all of that, it was still astonishing to someone so new to the sheer beauty and expressiveness of paint, and so hungry for it, as I. Those tiny flowered flecks, borrowed as they were from a technique of Corot's, were every bit as moving to me as my own childhood memories of lying on a sunlit lawn, breathing the fragrance of newly mowed clover, and having nothing to do but rest and dream. I remembered a particular time in my very early childhood when I lay on that same lawn, staring up into the soothing blue above me and wondering where the sky ended and what lay outside its boundaries. And what lay outside *those* boundaries. I remembered the struggle in my mind between the unsettling idea of infinity and the sensuousness of the afternoon – the lulling, fragrant warmth of the grass and the wash of sunlight on my skin. Thankfully, the immediacy of summer pleasures – an Impressionist moment – soothed away the anxiety of my very first bout with the impossible notion of eternity.

As a natural consequence of the art history class I was monitoring, I made a trip to the nearby Cleveland Museum, my first visit to such an institution. On display was the very same Morisot I'd seen in slide form, along with many other works by artists with whom I was becoming familiar. I had always regarded a trip to an art gallery as about as exciting a prospect as a tour through a tire factory, but the moment I arrived I reacted as if the Cleveland Museum were simultaneously a home and a shrine – if one can imagine such a mix of familiarity and awe, an oxymoron of the emotions.

Some people are put off by the elitist, palace-and-velvet-rope impression many museums liked to create, but I wasn't. I wandered around in a kind of blissful daze, rushing from one quiet room to another like an Eskimo in Paris. In 1950, museums such as the Cleveland were sparsely attended, and I found myself virtually alone with treasures I'd seen only in slides and color reproductions. I spent the whole day there, devouring the nourishment of a new life.

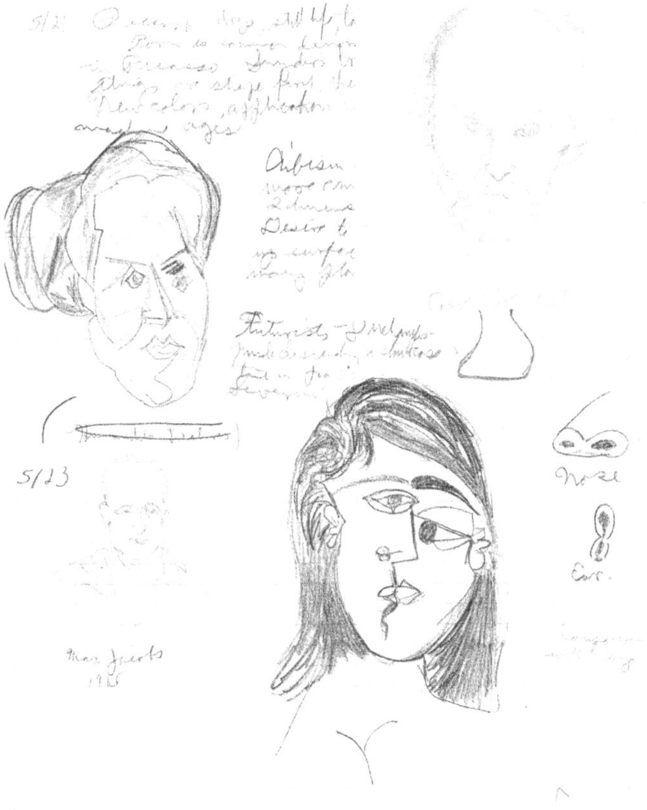

Quick sketches done from slides shown during art history class. Clockwise from top right: Cezanne drawing, Self-portrait; Picasso painting, Head; Picasso portrait drawing, Max Jacob; Picasso painting, Head of Fernande.

Back at Oberlin I enrolled in this same art history course for the second semester, taking it for credit and finally entering the dazzling world of modern art. As I recall, we began with Cezanne and moved on to other Post-Impressionists like Van Gogh, Gauguin, and Seurat, eventually coming to Matisse, Picasso, and Cubism. A few years ago I found some of my sketch-covered notes from this class, and as I pored over them I felt once more that same physically thrilling, damp-armpit rush of discovery. The pages are filled with drawings I'd made from the paintings shown on the screen, rendered as close to the style of the original as I was able to manage in the very few minutes I had with each. In my copy of a Cezanne self-portrait, a painterly pencil drawing, I imitated his oddly hesitant-decisive parallel strokes, while with Picasso's portrait of Max Jacob I tried to capture his spare, classical line. There are pencil renderings of Lautrec and Matisse paintings, versions of Cubist collages, and thick-pigmented early Cézannes. Fifty-some years later these pages of quick drawings by an untrained but awe-struck neophyte still look pretty good to me, steeped as they are in the yearning and headlong excitement of their discovery. Their execution is in no way impetuous, however; instead, they seem the careful products of reasoned adoration.

I suppose it was Impressionism – that quintessentially fresh new moment in French painting – that expressed most clearly the emotion I was feeling at the time. If Monet, Pissarro, Renoir, and Sisley together created the visual equivalent of a warm morning in May, I felt, at the age of nineteen, that it was the beginning of spring for me, too. Though my own work – and life – have long since moved past spring, I can still walk into a room of early paintings by Monet and Sisley and bask in their sunlight, their intoxicating air, their perpetual freshness and youth. When Monet was only 26, he painted *Dejeuner Sur L'herbe* (Luncheon on the Grass), a large work showing a sprawling group of picnickers who are themselves as young, as careless, and as obviously abrim with the juices of life as he must have been when he depicted them. I realize now that one of Impressionism's major gifts is its ability to stop time at a precious, youthful moment and remain ageless, though we, ourselves, are inexorably growing old.

In New York a few years later, when I came to know both the paintings and the persons of Abstract Expressionists like Willem De Kooning, Mark Rothko, and Franz Kline, I sensed a similar but opposite connection. The anguish visibly present in their work was as much a fact of their lives – older, bleaker, and more isolated – as was the relaxed sunniness in Monet's youthful Impressionism. It came to me, in that beginning art history class at Oberlin, that instead of "nature," it is the painter's own life and joys and restless discontents that together form Art's truest content.

When I first entered college, I brought with me the still unresolved quasi-religious and ethical issues that had bothered me at Lawrenceville. Sometime during my freshman year I met a small, friendly group of conservative Christian students who must have sensed my confusion and need, and who offered me their own religious doctrines as a solution. I have since read that cultists like the Reverend Moon's deliberately seek out lonely, spiritually confused freshmen in college and work to convert them before they have time to form friendships and become enmeshed in their studies. I was susceptible in the same way and for a while became involved in Fundamentalist Christianity.

As a child I had not been particularly religious; my parents paid lip service to the Protestant faith, but were never devout, and in fact when I was very young I had had a brush with atheism. My mother and father had always gone to great lengths to foster the illusion of Santa Claus: sleigh bells on the roof, half eaten cookies on a plate near the tree, "He knows what you've been thinking," "You'd better be good," etc., so when I learned that it had all been a hoax, my sense of reality and trust was temporarily shattered. No matter how benignly the Santa myth had been intended, for me its exposure had an immense fallout. My mother liked me to say a simple prayer at night – "Now I lay me down to sleep..." – but even as a very young child I realized that if Santa was a hoax that she and Dad had perpetrated for years, couldn't God be a hoax as well? After all,

I'd been told that both God and Santa were watching over me, and though I was aware of many similarities in their reported behavior, I'd never actually seen either one.

But at Oberlin it was Vincent Van Gogh who helped me to disengage from Christian Fundamentalism. As time went on, it became clear that my religious friends were far more concerned with a person's sworn fidelity to Jesus than they were with the moral imperatives that Jesus' teachings contained. The cruelty and loneliness I'd seen at Lawrenceville were of little interest to these believers, who concentrated instead on the issue of who was going to heaven and who was going to hell. And so one day, as I became more and more immersed in art, I asked one of their leaders about Van Gogh. The great Dutch artist was, in my opinion, an extraordinarily moral human being. I explained that his portraits showed a rare and moving concern for his fellow man, and his landscapes were filled, not only with great beauty, but also with life-giving energy and love for God's creation. I said that I recognized in Van Gogh's work a kind of humanistic spirituality that had been an inspiration to millions of people. And yet, I admitted, he apparently died without having accepted the kind of Christianity that the Fundamentalists professed. I asked them if, according to their beliefs, Van Gogh had ascended to heaven when he died. No, he had not, came the reply; without having made that avowal, he would burn forever in hell.

That pronouncement was all it took. I was finally out the door. It was obvious to me that all along my quest had been moral and humanistic rather than religious, pragmatic rather than doctrinaire. Having come to that realization, I felt a rush of freedom and joy. I saw that Van Gogh's kind of earthly spirituality was both more nurturing and more deeply ethical than a Fundamentalist religion that countenanced the burning in hell of good, non-Christian people who, despite their morally committed lives, had neglected to take the pledge.

IT WAS NOT LONG BEFORE my father began to show signs of regretting my enrollment in Oberlin. Early in the fall of my freshman year, my mother packed a picnic lunch centered on her delicious cold fried chicken and drove over with Dad for a visit. It was a warm Sunday afternoon, and I was very pleased to see them. I led them to a little park area that, as I remember, had the only hill in that part of Ohio – a very small one, I admit, but a sort of hill nevertheless.

We settled down, spreading a cloth on the ground, and unpacked my mother's thoughtfully prepared meal. From time to time as we ate, other Oberlin students wandered through the park, enjoying the fine weather, but at one point my father suddenly froze and stared. I turned to see what caused his grim expression, and there, perhaps twenty yards away, a boy and girl had paused to kiss rather passionately. I saw the problem instantly: the boy was black and his girl was white. Dad muttered something about how disgusting a sight this was, while I tried diplomatically to change the conversation. But by then our picnic had turned sour, especially when Dad noticed another group of young students, white and black, walking by and chatting amiably. Again he said how disgusting he found that kind of mixing.

This unpleasant incident was, in the long run, a very minor one in what was to be a four-year period of escalating strife between my father and me. Another tense moment arrived when I finally had to tell him that I was majoring in art and not in business. It was no surprise that he did not take it well, but I believe he took solace in the hope that I would finally shape up once I was out in the cruel world, jobless, and in desperation would gratefully come to him for a position selling cars. But the worst was yet to come.

The political situation in America during my Oberlin years led to a momentous clash between my father and me and greatly exacerbated the rift between us. The years 1949 through 1953 were marked by McCarthyism, blacklists, the Red scare, Alger Hiss, the Rosenbergs, and mindless, Cold War hysteria. My liberal political position was diametrically opposed to my father's intense, right-wing anti-Communism, and it all came to a climax during a vacation I spent back in Wheeling during the height of the controversy over the death sentences Julius and Ethel Rosenberg had received.

My parents and I were in the kitchen, as I recall, having a light

Sunday supper when the subject of the Rosenberg verdicts came up. I took as moderate a position as I could, putting it this way: I did not dispute the fact that during World War II the couple had passed documents containing atomic secrets on to Soviet agents, and that therefore they were technically guilty of treason. But I argued that no one had ever been executed in the U.S. for treason in peacetime, and that their death sentences should be reduced to life imprisonment. I pointed out that Ethel and Julius were themselves insignificant little people, the parents of young children, and that their death sentences had become an international issue unfavorable to the United States. Only a few women had ever been executed for anything in our country, and to kill one now would be a tragic mistake in the light of such powerful international opposition. Why should we give the Communists two such obvious martyrs? I asked my father. It was exactly what the other side wants.

With that Dad exploded in anger. "That's just what those Jew lawyers say," he shouted at me. "Those people shouldn't have even been given a trial. We should have taken them out and shot them!"

That did it for me, and I retaliated, enraged. "Well, that's what they do in Russia," I said, "and if you think we should shoot people without a trial, you don't understand anything about the difference between the United States and Russia!"

Dad was livid and close to tears, as was I. Never had our political differences been so raw, and never had I spoken to him like that. He turned and walked out of the kitchen without replying, as if he realized he had gone too far. My mother was weeping, and I was literally shaking with a profound rush of both anger and regret – regret that I had hurt my father and anger that he had deserved it.

My mother came over and put her comforting arms around me, and after a while she said, "There is something you should know about your father." Whispering as the tears ran down her cheeks, she said, "The year before you were born, your father had been taking care of his parents, giving them some money each month and renting a little house for them." She was having great trouble explaining this to me, but went on, despite her tears and mine. "Your grandfather – your dad's father – felt that he couldn't go on living in the Depression with no chance to make any money and so he decided... one day... sometime... to commit suicide. He wanted his wife – your grandmother – to kill herself, too, but she wouldn't do it... so he shot her... murdered her... and then shot himself. Your dad found their bodies... He managed to keep it out of the papers... but you can imagine..." Her voice trailed off.

I could imagine the horror, the blood, the abandonment it represented.

In the next few days, as I tried to think about what it all meant, I could visualize the shame my father must have felt, and the rejection, and the trauma. I could see, in my mind's eye, the bullet holes on the wall, the grotesque postures of his dead parents, the bloodstains everywhere, and my dad walking in to see it all. The more I thought about it, the more I could imagine that it fueled his need later on to hate someone, some race or group, anything or anyone he could look down upon in order to feel in some way superior, anything to offset his shame at having been abandoned, horrified, and disgraced by his own father whom he had tried to support and protect. And then there was the loss of his innocent, murdered mother.

In the days immediately following our battle over the Rosenberg case, Dad refused to speak to me unless it was absolutely essential, but gradually things began to cool down, eventually returning to something like normal. In the meantime I tried to consider everything about our argument in the light of my mother's shocking revelations, and I wondered if now I wasn't inventing a convenient psychological excuse for his virulent anti-Semitism. Was I merely creating my own way of rationalizing his past – or possible future – outbursts of bigotry? I knew that I loved my father and did not want to see him in that kind of state. I knew that he was proud of me and of my so far meager accomplishments. I was also aware that he was widely respected within Wheeling's business community, and that he had always been generous and openly loving to all of us. I realized that, like me, neither my brother, Stewart, nor my sister, Ellie, had grown up bigoted in any way, and that Dad had never tried to plant in us such reprehensible values. It was as if he had understood on some unconscious level that, despite Oscar Hammerstein's famous lyric, hate, like love, is an emotion that cannot be effectively taught. To believe that a child can be forced to feel real hatred for Jews or blacks is like believing that a child can be forced to feel profound love for a particular aunt or cousin. When we are dealing with emotions like love or hate, the rational mind can do nothing but sit on the sidelines while the heart has its way.

I thought a great deal about the tragedy of my father's parents, however, and realized why, as a child, whenever I asked about my unknown set of grandparents, I was given a vague answer. Essentially, I was only told that they both died before I was born, as if that explained anything. But now that I knew the truth, I searched several photo albums for pictures of this unfortunate pair. I found very few photos (had they been discreetly removed?), but in one shot of the family Dad's father stares out over someone's shoulder, looking quite insane. And many years later my sister, acting out of her own curiosity, visited the Wheeling courthouse to look up the death certificates of our grandparents. Dad's father's cause of death was listed on the document as "Suicide," but his mother's was listed as "Gunshot Wound."

After the Rosenberg battle there would be a number of other political disagreements between my ultraconservative father and me, but none were so drastic. In 1960, Dad supported Nixon over Kennedy, and during the campaign mailed me a virtually illiterate screed written by a southern preacher in which Kennedy's Catholicism was presented as virtually Satanic. I shouldn't have done it, but I decided to correct the many mistakes of spelling, syntax, and grammar and sent the hand-edited pamphlet back to my father. I explained that I'd spent so much time trying to straighten out the preacher's garbled writing that I hadn't yet had time to read the piece for content. In retrospect I see that it was a smart-ass thing for me to have done, but I was acting, once again, out of anger. I don't recall ever sending my father any liberal political material because I knew it would be hopeless. Dad rejected all Democrats out of hand, particularly Harry Truman, who some people thought he resembled, but then he often said that he despised *all* politicians: "They're all crooks. Every one of them."

Nevertheless he grudgingly supported Goldwater and Nixon, both of whom I gleefully opposed, and in 1965 and 1966 we argued about the strategic and moral necessity for the war in Vietnam. Dad's untimely death from a heart attack in October of 1966 preceded the country's most contentious split between pro-peace and pro-war factions, but had he lived it would have difficult for either of us to stay calm about such a divisive national calamity.

Nicki, The Motherwell Seminar, and Europe

My first real love affair (infatuation, late adolescent fling, sexual adventure, or whatever you want to call it) happened at Oberlin when I met Nicki, a magical creature two years younger than I. She was, to my love-struck eyes, not only beautiful but also extremely intelligent and creative in quirky, unpredictable ways. I was enchanted. She had a supple, sensual body, and when we finally made love it was the first time for both of us. We eagerly gave up our respective virginities one warm spring evening, by moonlight, on a hillside surrounded by fragrant pine trees.

We reached that milestone in our young lives during a weekend trip I'd arranged to Wheeling for the express purpose of making love under the most idyllic conditions. Early in the afternoon I stashed a blanket in the trunk of the car so that after dinner we could leave without raising undue parental suspicions. I told them that I was going to "drive around town to show Nicki the (meager) sights."

I drove straight to a place in the country, an old camping area from my high school years, which I knew intimately. I parked the car, retrieved the blanket, and led Nicki up a gentle hill and into a wide grassy area at the center of a circle of pines. I spread out the blanket and we embraced. Knowing that we had all the time in the world, I slowly undressed her, gradually unveiling her beautiful body, and then, under the stars, we made love. It was simultaneously magical, and passionate and erotic – everything one's first time should be.

Many years later, when my daughter Grace turned seventeen and began dating seriously, I took her aside for a fatherly chat. I told her that there was something she would only do once in her life, and that it was important she try to do it right. This experience was, of course, the first time she would make love. Don't let anyone pressure you into it, I said, and don't do it hurriedly or awkwardly in the back seat of a car. Try to make it as magical and as memorable as you can, with a partner you really love. Then I told her about my first time on that grassy hillside, under the stars, and how perfect it had been for both of us. I hoped that my little sermonette took, but I was secretly afraid that perhaps I had preached it a little too late. Nevertheless, I think Grace appreciated the advice, and the intimacy of our conversation.

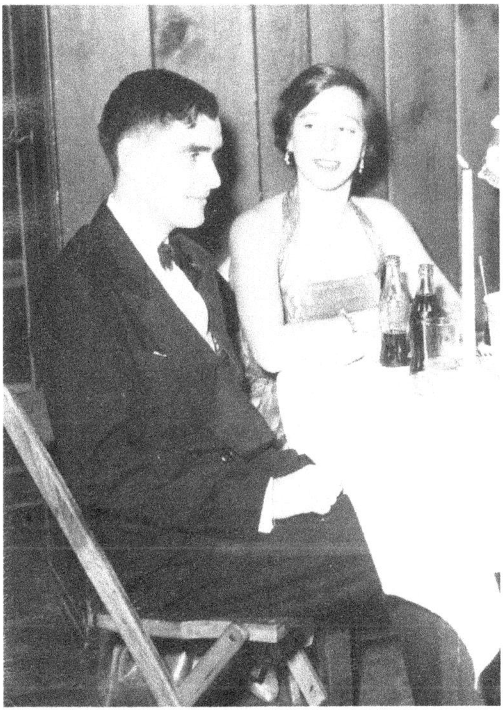

Nicki, gowned and sultry, and I with a bad haircut and a rental tux.

An interesting side issue about my parents' meeting Nicki had to do with the fact that even though she was Jewish, my father was very welcoming and even affectionate towards her, though she was shy around him. One mitigating factor may have been the fact that she was a beautiful, sensual young woman, and Dad was not blindly indifferent to attractive women. Leaving a movie theater he might use a guardedly neutral expression, such as, "Rita Hayworth certainly does have a beautiful figure." To me, Dad's euphemisms sounded as if he were describing a perfect circle or a lovely bit of calligraphy, rather than a sexually enticing woman, and though he naturally did not say such a thing about Nicki, I'm sure he noticed her obvious attributes.

The absence of any tinge of anti-Semitism, I think, was mainly the result of Dad's kind of bigotry. Though he disparaged Jews collectively, when he actually met an individual Jew such as Nicki, he was able to find her a charming "exception" to her race, in the same way that he regarded Russell Hicks, his black employee, as an exception to his. For reasons having to do with the shame of his parents' deaths, Dad's bigotry always seemed to me more ideological than personal. It was a style of belief one finds in certain racists and anti-Semites who carefully exempt particular black or Jewish friends from their bigoted condemnations.

IN THE SPRING OF 1952, the artist Robert Motherwell came to Oberlin for a one-man show at the Allen Art Museum and during his visit gave a series of lectures for art students. At the time I knew very little about contemporary abstract painting, so his exhibition and his seminars together came as a revelation. At 37, Motherwell was the youngest and most articulate of the leading Abstract Expressionists, and for several years he had been a kind of informal spokesman for the group. I'd seen reproductions of the work of some of these painters – Pollock, De Kooning, Rothko and Kline in particular – though I'd never heard anything very insightful said about them. But in 1952, in the person and words and art of Robert Motherwell, Abstract Expressionism not only came alive for me but became a magnet, a goal, and in many ways a future way of life.

After Oberlin and that seminar everything happened much more quickly than I could ever have imagined. Within a year or two I was living in New York and had begun using in my own work the kind of automatic, gestural approach that Motherwell espoused. I was attending the artists' club, hanging out at the Cedar Bar, and, miracle of miracles, becoming friends with the painters whose work Motherwell had spoken about so eloquently.

But in 1952, prior to hearing his lectures and studying his work, I had bumbled around Oberlin, taking studio and art history courses (all rather conservative) and even a philosophy class in esthetics, trying to absorb whatever I could from whatever sources were available. I was a thirsty sponge. When a film on the sculpture of Alexander Calder was shown, I was so affected that I began turning out wire and cardboard imitation Calder mobiles, one after another. For a while about half the college dining rooms had one of my fragile, short-lived contraptions dangling over their entranceways, gift of the artist, naturally. Any modern painting or sculpture I saw or read about affected me with almost equal force because everything was new. My esthetic sensibility was virgin territory.

Motherwell's lectures and exhibition changed all that. Speaking with a slow, almost halting eloquence, he was remarkably charismatic, and in his relaxed, off-the-cuff talks one sensed his commitment to precision, his struggle always to come up with the most apt and descriptive phrase. He would often stop in mid-sentence, back up, try out different words, hesitate, reject and then select yet another phrase. Then he would move on, still not completely satisfied. His way of speaking reminded me of a draughtsman sketching lightly, pausing, lifting his pencil, marking again, and then again in searching, parallel strokes, seeking the elusive, most expressive contour. Motherwell's sentences, like the lines in a Cezanne drawing, might seem irresolute at first until one realized that they had the authority of a solemn quest. Along with his unusually respectful attitude toward language, another reason for Motherwell's effectiveness as a lecturer had to do with the timbre of his voice: deep, resonant, and absolutely compelling. But it was, of course, what he had to say about painting that captivated me. He expressed the belief that art belonged on a plane where ethical and esthetic concerns were so intertwined as to become virtually indistinguishable. The range of colors he characteristically used – black, white, brown, blue, and red – had personal meaning for him: black for death, blue for the sky and the sea, red for blood, and so on. He tended to restrict himself to those hues, explaining that it felt somehow inauthentic to use colors for which he felt no strong personal associations. Painting was nothing less than a way of life in which authenticity of feeling was paramount.

It's not surprising, then, that Motherwell's most memorable lecture had to do with the life and work of the most ascetic of modern artists, Piet Mondrian. The authority of the Dutch abstractionist's drastically simplified, luminous paintings affected me like nothing

I'd ever seen, and I accepted their power as a miracle beyond my understanding. In their strange, distilled purity they were mystical, and yet at the same time they were fully physical: bright, clear, and precise.

Until my acquaintance with Mondrian's work, I had thought of mysticism in art as synonymous with vagueness and an indefinable, unfocussed yearning. Yet his paintings were rigorous, tough, classical, and the least hazy paintings I'd ever seen in my life. Though Motherwell talked about Mondrian's impoverished, ascetic life and his devotion to the spiritual logic of his work, his importance for me lay in the paintings themselves: their mysterious networks of simple black lines, their carefully-placed rectangles of brilliant primary color, and, dominating everything, the overpowering radiance of white. Pure, luminous, radiant white.

I immediately set about to find photographs and reproductions of his work and to try my hand at producing a Mondrian. I failed miserably at the latter, but though reproductions were hard to locate, I was eventually able to obtain the *Documents of Modern Art* collection of his essays, a thin, well-illustrated paperback book that took a central position in my growing art library. Robert Motherwell was the editor of this invaluable series of artists' writings, a collection which nourished hundreds of painters in the 1950s and beyond, and it is again part of the surprising trajectory of my life, that many years later, when Robert decided to retire from the editorship of the *Documents* series, he asked me to be his successor. I was honored, of course, but since I didn't regard myself as a scholar or editor and was not willing to take away from my painting the large of amount of time editing the series would require, I declined his generous offer and historian Jack Flam was named in my place.

My reaction to the Motherwell exhibition of paintings and collages at Oberlin's Allen Art Museum was to be both captivated and subtly instructed as to how Abstract Expressionist works came to be. I began, myself, to practice Motherwell's (or Kline's or De Kooning's) method of construction. I started each work with a series of spontaneous, "automatic" gestures which I then studied and responded to with still more semi-undirected marks, until the forming, shaping impulses took over and began to establish order from the open "chaos" of the field. Often, if I was lucky, I was able to achieve a surprising, unexpected order. It's as if, at the outset, the painting painted the artist, rather than the other way around.

I began to fill small notebooks with automatic drawings, little more than quick, deliberately blurred doodles, but which at their best contained a range of interesting, organic, even sexual forms. It would not be until I was in New York in 1953 with my own studio that I was finally able to turn these drawings – and I did hundreds upon hundreds of them – into related paintings, but I was on my way.

As a result of the Motherwell lectures, my interest in the other artists of the Abstract Expressionist group deepened, and I began to collect reproductions of their work, too. In 1951, Thomas B. Hess, the critic most closely identified with this movement, had published a book called *Abstract Painting: Background and American Phase*, which Motherwell recommended during one of his talks. I bought it and relished its color plates of paintings by Gorky, De Kooning, Pollock, Rothko, Motherwell, and Gottlieb. My copy, now more than 50 years old, is dog-eared and taped together from overuse, but for a while it provided a constant physical reminder of why I needed to get out of Oberlin and Wheeling and head straight for New York. When I graduated in 1953 that is exactly what I did.

It would be another twenty years before Robert Motherwell and I became friends and he learned just what an effect he'd had on my life and art. We eventually became gallery-mates in the same Provincetown Gallery – Longpoint – and our lives came together in many ways. But the simple truth was that his 1952 exhibition and seminar at Oberlin was the fuse that lit the rest of my life.

IN JUNE OF 1952 – a truly watershed year – there was yet another major event in my life: my first trip to Europe. The tour was meticulously planned by my father who had, of course, been in Europe during the two World Wars, and in the late 1930s had made another trip organized by the American Legion. I realize now that Dad, something of an explainer and teacher himself, obviously wanted to show his family the battlefield sites where he had fought and the European cities where he had spent his leaves. It was important to him that my sister and I go along, even though I was 21 and trying to be independent, and Ellie was almost nineteen. But since this European grand tour offered me a chance to see the great museum collections, I had a selfish reason to swallow my late-adolescent pride and accept my father's generous offer.

As it turned out, the trip delivered all the esthetic revelations I expected, but at the same time it demonstrated the enormous and depressing gulf between my parents and sister – the three of them on one side, the shoppers and sightseers – and I, the museum-goer and art fanatic, on the other. This pattern was repeated time and time again, in virtually every city we visited. In Paris the others shopped and saw the usual sights, while I spent hours in the Louvre, enthralled by its incredible collections. Not surprisingly, however, I believe the Louvre was the only art museum my parents and sister visited during the entire trip. They entered, asked where to find the Mona Lisa and the Venus de Milo, found them, looked at them, and left.

In Amsterdam or Venice or wherever we happened to be, I would depart in the morning to go to the museums and galleries and would rejoin the others late in the afternoon. And even though our dinners together were always stimulating because of the food and the settings, they were deeply frustrating because I was bursting to share with someone – anyone – the excitement and beauty of what I had seen that afternoon. No one in the family, however, seemed at all interested in my art discoveries.

In Rome I was lucky enough to meet a young art student who was far more sophisticated than I, and who introduced me to the gloriously bizarre churches of Borromini and Bernini and the powerful paintings of Caravaggio. The enthusiasm for the Italian Baroque that he instilled in me is still present now, after more than 50 years, and in fact, one of my greatest recent pleasures took place during a recent visit to Rome where I was able to show these same sculptural churches and overwhelming Caravaggios to Leslie, my companion, my colleague, and my partner. Since then she has become as enamored by Caravaggio's paintings as I, and as subtle in her judgment of their varying qualities as my young guide was in 1952.

Yet during the 1952 European tour my most personal quest was to locate as many Mondrian paintings as possible to satisfy the hunger that Motherwell's lecture and slides had so powerfully created in me. In a related way I sought out every work I could find by Vermeer because I felt an emotional connection between the two great Dutch artists. To me, it was as if Vermeer's classical seventeenth century calm and Mondrian's modern abstract purity and mysticism were subtly linked in a gentle, brotherly dialogue that enriched each.

ONE SIDE TRIP WE MADE to visit a farm where Dad had been billeted in World War I turned out to be a very moving experience, but it also provided me with an unusual glimpse into the complexity of his usually reined-in emotions. Shortly after the First World War ended, Dad, a young lieutenant of artillery, was part of what was called the Army of Occupation of Germany. He would have been 29 or 30 at the time and was quartered with a German family on a small, rather primitive farm. The farmer and his hard-working wife were a few years older than he, and according to Dad's recollections the couple had been very kind to him. Despite a huge language problem, they eventually became friends.

We had rented a small English car for our European trip, and so, map in hand, Dad drove along narrow country lanes until we finally reached a very modest little farmhouse. "This is it," he said, "and it hasn't changed much in 43 years." No one was expecting us, and for some reason my mother and sister declined to get out of the car with Dad and me to see who might still be living there. Though his German was almost nonexistent, Dad knocked on the door and called out a garbled greeting. A young woman opened the door, and the two tried to talk as she led us inside, with Dad struggling to explain who he was and why we were there. Eventually she understood that he was asking about the Frau of the house when he finally pronounced her name. The young woman then took us to a window and pointed out an elderly woman who was trudging along, reins in hand, behind a horse that was dragging a plow. The scene struck me as almost medieval.

The young woman – a granddaughter – called to her Nana in German, and in a few minutes, after she'd tied up the horse, Dad's friend of more than 40 years ago joined us. Somehow, despite the way they both had aged, they recognized each other and embraced, and I saw tears in my father's eyes. Conversation was almost impossible, of course, but the old matriarch led us over to a badly framed photograph on the wall showing a three-tiered family group posing gravely. From their period clothes I guessed that the picture dated from the later 1930s, and considering the era I was relieved that no one was wearing an armband or a uniform.

Between my father's few German words and her granddaughter's very sparse English, the elderly woman tried to make us understand the identity of the various family members in the photo. She pointed out her husband, the farmer Dad had known so long ago, and we understood that he had died before World War II. Then she pointed to a young man, a son, killed fighting on the Russian front; a daughter, now a doctor and living in Munich; and then another daughter, killed during a British bombing raid. There was also a grandson, a young teenager, shot by the SS for who knows what suspected crime, and so on, through the entire family. All were, in one way or another, victims of the Russians, Americans, British, or Nazis – all casualties among the millions who suffered or died during Hitler's maniacal war.

We left soon after the old widow finished showing Dad the photo of her now decimated family as it once had been, living together during the last gasp of peace. As we got into our car I could see how moved he was, how strongly his memories had been stirred, and that he must be aware that he would never again see this old woman. She was someone who, in their shared youthful years, had been kind to him, an old woman for whom politics and war and defeat had only meant death, destruction, and the loss of so many members of her family. We drove on, and it was a long time before either Dad or I managed to speak.

While we traveled from city to city, country to country, I also sketched and drew, and was especially intrigued by the old hilltop castles, ruined or restored, we passed on the way. It's not a surprise that this antiquarian interest of mine surfaced again decades later, in 1999, during a month-long stay in the south of France. Crouched on various hillsides, I made a series of small drawings of local castles, *chateaux*, and churches, influenced – deliberately – by memories of the work of Corot.

In retrospect I can see on many levels the continuity between the life-long preoccupations of my art and my four years in Oberlin. Those years began with an art history lecture about Corot and came to a climax in Motherwell's Mondrian lecture and the introduction to Abstract Expressionism he had provided. But there is a coda to that remarkable summer of 1952. When we returned from Europe, Dad had arranged a short stay in New York, and I was able to visit the Museum of Modern Art for the first time. Not only did I see a number of Mondrians, and, of course, the great, classic Picassos and Matisses that the Museum owns, but I saw and was astonished by the now-legendary *15 Americans* exhibition that featured works by Jackson Pollock, Mark Rothko, Clifford Still, and other Abstract Expressionists that Motherwell's lectures had introduced to me. At that exhibition I was a very young spectator standing in awe outside the velvet rope. But in less than two years I would be living in New York, painting and drawing obsessively, having lunch occasionally with Mark Rothko at a local drugstore, hanging out at the Cedar Bar, befriending Franz Kline, Bill De Kooning, and the other Abstract Expressionist painters, and aware that, as if by a miracle, my feet were now firmly planted well inside the velvet rope.

In 1952, however, I did not yet understand that my adult life had begun in earnest.

Manhattan, At Last

In September 1953, I bailed out of Wheeling, the small city where I was born, and landed on my feet in New York, the true metropolis, where I've lived ever since. As a compromise with my nervous father who had agreed to pay my tuition at Columbia University, I enrolled in graduate school to calm his worries about my future. I told him that I would study art history under the great Meyer Schapiro, whose books on Cezanne and Van Gogh I had devoured at Oberlin, and that a Columbia Masters Degree would eventually lead to a teaching job. My secret hope, of course, was that things would work out differently, and that graduate school would represent a halfway house on my way to becoming an artist. And that is exactly the way it turned out.

In 1953, Eisenhower was president and the Korean War was winding down, but I was aware that even if peace were fully upon us, graduate school could provide me a year or so of deferment from the draft. I am not proud of this self-serving calculation on my part, especially since types like Dick Cheney, George W. Bush, and Donald Rumsfeld later all availed themselves of similar deferments to evade service in a dangerous and very bloody war, but in 1953, in peacetime, deferment is what I sought. Ironically, when I finally took my pre-induction physical, I was 4-F and had worried needlessly.

From the first day of my arrival, New York was a revelation. Despite four years at Oberlin, I was still pretty much an unsophisticated West Virginia hick, so everywhere I turned I found new things to explore. Nicki had transferred from Oberlin to Barnard College, so together we set out to sample the pleasures and cultural enticements of the city. In the first few months we joined the Poetry Center at the YMHA, attending readings by W.H. Auden, Marianne Moore, Truman Capote, Dylan Thomas, and other major figures whose works I had read as a student. We spent hours in museums, especially MoMA (the Museum of Modern Art), where I later obtained a lowly job selling admission tickets, memberships, postcards, and so on. We explored the world of foreign films at the Thalia on the upper West Side, and the classic silent comedies of Chaplin, Harold Lloyd, and Buster Keaton at the MoMA's repertory theater. I couldn't get enough of the feather-light films of Rogers and Astaire, and laughed myself silly when the subversive W.C. Fields hurled outrageous gags at middle-class prudes. Like truly besotted novices, Nicki and I explored and relished everything available to us: sex, art galleries, restaurants, the Village (where I finally found a tiny place to live on Waverly Place), as well as bars, used-book stores, film clubs, and whatever else we discovered that was fascinating, free, or at least very cheap. Oddly, it would be several months before I first visited the Cedar Bar, the saloon that would eventually become extraordinarily important to a beginner like me as an art-world hangout, a source of friends, and a makeshift schoolroom of a peculiar kind.

Everything I discovered in New York seemed to marginalize my memories of the safe and conventional life I'd lived in Wheeling. My previous sense of the possible had expanded exponentially. Food, for example, was a minor but telling example. My mother was a good cook and we were always well fed, but in New York I encountered, almost daily, delicious new things to eat in the Chinese and Italian restaurants we frequented because they offered the best inexpensive meals we could find. There always seemed to be unusual flavors and foodstuffs to try – unusual because my mother never used them in her cooking. Garlic, for example, was regarded in middle-class Wheeling as fit only for immigrants, people who were often contemptuously called "hunkies," a bastardized version, I presume, of "Hungarians." Cheeses were severely limited to cheddar, Swiss, and American, and I don't recall ever seeing an avocado, an eggplant, or an artichoke at our table. In New York, these, along with a staggering array of pasta dishes and omnipresent staples like pizza, bagels, cheesecake, and even pistachio nuts, were discoveries, as exotic to me as papayas or breadfruit might be to a Pacific castaway.

In retrospect, I see that my mother's cooking constituted what might now be called "Red State Cuisine." Our standard Wheeling fare was beef, pork, or chicken, served with mashed or baked potatoes, peas, green beans, or corn, and ice cream, cake, or pie for dessert. Seafood, partly because of its unavailability, was rare. I don't recall having lobster until I came to New York, and though we occasionally had scallops or a piece of swordfish, peculiar-looking things like oysters, clams, and mussels were not to be seen in our house. (For some reason Dad liked to make fried oysters just for himself at Christmastime, but I first discovered the glories of raw shellfish on Cape Cod a few years later.) Breakfast was usually bacon and eggs or pancakes, and Sunday dinner featured a stuffed roast chicken or a beef or pork roast, which my father carved with his usual deft authority. The truth was that although my mother was skilled at preparing a meat-and-potatoes menu, and I had consumed it with gratitude and pleasure, my new life in New York meant that pesto and paella were in and that iceberg lettuce and meatloaf were out.

Despite all of this exploratory excitement, my passionate relationship with Nicki was gradually becoming more difficult. I had begun to notice signs of serious emotional strains, troubling moments in which her behavior seemed irrational and which led one evening to a major and final crisis. We had met for supper at a cafeteria, intending to see a movie afterward, when Nicki told me of a dream she'd had that I was having an affair with a classmate of hers at Barnard. I treated the mention lightly, as an amusing dream, but she soon began to change her story, claiming that it was not a dream and that I was romantically involved with her friend. I patiently explained that I'd never even met her friend and had no idea who she was, but Nicki insisted, with mounting anger, that the affair was real and that I was, in fact, in love with her classmate.

The whole thing was bizarre, particularly since she had said at first that it was only a dream and I knew I'd never met this friend of hers, but now it was becoming serious. We had just left the restaurant and started for the theater when suddenly a fist crashed into my face. I spun around, stunned, trying to see who had hit me, and was aware that Nicki was weeping loudly; it was she who had struck me, cutting my lip. A group of astonished passers-by stopped and stared at me as blood dripped off my chin. One Good Samaritan fished out a couple of tissues for me to mop up my face. Nicki was in an extraordinary state, crying uncontrollably like a child as I turned and, to avoid the gawkers, took her arm and steered her into the nearest subway entrance. She finally dried her tears as a train came and we headed uptown, back to her dormitory at Barnard. I tried to console her, but she said nothing about why she'd attacked me. Most unnerving of all, before we reached the subway stop at Columbia, she began to laugh, as if in her mind she was viewing the incident and my swollen lip as a crazy joke.

I knew that night that I had to end our relationship. I was self-protective enough to realize that I was unable to handle what seemed to be her very real emotional problems, and that her behavior towards me could become even more dangerous. And yet, despite everything, I was still infatuated with her. She had been my first real lover. She had an odd, entrancing intelligence and was so deliciously sensual. Yet I knew I had to leave her. I grieved for a long, long time afterward, and have never forgotten her – or the magical time we had together when we first made love on that hill, in Wheeling, in the moonlight, surrounded by a ring of tall, fragrant pine trees.

Half a century ago, the broad, magnetic pull that drew so many of us Middle-Western refugees to New York City was, for me, obviously focused on the Abstract Expressionist painters living here: Willem De Kooning, Jackson Pollock, Franz Kline, and their illustrious colleagues. But along the way, I admit I fantasized that in its glamorous riches, Manhattan would also provide me with myriad other surprises and rewards: sexual, emotional, and financial. Except for the financial part, I was right, of course, almost from the beginning.

During my first months in New York, I shared a small, furnished apartment with two fellow Oberlin graduates. For spending money I took on a variety of mundane jobs, such as clerking in a bookstore and working briefly at Gimbels department store. At Columbia, I began attending Meyer Schapiro's art history course, which held me spellbound. Beyond any doubt he was the most compelling lecturer I have ever listened to, and eventually we formed a casual friendship.

A few months after my breakup with Nicki, I somehow met a group of young New Yorkers, perhaps five or ten years older than I, who were living an amazingly unfettered existence. Their freewheeling life style was partly due, I realized, to the fact that some of them seemed to have quite a bit of money. They were not artists, though one of the women, Annie, plump and sexy and very funny, made thinly-painted, semi-surreal works that had a peculiar charm, somewhere between Edward Gorey and Rene Magritte. I remember one work entitled *Young Girl Taking Her Whale for a Walk*. She'd painted an Alice-in-Wonderland child holding a ribbon, a pink leash around the waist of a gigantic, accurately drawn whale that floated calmly through most of the sky in what was otherwise a conventional landscape.

Annie and her philandering husband, whose name I can't recall, introduced me to Joanne, a beautiful, clean-limbed but hard-eyed beauty whom I fell madly in love with, and who, I believe, enjoyed me for my obedience and naïveté the way a young matron enjoys her poodle. I remember making love to her with the ardor of an infatuated teenager, while she coolly informed me, as she lay back passively, exactly what it took to get her off. Years later I was told that Joanne had been a drug addict and that she had died of an overdose in her thirties, but at the time I knew her I was too captivated to even notice.

Annie and her husband and Joanne introduced me to many things, including marijuana, which I enjoyed even though I had been a non-smoker, and Café Society, in the person of the great Mabel Mercer. We went a number of times to the Plaza Hotel to hear this nonpareil of cabaret singers, who performed while regally seated and who resembled a British mulatto version of Eleanor Roosevelt. Mabel Mercer's extraordinary diction and clarity and controlled passion made her the greatest singer I've ever heard,

Joan Sutherland and opera aside.

The very first evening I spent with the bibulous trio of Annie, her husband, and Joanne, I was also introduced to Drambuie, the Scotch-based liqueur. Already a Scotch drinker, I found Drambuie to be a delicious, syrupy, extremely aromatic version of the real thing. The impromptu party where I first tasted this ambrosia was held in the Village apartment of someone who had sublet the place to a friend of Annie's, and we managed to pry open his locked liquor cabinet to find three or four bottles of the golden stuff. Now Drambuie is not something you can drink in any quantity without making yourself sick. I drank a lot of it and made myself sick, but I've never gotten over the rich, effusive aroma and taste of this special liqueur. I think that if it were to be served straight up in a really huge brandy snifter, you might be overcome by the glorious fumes and pass out happily before ever putting mouth to liquid.

Often when this free-living group partied, there were orgies going on in various bedrooms – discreetly, one might say, if that word can ever be applied to an orgy. I didn't participate. Unfortunately (or fortunately) I was never asked, and God knows what they did to one another, and in what combinations, behind those closed doors. I was content to sneak my blond, pony-tailed, hard-bitten but beautiful Joanne out of the party before it ended, and take her back to my pathetic little apartment to make love, just the two of us. I have only one picture of her now, a grainy shot taken in a 42nd Street photo booth. In it she looks sleek and elegant – she had exquisite cheekbones – but very unhappy. That cheap photograph, unfortunately, documents exactly the way she was.

We went together for three or four months before Joanne evidently decided she wanted someone more worldly, and wealthier, than I. On one of our last bar hopping excursions, the two of us were sitting in the San Remo, nursing our third Scotches, and she was telling me an enticingly lurid story about a party that she and Annie had attended recently. I was listening with rapt attention – she had a nice, terse way with words – and studying her serious, patrician face. I was infatuated with her, her adventures, and her sybaritic lifestyle. Interrupting her suddenly, I told her I thought we should get married. She gave me a quick, surprised smile, not entirely lacking in warmth, and then resumed her story. She paused only to order another round of drinks, and that was that. The subject never came up again.

I guess everyone is entitled, at least once, to run with the fast crowd, and that time, back in the winter of 1953, was my time. In retrospect, my affair with Joanne was so cockeyed and one-sided that I'm surprised it lasted as long as it did. Like most of her many friends, she was an alcoholic, and apart from that and drugs she had a core of bitterness and disappointment that seemed to make love impossible for her. I think she liked me because I was so bedazzled by her, and perhaps because my West Virginia innocence, though fading fast, must have seemed an attractive novelty.

At any rate, life in Joanne's fast lane was, for many reasons, impossible for me to maintain for very long. Obviously I didn't have the money to support the trips to the Plaza, the long taxi rides, or the expensive dinners out that she and her friends enjoyed. At every party, cheap champagne flowed in abundance, but it was noticed that I rarely contributed cash to the flow. Even worse were the inevitable hangovers. My Meyer Schapiro lectures and my paltry day jobs required that I show up clean and bright, and be able, at least to some extent, to think clearly and make the correct change. And so my brief fling with glamour and decadence eventually just petered out, allowing me once more to live on my normal starvation wages and be able to face myself in the mirror in the morning, headache-free. My world of Weimar wild oats was soon replaced by the community of artists I met in the galleries and at the Cedar Bar, the reason I had come to New York in the first place.

IT'S DIFFICULT, NOW, so many years later, to recall exactly where and how I met each of the many artists, critics, collectors, and general hangers-on who collectively made up the New York art world in the early 1950s. I know I met Franz Kline at the opening of one of his shows at the Egan Gallery, and that I introduced myself to Mark Rothko at the Museum of Modern Art's cafe. I also know that I met

Bill De Kooning, Earl Kerkam, Jackson Pollock, and many others at the Cedar Bar, a place that drew artists the way Istanbul attracted spies.

One of the first things I learned was that no matter how well-known and successful I thought these Abstract Expressionist (AbEx) artists were, based upon my having seen articles and photos about them in *Life* magazine, hearing Motherwell's lectures, and seeing paintings by a number of them in the Museum of Modern Art, I discovered that almost none of them had sold very much, and most were hurting badly from lack of money. In other words, these middle-aged, well-known artists and I – a kid in his early twenties, a mere beginner – were in some ways floating around in the same leaky boat.

The second thing I learned was that the New York art scene was much smaller than I had imagined, containing perhaps 250 people: artists, critics, curators, collectors, and committed kibitzers.

And third, I realized that the Abstract Expressionist movement, which I had assumed was familiar to most educated people, was about as familiar to them as the administration of Chester A. Arthur, our 21st American President. As an example of this lack of cultural information, a good friend of mine, Herman Somberg, a painter for whom art was everything, came to my 15th Street loft one day after I'd told him that two attractive young women, recent college graduates, had moved into the building. Hoping to score something or other, Herman had me take him upstairs to meet them.

Now an unavoidable fact about Herman was that he had some kind of speech defect and always pronounced "S" as "Sh." This rendered his most common interjection, "Christ sakes," as a saliva spouting "Chrisht shakes." When the ex-coeds invited us in for a beer, Herman began talking to one of them while I chatted with the other. After a while, when the young woman he'd been talking to went to fetch him a second cold one, he came over to me and wetly whispered, "Chrisht shakes, I jusht mentioned Pollock and Bill De Kooning to that girl and she'd never heard of either one of them!"

After she returned and handed him his beer, he resumed his name-riddled art conversation. But a few minutes later an even more exasperated Herman came over to me and whispered, "Chrisht shakes, Budd. Letsh get the hell out of here. I just mentioned Shezanne and Gauguin and she'd never heard of them either!"

When art is your life, it's hard to accept another person's indifference, a painful lesson I had learned travelling with my family in Europe.

Herman Somberg was a denizen of the Cedar Bar and for years had been a close friend of Franz Kline. An autodidact who could talk endlessly about Cezanne or Picasso or, for that matter, Proust or the films of Rene Clair, Herman seemed to have no ego of his own. "I've never known anyone who talked less about himself than Herman," Kline said to me one day. "I've known him for years and still don't know anything much about him."

That kind of selflessness was truly rare in the 1950s, and particularly among Cedar habitués. As an example, the place had an old-fashioned phone booth near the bar, and certain painters, afraid that their names weren't being mentioned enough, sometimes disguised their voices and made anonymous calls to the Cedar, asking whoever answered to page them. This guaranteed that the caller's name would be shouted out, perhaps several times, before the unwitting shouter came back to the phone to report that the person the man sought wasn't there that night. This tawdry trick must have satisfied a certain kind of egotist who could be sure, at the very least, that everyone in the Cedar had heard his name loud and clear.

Physically, the Cedar Bar – technically the Cedar Street Tavern, though it was located on University Place near 8th Street – was a workingman's barroom so nondescript, so utterly lacking in even a touch of visual interest, that it drew artists by the score. This might seem perverse, but the truth is that, away from their studios and in search of a clubroom that sold cheap beer, visual dullness was just what the artists wanted. Paradoxically, this drab barn of a place was to become the scene of many legendary events and oft-told stories from the history of Abstract Expressionism: brutal arguments; glamorous fistfights; seminal conversations; broken, mended, and newly-minted friendships; plus a thousand other familiar incidents, both historic and trivial.

The 1950s art world, as exemplified by the regulars at the Cedar Bar, was an amazing collection of vivid personalities: ego-ridden wannabes; great, innovative artists; hopeless drunks; witty raconteurs; shy, private people; and restless satyrs constantly trolling for women. (Naturally, some of these categories overlapped.) As one might expect, painting, sex, and art-world politics were the main topics of conversation, with jokes as part of the leavening. At a given night at the Cedar, Franz Kline, wearing an expensive tweed sport coat and frazzled khaki pants, would be standing with friends near the door, smiling, telling stories, making wisecracks, and dazzling everyone with his descriptions of, say, Rembrandt's brush and ink drawings or the velocity of Lautrec's line. De Kooning, in a knitted Dutch seaman's cap, might be seated nearby at the bar, quietly talking with a friend in his intense, cryptic, and poetic way, while in a back booth, Barnett Newman, decked out like an aging British dandy, monocle tightly in place and his cavalry officer's mustache beautifully trimmed, would be speaking to his coterie about transcendental art and the Sistine ceiling. At the edge of this group, a younger artist, one of the envious lesser-knowns who was obviously irritated by Newman's haberdashery, would look him up and down and mutter, "What, no spats?" To which Barney would smile, unoffended, having succeeded in grabbing and holding the man's attention.

Back in one of the crowded booths towards the rear, Steve Pace, in his flat-crowned farmer's hat, might be gazing down into his now-empty beer glass as a friend mentions Pierre Bonnard. "Bonnard..." Steve would murmur softly. "I like him. I bet he never shined his shoes." And there was Earl Kerkam, a senior, much-admired figure painter, having his dinner with a group of younger artists. He would sit with his bald pate gleaming, his hands trembling, and his false teeth on the table beside him as he gummed a plate of ketchup-drenched spaghetti. "What about Max Beckman?" someone might ask, and Kerkam, without a moment's hesitation and with his mouth full of spaghetti, would answer, "Max Beckman is the greatest modern painter around that nobody likes."

And so it went. During those tense, repressive Eisenhower years, the Cedar Bar was host to every kind of personal style, of painting, of esthetic discourse, of costume, facial hair, argumentativeness, and so on. Artists adopted social poses that ranged from the embittered to the theatrical, the grandiose, the defeated, the vicious, the helpful, and the condescending. It was into this heady mix that I threw myself, in 1954, at the tender age of 23.

In the meantime I had been accepted by the Museum of Modern Art, literally in the entry position of selling entry tickets, at 60 cents each, and handling book, membership, and postcard sales at what we called the front desk. The MoMA had only one ticket booth at the time, and I was usually asked to man it because I could punch out tickets and make change more quickly than most of the front-desk serfs. However lowly my job actually was, it had certain secret perks. I could quietly let my artist friends in free and use my judgment about others.

One day I was startled to see the very tall and stately Eleanor Roosevelt standing at the booth, having just placed her 60 cents on the counter in front of me. I handed the money back and informed her that she was my guest today. Leaving my post – a big no-no – I came around, took her by the arm, and led her into the museum. I told her, shyly, that I was honored to do so, and, giving me her famous, beatific smile, she replied, "Thank you very much," as if she were almost as shy and embarrassed as I was. Unfortunately, I never found out what she thought about the Modern's collection.

Another day it was the famous Nobelist William Faulkner and his daughter at my ticket booth. After accepting their $1.20, I signaled someone else to take my post for a few minutes while I went AWOL to follow them into the museum. Having read and admired a number of Faulkner's novels, I was curious about his visual enthusiasms and was soon disappointed. He walked right by many great Matisses and Picassos and lingered inordinately long before Pavel Tchelichew's gaudy puzzle painting, *Hide and Seek*. Oh, well, I rationalized, at least he's a great writer. One odd detail I recall about his appearance, apart from his small stature, was his green, narrow-brimmed forester's hat, which sported a neat little feather in its band and made him look rather like a short English Lord on the alert for potential poachers.

Sooner or later, it seemed, every writer, painter, actor, or personality in the Arts came to the Modern, though apart from Mrs. Roosevelt I remember seeing few figures from the world of politics. Another time when I was in the booth selling tickets, the very tall and nearly blind British author Aldous Huxley appeared next in line before me. Like everyone else, I had read his famous novel *Brave New World*, but I also knew that he had written a vicious diatribe against modern art. Yet here he was, with a friend, at the very temple of Modernism. Huxley pulled a hand from his trouser pocket and dumped a mass of coins on the counter in front of me; unable to see, he'd trusted me to fish out two quarters and a dime for his admission. I put the ticket into his hand, shoveled the pile of coins back to him, and watched as, cane in hand, he and his friend slowly entered the museum. I wondered two things: if he hated modern art, why was here, and, second, what on earth could he see anyway?

About fifteen minutes later he came back down to the lobby, muttering angrily to his companion, and left the building. In that short time he'd either had his prejudices reinforced or realized that he was unable to see any of the work on view – or both. Opinions rarely need cogent reasons to be strongly held.

But essentially, during those first years in New York, my job at the Modern was quite marginal. My life revolved around my own developing art, along with regular trips to galleries and other museums, attendance at Meyer Schapiro's lectures, visits to friends' studios, and of course, in the evening, hours spent hanging out at the Cedar Bar. In my work I was slowly developing a more expressionist way of handling paint, though my color tended toward the landscape hues of earths and greens. It was as if memories of the West Virginia hills, of our high school camping trips and the thick, brushy woods I'd lived near for years, were still present in my head but expressed now with some of the energy and daily velocity of New York City. Though it was all still a bit unformed, I knew it was gradually all coming together.

Three Painters

Mark Rothko

DURING A LUNCH BREAK shortly after I began my job at the Museum of Modern Art in 1954, I noticed a large, familiar, and somewhat rumpled man sitting alone in the museum's garden, nursing a coffee. From pictures I'd seen in *Life* magazine and elsewhere, I recognized the stern, frowning face of Mark Rothko. Approaching warily, I told him I was an artist and that I'd seen his extraordinary paintings for the first time in the *15 Americans* show at the Modern in 1952. He seemed pleased, and permitted himself the closest thing to a smile that his depressed personality would allow. He asked me to join him, and that afternoon we began a casual, intermittent, but lifelong friendship.

In conversation Rothko had an intense, intimidating gaze, staring at his companion through round, plastic-rimmed glasses. He had very little small talk and none of the bantering, barroom palaver and wit of Franz Kline, nor, for that matter, the elegantly relaxed fluency of his friend Robert Motherwell. With Rothko, one would never use the word "charming" anywhere near him. Not surprisingly, many of the regulars at the Cedar Bar felt that although Rothko was a terrific painter, his personality was more that of a melancholy rabbi or a dour, censorious priest. I found him magnetic, nevertheless, and on that first day of our meeting he related a personal story that he obviously liked to tell.

During the *15 Americans* show, he said he'd been standing in the room displaying his work when a stranger came over to him and, unaware he was the artist, said something like, "You look like a sensible man. How can the Modern put up such empty, pretentious, fake things as these paintings about nothing?!"

Rothko didn't tell him that they were his, but instead asked the man a few probing questions: "Do you think the color lacks any kind of feeling?" and "When you look at these paintings, do you sense *nothing*... or *something*?" The man seemed confused, and studying the works a bit more carefully, admitted that there was, perhaps, *something* about them, though he wasn't sure what. Mark suggested that they go downstairs for some coffee and talk a bit more about what disturbed the stranger in these "empty" paintings.

After more conversation at the cafe, Mark finally told his companion that he was the artist, though at first he wasn't believed. "But you seem so sensible!" the man said. "So sane."

A few days later the man called him and said he was having trouble getting the paintings out of his head and asked if he could come to Rothko's studio to see some more works and to talk about them. At this point in Mark's story, he paused and then made the point he'd been waiting to make: "So, do you know why I'm here in the café? I'm waiting here because I have an appointment to meet that same man. He's coming again to my studio because he wants to buy his third painting of mine. We've become friends."

ROTHKO'S LARGE, STACKED, delicately brushed and colored rectangles, though undeniably beautiful, arouse in me a variety of unusually somber feelings. Like most of the world's religious art, Rothko's paintings are symmetrical and orderly in a way that suggests the hieratic. I've also thought that his warmer-hued paintings of the early and middle 1950s manage to suggest an unlikely blending of the exquisite color sensibility of Bonnard with the geometrical purity and mysticism of Mondrian. (It was no surprise to me that years after Rothko's death the Pace Gallery mounted a beautiful Bonnard-Rothko exhibition, but I'm still waiting for a knockout Mondrian-Rothko show.)

When I first got to know him, I naturally assumed that he was extremely successful. With collectors beginning to buy and the imprimatur of MoMA behind him, he seemed as solidly established as a New York artist could be. Yet again I underestimated the insecurities that earlier decades of neglect could breed in an artist, as an incident with Rothko clearly demonstrated. He had recently joined the prestigious Sidney Janis Gallery on 57th Street, a place I visited frequently. I was friendly with Sidney himself and asked one day whom he would be showing next. Sidney replied that he was having a Rothko show, and then made the casual comment that the paintings were too big to fit in the elevator. "He'll have to take them off their stretchers, roll them, and bring them up the stairs, and then re-stretch them in the gallery." We chatted a bit about other things, and then I left.

As it happened, a few minutes later I ran into Rothko on the street – East 57th Street had become art gallery row – and told him that I was looking forward to his upcoming show. I mentioned that I'd been talking to his dealer about it, and he immediately burst in: "What did he say?" He seemed desperate to know, so, after telling him that Sydney was very pleased, and trying to remember so casual a conversation, I repeated his remark about the paintings having to be taken off their stretchers and rolled.

"Was he upset by that?" Mark asked, now very anxious. "Did he say it was a problem? Do you think he was upset that the paintings were so big?"

I tried to reassure him that everything was fine, that Sydney was looking forward to his show, and that he'd only made the comment about the paintings' size in relaxed conversation. Still agitated despite my attempts to calm him down, Mark said a curt goodbye and hurried off. I realized then that despite his growing fame and critical acceptance, his many years of art world neglect and his still ongoing financial worries had left him permanently insecure. Sadly, all of the AbEx painters of Rothko's generation suffered in exactly this way. Many, if not most, became alcoholics, and despite the eventual fame and financial success of some, their lives seemed, from the outside, to be profoundly unhappy.

In 1954, the Rothkos lived in an apartment on 54th Street, close to the Museum of Modern Art, and he often lunched at a small, old-fashioned drugstore on Sixth Avenue. It was the kind of place that still had a soda fountain, wire-backed chairs, fancy globes of colored water in the window, and an elderly counter-man who served up grilled cheese sandwiches. Mark and I began to meet there during my lunch break, and like a willing student I listened to him recount his wide-ranging ideas and recollections. He told me about the time he'd spent years before with a theatrical group and his friendship there with the young, unknown Clark Gable. Mark was also acutely interested in politics, and I remember a long conversation about the Supreme Court, as well as many despairing observations about the Eisenhower-Nixon administration.

I've often wondered why he seemed so willing to chat with me; why he, a seasoned man in his fifties, ever bothered with a beginning artist like me, still in my early twenties. I decided that there were, perhaps, several reasons. I was a good listener, for one thing, and a great admirer of his work. And since he lived a somewhat isolated life – he did not approve of the raunchy, alcohol-fueled Cedar Bar crowd and rarely showed up there – perhaps the presence of a young, sober, and still somewhat unformed painter like me was a welcome change. I also think that he wanted to make sure that artists of a younger generation fully understood the meaning and importance of his legacy. But whatever his reasons, I felt lucky to have these casual lunchtime chats with a highly intelligent artist I greatly respected.

At this time, at Columbia, I was auditing one of Meyer Schapiro's legendary graduate classes on modern art. During a lecture about the expressionist painter Chaim Soutine, he pointed out the fact that Soutine, Marc Chagall, and Mark Rothko had all been born in Jewish enclaves in the same general area of pre-revolutionary Russia. He spoke about the rich, colorful Jewish culture that all three had known and which, he believed, had had a great deal to do with forming the emotional content of their art. Then he said that unfortunately the current leaders of the state of Israel had no interest in preserving the ethnic riches of this heritage, opting instead to form a modern industrial state with all the trappings and tawdriness of a typical Western capitalist democracy. Schapiro paused a moment and then went on to say that within Russia most traces of this marvelous traditional culture had been wiped out, first by the Stalinists and then by the invading Nazis. The Holocaust, of course, marked the virtual end of it all.

Then he stopped speaking. He bowed his head and after a moment we could see that he was quietly weeping. The lecture hall, containing perhaps 60 or 70 students, was absolutely silent. Meyer Schapiro, an intellectual whom we all respected to the point of adoration, stood at his desk with tears flowing down his cheeks for what seemed now like many minutes. Finally, Gandy Brodie, a painter friend who, like me, was auditing the class, walked down to the front and put his arms around Schapiro's shoulders, and the class ended.

I was profoundly affected by this experience. Schapiro's limpid humanism was something I'd always known about him but had never seen with such clarity. I was also amazed to have learned of the subtle cultural connections between Rothko, Soutine, and Chagall. What the latter two artists shared was obvious to me: a deliberately Jewish subject matter of villages, rabbis, and simple folk, whimsical in the case of Chagall and deeply anguished in Soutine's. But to know that their lost heritage was also Mark Rothko's gave a new resonance to his austere paintings.

It was only a day or so after Meyer Schapiro's Soutine lecture that I met Rothko at the drug store for a quick lunch and began to tell him what had happened. He listened intently, and rather than seeming to be affected by what was, to me, a profoundly moving incident, his face took on an almost steely coldness. I finished relating what had happened, that after linking him with Chaim Soutine and Marc Chagall, Schapiro broke down in tears for what was also his own lost culture. Mark then looked past me out into the room and said with disdain, "Meyer Schapiro is always so sentimental."

I was so shocked I said nothing. I was too surprised and disappointed to make any kind of comment. It took me a few days to mull over what had happened, and to realize that he was probably working to keep his own personal truth at arms' length. For him, the austerity of his dark rectangles might have represented an attempt to *avoid* being Soutine or Chagall, or, for that matter, Meyer Schapiro. "Sentimental" was Rothko's most damning term of condemnation. Naturally, he couldn't deny that his simplified abstract style was a method he'd developed years before to simultaneously express and transform his own most powerful feelings. But unlike Soutine and Chagall, he chose not to spill his emotions nakedly across his canvases, but instead imbued his ostensibly neutral abstract shapes with an undercurrent of melancholy that often approached the tragic.

His friend, the painter Al Jensen, once told me about one of Rothko's late-night, self-revelatory stories, which seems to confirm this theory. They were drinking together and talking about Mark's earliest years in Russia, before his emigration to America at the age of ten. He told Al that the elders in his village often spoke about the pogroms carried out by the Cossacks in small, isolated Jewish villages, and that the descriptions he heard were so vivid that as a child he had almost come to believe he'd witnessed the killings himself. According to the elders' stories, the Cossacks would sweep into a village and round up all the men and older boys and march them out to a nearby field where, before they were slaughtered, they were forced to dig a large, rectangular hole… ultimately their mass grave.

Mark told his friend that through all his adult life he'd thought about that large, rectangular grave, never being able to get it out of his mind. Then he paused a few moments, and said: "I think I've been painting that grave all my life."

Though I felt that this story was far too personal for me to mention to him, in our conversations about his work he had always insisted that his paintings were concerned with the tragic. This seemed to be true even when he used colors that ordinarily suggest warmth and lyricism. By some emotional alchemy he was able to make even Bonnard's characteristic hues – yellow, orange, and pink – seem deeply pessimistic. Beautiful, undeniably, but still pessimistic.

MY LAST PROLONGED MEETING with Mark Rothko occurred late in 1969, only a few months before his death. I was aware that for years he had been severely depressed and that he had been drinking heavily. Since I was fond of him and enormously respectful of his work, when my friend, the Swiss film actor and collector Maximilian Schell, said he would like to meet him, I arranged a small dinner for just my wife Joan and I, Max, Mark, and Rita Reinhardt, the painter Ad Reinhardt's widow who was Rothko's companion during his final years.

When we gathered in our living room, Maximillian Schell was, as usual, charming and genuinely interesting. He told Rothko about being taken as a boy by his father to meet Herman Hesse, and went on about his experiences with various European intellectuals and writers, obviously hoping to engage him in an absorbing dialogue. Mark would listen for a while, obviously enchanted, and then his eyes would suddenly shift to middle distance and he would seem to leave us all. I was afraid that he might be in physical pain, since I knew that he had recently had serious heart trouble. I was aware that people who have been gravely ill sometimes seem to suddenly tune out, as if they are momentarily compelled to listen for any ominous throbs and ticks within their own bodies.

As the evening wore on, we went down to the studio and I showed Mark, Rita, and Max some of my new paintings, Rothko continued to alternate between genuine interest and this same disconcerting sudden absence from the world. Despite his supportive comments about my work, I was never sure at any given moment if he was actually in the room with us, participating, or away in his own distant space.

It grew late. Mark finally said that he must go, and so he and Rita departed, leaving Joan, Max, and me feeling quite uneasy about the state of his health. I saw him just once again, briefly, at an artist's party in the Village.

A number of weeks later, in early February, Joan brought me *The New York Times* with a front page story about Rothko's suicide. He'd poured himself a glass of Vodka, seated himself in a chair in his studio, and slit his wrists. He bled to death.

In retrospect I realized that his frequent lapses of attention at our small dinner were not because he was listening to the quirks and pangs of his body. Most likely they occurred because he was preparing to leave us – and life – altogether. Suicide, I imagine, is rarely a sudden decision. It must be debated, rehearsed, imagined. Even in the company of friends, oblivion, the absence of life, must be tested. The glowing, soft-contoured rectangles that Rothko painted will always be, for me, graves. Pulsing often with the rich, fragile colors of repressed life, but graves nevertheless.

Jackson Pollock

DURING MOTHERWELL'S LECTURES AT OBERLIN, he spoke about Jackson Pollock, particularly his so called "drip" paintings. Viewing them in the form of color slides, I thought they were uniquely beautiful because of their intricate, dance-like rhythms and resonant color, but since I'd never actually seen one in the flesh, I had no idea of their power and complexity. It wasn't until the summer of 1952, when I was face to face with a number of them in the Modern's *15 Americans* show, that I felt their emotional force and what I

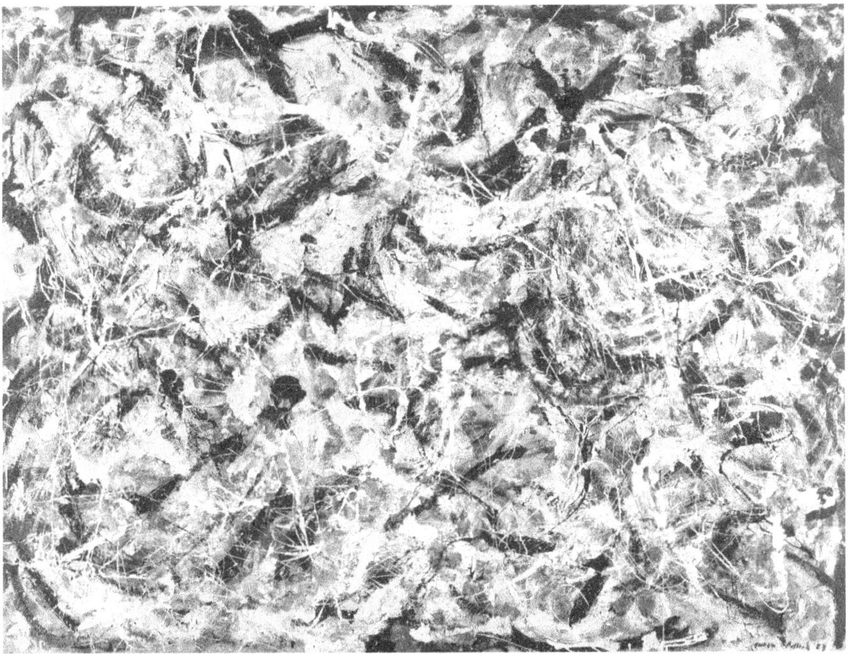

Jackson Pollock, Greyed Rainbow, 1953, oil on canvas, Chicago Art Institute, Gift of Society for Contemporary American Art. Photo: Bob Hashimoto. Reproduction, The Art Institute of Chicago.

can only describe as their underlying torrent of lyrical desperation. I began to understand that the layered intricacy of Pollock's paintings was not merely decorative but was also a way of conveying, beneath the surface beauty, his own very personal anguish. Like De Kooning and Kline, Pollock painted as if his very life depended upon it, which, in retrospect, it possibly did.

By 1953, the year I moved to New York, Pollock was America's best-known modern painter by any measure. The reason for his fame was two-fold. First was the legendary spread in the August 8, 1949, issue of *Life* magazine, headlined "Jackson Pollock: Is he the greatest living painter in the United States?" *Life's* article must have reached many hundreds of thousands of readers who had probably never heard the name of *any* living American artist, nor glimpsed a color reproduction of an abstract painting. Now, however, they had three classic Pollock "drip" paintings in full color to gaze upon, uncomprehendingly. Can these chaotic-seeming works even be art, thousands must have mused, let alone be the productions of the greatest artist in the country?

As if to hedge its bet, *Life* pitched their coverage somewhat negatively, informing the article's inevitably irate readership that despite the claims of a "formidably highbrow New York critic" [Clement Greenberg] who praised his paintings, "others condemn them as degenerate and find them as unpalatable as yesterday's macaroni." Thus the implied score was: one New York egghead versus everybody else who despises degeneracy and cares about the kind of painting where you can see things in it and understand what the heck it means.

Nevertheless, millions of people had seen Arnold Newman's glowing color shots of Pollock's work, and in one photo, the image of Pollock himself, fashionably clad in paint-spattered denims and depicted casually leaning back with his arms folded and a cigarette dangling from his lip. It's difficult to read his posture and demeanor as conveying anything but supreme tough-guy arrogance. In fact, the pose was so strong and defiant that it more or less created the template for later, similar photos of actors like James Dean and Marlon Brando.

The second reason for Pollock's immediate renown was the unique, so-called drip technique itself. After seeing the photos in *Life*, anyone, no matter how esthetically blind, could instantly recognize a Pollock for the same reason that thousands could identify any wire sculpture with oval planes that moved with the breeze as a Calder mobile.

A number of other extra-esthetic issues lent Pollock enormous visibility and acceptance among intellectuals and the art community in general. There had always existed a kind of latent nationalistic desire to have a "Great American Painter" in the same way that Hemingway had become unofficially anointed as the "Great American Novelist," and Robert Frost, the "Great American Poet." (In rather the same way, Alexander Calder was well on his way to becoming the "Great American Sculptor.") There were, of course, many personal standards to be met in order to be thought of as *the* Great American anything. Obviously, like Hemingway, Frost, and Calder, you had to be a "real" American, actually born here. Among Pollock's AbEx contemporaries, Rothko was born in Russia, De Kooning in Holland, Philip Guston in Canada, and Hans Hofmann in Germany, so all four were automatically out of the running. Pollock, however, was not only wholly American but had been born in Cody, Wyoming, a place named after Buffalo Bill Cody, and thus he, Pollock, was even, possibly, *a real cowboy*.

And, lest we forget, in the still subtly anti-Semitic United States, distinguished Pollock colleagues like Barnett Newman, Adolph Gottlieb, Mark Rothko, and Jack Tworkov, being Jews, were as unthinkable in the role of "Great American Painter" as they would have been in the role of Republican presidential candidate.

A second and more relevant credential had to do with the perceived "American" qualities of the various media. Hemingway's stripped-down prose was a far cry from, say, the elaborately nuanced, clause-clogged sentences of the more European Henry James; by comparison, Hemingway was thought to write "like real men talk." And if Pollock was often reticent or seemingly inarticulate, he might bring to mind certain all-American film stars like John Wayne and Gary Cooper, whose style of speech also tended to be halting and quietly spare. By comparison, Robert Motherwell, though properly American and WASP in origin, was far too articulate and literary in the European sense to be a contender in the "Great American Painter" sweepstakes. And Franz Kline also disqualified himself by being too ironic, complex, and humorous in his personality and style of banter, as well as by being the creator of stark black and white images that had little appeal to the unsophisticated. At least Pollock's work had color.

In yet another nativist trait, after the glut of ploddingly traditional American Scene paintings in the 1930s, Pollock, like Calder, had developed a wholly new art technique. Americans like to think of themselves as creative inventors – we revere the Edisons and the Henry Fords among us – and we like to downplay any indebtedness to Europe. The radically new painting technique that Pollock created not only flew in the face of European virtuosity, but its creator also liked to suggest that he'd been influenced by *Native American* sand painting and *Mexican* muralists. Any hint of a Picasso (European) influence in Pollock's work was quickly squelched, while he advertised his friendship with the famous American Scene painter, Thomas Hart Benton. From every perspective, Pollock's Great American credentials were top of the line.

And there were still other issues. Though Pollock had been a notorious alcoholic, in a certain American scheme of things this was viewed less as a personal failing than as an inevitable trait in the authentic creative personality. Famous *European* painters like Monet and Cezanne, or Matisse and Picasso, though not teetotalers, were never renowned drinkers like Ernest Hemingway or Edgar Allan Poe or F. Scott Fitzgerald. Or, obviously, Jackson Pollock. And though at a later time he was perhaps more sunk in the mists of alcohol than his bibulous contemporaries, on balance Pollock's drinking probably did more to support the idea that he was the "Great American Painter" than it did to damage that claim.

And finally, in a kind of self-fulfilling prophecy, one might have speculated that whoever is anointed with that unofficial title will not only have the support of important art critics, but will also turn up in the pages of *Life*, the most popular and successful general magazine in the country. (Years later, Pollock also became the first American artist to become the subject of a major motion picture, one that was seen by an audience of many more millions.)

If, in 1949, "*The* Great American Painter" was Pollock's unofficial title, by 1953, there were many artists who questioned it. In my various encounters with him it was clear that his alcoholism was now out of control, that he seemed desperate to do whatever he could to maintain his preeminence, and that he sensed, accurately, that Bill De Kooning was replacing him as the stronger presence for younger artists. Even more personally tragic, Pollock, apparently drowning in self-pity, was not painting very much, or very well. Logically, if he, a man still in his early forties, was truly The Great American Painter, he should still be painting, and producing masterpieces.

I went to the opening of what would be his last show of new work at the Sidney Janis Gallery, in 1954, and, to me, the wide stylistic range of the works suggested a disturbing confusion of purpose. Though most of the paintings were quite beautiful, it was obvious to everyone that his greatest work lay behind him: the extraordinarily powerful and classic drip paintings of the late 1940s and very early 1950s, a period in his life when he was not drinking. After his 1953 Janis show he would complete only two more paintings before his death in 1956.

By the time I came into the New York art scene, Pollock was a profoundly damaged man. Though he had never been emotionally sturdy, his decades as an alcoholic had physically and psychologically taken a terrible toll. His face and body were bloated, and when he saw his glory waning he redoubled his efforts to be outrageous, to be talked about, to remain *famous.* I tried to avoid any contact with him because it almost always spelled trouble. He radiated so much violence and drunken anger, sweeping his arm across the bar to crash the empty glasses onto the floor, starting fistfights, and grabbing women by their breasts that the Cedar's far from conventional bartender-owners periodically banned him from the premises. The front door to the Cedar had a tiny, speakeasy-sized window, and I vividly recall several times seeing Pollock's pleading face through the glass after Johnny the bartender had locked him out.

But there were many nights when he was there, having come in from his home in Springs on Long Island to visit the galleries or see his therapist. One afternoon, my Oberlin friend, George Lubasz, called and asked me to take him to the Cedar, which at the time was starting to be known as an artist's hangout. When we entered, we sat at the bar and ordered our beers, while George, always shy but ever curious, asked if Jackson Pollock was there. "Don't look now," I said, "but that's Pollock, the balding, grizzled guy standing back there by the men's room door."

Pollock's *modus operandi* was to locate someone looking at him, and, once there was any eye contact, he would glare fiercely and advance on the gawker to make some kind of memorable scene. The rule with Pollock was to act as you might in a subway car if you noticed a disheveled, slightly psychotic fellow passenger boldly searching faces for someone foolish enough to return the stare. In a closed subway car – or in the crowded Cedar Bar – you simply didn't look directly at that kind of volatile person. Eye contact involved too much risk.

Despite the warning, my pale, timid friend glanced at Pollock, who locked onto George's gaze before he had a chance to avert his eyes. Pollock began to advance ominously, like a gladiator striding slowly into the ring, as George hunched down over his beer glass as if he were trying to climb inside it. In a moment Pollock reached us, looming up behind my friend and clamping his beefy hand down on George's shoulder. In his gravelly voice, he said, "What's your name?" When George answered in a virtual whisper, Pollock asked another question, the wording of which I found astonishing. "What are you doing," he said, "to bring notoriety to your name?" His peculiar use of the word "notoriety," I guessed, must have come from an article he'd read about himself. It was one of the strangest, most unlikely things I ever heard him say.

George gulped and answered as best he could. "I work as an editorial assistant at a publishing house."

"You're lost," said Pollock, with utter disgust. Then, with a push he released his terrified captive and strode away, looking around the bar for another victim to humiliate.

The other side of Pollock's emotional nature during his last few years was one of extreme self-pity. At those times, tears, confessions, and brutally self-lacerating comments replaced aggression and macho acting out. On one such night, I was in the Cedar with Christie Poindexter, the attractive young daughter of my art dealer, Elinor Poindexter, and as we sat together, nursing our beers in a booth toward the back, Pollock, drunk as usual, wandered over and, uninvited, joined us. I was instantly on the alert, but as he talked to Christie, I saw that he was in one of his quiet, depressed moods and was therefore at least temporarily well behaved. I knew that though Christie had heard a great deal about him, she'd had little or no personal contact with him before this encounter. She seemed, however, to be absorbed by Pollock's sad, downcast conversation, so after a while I left the two of them and wandered off to sit with some more cheerful friends in a nearby booth.

From time to time I looked over at Pollock to make sure he wasn't becoming crude or aggressive with Christie, and noticed that tears were beginning to stream down his face. As he talked to her in a low, confessional voice, his big cowboy hands were mindlessly handling and bending the cheap, diner-grade silverware on the table. Suddenly, a knife snapped in half, and, dropping the two pieces without taking his morose, teary eyes away from Christie, Pollock picked up a fork and resumed his nervous manhandling of yet another crummy piece of Cedar Bar property.

Later, when he left the booth, I asked Christie what he had been talking about and was not surprised when she said he'd been telling her that he was a fake, that his paintings were worthless, that he was an utter failure, and so on. It was the same litany of woe that he often repeated in his last years when alcohol had taken him down to the very nadir of his soul – as opposed to the many times drink had turned him, instead, into a ragingly high and monstrous Mr. Hyde.

His artist friends and acquaintances were aware that much of Pollock's Cedar Bar behavior was a kind of public showboating, designed only to attract attention and thus to reassert his diminishing celebrity. Once, when he seemed genuinely angry and forced his friend Franz Kline into a wrestling match, Kline, who was soberer and quicker, shoved him sharply back against the bar. Pollock roared in pain and embarrassment but soon managed to get his opponent down on the floor. Kline told me later that as they grappled and rolled around with everyone watching, Pollock whispered in his ear, "Not so hard, Franz." Apparently he did not want his show of macho retaliation to involve the real thing.

In 1955, Elinor Poindexter, a kind, generous, and rather shy woman, opened a temporary art gallery in her townhouse in the Murray Hill section of New York. (She later moved the gallery to a more permanent space on West 57th Street, where, in 1956, I had my first exhibition.) In the opening show at her home, Pollock arrived, loaded as usual. I was talking to Nancy Ward, Kline's companion at the time, when Pollock approached, muttered hello, and in front of everyone, grabbed Nancy by her breasts. She cursed and pushed him away. He released her and, grinning his satyr's grin, staggered off, in search of other prey.

Sometime later I was talking to a young woman named Josie Wilkinson, a college friend of my sister's, whom I had invited to the opening. Out of the corner of my eye I noticed Pollock looking at me and signaling, so I excused myself and walked over to him, wary as usual. He told me he wanted to meet the young woman I'd been chatting with.

I explained the situation. "Jackson, she doesn't know you, she's never even heard of you. She's a conservative person who's never been around artists."

"I gotcha," he replied, and again said he just wanted to meet her. He walked back with me and I made sure that I stood between them to make the introduction, but this time there was no grabbing, no crudeness. He addressed her as "Miss Wilkinson," and seemed on his best behavior. After a while I turned to talk to some other people, and a few minutes later a red-faced Josie told me she had another appointment and was going to have to leave.

A year or so later, my sister said Josie told her about meeting Pollock, and that in the middle of their conversation he had politely excused himself, walked about ten feet away, unzipped his fly and urinated into one of Ellie Poindexter's tall potted plants. Then he zipped up and returned, attempting to continue the conversation. It was then that she announced she had to leave, not knowing what might happen next. I realized that there, in microcosm, were three of Pollock's basic moods: macho-aggressive, grabbing Nancy Ward; well behaved, chatting politely with Josie Wilkinson; and outrageous, pissing on Ellie's potted plant in a room full of people.

As much as I admired Jackson Pollock's paintings, I avoided him and therefore never really got to know him. Obviously, I didn't want to become yet another victim of his drunken rampages. By the time of his suicide-like death at the wheel of his car (one young woman passenger who had begged him to slow down, died with him; another survived), he was a ruined man. He had never been very stable, but there were two major things in his life that he absolutely could not handle, and together they destroyed him. They were, of course, fame and alcohol, each of which he had in lethal abundance.

Yet Pollock's importance in the history of American Abstract Expressionism is fixed and gigantic. He was the first painter of the New York School to enjoy a national reputation, the first to receive substantial financial rewards for his work, and throughout his life, he was the central target of ridicule and virulent know-nothing attacks against abstract art. De Kooning famously remarked that Jackson "broke the ice," but my friend Bill Sebring put it more dramatically: "Pollock," he said, "was the guy they shot out of the cannon without a net in order to know where to put the net for everybody else." Pollock was 44 when he lost control of his speeding car, and his death, though not a surprise to anyone, was nevertheless a shock to all of us. It was also felt as more of a personal loss than any of us might have expected.

Many years later, the Museum of Modern Art mounted a huge Pollock retrospective, which I went through several times. The impression lodged most firmly in my mind was that of Pollock's apparent need throughout his life to fill every square inch of his canvases with emotionally wrought marks, strokes, colors, or shapes, as if he felt a responsibility to charge the entire field with his own boundless and passionate energy. There are almost no tranquil areas or moments of serenity in any of his works. Everything is unsparingly alive… moving… restless. In the late 1940s, when he came upon a method that disposed of physical brushstrokes, he was able, by tossing and dripping the liquid paint, to create dense, writhing surfaces almost instantly. And as if speed of execution were essential to him, these paintings remain his greatest works.

Pollock's obsessive, all-over intensity reminds me of Van Gogh's similar need to charge every square inch of his paintings with emotional energy, while somehow achieving, in the end, an unexpected feeling of near-classic tranquility. Tragically, like Van Gogh, Pollock had the same far too brief a run as a great artist – about three or four years.

Throughout their very different lives and levels of accomplishment, both men were emotionally disturbed and eventually suicidal, though Van Gogh was more direct about it. Both were consumed by an almost pathological need to lay their emotions bare through their art. But now, decades later, as we have become familiar with their work, the disturbing urgency and agitation viewers originally sensed in their paintings have receded enough to reveal the sheer beauty and life-giving energy that were there all along, and which each artist so generously bequeathed to the world.

Franz Kline

There are many reasons why, among the many senior artists I met during my first few years in New York, I formed the closest bond with Franz Kline. First of all, because his paintings, when I finally saw them in the flesh, spoke to me more powerfully and with more unforgettable impact than those of any other AbEx artist. Though I was ultimately drawn at least as much to De Kooning's work, when I first saw the Women series of paintings in 1953, I was put off by what I took to be De Kooning's barbaric violence. At the time I was probably too inexperienced and too immersed in the more classical French traditions of Matisse and Picasso to really grasp their painterly richness and subtle control. On the other hand, Kline's black-and-white paintings, though equally intense and loaded with expressionist energy, possessed a clarity that touched something in me and brought to mind Mondrian's far more precise use of sharp black-and-white contrasts. Earl Kerkam once called Franz a "drunken Mondrian," a clever but not entirely esthetic remark since Kline, like so many others of his generation, also had a drinking problem.

A second reason for my fondness had to do with Kline's warm, open sense of connection with other artists, even young ones like me. I avoided Pollock because of his chaotic behavior; Rothko was often rather chilly and forbidding; and De Kooning, at least in the early 1950s, tended to be rather private and inward, and was thus somewhat unapproachable. Franz, however, was the very spirit of painterly bonhomie.

The critic Tom Hess once remarked that the Abstract Expressionists consisted of two groups: the "uptown intellectuals" – meaning Rothko, Motherwell, Newman, and Gottlieb, among others – and the "downtown bohemians" – centrally Kline, Pollock, and De Kooning. The former group, he said, lived in apartments and tended to paint calmer, more "imagistic" paintings, while the downtown bohemians lived in lofts, hung out at the Cedar, drank a lot more than they should, and painted with a greater degree of expressionist violence. Since I lived in a loft on 15th Street and hung out at the Cedar, I was, by default, more of a downtown bohemian than an uptowner, and therefore had not become particularly friendly with Newman or Gottlieb or Motherwell. (In 1976, however, Motherwell and I connected as gallery-mates in Provincetown's Longpoint Gallery, and over the next twenty years our friendship blossomed.)

But in 1954, I was a 23-year-old neophyte crazy about painting, and Franz Kline was an experienced artist in his mid-forties. Despite these huge gaps of age and experience, he accepted me with warmth and friendship. Since the late 1940s, Franz had been *the* central figure at the Cedar Bar, where he held forth night after night, drink in hand, offering surprising insights into the art and artists we all cared deeply about and punctuating his remarks with jokes, elliptical personal stories, and his own unique style of banter. For example, he told me what his mother said when she first saw his black and white abstractions. For decades he had only painted representationally, usually romantic landscapes and portraits, but now, when he showed his mother his new work, she said, "There you go again, Franz, always trying to do it the easy way." He smiled about her no-colors-no-problems remark, while he wrestled daily with the daunting new spatial and painterly issues posed by his black and white abstractions.

In the Cedar he liked to talk about certain painters whose drawings were made with speed and assurance, the line denoting a mixture of clarity and velocity: Toulouse-Lautrec, Rembrandt, Picasso, and Hokusai were four he referred to often, as well as a number of British caricaturists and illustrators unfamiliar to me. (When I mentioned Matisse one night, he snapped, "Who said Matisse could draw?")

Virtually all of us were dazzled by Kline's range of art knowledge, his wit, and his quirkily inventive way of expressing himself. One thing I obviously shared with him was a sense of humor. Both of us liked jokes – usually smutty ones – and each of us had an extensive personal collection that naturally leavened the Cedar's usual sour, late-night bitching about dealers, collectors, and the art world in general. Franz and I enjoyed trying out our jokes on each other, and though his delivery was full of expressive gaps and was sometimes slurred and a little surreal, his stories were hilarious. Unfortunately, because of his odd ellipses and outrageous leaps of imagery, they were often almost impossible to remember. The critic Irving Sandler managed to recall one of them: Two men go into a bar and start drinking. An hour passes and one of the now drunken friends announces a trip to the men's room. More time passes and he doesn't return. His companion, worried, goes looking for him and, on the way to the men's room, passes an open door on the elevator shaft. He looks down to the basement floor below and sees his friend squatting there. The man looks up, and in a panicky voice shouts, "No! No! Don't flush!"

Physically, Kline was – surprisingly – a bit less than medium height, but with the broad, powerful shoulders of the high school football star he had once been. He had a large, handsome head that sported a narrow, down-sloping mustache and a thick mop of dark hair, which he brushed straight back. His style resembled that of a 1930s or 1940s movie actor of the Ronald Coleman/John Barrymore type, except for Franz's frequent display of a happy, wide, and generous grin. For all of these reasons, and apparently throughout his life, he had been catnip to the ladies.

Despite his thick, athletic body, Franz was graceful, dexterous, and quick in his gestures as he told his stories and mimicked the various characters they featured. He was, in fact, a great mimic, and one day I was convulsed by his imitation of our mutual friend, Herman Somberg. Later I told Herman that "in the Cedar last night, Franz had you down to a tee."

"I'm not surprised," Herman replied. "You should see him when he does you."

However, along with his playful humor, his sense of camaraderie, and his ebullient energy as a painter, one always sensed a profound sadness in the man. He had had a difficult life, living often in solitary poverty and extreme discouragement, though he once quipped that a bohemian like him was someone who could live in a place where an animal would die. To make matters worse, Elizabeth, his British wife, whom he managed, irregularly, to care for, ended up spending most of her life in mental hospitals. Though Franz, in the Cedar Bar, was typically smiling and obviously enjoying the company of his (mostly male) friends, at more private moments, his expression was often quiet, depressed, and brooding. It was a face he rarely displayed in public, but the dark emotion behind it was perhaps a source of his stark black and white paintings.

The 1950s – the reactionary Eisenhower years – were not favorable to women in general, or, obviously, to blacks, gays, Latinos, and other minorities, and it would be decades before some of these problems were even recognized. I recall sitting with Franz one afternoon in a neighborhood bar when he told me about an incident that had happened the day before. An ardent collector of his, a wall-street impresario of some sort, had come banging on his studio door, pushing in front of him a beautiful, well-dressed young woman. "The guy told me," Franz said, "that I could have the girl for the afternoon, and that he'd already paid her. He said he would come back around five to get her and that he wanted to pick out a drawing as an exchange."

The collector left the woman with him, and, somewhat perplexed, Franz sat down with her on the couch. "She was young and very pretty, but sad," he went on. "I asked her how she had gotten into this business. She said that she had come here from London, wanting to be a model, and that things hadn't worked out. She'd met some men and needed money, and one thing led to another. She seemed very down and started to cry, so I made her a cup of English tea and told her I'd once lived in London, and sort of calmed her down. She was so young and so unhappy…"

He looked down at his beer glass and then took a meditative sip. I was quiet, too, thinking about the whole scene he'd described, and the poor young woman who had so recently become a call girl. After a minute or two I looked up and asked, "Well, Franz, what happened then? Did you make love with her?"

He grinned and his eyes sparkled. "Sure. Of course. And she was great, too." It was a man's world in the 1950s, and this was a very 1950s encounter.

Kline's conversation ran to oblique cracks, which nevertheless hinted at great buried complexities. When asked how he, a native of rural Pennsylvania, liked living in New York, he answered, "If you've been here longer than a year, you're beyond answering that question one way or another."

Another time, he and a group of his contemporaries were recalling the risky things they had done when they were young. "How could we have ever tried such crazy stuff?" one asked.

"Oh, hell," Franz explained. "When I was young I was nineteen."

He had a marvelous way of describing bad painting. Of a botched still life, he said that the vase was there to hold up the table and the flowers were there to hold up the vase, and in a similarly bad landscape, that the mountains were there to keep the sky off of the river.

He never liked to talk about his own painting, and particularly avoided serious comments about his working methods. (His interviews with critics are painful to read.) When asked how he managed to keep the space in his black and white paintings so flat and consistent, he said, "it's like stuffing mattresses. You keep stuffing and stuffing and then you see a bulge, so you start pulling the stuffing out for a while and then you see more hollows, so you start stuffing again. You do this for awhile, and then, out of the corner of your eye you notice that the damn thing is flat, so you tiptoe away and leave it."

When Franz had his first show at the prestigious Sidney Janis Gallery, he asked me to help him stretch some of the paintings that were too large to fit in the elevator, and had to be brought in rolled up. Philip Guston was there, too, and after we'd stretched all the paintings, Kline stood them up around the room and took out a piece of notepaper. It was a list of potential titles, and our job, now, was to assign names to the works. One smallish painting had a flat, simple shape taking up much of the surface. That painting, we decided, was *Thorp*, the name of the great Native-American Olympic athlete Franz admired and liked to talk about, because the sound of his name was also simple and flat. *Mahoning*, another title on the list, was the name of a river in Pennsylvania, where Franz had grown up. One of the largest paintings had a series of bars flying through a complex space, so that became *Mahoning*. By the time it was over, all of the works had titles, and none of us could recall who named what. In retrospect, I saw that the process had been Franz's ingenious way to link his abstractions with the intricacies of his own life.

His final studio, on West 14th Street, was two short blocks away from mine, and I visited him often. When we'd first met, he'd been living in a large loft on East Ninth Street, but after that, his successive studios – on Tompkins Square in the East Village, on Sixth Avenue near Eighth Street, and finally, on West 14th Street – were far less spacious. This is an important aspect of the effect of his paintings, because his huge, powerful black-and-white abstractions often look as if they were bursting out of their frames, and that neither their edges, nor the walls they were on, nor even the rooms they were in could comfortably contain them. I recall once visiting Franz's friend Jackie Martin in the East Village apartment she had sublet from W.H. Auden. There, in the poet's cramped living room, a huge Kline black-and-white was precariously and aggressively resting along the back of the sofa, as if someone had parked a steam locomotive in a village bookshop. When the Whitney Museum held a memorial retrospective of Kline's work in 1968, the big paintings hanging in the Whitney's grand, impersonal, high-ceilinged spaces lost some of their compressed power, while the works in the smaller, low-ceilinged rooms, more typical of the space they had been painted in, retained all of their aggressive force. The drama of Kline's paintings had a great deal to do with the real-life, limited space from which they seemed to want to break free.

Though Franz had restricted most of his mature production to black and white (there are many magnificent color paintings, too), his formal range was extraordinary. Some works were almost minimalist in feeling, suggesting Malevich or Mondrian, while others were wildly baroque, and made up of drips, splashes, and thick, rushing brush strokes. Some were stark, while others were luscious and painterly, and some even included areas of gray tones between the black and white. Many of us saw a kind of precarious architecture in his paintings, and when one large abstraction, made up of a few out-of-plumb horizontal and vertical beam-like forms, was hung in a show at the Whitney Museum, his good friend Bill De Kooning looked at it and said, "My God, Franz, that painting is holding up the building." This same work – one of Kline's finest – is now in the collection of the Art Institute of Chicago where it hangs next to De Kooning's masterpiece, *Excavation*, and efficiently holds up the entire lower floor.

Franz Kline died on May 13, 1962, in a New York hospital, of heart failure. My wife at the time, Joan, and I attended his funeral service with our suitcases at our side because immediately after the

Franz Kline, Painting, 1952, oil on canvas, The Chicago Art Institute, Bequest of Signund E. Edelstone. Photo courtesy of The Chicago Art Institute.

formal, Episcopalian rites we had to take a train to Chicago where a show of my work was scheduled to open at the Kasha Heman Gallery. We left New York in a mutually grieving silence. The next day, when we arrived, I learned that my friend singer Tommy Leonetti was performing at Mister Kelly's, a leading Chicago nightclub. We met him there after the last show, and he and his wife insisted that we accompany them to the Playboy Club, then in its heyday, where we were introduced to Hugh Hefner. "Hef" was friendly and surprisingly knowledgeable about art, and he promptly invited us to a late-night party at what was then called the Playboy Mansion. Momentarily taken aback by this ongoing wave of showbiz glitz during our first 24 hours in Chicago, we entered the Mansion with an upbeat sense of excitement, but the first thing we saw in Hefner's vast living room, hanging above the noisy party-goers, was a huge Franz Kline abstraction. Memories suddenly flooded back and I saw that Joan had to turn away to hide the tears running down her cheeks.

A few weeks later, we drove to Provincetown to set up house for the summer in a ramshackle cabin I'd rented. Beside Joan and me, our overloaded car contained a wailing cat and enough art materials and clothes for the three-month stay. We found that the place we'd rented had been recently involved in a propane gas explosion and was topped by a colander-like leaky roof, so we had our work cut out for us. Within a short time my friend, the painter Herman Somberg, called to say he was coming to the Cape on a mission for which he needed my help. Elizabeth Zogbaum, Kline's companion during his last years, had asked Herman, an old and trusted colleague, to go to Provincetown and open Franz's West End studio to make an inventory of any artworks that remained. No one had been there since his death.

Herman arrived a few days later with the key and a sense of foreboding at how it might feel to be in Franz's studio and to wander among all the things he had so unexpectedly left behind. He, Joan, and I gazed through the windows of the main part of the white, nineteenth century house, and into a wide, shallow room that contained a number of antique rocking chairs – such chairs having been for years one of his most frequently painted and drawn studio props. He had obviously sought out these antiques and collected them with love, so the row of rocking chairs, sitting empty and abandoned and eliciting memories of his early work, powerfully underlined his absence.

The studio, for which we had the key, was behind the house and far more difficult to face. Franz apparently slept here often, and his bed looked as if it had been vacated only moments before, the covers carelessly thrown back and his tattered bathrobe limp on a nearby hook. His paint-spattered jeans were draped over a chair, a pair of his sneakers and two rumpled socks lay abandoned on the floor by the bed, and several empty glasses and coffee cups all came together to underline what seemed like a momentary absence. It was as if he had just walked down to the Studio Shop to buy a sketchpad and would be right back.

Lying on his worktable was a small stack of black and white drawings – studies, perhaps, for future paintings – which Herman and I carefully measured, initialed on the back, and catalogued. Nearby were some flat pans partially filled with drying paint, a row of his typically wide house-painters' brushes, and a roll of canvas – everything he needed to resume painting. Franz had left the studio in the fall, obviously planning to return, but his illness and death came before the summer began.

About fifteen years after Kline's death, I awoke from a remarkably vivid dream about him, and rousing myself, found paper and pen on my bed table and recorded it. I had rarely, if ever, had such a realistic and emotionally accurate dream about another person.

As it opened, I was walking along a path on the ridge of a long hill, when I saw someone coming towards me from the opposite direction. I knew that it was Franz and was startled because I also knew – even in the dream – that he was dead. As he approached, I resolved to ask nothing about where he'd been but just to pick up where our friendship left off, back in 1962.

He greeted me in his usual friendly manner, smiling broadly, and asked where I was going. I explained that I was headed to a party I'd been invited to, at a collector's house, and asked if he wanted to come along. "Sure," he said with a shrug, never having been one to pass up a party. In a moment we were above a valley where the collector's impressive house and grounds lay spread out below. In front stood a sculpture of a female nude, a typical French garden decoration.

"I see he has a Dujardin in his yard," Franz said. I asked who Dujardin was, never having heard of him, and he replied that he was a nineteenth century academic sculptor. I was amazed once again, as I had been many times in the past, by his knowledge of the obscure artists of many countries.

We walked down the hill and into an area behind the manor house, where a curving flight of stone stairs led down to the collector's open-roofed "party area." As we descended the stairs, a young man and his girlfriend, arguing fiercely, were coming up. Suddenly the young man threw his drink at his girlfriend, which immediately soaked into her blouse, rendering the fabric across her breasts almost transparent. Franz, smiling mischievously, gave me a nudge and we both gaped at the spectacle. I thought, *He hasn't changed a bit. He's the old Franz I remember.*

The party area was filled with guests, and for a moment Kline disappeared, apparently heading for the bar. The collector took the opportunity to come over to me and whispered, "Isn't that Franz Kline you're with?" I told him it was, and he looked dumfounded, saying, "But isn't he dead?" I put my finger to my lips, implying that he was not to say anything about it. Franz came over, drink in hand, and I told the collector that he had identified the Dujardin in front of the house.

"That's amazing," the collector said. "There aren't five people in the United States who would recognize a Dujardin."

"Well, I recognized it," Franz said. "And it isn't a good one, either."

Soon we left the party and as we ascended the curving stairway, Franz asked, "What ever became of old Hans?" meaning Hans Hoffmann, who, in the 1950s, had been unfairly overlooked by the Museum of Modern Art.

"Oh," I said, "the Modern finally gave him a big retrospective, and they even had Clement Greenberg write the essay for the show."

"That's the trouble with those guys," Franz said. "Give them half a chance and they'll catalogue you to death."

We went back up to the path that ran along the ridge, where a man approached us. We both noticed a certain look in his eye that suggested he was a panhandler about to ask for a handout. He was wearing a suit and tie, but his shirt collar and sleeves were frayed and his jacket badly worn. "Excuse me," he said to Franz, speaking in a slightly unnatural voice, "I'm very embarrassed to have to ask a favor, but I left my wallet at home and I find I don't have enough money for the train back to Westchester. If you could possibly lend me five dollars, I'll get your name and address and mail the money back to you." Franz was already taking out his wallet as the man went on with an attempt at profound sincerity: "I'm really embarrassed to have to ask such a favor. I've never had to do this before."

"Don't worry about it," Franz said, handing him a five. "You do it very well."

At that the man wandered off and Franz turned to me to say goodbye. We shook hands, and I knew that meeting him had been some kind of miracle, and that, sadly, I would never see him again. I watched as he walked away, heading along the path, back to wherever or whatever he'd come from.

There my dream ended and I woke up, stunned at the realism of the entire experience. It was as if Franz had been there in person, as his usual generous, aware, amusing self, making wisecracks and commenting on obscure works of art. His gift of a five-spot to the panhandler, whom he'd seen through in an instant, was at one with his ironic assurance that the man shouldn't worry about asking because, "You do it very well."

I lay awake, wondering where all of this had come from. I could not recall any of Kline's remarks in the dream as actual quotes from the past. And who, I thought, was Dujardin? Even in my waking state I'd never heard of him. Where did I get that name? Franz's concern about Hans Hoffman – a man much older than himself whom I was aware he barely knew – was also typical of his care and respect for his fellow artists. To me, the whole experience seemed like an extraordinary gift, and I found it almost impossible to believe that I'd imagined it all, that I'd been a kind of ventriloquist for everything he'd said.

A year or so later, I visited Elizabeth Zogbaum, Franz's companion in the last years of his life, and related my dream to her. She seemed as stunned as I had been by the way my unconscious had created such a three-dimensional image of the man, exactly as we both remembered him. She also seemed as touched as I had been by the final scene of the dream, when he'd said goodbye and wandered back to the place or the existence – whatever it was – which he'd so memorably, and temporarily, left behind.

It has now been over four decades since Franz Kline passed away. Presently, his paintings look even more powerful, and, remarkably, even fresher and more spontaneous than almost anything around. The farther we move away from that time in the 1950s and early 1960s when Abstract-Expressionism ruled the day, the more his stature seems to have grown. I think, now, of that distant time as being like a long, dimly-lit corridor, at the end of which, behind a half-open door, I can still glimpse lights and talking, and laughter – edged with despair – and in the middle of that crowd of artists stands Franz, drink in hand, cracking wise, and making quick, incisive observations about the artists we all revered. The corridor between that place and me is long and dark and empty, but the distant room at its end still glows with life.

Struggling Through the 1950s

Over the decades I've pondered the question of why, surrounded as I was in my formative years by senior artists whom I respected enormously, I never fell into the alcoholism, depression, and suicidal behavior that I saw all around me. There was nothing heroic about my survival, of course, nothing consciously willed to keep me from that kind of self-destructive lifestyle. Many factors of time, place, and personality must have been involved, but the most important, perhaps, were the lucky circumstances of my upbringing. Unlike my own conventional, middle-class family, Kline, De Kooning, and Pollock were all from dysfunctional, blue-collar backgrounds. Elaine De Kooning famously described the mothers of all three as "the toughest women I've ever met. They were the only women I know who I think could walk straight through a brick wall." Both Kline and De Kooning had been on their own in every way since their teenage years, with virtually no financial or moral support from their families. Kline was the son of a tavern owner in rural Pennsylvania, and De Kooning, as a very young man, left his native Holland, sailed to America, and jumped ship to live the life of a non-English-speaking illegal immigrant. Jackson Pollock was the only one of the three to receive encouragement and a bit of financial help from his family, particularly from his generous brothers, but ironically it was Pollock who ended up with the most intractable emotional problems. To make things even worse for all three, there was virtually no public interest in any of their paintings for decades, so they worked in a dispiriting vacuum, supported only by each other and the enthusiasm of a few close friends. As a result, each had to face the massive problem of trying to get by, day by day, on almost no money.

My situation was totally different. I grew up in a comfortable, ultra-bourgeois home, with nurturing parents who supported me with unfailing generosity. I was able to attend a good liberal arts college, an advantage neither Kline, nor De Kooning, nor Pollock had enjoyed, and even after I left Wheeling and moved to New York my disappointed father still sent me a little money from time to time.

Equally important, the art world I came into in the early 1950s was dramatically different from that of the cold, Depression-Era Thirties and Forties. In 1953, when I moved to New York, things had begun to change, but it was Pollock's death in 1956 that marked the turning point. Suddenly this roistering, alcoholic "drip" painter was gone, and his life's work had now become a closed chapter demanding serious examination. His canvases and those of his colleagues began to be talked about and acquired by an ever-widening circle of critics, curators, and collectors, and consequently their prices began to rise. More and more people had correctly concluded that this band of radical, contentious New York artists might together comprise a major movement in the history of world art.

Because of this post-1956 shift of taste, more galleries were showing recent abstract work and things were easing up for all of us – even for very young artists like me. And when I had my first one-person show in 1956 at the age of 25, it was an event that would have been unheard-of even a few years earlier.

If the difficult circumstances they'd endured in the past led many senior artists to take refuge in alcohol – Pollock became dependent at the age of sixteen – I had no such need. Though I guzzled at the Cedar's trough with the real drinkers, it was rarely to dangerous excess. For that matter, I never developed much enthusiasm for beer, the very lifeblood of the place. Another reason I resisted drunkenness was because I dreaded the hangovers, a ghastly side effect to which I was hopelessly prone. And besides, who would want to end up like Pollock?

Obviously, my relative sobriety had a variety of other causes, too, but whatever they were, I tended to be optimistic by nature rather than morose. I was genuinely excited by the art I was making and by the work of others that I saw around me, and I felt that my future looked good rather than bleak. I had no need for the oblivion of alcohol that the older artists had used for years to blot out decades of justified despair.

Ironically, when fame and a degree of fortune finally arrived for a number of these now middle-aged artists, an entirely new set of problems often arose. One such problem, welcomed to a certain degree, had to do with the appearance on the scene of eager young women – proto-groupies, one might say – who were more than willing to bed the increasingly well-known AbEx artists. This led to a raft of personal difficulties along with the more obvious pleasures, since De Kooning, Pollock, and Kline, for example, were all technically married and often simultaneously involved in extended extramarital relationships. One afternoon I dropped in on Franz Kline and saw that he was with a young woman from the groupie group who was clearly making herself at home. "Budd, let's go out and have a beer," Franz said rather quickly, and off we went, leaving the girl behind.

"I wanted to get away," he told me a few minutes later. "She came here yesterday and I can't get rid of her. I can't get anything done." We went to a local bar, ordered our drinks, and began to talk – interesting art-talk, as it turned out. Though he mentioned his affection for Mondrian's work, I have only the dimmest memories of the hours of relaxed, beery conversation that followed. But each time I said I had to leave, Franz would grab my arm, order another round, and ask me to stay. Finally, about three hours and too many beers later, I said I really had to go back to my place since it was getting close to suppertime and I was expected. Franz had told me a little about the young woman whom we'd left behind, none of which was very complementary, and when he asked me to walk him back to his studio I began to get the picture. As we went up the stairs, he fumbled with his keys and looked unusually apprehensive.

We entered the place quietly, two cat burglars breaking into someone else's studio. It seemed empty at last, but suddenly a curly-haired female head popped up on the other side of the couch. "Hi, Franz," she called out. "Where've you been gone so long?" He gave me a quick, trapped look and I left, smiling to myself at the unwelcome bonus of fame that he now had to deal with.

During those years, none of us, famous or not, were free from a certain super-casual attitude toward sex. Late at night at the Cedar, if there was a lonely woman still sitting at the bar, some horny artist would approach her because, our feeble rationalizations firmly in place, it seemed almost ungentlemanly to let her go home unaccompanied and unpleasured. The following night, if the two accidental lovers happened to run into each other, they might exchange polite, even friendly greetings, but often nothing more than that. After all, last night's intimacies were last night's and this was a different day. No wonder the feminist movement was like a freight train idling in a tunnel, slowly building up steam to finally thunder out to devastate the Eisenhower-era's macho morality.

IN JUNE OF 1956, Nat Halper, a Provincetown art dealer, hired me to gallery-sit the following month, during the hot afternoons when most people went to the beach and business was slack. In return I was paid a modest sum and given a small room to use as a studio. Since the New York galleries shut down during the summer months and Ellie Poindexter, for whom I had been working, was not paying me, I needed the money, though I was also eager to explore the Cape Cod art colony I'd heard so much about. The famous Abstract Expressionist Hans Hofmann lived and taught in Provincetown; Edward Hopper had a studio in nearby Truro; Robert Motherwell owned a house on the bay; and numerous other artists either visited regularly or had their own studios in the small, sun-drenched community. Nat's gallery, named the HCE for arcane reasons involving James Joyce's impenetrable *Finnegan's Wake*, showed a number of off-Cape AbEx artists in addition to local residents like Motherwell, Hofmann, and Jack Tworkov.

That July, David Smith, who was then, after Calder, the best known American sculptor, exhibited several beautiful small works in steel at the HCE, which he priced at $750 each and which nevertheless found no takers. Smith had had a powerful show of his work that spring at the Willard Gallery, and not only had he sold nothing there either, but he said that one largish work had been stolen. Despite his national reputation, things were particularly difficult for him because at that time almost no one collected sculpture.

One afternoon David mentioned that when a school of small squid swarmed into Provincetown harbor, he netted quite a few, and as a result had a delicious free calamari dinner, which came at a needy time. Ultimately, David Smith, a huge, gregarious, bear-like man with appetites to match, was another of his generation's too-long overlooked victims. Though he was a major artist, he was also a man with a troubled life and a drinking problem. He died in 1965, at the age of 59, when he lost control of his speeding car.

My part-time gallery job provided time to paint very small scale works in my cell-like room, and to bum around the town, swimming in the bay, devouring an occasional (expensive) lobster roll, and hanging out with other artists at the Old Colony Tap – Provincetown's version of the Cedar Bar. Like many other younger painters that summer, I began dropping in on the various informal late-night parties, some of which were wild, even by New York standards. In 1956 Provincetown was not yet the national Mecca for gays and lesbians that it has since become, but the sexual freedom of the place wafted an atmosphere impossible to avoid. I remember going to one dimly lit party in a small shack on the bay, crowded with drinkers, pot-smokers, and people of every age and sexual orientation. When I wandered into the cramped kitchen-bathroom area to get another beer, I heard rustling and bumping sounds coming from the shower stall. There was no water running, but the shower curtain fluttered and swung with the obvious movements of a couple busy behind it. "I love you, I really love you," a man's voice whispered, and a woman's voice answered, "Okay. Okay. Just fuck."

Apart from dipping into the bracingly chaotic Provincetown nightlife, I also met another group of artists my age and older who gave me helpful suggestions about my work. A couple of times I dropped in on Hans Hofmann's fabled art-class criticisms, though I didn't submit any of my own work. I found his teaching almost incomprehensible, since his German accent was so strong that I couldn't understand a word he said. His regular students seemed to listen with rapt attention and masochistically offered no resistance when he took large pieces of colored paper and brusquely thumbtacked them to their still-wet paintings, the better to make a spatial-coloristic point I was unable to decipher.

In relation to the other Abstract Expressionists, Hofmann occupied an ambiguous position. He was a generation older than the others, having lived and painted in Paris where he had befriended both Picasso and Matisse. He settled in the United States in the 1930s, and established a successful art school in New York. In 1956 his paintings suggested a blend of American full-tilt expressionism and European order, so, despite their ebullient paint handling and intense color, there was always something about them that suggested the reassuring hum of the machinery.

Physically, Hofmann was a large, rosy-cheeked, Santa Claus-looking man whose consistently upbeat work avoided the darker emotions that Rothko, De Kooning, and their contemporaries seemed unable to escape. His best paintings date from the 1960s, after he gave up the grueling routine of running a large art school, and in his final years he surprised us all by soaring freely with the innovative energy of a very young man.

But it was not art, Hofmann's or anyone else's, that I found so inspiring during my month on the Cape. It was the landscape itself, the glorious sea and dunes and the limpid light, "like the light of the Greek islands," as Motherwell described it. Without exploring any other seaside art community, I have returned to the Cape virtually every summer since then, and in 1964 I built a studio in Truro, a few miles from Provincetown, and, later, a second house in Wellfleet, where I now spend every August and September. After the pace and energy and complexities of New York, my yearly time on Cape Cod never fails to help clear my head and steady my hand.

At the end of my July stint at the HCE Gallery, I reluctantly left the art and the sun and the erotic ambience of Provincetown, and sailed aboard the *Boston Belle* for the first leg of my trip back to the heat and the dirt of a New York August. It was a warm day and I was strolling around the deck when I spotted a beautiful young woman, sitting on a bench and playing with a boy I assumed was her much younger brother. She radiated a warmth and gentleness that captivated me, so I sat down nearby to study her. Her hair was a light, almost reddish brown shade and her guileless features showed an unusual combination of innocence and strength. The qualities I felt in her, as she played and laughed with her little brother, made her instantly appealing in contrast with the bored, careless promiscuity of the women I'd met in Provincetown.

Eventually, as she and her brother were standing at the rail, looking out over the bay, I approached her and we began to talk. Her name was Joan Rich. She was nineteen years old, she told me, and lived in Winthrop, a suburb of Boston. Currently she was training to become a nurse, but she added that she was very interested in art. Amazingly, one thing quickly led to another, as often happens in such situations, and we fell in love. Within a few months she moved in with me in New York and we were soon happily married. We would be together for the next thirteen years.

The loft where I lived at the time was in a broken-down former townhouse, with a grandiose street door that could be neither firmly closed nor locked. Sometimes a homeless man and/or a wino would curl up on the floor just inside the vestibule, so Joan and I occasionally had to step over an inert body on our way into the building. It was positively Dickensian. There was one bathroom for three floors so we had to wander upstairs in the middle of the night to use the single john that also serviced tenants in three of the other lofts. In fact we occasionally passed each other in the hallways or on the stairs, edgily hurrying toward the same goal. One amenity we did

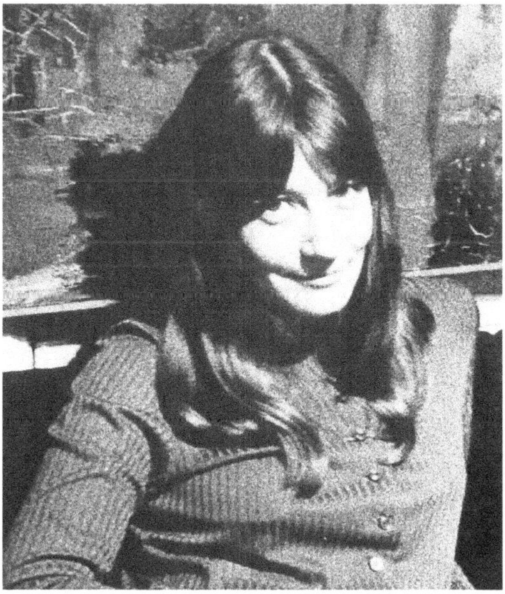

Joan at a party in the 1960s.

have in our loft was a sink, which, under emergency conditions, I sometimes put to unorthodox use.

Joan was tolerant of all this, however, and showed an intelligent interest in the paintings I was producing. Early on I was immensely pleased to discover that she had an acutely discerning eye, remarking to me once that a Kline we were looking at in an exhibition seemed somehow wrong. "Maybe it's hanging upside down," she said, and in fact it was. She got along well with my friends and colleagues, taking it in stride one night shortly after we were married when a sudden pounding on the door awakened us. Herman Somberg, Franz Kline, and another friend, bearing a couple of six-packs of beer, burst in, in what they thought of as a boisterous Western-style party ostensibly designed to interrupt newlyweds at their love-making. Joan donned a robe, someone turned on the phonograph, beer glasses were produced, and the subsequent raucous dancing roamed around, up, and over our bed.

Eventually, however, my inborn West Virginia commitment to domesticity kicked in – along with deepening guilt about having subjected my bride to such primitive conditions – and we moved to a more conventional apartment nearby, on Eighth Avenue, a flat that included a real bathroom.

The year of our marriage, 1956, was also notable because it was the year of my first one-man show. It came about because of a series of fortuitous meetings and conversations with Elinor Poindexter that had begun the previous year. We had become friendly just as she was planning to open her own gallery, and in 1955 she hired me on a part-time basis to help her with some of the inevitable chores and to offer whatever advice I could muster. One of my first suggestions was that she take on Richard Diebenkorn, a young California artist whose relaxed but oddly intense work I had seen at the Guggenheim Museum. Her decision to act on my suggestion and include him in her stable was an important one, for Ellie, for the New York art world, and for Diebenkorn himself, because eventually he became one of the most sought-after American painters.

This piece of advice also turned out to be a lucky break for me, because it fortified Ellie's faith in my judgment, and led her to offer me a one-man show at the end of 1956. I had been working for a year or so on a group of modestly scaled watercolors and drawings that were somewhat influenced by Arshile Gorky. A subtle and delicate artist whose tragic life ended in suicide in 1948, Gorky made drawings and paintings that suggested abstract tangles of organic, even sexual forms, seen close up. His example offered me a way to marry my early love of nature with a more aggressive handling of the brush and a range of hot, high-keyed greens, reds, and yellows.

The day after the opening, I came up to the gallery and heard voices coming from the front room where my show was hung. One voice was familiar: Meyer Schapiro's. I was stunned because I hadn't seen him or attended any of his lectures for several years, yet he was enthusiastically discussing my work with someone, and saying very kind things about it. When I gathered my courage, I joined them, and a smiling Meyer congratulated me on my exhibition and introduced the man he had been talking to: Stuart Preston, the chief art critic for *The New York Times*. It was an astonishing coincidence because the next day, in his review, Preston referred to my show as "an unusually promising debut." Temporarily, at least, the gods were smiling at me and I was on my way.

In the meantime, I had a variety of part-time jobs, while Joan worked full time in an office so that we could pay our bills, but as a result of my Poindexter show, I had begun to sell a few works, mostly small and mostly cheap. In 1958 we moved again, to a loft floor in the Chelsea building I currently live in. When the summer arrived, I sublet the place for extra money and we went back to Provincetown, renting a small shack near the bay. I was asked to exhibit at the new Tirca Karlis Gallery, making my work slightly more visible in the Cape art scene,

Meanwhile, Walter Chrysler, Jr., son of the founder of the eponymous corporation, had opened a museum in Provincetown to show his collection, a mix of great works such as Matisse's *Dance* (now owned by the Museum of Modern Art), interspersed with a number of obvious fakes. The new head art critic for *The New York Times*, John Canaday, had printed a number of vitriolic attacks against Abstract Expressionism, so we were delighted when he wrote approvingly of Chrysler's collection *en toto*, eventually having to print a humiliating *mea culpa* at having accepted such glaring forgeries. "Too many lobster dinners," he claimed, as if good food had made him temporarily blind. This public admission of faulty judgment on the part of the *Times* anti-AbEx art critic marked yet another milestone in the growing acceptance of the kind of work that many of us were producing.

Walter Chrysler's presence in town was fortuitous for me in another way because he eventually bought a number of my paintings. I was aware that he was famous both for purchasing art in quantity and for shamelessly trying to talk artists down in price, so when he came to my studio one afternoon to look at my work, Joan sat demurely nearby with a notepad and pencil. "How much is that one?" Chrysler would ask, and as I quoted a price, she would jot it down. "And how much for that one?" he went on, through about fifteen more paintings. "Now, how much would it be if I took all of them?"

Joan was good at math and immediately gave him the running total of the prices she had been recording. Chrysler turned to her, shocked, and after we discussed a reasonable discount – far from the one he had hoped for – he bought the paintings and left. But on the way out, he whispered, "Budd, you and I can work things out, but in the future please try to keep your wife out of our dealings."

The sales I made that summer to Chrysler and to a few other collectors, including the philanthropist J. Patrick Lannan, enabled us to go to Europe in 1959. We managed a glorious trip on a shoestring, visiting Italy, France, and England and spending almost a month in Paris.

Also that year I was given a substantial one-person show of large paintings at New York's Zabriskie Gallery, where I was reviewed favorably in *Art News* magazine by the poet James Schuyler. I even sold a few things. So, when the 1960s arrived, marking my last year of being a twenty-something, I was feeling both hopeful and excited about the way things were moving along.

Politicians, Writers, and Musicians

One of the first things I noticed from the early days of my immersion in the New York art world was a general indifference to politics and the non-visual arts. Ideologically, most artists, like most intellectuals, were liberals, though for a very good reason few actually voted. Since most artists lived in lofts zoned for industrial use only and were illegal to occupy as residences, registering to vote meant having to provide one's real address and thus risking eviction. All of us living under these conditions dreaded an unexpected visit from the buildings department even more than we feared an audit by the IRS.

There were many harrowing stories about such official encounters. Once, an inspector climbed the stairs in De Kooning's building and knocked on his door, but Bill was evidently too preoccupied with his work to check before he let the man in. Few artists were ever prepared for this kind of stark encounter, and De Kooning, an illegal alien, had no idea what to do.

Frowning ominously, the inspector wandered around the studio, noticing the unmade bed, the simple kitchen area, and the other unmistakable signs of illegal habitation. "Are you Willem De Kooning?" the man asked, having read the hand-lettered name on the door. "Do you live here?"

"Nope," Bill answered in his unmistakable Dutch accent. "I'm not Mr. De Kooning. Mr. De Kooning lives in New Jersey. I'm da caretaker."

The inspector must have appreciated such a pathetic improvisation, because he nodded (smiling perhaps?) and departed, leaving Bill trembling but happily unevicted.

Cedar Bar art talk rarely ventured into national politics, and throughout the 1950s President Eisenhower was rarely referred to, except with casual derision. One popular story had it that when Ike, the unlikely President of Columbia University, quit his job to run for president against Adlai Stevenson, someone said that this would be an interesting election because for the first time in history it would pit a college president against an educated man.

A number of painters showed a bit of arrogance in demonstrating (and sometimes feigning) their ignorance of world affairs. For them, painting and art world politics were all encompassing, and international issues were beside the point. As an example of one artist's prideful lack of information, some time after the accused spy Alger Hiss had been released from prison following his spectacular conviction in the 'Trial of the Century," I left the bar with several friends and was walking home. Earlier, an acquaintance had pointed out the place near the Cedar where Hiss had reputedly rented an apartment, and as my friends and I were passing by, I interrupted our heated art-world talk and said, "You know, by the way, Alger Hiss lives over there, in that building." One of my companions turned to me and sharply asked: "Hiss? Hiss? What gallery's he with?"

If not many followed political developments or even bothered to vote, when it came to literature, only a few were great readers. Motherwell, of course, was a true intellectual with broad interests, and several others, such as Gottlieb, Newman, and Tworkov were also widely read. Philip Guston cared particularly about poetry, but there were also a number of others, such as Pollock and Kline, whom I never saw with a book, nor did I have a reason to believe were habitual readers. De Kooning, apparently, read and reread certain favorite books, but it is accurate to say that literature was not a popular topic at the Cedar. In fact, the one art form other than painting and sculpture that unfailingly occupied our attention was that of the motion picture. In the 1950s, the current films of De Sica, Fellini, Rossellini, Goddard, Bergman, Truffaut, and many other *auteurs* were widely talked about, dissected, and argued over, as well as the classics of earlier times. Buster Keaton seemed to be the favorite over Chaplin, and I recall heated arguments about the relative merits of Rene Clair, Jean Renoir, Josef von Sternberg, and the masters of film noir, among others. Despite these serious discussions of the cinema, classic and otherwise, I don't recall ever hearing from my colleagues the names of writers such as William Faulkner, Robert Frost, or Andre Gide, for example. We were movie buffs first – classic films were regularly shown at the Museum of Modern Art – while the written word received much more scattered attention.

However, in the wake of Jack Kerouac's *On the Road*, the Beat Generation elbowed its way onto the stage and some of its writers occasionally dropped by the Cedar. In retrospect it seems to me that Kerouac was always searching for role models, Neal Cassady and William Burroughs being among the first, but for a time he apparently idolized Franz Kline and, welcome or not, hung around his studio. In the long run, however, the self-dramatizing quality of the Beats, and their desire to outdo everyone in anti-bourgeois behavior, did not sit well with the painters who were made to seem, by contrast, hard-working drones – more like nine-to-five hirelings than free-living "white hipsters," in Mailer's currently popular phrase.

After *On the Road* appeared in 1957, Kerouac hyped up the misbehavior, and I was forced, one night, to become his bourgeois enemy. The confrontation came about when David Amram, the crossover musician and composer, invited Joan and me to an impromptu party at his apartment. It was, I recall, on New Year's Eve, and the place was filled with jazz musicians and some of the Beats, including Kerouac, Corso, and Ginsberg. Since there were almost no other painters there, I felt a little out of place. Joan was not only the youngest and most attractive woman at the party, but she was also one of the few women there. I left her for a few moments to go to the bathroom or to get us some drinks or whatever, and when I came back Kerouac was standing inches away from her, leaning in, and coming on like the recently best-selling radical novelist he actually was. As I came into the conversation and handed Joan her drink, he turned to me with a "fuck-off" look and, elbowing me aside, continued hitting on her.

When I told *him* to buzz off, that Joan was my wife, he became enraged. A fight was in the offing, a fight I would certainly lose, because Kerouac, once the recipient of a football scholarship at

Columbia, was big, tough, and drunk, and I was none of the three. I took Joan's arm and led her away toward the door, with a furious Kerouac following and cursing me. Apparently, Dave Amram intervened, and though it was a close call, I got her out before anything worse occurred. Though it all happened very quickly, I understood that from Kerouac's point of view, the situation was clear. He saw himself as an entitled, radical Beat and current literary star, while I was everything he detested – a "nonentity" acting as the protector of "family values." Joan, in Kerouac's scheme of things, should have been his merely for the asking. The incident nicely illustrates why the AbEx painters and the Beats never really got along, despite attempts by several critics to put us in the same box. The painters and the Beats were like ships that merely pass in the night, despite an occasional ramming and a grandiose waving of flags.

Around the same time, I had another encounter with a well-known writer, the wild and wooly Irish dramatist, Brendan Behan. In 1956 his first play *The Quare Fellow* opened, and two years later, the much acclaimed *The Hostage*. Both plays appeared in New York and London, and the same year *The Hostage* opened, Behan published *Borstal Boy*, his memoir of the rough times he spent in the British reform school system, the "borstals."

Behan had come to New York with his wife for the opening of his play and became an instant celebrity, noted for his gift of gab and serious problem with alcohol. In the 1950s, long before Rupert Murdoch got his mangy hands on it, the *New York Post* was a widely-read *liberal* tabloid, and one of its popular features was a gossip/theater column written by a man named Leonard Lyons, whose unfortunately named contribution in the style of the times was *The Lyons Den*. For some reason, Leonard Lyons took a liking to Behan and hardly let a day go by without including an item about the playwright's various shenanigans and memorable quotes. Before he left the U.K., Behan must have French-kissed the Blarney Stone, because he was the source of an endless stream of great Irish tales, jokes, wisecracks, and misadventures, many of which, accompanied by photographs, eventually turned up in the *New York Post*.

Though I had seen neither of his plays, nor read *Borstal Boy*,

I thought knew a lot about Brendan Behan from Lyons' column, and when I found myself face to face with the man himself in a tiny Village bookstore one night, I had no doubt who he was. The bookstore, which I recall was on West Fourth Street, was showing a few paintings, including a large 1957 oil of mine, and as I looked from my work to Brendan Behan standing across the room, I was a bit flabbergasted. The feeling deepened when I saw that he was coming over to me. "Excuse me," he said in his marvelous brogue, "but you look like a person who can help me. I'm tryin' to find a man named Allen Ginsberg. Would you be knowin' where I can find 'im?"

I replied that I didn't know exactly where the poet lived, but that he sometimes came into a bar where I was intending to go. Having read that Behan's wife was a painter, I added: "The bar Ginsberg sometimes drinks at is called the Cedar, and it's a hangout for artists. Since your wife is a painter, maybe if I show you the place you could bring her there, sometime. She'd probably enjoy it."

He smiled and said, "Well, seein' as you know who I am, who would you be?" I introduced Joan and me, explaining that I was an artist, and in a moment or so the three of us headed for the Cedar.

It was only about nine o'clock and not crowded, so we took a booth, and Herman Somberg soon joined us. Almost from the instant we sat down, Behan, the consummate raconteur, was off and running. He was an unforgettably odd-looking man, with a large, asymmetrical, meaty face, and a nose that seemed to have been bent in several directions simultaneously, the obvious results of fistfights at the borstal. His mouth was wide, very wide, and his several irregular teeth were a truly strange assortment, growing here and there like the teeth carved into a Halloween pumpkin by an unsteady ten year old.

Behan had a wild thatch of hair that looked as if many a month had elapsed since a comb was pulled through it, and when he laughed, his head tipped back and he uttered a full-throated, happy guffaw, his mouth elastically agape and his remaining teeth easily counted. Sadly, his complexion was florid in an obviously unhealthy way, the result, I guessed, of too many hours with too many bottles. And yet the man was a charmer.

Herman, Joan, and I ordered beers, but this was evidently a period in Behan's life when he was trying to stay off the sauce. In the place of an alcoholic drink, he gave elaborate instructions to the waiter to bring him several non-lethal ingredients that he would prepare himself. He explained that a doctor had told him that if he went through a lot of complicated rituals he wouldn't miss the alcohol in the final concoction. As I recall, the waiter brought him things like grape juice, ginger ale, seltzer, bitters, and a wedge of lemon, which he carefully mixed and stirred and fussed with, but clearly was hesitant to actually drink.

He told us how, as a lad in Ireland, he had first become fascinated with the theater. Apparently a relative (an uncle?) owned a small movie theater in a nearby town, and during the Easter season a simple *Passion Play* was put on between showings of the regular film. (According to an old story, the *Passion Play*, dealing with the Last Supper and the betrayal of Jesus, was staged far more frequently than the *Nativity* because the *Nativity* required a cast almost impossible to find in Ireland: three wise men and a virgin.) As Brendan described his uncle's theater, he said that the apron of the stage was shallow, but the locals did their best as disciples, wearing homemade robes and speaking lines they had learned from the Gospels, an effect probably more impressive to little Brendan than to anyone else. Each year the same man was tapped to play Jesus because of his genuine beard and somber but saintly face, though in his daily life, Behan said, he was the town drunk. Apparently the various disciples took turns minding him, and worked diligently to keep him sober for his central role. A rather mousy little man had been drafted in the role of Judas, and each time when the *Passion Play* ended and the film went on, the costumed actors repaired to the pub across the street for a spot of refreshment. Little Brendan, fascinated by the actors, always went along so he could watch them chatting in their multi-colored robes as they consumed their pints. Several disciples kept their watchful eyes on the man playing Jesus, but sadly, no one wanted to drink with Judas. The poor man was forced to stand alone at the bar, ale in hand, a social, theatrical, and religious outcast.

One day, all was going well, Brendan told us, when suddenly two burly men, well-liquored up, came through the pub's front door. They had been in the audience for the *Passion Play*, and as they glanced around the room they spotted Judas, drinking quietly alone. "Look at 'im," one of the men bellowed, pointing a callused finger. "There's the fucker who betrayed the Lord Jaysus!" They began to advance menacingly on poor Judas while the other eleven disciples formed a protective, biblical wall around him. And since the distinguished, colorfully robed apostles outnumbered them eleven to two, the drunken pair was unable to avenge Jesus' terrible betrayal and finally decided to leave. It was a close call.

One of the most endearing aspects of Brendan Behan as a raconteur was his own obvious enjoyment of these stories. He would laugh uproariously at the funny parts, tossing his head back, and letting go with a full-throttle belly-laugh, his strangely shaped mouth so widely agape that both Joan and I found ourselves unconsciously staring at his arbitrarily arranged teeth. But it was also impossible not to be swept along with his infectious storytelling. He obviously loved to tell about his misadventures as much as we loved to listen, and as the evening wore on, our hilarity attracted some unpleasant stares from a few morose types seated in a neighboring booth.

Brendan told us that when his play, *The Hostage*, opened in London, it was a major hit, and that one night the great Noel Coward was in the audience. Afterwards he came backstage to meet the author and offer his best wishes, and as Brendan described the scene I was hard put to imagine a more disparate pair of playwrights: the immaculately British Noel Coward, as stiff-upper-lip as they come, elegantly attired, precise in speech, witty, erudite, and gay on top of everything else, and Brendan Behan, the unkempt, roistering, working class Irishman, profane in conversation, politically radical, and voraciously heterosexual.

Imitating Noel Coward's clipped, upper class voice, he repeated the great man's words: "Congratulations on a fine play, dear boy, and now that you've got some money, for God's sake *get yourself some teeth!*" At this Brendan once more threw his head back, opened his still unrepaired mouth, and let the laughter roll out.

It crossed my mind that Franz Kline should come over to the Cedar and join us, and when I suggested it, Herman obliged by phoning him. Unfortunately, Joan and I had made plans for the evening so we were not at the bar when Franz finally arrived. I heard the next day, however, that this mini-summit turned out to be yet another of the fabled great nights at the Cedar Bar.

Unfortunately, Brendan Behan could not maintain his sobriety, despite the peculiar substitute beverage he assembled that night at the Cedar. It was a foolish strategy at best, and as such never had a chance. Ironically, in Behan's last years, a reporter, thinking he was asking a literary question, wanted to know what Behan would like people to be saying about him in 50 years.

He answered quickly. "I'd like them to be sayin' 'How did that old drunk live to be 87?'" Sadly, he only made it to 41, a victim of severe alcoholism.

I recently came across an early quote by another, more famous Irish playwright, George Bernard Shaw, whose words helped me to understand Behan's doomed and chaotic life. "An Irishman's imagination," Shaw wrote, "never lets him alone, never convinces him, never satisfies him; but it makes him that he can't face reality, nor deal with it, nor handle it, nor conquer it... imagination's such a torture that you can't bear it without whiskey... and all the while there goes on a horrible, senseless, mischievous laughter."

IN THE 1950S, because the New York art and literary worlds were both relatively small, there were, inevitably, accidental encounters between members of the two groups, at openings, at unplanned, bring-your-own-booze parties, and on other informal occasions. I remember once having a brief chat with Saul Bellow, in the host's bedroom, during this kind of impromptu gathering. The conversation was memorable to me because I had recently read and admired Bellow's *The Adventures of Augie March* and *Seize the Day*, though, stupidly, I was too abashed to tell him so. In a similar situation, I once spent an hour, sitting in the garden at the Museum of Modern

Art and talking with Carson McCullers, whose novel *The Heart Is a Lonely Hunter* was a favorite of mine. At that very moment I had, in my hip pocket, a paperback copy of her *A Member of the Wedding*, but again I was too embarrassed to pull it out and show her the proof of my affection for her work. I thought it would seem too hokey or premeditated, so I kept the book concealed.

"Do you like this kind of art?" McCullers asked, pointing to the sculptures in the garden. Before I could answer, she told me that she didn't understand it at all, and so she didn't care for it. In the 1950s, the gap between writers and visual artists always seemed disappointingly stark. Even the marvelous short-story writer, Grace Paley, with whom I became quite friendly, never showed much interest in my work or that of my fellow artists.

There was, however, a small group of poets, friendly with some AbEx artists, whose writing ostensibly shared a similar esthetic, such as free-wheeling improvisation and emotional free-association. John Ashbery was the most important of these poets, though his work eventually diverged from that of Frank O'Hara, James Schuyler, Kenneth Koch, and a few others of the "New York School." But the central point is that very few of the AbEx artists paid much attention to poetry of any kind, old or new. Thus, the audience for Frank O'Hara's New York School writers was that of those few who regularly sought out and read poetry, and not the relative many who produced New York School paintings. There were, however, a few artists, such as Grace Hartigan, Jane Freilicher, and Larry Rivers, who were intensely interested in the poetry of O'Hara's group, but overall, this poetry, like that of, for example, W.H. Auden or Robert Lowell, went largely unread by the painters.

Music, however, was another story. All the artists I knew in the 1950s had phonographs and many played records while they worked. For Franz Kline, it was jazz and the music of Wagner (he had titled one of his major paintings *Siegfried*). And in 1954, when my girlfriend Nicki and I first visited Mark Rothko's apartment (we were babysitting his daughter Kate), Mark handed us an album of

Mozart's *The Magic Flute* to listen to. (Nothing but the best for Mark Rothko!) Pollock liked the small-band swing of the 1940s, and everyone adored Billie Holliday. There was not, however, a great deal of concert-going or opera-attending among the painters that I was aware of. Such expensive pleasures were out of most everyone's reach. Jazz joints, however, were another story. Many Cedar Bar regulars went to the Five Spot to hear Thelonious Monk and John Coltrane, and to the Half Note for Zoot Sims and Al Cohn. But in their studios, just about everyone listened to jazz records.

During my first stay in Provincetown in 1956, Zoot Sims was playing at the Atlantic House, and it was there, between sets, that we became casual friends. In my clichéd thinking, I assumed that a jazz musician like Zoot had to be the coolest of the cool, but one incident that summer proved me wrong. In those years, stag films – 8 mm pornos – were a great rarity and all of us were avidly eager to see one, so, one night, when Zoot joined our table between sets and started talking about having some "home movies" that we might be interested in, everyone felt they knew what he meant. We said we very much wanted to see his films. Zoot was pleased and made arrangements, after the Atlantic House closed, for us to come to the place he was renting where he would screen the movies. At the last minute, something made me hesitate, because I began to think he really meant *home movies*, family scenes like the ones my father used to make from time to time. I decided not to take the chance and stay up so late, but when the A-House closed, my excited friends, full of lewd expectations, all hustled out with Zoot. The next morning they sheepishly told me I had been right. Zoot's badly-shot home movies depicted things like his wife waving in front of a parked car, some shots on a beach somewhere, again with his wife waving, and many of the other boring, generic home movie images I knew so well from my own family's films. This cool jazz musician was, as I had sensed, really innocent in many ways.

Another time, in New York, Zoot came with some friends to my studio and asked to see my paintings. As I was showing them to him, I could see that he had no idea what they were about, or what he should say about them. I sensed the wheels in his head working to come up with the kind of complement he thought I would be pleased to hear from a jazz musician. "I like your paintings Budd," he said, straining for the right word. "They've got… they've got… *rhythm.*" It was an innocent try from a not very articulate but immensely talented musician, and as such I appreciated it.

As a young man the painter Larry Rivers had once played sax in a big band, but after he changed professions he kept at it, carrying his horn around and asking to sit in with experienced pros like Zoot Sims. One could tell that that they were usually not too pleased by his pushiness. "You know this painter Larry Rivers?" Zoot once asked me, and I said I knew him but not well. "Does he paint good?" he asked.

"Pretty good," I answered.

"He better," Zoot replied.

Aside from the jazz world, there were two composers of radical music, John Cage and Morton Feldman, who befriended the AbEx artists and came to the Cedar Bar rather frequently. Cage had famously "composed," in 1952, a piece called *4'33"* (4 minutes, 33 seconds), which was completely silent except for any random sounds that occurred during that time in the room in which the piece was being "performed." Morton Feldman, in his work, employed actual musical sounds, interspersed with fairly substantial pauses and silences and was generally thought of as a follower of Cage. In the 1950s a Japanese painter named Hasegawa came to New York, mainly to meet Franz Kline whose work he had seen in reproduction. One night, Hasegawa was sitting in the Cedar, talking to Feldman, when the composer brought him up to date.

"You know, Hasegawa, that we American composers, John Cage and I, have discovered and are exploring a musical element that has long been overlooked. We have discovered… *silence.*" He let that sink in, as Hasegawa rubbed his chin thoughtfully in search of a Zen reply.

"Feldman," he said finally, "the young Japanese composers are ahead of you Americans. In Japan we have discovered and are exploring… *deep* silence."

And so it went in the 1950s. The painters and sculptors more or less kept to their particular crafts, and apart from going to the movies and listening to recorded music – mainly jazz – left the other art forms (and politics) pretty much alone.

Dodging Hits

As someone brought up in repressed, genteel Wheeling, West Virginia, I'm now well aware that my family never discussed the subject of homosexuality – as well as anything else remotely controversial. I can't recall what we really did talk about at the dinner table, but whatever it was it would seem in retrospect to have been numbingly boring: family affairs, schoolwork, Jack Benny, mild gossip about friends, and so on. My parents liked it that way, and if they ever had to refer to one obviously gay cousin of ours, they were ready with a euphemism: the poor man was "a sissy." I realize, now, that their idea of a gay man was someone who knitted and lisped and extended his little finger when he drank tea – in other words a stereotypical object of humor. Lesbians, naturally, were "tomboys" – loudmouth tree climbers and football players who wore ragged shirts and pants and whose hair always needed shampooing. (For some reason my mother was extremely hair-conscious; it should be short, parted, combed, and extremely clean. Naturally, she hated the 1960s.)

Over the years, the Chelsea area of New York has become a kind of gay Mecca, and if my father were alive today and visited me at my Chelsea studio, he would be astounded by the buff gay men who swagger out of the gym across the street, wearing tiny muscle shirts to display thigh-size biceps, which look as if they could lift a school bus without raising a sweat. Macho has become the new gay, and sissydom seems gone for good.

At Oberlin I was aware that there were closeted gays – it was the Eisenhower-Truman era, remember – but I had no friends of that persuasion and came away almost as ignorant of the phenomenon as I had been when I enrolled as a freshman in 1949. However, through an unexpected encounter with a university professor, I was soon to learn a few things about one aspect of the gay world.

In 1952, returning with my family on the liner *Niew Amsterdam* after my first trip to Europe, I was, as usual, holed up, reading in a corner of one of the ship's capacious lounges to avoid the distractions of my family. Ever the intellectual sponge, I had begun a paperback book, Irwin Edman's *Arts and the Man*, a fairly dense discussion of esthetics, when an elderly gent approached me. He was smiling and quivering slightly, as if he was unsteady on his feet. Noticing that his skin was unusually pale and his watery eyes seemed also to wobble, for a moment I thought he might be an albino. He asked me if I was enjoying the book, and I said that I was – a partial truth – when he announced that he had written it.

He was Irwin Edman and asked if he could join me on the banquette. I was naturally thrilled to meet the author of the book I was reading and saw that he was pleased as well; this work on esthetics was not typical subway reading – or ocean liner reading, for that matter. Edman was charming and told me that he was a professor of philosophy at Columbia University. When he asked about me and my future plans, I explained that I wanted to be an artist but was first planning to take some graduate courses with Meyer Schapiro at, of all places, Columbia University. Edman said that he knew Schapiro and hinted that perhaps he could help get me admitted into graduate school. I was elated, and when I told him that I would be staying in New York a few days after we docked, he said he would like to take me lunch at the Columbia faculty dining room. We exchanged addresses and I went back to our stateroom to report this amazing and serendipitous event to my parents.

When the great day arrived, I walked across the Columbia campus to the philosophy building, bursting with optimism. The professor ushered me into his office with a broad smile and an extremely warm greeting. He offered me a chair, as he moved behind his desk, and, comfortably seated, we chatted for a few minutes. He mentioned that there was a marvelous view of the campus to be had from the office window behind his desk and gestured for me to come around and take a look. For a moment we stood side by side as he pointed out that a cast of Rodin's *The Thinker* was located below "with its back turned on the philosophy building." I assumed that this ivy-covered joke had for decades been used by academics to prove their cleverness, so I rewarded it with a modest chuckle.

But then I felt something moving at my side. An arm, Irwin Edman's arm, had encircled me from the back and his hand had begun hugging me against him. I pulled away and in a state of slowly building shock moved quickly to the other side of the desk. He came after me, and I darted away, as we began to circle his desk like a couple of characters from a French farce. He would feint to the right and then come quickly after me clockwise, and though I was quite a bit faster, he seemed determined to catch me. The weirdest aspect of this chase around his desk was that through it all we maintained an inanely civilized conversation, as if two radically different things were going on at once.

"Is that colonnaded building the library?" I asked as I moved quickly away from him.

"Yes, it was, but it's not used as a library any more," he replied, lunging towards me with surprising speed for such a wobbly old gent.

"It reminds me of the Pantheon in Rome," I said, passing again to the other side of the desk, and he agreed that the Pantheon was its inspiration as he circled after me.

This bizarre cat and mouse game continued until it apparently became clear to him that he would never be able to catch me. He finally stopped, a bit winded, and suggested that we go have lunch. I agreed and moved to the hall door in case he tried another lunge. With no mention of what had just transpired, we then proceeded to the faculty dining room, but I walked as far away from him as I possibly could while still maintaining the illusion that we were having a conversation.

The reason I did not excuse myself and leave was that I had looked forward to seeing the dining hall and perhaps encountering there a few of the famous people who taught at Columbia: Lionel Trilling, Meyer Schapiro, Jacques Barzun, and many others with whose work I was familiar. But at the door of the room, I had a sudden unpleasant realization. If Irwin Edman was as promiscuous and careless in his pursuits as his behavior demonstrated, his reputation could hardly have escaped the attention of the other faculty members, and now I, a relative innocent of 21, was about to enter the dining room as the guest of a notorious predator some 40 or 50 years older than I. It would look awfully suspicious, I knew, but since there seemed to be no way out, I decided I would sit with him at his table and have lunch. At least he owed me *something* after what he'd put me through. A tuna fish sandwich, at the very least.

The meal, as I recall, was only so-so, and I saw no celebrity academics. But as I sat with the old satyr, trying to make civilized conversation, my anger built to a level equal to the profound disappointment I felt. I realized that all along Edman had been interested in me only as sexual fodder, and never as a promising young student whom he could help in his career. I went back to my parents' hotel rooms a few hours older and a lot wiser, but deeply depressed and unwilling to tell them what had happened during my supposedly triumphant visit to Columbia University.

My next such experience was infinitely more benign, but in its own way, equally depressing. A few years after being chased around Irwin Edman's desk, I was living in New York in a tiny furnished room on Waverly Place in the Village, only four blocks away from the Cedar, and was painting small works in an organic style somewhat influenced by Arshile Gorky. I was hanging out at the Cedar Bar, which, as I've described, was a tough, macho place, but there were a few gay men – mostly poets – who also hung out there. Along with John Ashbery, the best-known poet of this New York school was Frank O'Hara, who was, in addition, an important art critic, a curator at the Museum of Modern Art, and a friend of De Kooning, Kline, and the other major abstract painters. All of us younger artists were eager to get O'Hara to our studios to see our work and then to write about it or at least help it along within MoMA's hierarchy.

Frank O'Hara, who was openly gay, had a kind of relaxed, unthreatening grace about him that made him very likeable, so one slow night at the Cedar we began talking at the bar as we sipped our beers. He asked about my work, of which he was unaware, and seemed genuinely curious about it. He asked where my studio was, and when I told him it was a very small place nearby on Waverly

Place, he brightened and asked if we could go there when we finished our beers for a look at my paintings; he had to meet some friends in an hour or so and would have some time to see what I was doing. I was thrilled, but after my experience with Irwin Edman, I was still a bit uncertain as to whether his interest was in my art or me. On the one hand, Frank was open about his sexual orientation, but on the other hand nothing in our conversation had the slightest erotic overtone. It was all about art.

As we walked along Waverly Place, we talked about the current gallery scene and the shows we had liked, and I began to feel very much at ease. When I opened the door to my tiny studio, Frank seemed surprised, remarking that it was one of the most cramped places he'd ever seen. "You've got to find a bigger studio," he said, "because no one can work in a tiny place like this. Anyway, you've got to work on a larger scale."

When he sat down on the narrow bed and faced my painting wall, I began to go through my drawings and paintings slowly, displaying each on a small folding easel. From time to time he made a perfunctory comment or two, which caused me to feel a rush of optimism; for the first time in my life an important curator at the Museum of Modern Art was examining my very young oeuvre and giving me some criticism. After I'd shown him ten or twelve small works, he turned away from the painting wall and looked at me with an ambiguous smile. "Budd…" he said. "I'd like to know… Are you straight or gay?"

"Straight," I said, as my heart sank.

"I just needed to know," he said, and a few moments later glanced at his watch. "It's getting late and I think I'd better go and meet my friends. But thanks for showing me your work. I think you're on the right track," a bland remark that meant nothing.

When he left my room and closed the door behind him, I leaned back on my bed, thoroughly depressed. Once again I felt crushed by someone from whom I had hoped for a hand up, but who apparently hoped only to get his hands on me. It seemed fairly obvious that it was not so much his curiosity about my work that had intrigued Frank O'Hara, but the possibility of a new sexual conquest. I faced a terrible question: What was it about me that seemed to embolden gay men?

I realized, of course, that I was both young and relatively innocent and looked it. Old habits die slowly, and as I glanced in the mirror I was reminded that I still kept my hair cut neatly short and well brushed, Wheeling style, and, not having the money for new clothes, I dressed in my old, generally conservative way. Such was also the style of choice for many gay men in those closeted days, men who did whatever they could to avoid attention in the conventional world. Did gay men misread my conservative appearance as a signal of sexual alignment? In Frank's case, those same conventional features also made me stand out at the Cedar Bar, where most of the grizzled habitués were 20, 30, or 40 years older than I and whose chaotic styles of dress and facial hair would have driven my mother up the wall. It was time to dump my bourgeois haberdashery. But in the meantime it was painful to realize that a major art critic had come to my studio, looked at my work, uttered a few *pro forma* comments, and then made a subtle, verbal pass at me. Unlike the professor, at least Frank had been a gentleman about it, and I was not chased around my easel. Yet it still hurt – badly.

Within a year or so I had accepted a new level of non-Wheeling grunge and was living in the battered loft in Chelsea, which I've described earlier as having only a sink as an amenity, with a shared toilet and shower in the upstairs hall. To put the best face on it, it was colorful, and when I moved in, I discovered that the tenants, two men and a woman whose loft was directly above me, were practicing sadomasochists. One evening when I went upstairs for a drink, I noticed that their old-fashioned umbrella stand contained ten or fifteen canes, though none of the three was lame. And then several times I was awakened late at night by screams coming from their floor. One night the screams became frighteningly excessive, and in the morning as I went upstairs to the shower I discovered a series of bloody handprints along the wall. That did it. Several of us tenants went to the landlord, threatening to call the police, and the noisy torturers were forced out.

A nuclear family moved into their loft: a man, his attractive wife, and their toddler son. But I soon learned that the wife, who supported the ménage, was a call girl who worked out of a classier apartment somewhere uptown. Because of her ever-suspicious husband, I was careful to keep my distance, but my description of her greatly intrigued Franz Kline. One night, at a party I gave in my loft, Franz asked me to introduce him to the call girl. I saw them talking, and later, when I asked what he thought of her, he seemed a bit downcast. "Well, she's good looking," he said, shrugging, "but then you'd have to pay her a wad of money, and it would end up just the same old thing."

It was to these strange living quarters that I brought my innocent wife-to-be, as I've described earlier, but in the summer of 1956, just before Joan and I met, I had left New York for a job working at the HCE Gallery in Provincetown. And it was in P'town that I had another depressing experience like those I'd had with Irwin Edman and Frank O'Hara, except that this time, instead of a philosopher or a poet, I was dealing with a tycoon, a man who came to the HCE Gallery ostensibly to buy an artwork. In a marginal way, Joan was involved this time because I had warned in her in advance how I feared the ensuing situation with the tycoon might pan out.

Mr. T, as I will call him for reasons that will become obvious, entered the gallery one afternoon and began asking prices of the works on exhibit. I remember that he was dressed in high style summer clothes, Bermuda shorts in the Abercrombie and Fitch style, a matching shirt, and expensive sandals; nothing about him, not a hair, was out of place. He was handsome and fiftyish, and later, when he signed the guest book, I recognized his name because of the eponymous company that bore it. A real tycoon.

He made easy conversation and soon learned that I was an artist temporarily minding the gallery. Amazingly, he asked if he could see some of *my* work, and since the little studio my employer provided me was some twenty feet away, I immediately took him there. He casually examined the watercolors I was doing that summer and seemed to like them, and then he asked if my regular studio was in New York. He explained that he wanted to see more of my work and, since he made frequent business trips to the city where he kept a *pied-à-terre,* he would visit me there when I returned. In a moment we were exchanging addresses and phone numbers while my heart did a little hopeful racing.

Still, it was perplexing. Though I had some rather good paintings in my Cape studio, Mr. T had asked no prices and made no effort to buy anything, potentially an ominous sign. The old question again: was he interested in my work or me? Though I was a bit more rumpled than before, I looked younger than my 25 years, and, for many of my friends, still seemed appallingly innocent. Despite the fact that I'd been stung twice before, by a philosopher and a poet, I allowed myself to hope that now, with this obviously wealthy tycoon, something good might come of it.

Meanwhile, before Joan moved in with me in New York, we eagerly communicated by phone and letter. I told her about my encounter with the tycoon and my uncertainty about what he really might have in mind. I called her immediately when a plain little postcard arrived in which Mr. T invited me to come to his *pied-à-terre* – actually a hotel suite – for drinks on a certain night. He would take me to dinner at a restaurant of my choosing near my studio, and afterward we could go there for a good look at my work. I called him and accepted, and later that night phoned Joan again to discuss the still ambiguous situation. "Maybe he really will buy something," she said, hopefully, "even though he might be gay. After all, gay people collect art, too."

So far I had seen no obvious reason to think he was gay, let alone another predator, but his lack of interest in the works I showed him in Provincetown still made me wonder. If he didn't like them, why would he want to visit my studio and see more of the same? Just before I left to meet him for drinks and dinner, I called Joan and told her that I saw my chances as 50/50 that he was considering buying a painting of mine, but that maybe, even if he was gay and had set his sights on me, he might buy something out of sheer guilt. I knew that he had a distinguished art collection and we certainly needed the money. I asked her to cross her fingers and hope.

That night I wore a jacket and tie, but when Mr. T opened the door to his suite he was informally dressed with his shirtsleeves rolled up. As we shook hands, he continued to hold my hand so forcefully between both of his that I had to strain to withdraw it. So that was it: another disappointment. My heart sank but I made a series of quick decisions. I would enter his comfortable-looking living room as if I hadn't had to wrestle my hand away from his, I would have a drink with him, and then I would make it clear that I was not gay but had no objection if he was. I would hold him to his dinner promise – I had a local steakhouse in mind – and insist that he visit my studio after supper; then, maybe I could shame him into buying at least a small work. It was utterly cynical of me, but I was angry, I felt tricked, and he could easily afford the purchase.

Mr. T poured us each a Scotch, and as we settled down to make polite conversation he told me that we would not be alone for dinner. He had invited "another couple," two men he had met the night before – and he looked away as he said it – "at a gay bar." As I was trying to decide how to handle this new announcement, there was a knock on the door and Mr. T ushered in the pair – one man about his age, fiftyish, and a younger man, like me, in his twenties. A planned symmetry, I guessed. Introductions were made, and when our host went into the kitchenette to prepare drinks for the new arrivals, I followed him in. He was carefully pouring Scotch over the ice when I said something like this: "Mr. T, I don't like to be anyplace under false pretenses, so I'd better tell you right off that I'm straight."

His hand shook and he spilled the liquor, but he quickly cleared his throat and said, "Oh, well, I'm straight, too… we're all straight here… No one's gay."

I made it clear that I had nothing against gay men, and that I didn't view someone's sexual orientation as an obstacle to friendship. Mr. T wiped up the spilled liquid and unsteadily carried the drinks into the living room. "Friends," he said, speaking a bit nervously, "Budd just told me he's straight and I told him that we're all straight here. No one's gay."

The guests looked shocked but recovered themselves quickly. "Of course," the older man said, "We're all straight here. No problem."

This was, after all, 1956, and closeted wealthy gays like these men probably lived with an ever-present fear of blackmail. So, to further prove his "straightness," Mr. T showed me some small, framed photographs on the mantel above the fake little fireplace. "See, Budd, this is a picture of my wife and me and our three children. This baby is one of my two grandchildren. I've always been straight." I realized that his frequent "business trips to New York" were probably the excuses he gave to his wife, his cover stories for the days and nights he spent cruising the city's gay bars.

As his older guest fumbled through his wallet in search of similar snapshots of wife and family, I said, "Don't bother. It's not necessary. It's O.K."

The three men were apparently relieved, and eventually Mr. T served another round of drinks. By the third round they had let down their guard and relaxed into talk about dinner, the older man recommending "a gay restaurant" he liked. I stepped in and announced that I wanted to eat at the steakhouse near my studio, so we could visit it as planned, after dinner. The guest said that he really wanted to go to the restaurant he'd mentioned, whereupon Mr. T said that perhaps the four of us had better dine separately because "I told Budd I wanted to visit his studio after dinner, and he has a particular neighborhood steakhouse in mind." It was a gracious decision in my favor.

So it was settled, but before they left, the two guests had yet another round of drinks. All pretences gone, the older guest put his arm around his companion's waist and asked Mr. T, "What do you think of Michael, my young man?"

His host replied that he found the young man "very attractive, and quite nice," though I realized that so far Michael had seemed rather sheepish and had said very little.

"Well, he should be nice," the older guest said. "He costs me $250 a week." Obviously embarrassed, the young man turned to me, and said in a quiet voice, "I'm trying to get through medical school."

The rest of the evening was in every way unpleasant. All during dinner at the steakhouse Mr. T kept sneaking glances at his wristwatch, and generally behaving like a reluctant prisoner. I knew that the studio visit was out, and that in fact he had probably never intended to look at my work. As he paid the bill I decided to free him: "Why don't you just go now and rejoin your friends at the other restaurant. It's late and you can visit my studio another time." He smiled like a fourth grader at the announcement of a snow day, bouncing up from the table, saying goodbye, and leaving as politely as his joy permitted.

I went home depressed in this way for the third time, but far less so than before because I had suspected from the outset that this might be the denouement. I phoned Joan and told her the bad news, and it felt good to hear her commiserations. Life goes on, she said. There will be other times when the interest really is in your work. And, I thought gloomily, not in my sad, young, heterosexual self.

Earlier I've described my first one-man show, which took place shortly after my encounter with Mr. T, and the encouraging review the show received in *The New York Times*. Stuart Preston, then the chief art critic for the *Times*, described my exhibition as "an unusually promising debut," and as a result I actually sold a few works. I've written that I met Preston in the gallery the morning after the opening, when I found him talking about my work with Meyer Schapiro. Under these happy circumstances, I felt very lucky to be introduced to the critic, a tall, friendly, serious-looking man, but it was all to get even better.

A few months after my first one-man show closed, I was told that Preston had bought a large but inexpensive painting of mine (my prices were still quite modest), giving Joan and me a reason to celebrate this first sale to a major critic. A few weeks later he called to invite me to his apartment for lunch on a Friday, and to see how my painting looked hanging where he had placed it. Thrilled, I immediately accepted for myself, aware that since Joan had a fulltime job at the Whitney she wouldn't have been able to come. But there was one thing Preston said that gave me pause. He told me that he had hung my painting – a horizontal – vertically, "because that way it brought out the phallic nature of the forms." I was stunned that an art critic would take it upon himself to change the clearly stated orientation of a painter's work. And what was this stuff about the "phallic nature" of the painting's forms? As far as I was concerned, the forms were organic and made vague references to nature, but phallic they weren't. The problem for me was that I was still a shy and very young artist, and Stuart Preston was the *Times*' chief art critic who actually owned the work. Perhaps, I thought, when I got to his apartment, I could gently persuade him to hang it properly.

Though he had made a point of saying that it would be just the two of us for lunch, I still did not suspect that the invitation might have a covert purpose. This kind of lingering innocence is proof, perhaps, that I was either very stupid or overawed that such an important critic had actually invited me to his apartment for lunch. Still, after the debacle with Mr. T., I should have learned *something.*

In his personal style, Stuart Preston turned out to be a very different kind of would-be seducer. When we shook hands, I did not have to struggle to extricate mine, and there was no conversation about gay restaurants or gay anything. The word wasn't used. After serving some chilled white wine, he showed me how he had hung my painting, and I argued for its original orientation. The issues of placement and so-called "phallic forms" were still unsettled when he invited me into his large kitchen and offered me a chair at a table elegantly set with his best silver and china. As he began to prepare the lunch, he refilled our wine glasses, and while he worked we talked about the art world and various shows he or I had liked particularly.

Then, with a proud gesture – what we would now call a ta-da presentation – he took from the refrigerator a silver platter on which lay, carefully arranged atop a bed of lettuce, a dozen raw oysters glistening in their juices. "You know that oysters are an aphrodisiac," he said with something of a wicked smile. Only then did I get the point that it was happening yet again. I withstood a perverse impulse to say that I hoped the oysters' aphrodisiac effect would last until I could get home and bed my wife, but I realized that I had to handle things as delicately as possible. I told him I had never had raw oysters before, and when I tried them I found them delicious. Privately, however, I felt uncomfortable by the way he watched me devour my half dozen.

We had a fine, gourmet lunch with a lot more wine – my host kept refilling my glass – and it became clear that he had put a lot of time and effort into a meal that he must have hoped would be the prelude to a postprandial sexual romp. I stayed at his apartment for what I thought was a polite period of time, but then announced that I had to leave because my wife would soon be due back from work.

As a flicker of sudden disappointment washed over his face at the word "wife," I felt a rush of sympathy for him because all of his elaborate preparations had come to naught. No one was going to stay at his party. He had said nothing or done nothing overt or predatory, but I left the apartment feeling depressed about the obvious purpose of his elegant repast. Still, I was extremely grateful to him and bore him no ill will since he had written so favorably about my work and had purchased a painting. Stuart Preston was a gentle, somewhat shy, but goodhearted man, and despite my unhappy realization that his lunch invitation was not a matter of simple, collegial friendship involving the painting of mine he had acquired, I regretted having saddened him. In retrospect I can see that in those repressed and closeted times, sadness and disappointment must have been everyday companions for multitudes of gay men like him who were trying, as "bachelors," to live two very different lives.

My fifth and final such incident could have popped out of a bizarre slapstick comedy, but it ended successfully – with the sale of a number of paintings. It did not involve a philosopher, poet, tycoon, or art critic, but instead the famous art collector, Walter Chrysler, Jr. Elsewhere, though I described my dealings with Chrysler, I did not mention his gay, forthright boldness, a much talked about trait in Provincetown where he had established a museum for his large collections. Like Mr. T and his older guest, Chrysler was also married but obviously much less concerned about hiding his homosexual activities, so when he asked to come to my studio to look at my work, I more or less knew that, in the immortal words of Bette Davis, I would be in for a bumpy ride. He was aware that I was married, but marriage was apparently never an obstacle to him, a male being a male and thus another potential target for conquest.

Walter – we were on a first name basis – asked me to meet him at his museum and drive him the half mile to my studio, just off Commercial Street. Since he had bought the work of many P'town painters, I assumed, correctly, that he would actually buy some paintings of mine. I double-parked and found him waiting for me in the museum lobby, and as he got in the car on the passenger side I noticed that he sat toward the middle of the seat, close to where I, the driver, would have to sit.

As we started off, unavoidably pressed hip to hip, Walter began speaking in somewhat grandiose terms about commissioning me to paint a large work for the lobby of the museum. He was gazing out the passenger-side window and gesturing grandly with his right hand, while his left arm flopped behind me, on the back of the seat. As he droned on about the great things he foresaw for my work, his left arm seemed to accidentally fall forward until it rested on my shoulder. I leaned towards the steering wheel to break the unwelcome contact, but the arm dropped further, touching my lower back. I sped up to shorten the trip to my studio and slid forward into a kind of protective crouch as he discussed the possibility of a one-man show of my work at the museum.

He never once glanced in my direction or slowed his rap about all the good things he could do for me, but now, behind my back, his left hand touched me again at belt level. Luckily we were almost at my studio. I was driving much too fast with my face embedded in the steering wheel and my knees cramped up against the dashboard. I could no longer avoid his arm, but I was finally home. I brusquely stopped the car, yanked on the handbrake, and opened the door, flying out of the front seat like a boulder from a Roman catapult. On his side of the car, Walter, a portly, awkward man, slowly emerged, still describing the grandiose future he could foresee for me.

Since Chrysler actually did buy a number of my paintings that day, my obvious avoidance of his ever-descending arm didn't interfere with the outcome of his visit. Because this last of my depressing encounters with gay, would-be seducers took place in 1958, three years before I would leave my twenties behind and turn 30, I wondered if this welcome drop-off in attempted seductions might have an age connection. I certainly looked less innocent in 1958 than I had in those earlier times. After all, we live in a youth-saturated culture, and maybe for some people, I was getting too old and too wise to bother with.

I'm reminded of a very heterosexual story about Hugh Hefner, who, at the age of 60 or so, married a beautiful 25-year-old girl. After the wedding a reporter asked the bride what it was like to marry someone so much older than she. "I don't know," she answered, somewhat tentatively. "I've never dated anyone over 29 before."

"Neither have I," Hefner added with a smile and a puff on his pipe.

My youthful encounters with these five accomplished older men, each of whom was quite well known in his profession, taught me several things about the gay underworld in the 1950s. Apart from the uncloseted Frank O'Hara who, early in the game, at least had the foresight and courtesy to ask me about my sexual orientation, each of the others ran a major risk in pursuing me. To them, I was an unknown quantity who might, as I did, refuse their advances, but I was also someone who, if I wished, could have reported them to the Columbia faculty, to their wives, to *The New York Times*, or to whoever could cause them serious trouble. Judging by my experiences, most of these men seemed to live fairly reckless lives, since each apparently preferred to seduce the young, the innocent, and the unknown, rather than settle for safer, known quantities within the gay world.

Though it's no excuse for their behavior, all of them were living in an intolerant society that forced them to accept a closeted, hypocritical lifestyle, so occasionally they may have felt the need to break out and risk dangerous new adventures. Fortunately, as I write these words, most all of this has changed for the better, and thousands of gay men and women have "come out" without serious consequences. Nevertheless, during those long ago benighted years, many innocent young men must have suffered from the kinds of unwanted intrusions and disappointments that I went through with men who should have known better.

The Start of a New, Life-Changing Decade

After writing about the 1950s and thinking ahead to the incidents and events of the following crucial decade, my train of thought was interrupted from time to time by strong sensory recollections that seemed unattached to anything significant. Apart from wondering what an incident has to do to qualify as an event, I realized that many of my most vivid childhood memories are neither. Instead, they are free-floating but powerful bits of sensory detritus that pop into the mind unexpectedly and are anchored only haphazardly by circumstances. They appear in such things as memories of the particular feel of physical surfaces... the resonance of oddly familiar odors... sudden, internal spasms of intense emotion. What they have in common, despite their strength, is that when weighed against the world of material events, they are utterly trivial.

For example, from my earliest years I have vivid memories of simply holding a certain toy, a little red truck or a car, and turning it over to look at it from underneath and spin its midget wheels. When I held it close to my nostrils, the metal such toys were cast from (lead, possibly?) gave off a dull, machine-like odor, especially if I had been playing outside and the metal had been sufficiently warmed by the sun. From another vague time early in the war I recall a toy warplane, a fairly realistic Bell Airacuda with a rounded fuselage that fitted perfectly down into the curved palm of my pint-sized hand. I loved to hold that little plane and pretend it was flying around the room, accompanied by the steady drone of my aircraft-engine imitation. I can't explain why this particular toy felt so good in my hand, or why the sensation of holding it is so memorable, but I know I could barely bring myself to put it down at suppertime.

And there were the times during the war, in the years just before we moved to Memphis, when I commanded an army made up of my little sister, Bobbo Weiler, and Eddie Stiefel. We would take up play weapons and slip into the thick autumn woods near Wheeling Creek to hunt Nazis, but my recollections have mainly to do with the sharp, musty smell of the moist, decaying leaves beneath our feet as we crept along in wary silence. Suddenly, someone would whisper an urgent "Down!" and I'd feel a sharp stab of adrenalin-laced fear as we dropped to our knees. The invisible Nazis were about to take us in ambush!

This kind of vivid but insignificant sensory recollection, based on nothing more than trivial moments of play, continued into adulthood, but there it usually seems connected to something more meaningful. For example, I can remember the mixed rush of sensations I felt one warm summer night in 1964, when Joan and I and three friends went skinny dipping – a first for the two of us – in a Wellfleet pond. There was the element of daring, of being naked in the moonlight in front of our friends, and the initial shock of the cool water against our skin. Then there was a liberating sense of utter freedom as we swam near one another, laughing with amazement at our happiness and audacity, and, underlying everything, the intensely erotic thrills we felt when body touched body, hands brushed breasts, and Joan and I embraced in the silken water.

Much later in my complex life, at a time when I was regularly giving lectures about the UFO phenomenon, I recall the daunting moment when I took the podium in Istanbul to address an audience of well over a thousand people, feeling a strange blend of elation and unease as I stared out over what seemed to be an unending sea of faces. All were waiting to hear what I had to say, so the thrill of the moment was intermixed with uncertainty as to whether they would be receptive to my talk, or if they even cared. But, like diving into the chilly water of an ocean surf, once I got going it turned out well, even though in the pregnant first few seconds after I was introduced my knees were weak and my heart was racing.

And then there were the many times in the early 1960s when, as I painted loosely and without a guiding plan on small Bristol Board sheets, a composition would suddenly come into focus and I would gasp at its unwilled coherence. At such a moment, I would have to put my brush down and stare at the painting for a while, afraid that, for the time being, anything I would do to it would destroy its mood and its magic as rudely as if I'd coughed during a piano recital.

Internal sensations of failure were just as acute. In the late 1950s, a friend of mine, the painter Jan Muller, died, and I began to paint a portrait of him from memory and the help of a few old photographs. At one point the painting came into focus, and I achieved a startling likeness. I pushed on, but it began to get away from me, the likeness fading with each touch and my would-be memorial gradually turning to mush. The slow, deepening sense of helpless failure was one I'll never forget, and a day or so later I gave up completely and destroyed the canvas. Though the wasted effort barely qualifies as an incident, the inner emotion I experienced is one I can recall with uncomfortable sharpness.

Though these pungent, irregular Proustian recollections, like the faint leaden aroma of a sun-warmed toy, often come unattached to anything significant, they are both unexpected and welcome links between past and present. But naturally, life in the 1960s also came laden with many complex memories of real substance. In September, I recall my excitement when a number of my paintings were included in the Whitney Museum's exhibition *Young America, 1960*, which later traveled to major museums around the country, providing me a welcome degree of national exposure. In 1958, I had already been included in my first Whitney *Annual Exhibition* and had begun to sell a few larger paintings at slightly higher prices to serious collectors. My work was shown in several group exhibitions that year, and was favorably reviewed in *Art News* magazine by the poet John Ashbery, then at the beginning of his distinguished career.

More important to me was the way my work was evolving. I was gradually abandoning the densely packed organic style of the middle 1950s and simplifying my imagery by using larger, more stabilizing forms. To the extent that they relied on fewer moving parts, my new paintings were gaining power. Though still somewhat indebted to the work of Franz Kline, I was trying to achieve a more classical sense of order without sacrificing the life-giving energy that lay at the heart of AbEx painting. My color moved away from the hot reds and greens I'd been using and shifted towards a cooler, more neutral range in which blue, black, ochre, and gray made up a very different chord. During our European trip in 1959, Joan and I had seen the great Piero della Francesca frescos in Arezzo, and I had been carried away by his limpid color, his majestic calm, and his infallible sense of structure. He had obviously influenced the direction of my work, which was beginning to slide away from one polarity – the expressionist – and slowly to approach the other – my long-term fascination with Mondrian's classicism.

In 1961, I received a studio visit from Joseph Hirshhorn, the fabled collector who eventually donated his enormous holdings to the United States government and provided funds for the museum that now displays them on the Capitol Mall in Washington, D.C. Hirshhorn was a short, stocky man who seemed as much a Borscht-belt comedian as the eminent collector and astute, self-made millionaire he actually was. Whenever he asked me the price of a large painting and I quoted it, he would slap his forehead in mock horror, spin around on his toes, and begin singing the song, "Say It Isn't So." Nevertheless he bought six major works, providing Joan and me with the funds we needed for another trip to Europe.

This was also the year of John F. Kennedy's inaugural, but ever since my epic battle with my father over the Rosenberg case, and my knowledge of the personal tragedy Dad had suffered years before, I had been trying to mute our political disagreements. Some clashes, however, were inevitable. One of his *bêtes noires* was the civil rights movement – to him, Martin Luther King was nothing more than a left-wing (Communist?) rabble-rouser – and another was national health insurance, eventually voted into law as Medicare. In my father's view, such a national health program, like FDR's Social Security system, was nothing more than an example of a socialist victory over capitalism. Dad still occasionally sent me right-wing tracts warning about the "Communist-Socialist" plot to take over America, but I did not respond in kind; I knew how futile it would be.

Ironically, the two things that Dad regarded as the most deplorably socialistic – a national program of health insurance (Medicare) and the Social Security system – have turned out to be the two programs that have kept me alive and relatively solvent over these later years of continuous health problems and consequently lowered income. I sometimes wonder, had Dad lived longer, if he might not have eventually changed his mind about these two life-saving liberal programs and doffed his hat to FDR and Lyndon Johnson.

But in the early 1960s there was a second reason I held back somewhat from stating my more liberal views: I was the only member of my family who held them. As I mentioned before, while I was growing up, Dad's political outlook not only dominated but was also sacrosanct, and the topic of politics – as well as sex and religion – was banned from family conversation. At any rate, no one I knew in Wheeling was well informed about the crucial issues the country faced, and the local newspapers were a joke, so it was only when I moved to New York that I met people, on both the left and the right, who had enough facts at their disposal to buttress their points of view. For me, this was a refreshingly new state of affairs.

As for my life in the career that my father had originally opposed, I developed a new tactic to keep things calm. Whenever I sold a large painting or one entered an important collection, I immediately telephoned him with the news. Since his business handled Dodge and Plymouth cars, both Chrysler Corporation products, he was immensely pleased when I told him that Walter Chrysler, Jr. had purchased fifteen paintings. And when the Whitney Museum acquired a large canvas in 1963, I was on the phone in an instant. The tactic worked, and I could tell that Dad was becoming, reluctantly perhaps, quite proud of me. He had also become very fond of Joan, once he and my mother got over the shock that we had been married in private without first having discussed the situation with them. ("Thank goodness she's white," Joan heard my mother whisper to Dad, as if the two of them had been dreading what to them would have been the worst possible outcome: an African-American daughter-in-law.)

There were, of course, many other things that I kept to myself because I knew they would upset my aging father. One of them was my casual friendship with Alger Hiss in the late 1950s, shortly after his release from prison. Hiss had been accused of spying for the USSR, but he had been tried and convicted on perjury charges in what the tabloid press called the trial of the century. Having fallen from the heights of a State Department position as one of the architects of the United Nations, his status now was that of a convicted felon and suspected traitor. When I met him, he was reduced to selling stationery products from company to company in order to make a living. I had no real idea about his guilt or innocence of the spy charges, but I found him to be a highly intelligent, principled man whom no one, not even his worst enemies, ever accused of acting from mercenary motives. He was also someone with a surprisingly acute interest in art, and I first met him at a supper party given by an art collector and his wife.

One evening, when Alger and his wife came to my studio for dinner, he spotted a reproduction of a Piero della Francesca painting I had tacked up on my wall. He remarked that years before, when he was a student, artists pinned reproductions of Giotto on their walls when no one else seemed interested in Piero. But now, he said, since the "anecdotal" was passé and abstraction was dominant, the more formal, more abstract work of Piero had replaced Giotto's emotional storytelling. It was a subtle observation and typical of his finely-tuned esthetic sensibility.

Throughout our casual friendship, I never mentioned the subject of the charges against him, though I was aware that among the complex mysteries of "the case," as Alger referred to his situation, one crucial detail had to with a typewriter that he had allegedly used to type incriminating documents. I knew that after a long search, his lawyers had managed to locate the disputed typewriter and entered it into the trial as evidence of his innocence. In fact, it proved the opposite and helped to convict him. He responded that the typewriter must have first been found by the FBI, which then doctored it and planted on his lawyers, but it was a convoluted explanation that went nowhere.

In casual conversations about political subjects, such as his admiration for President Kennedy, Hiss was always very circumspect, speaking carefully in a way that suggested a habit of hyper-vigilance. This caution was a quality that could be explained either as the product of having for years lived a double life, or the opposite, that he had to be constantly on the alert for government eavesdropping and surveillance. I simply didn't know which was true, though I found him personally to be a sensitive, highly intelligent man who for whatever reason had come to a tragic pass, and I felt deeply sorry for him and the utter waste of his now quite useless talents.

Meanwhile, in 1962, Franz Kline lay dying in a New York hospital. When his death came, Herman Somberg, one of Franz's closest friends, arrived at my studio in a state of profound mourning. We commiserated with each other, both of us intensely moved by the loss of a good friend and a great painter. I suggested that we go to the Guggenheim Museum to look at some art in order to lift our spirits, particularly since a Philip Guston show was on exhibit and Guston had also been one of Franz's close friends. As Herman and I walked around the rigid ramps of Frank Lloyd Wright's weird, curving display areas, we became even more depressed because most of the Gustons in the show were his recent, rather gloomy dark paintings, which avoided the lush color of his earlier work. We were sitting on one of the few benches in the Guggenheim, feeling really down, when suddenly Alger Hiss came up to us, beaming with excitement.

"Budd, did you see the front-page article in today's *Times*?" he asked. "It's about Nixon's new book on his six crises, where he writes that the big break in my case came when the FBI located the alleged typewriter. He says that the *FBI found it*! It's virtually an admission that they planted a doctored typewriter, just as we claimed!"

Alger was overjoyed at his news, while Herman and I, still consumed by our personal sense of loss, made a few feeble efforts to share his happiness. A few days later, Nixon announced that he had "misspoken" in his book, and retracted his claim that the FBI had originally found the typewriter in a statement that seemed to put Alger's case back on square one.

I still have no fixed idea of the extent of Hiss's guilt or innocence, beyond the fact that he had obviously committed perjury. But, in retrospect, the grief and sense of loss I was feeling in the Guggenheim that afternoon when I faced the sadness of Franz's passing, combined with the depression I saw in Philip Guston's latest work (he was another senior painter with a troubled life and a drinking problem), and the obvious elation Alger expressed at Nixon's "error," remain in my memory as a vivid example of the complexity of my life and its unusual crosscurrents during those tumultuous years.

There were, of course, many other moments of unadulterated happiness and good fortune. Malcolm and Janice Fleschner were wealthy art collectors who bought a painting of mine from the *Young America 1960* exhibition at the Whitney. Subsequently we met, they came to my studio, and we became good friends. In the next few years they bought several more works, and when they visited the Cape one summer, aware of its beauty and the love Joan and I felt for it, Malcolm made a characteristically generous proposal. As the four of us were swimming in the bay, he asked me why I didn't buy land and build a studio instead of renting one shack after another. I explained that I didn't have that kind of money, but he said he was sure the local bank would give me a mortgage. "Anyway," he said, "if they don't think you can swing it, I'll countersign it for you."

I was astonished at his offer, but within the year I had bought land in Truro, hired my friend, the architect Charlie Zehnder, to draw up plans for a spacious studio with an adjoining compact living area, and had been granted a loan to build it. "This is the biggest two-room house we've ever written a mortgage for," said a smiling bank official, more used to funding cramped, six-room Cape Cod cottages than spacious two-room, loft-style studios.

In late November 1963, I had another exhibition at the Poindexter Gallery and received a rave review from Brian O'Doherty, the recently appointed chief art critic of *The New York Times*. "One of the year's best shows," he wrote, adding that my work provided an answer to the question of what kind of painting should come after Abstract Expressionism. He implied that in bringing a new classicizing order to AbEx energy, I was a "master of a movement *manqué*," a description of me as, in effect, the leader of a movement that as yet had no followers. But this extraordinary review went almost unnoticed, even by me, because it appeared the same day the *Times* printed its extensive coverage of the Kennedy assassination. My personal and therefore almost insignificant triumph disappeared beneath the immense national tragedy of the President's death.

The August UFO Sighting

LIVING IN NEW YORK, I've always felt an edgy impatience in the early spring when each tender breeze and smogless patch of blue sky makes me yearn for Cape Cod. My mind becomes fixed on escape, on driving north to the calming beauty of the Cape's pinewoods, sand cliffs, and endlessly lulling sea. Wandering down Eighth Avenue amid its sirens and horns and acrid fumes, I temporarily morph into a caged prisoner, rattling imaginary bars and crying out for sunlight and parole.

In 1964, Joan and I made a particularly early exit, leaving for our new Truro studio at the end of May because we just couldn't wait any longer. The blessed change of mood from New York to the Cape happens quickly, and in a day or two, after unpacking and arranging things in our brand new house, we fell into a quiet routine. Joan and I worked in the morning, swam at Balston Beach in the afternoon, and then later, at home, watched the stunning sunsets from our deck high above the tiny, meandering Pamet River.

What I think of now as the August UFO incident began on yet another uneventful but productive summer day. I worked in the studio while Joan, sitting in the sunlight that streamed in through the big glass doors, wove beautiful things on her Swedish loom, and our houseguest, Ted Rothon, lounged outside on the deck, reading. We had met Ted, a young English social worker currently living and working in Chicago, during our 1959 trip to Europe and subsequently maintained our friendship. He was interested in my work and had recently bought a major painting that I dedicated to the memory of Medgar Evans, the murdered civil rights leader. Joan and I got along very well with Ted, an intelligent Brit with an engaging sense of humor, and he had been staying with us for a while, bunking without complaint on the built-in living room couch.

August in the Cape art colony is dense with gallery openings, cocktail parties, and small dinners at one another's studios, so when we were invited to a party at the Provincetown home of Hudson and Ione Walker, we asked if we could bring Ted with us. Naturally, they said that he would be welcome, mentioning that several other people were also bringing houseguests. Hudson Walker was a devoted art collector and a fixture in the Provincetown art scene, so I knew that his guest list would include some artists I thought Ted would enjoy meeting.

About 5:15, the three of us, all sitting in the front seat, started the twenty-minute drive to Provincetown. I was at the wheel with Joan beside me and Ted next to her. The sky above us was clear, containing only a series of small clouds that blew in rather quickly from the sea. An earlier storm had broken up, and these fast moving puffs were its low-lying remnants, though a distant cloud mass still lingered to our right, out over the ocean. As we drove along High Head on Route 6 in Truro, just before the highway dips down to only few feet above sea level, we were carrying on an animated conversation when, as Joan recalls, we were all silent for a few moments.

"Are you seeing what I'm seeing?" she asked.

The three of us were looking at a small, lens-shaped object in the sky ahead of us, a bit off to our left but clearly visible through the windshield. Whatever it was, it seemed stationary, but since we were moving and the small clouds were scudding by, it was difficult to tell if the object was standing still or gliding very slowly. I thought for a moment that it might be some kind of flatish balloon with a surface like dull, brushed aluminum, but then I realized that it was not keeping pace with the nearby clouds. If it were an oddly shaped type of balloon, it would have to be tethered to the ground or it would surely be blowing in the same trajectory as the clouds. As I eased up on the accelerator, a small cloud passed rapidly across it, temporarily blocking our view. A second later, as that cloud moved on, another passed behind it, silhouetting it nicely. Then, after a moment, another cloud seemed to swallow it up, so that for a few seconds we could see its dark shape within, as one might observe a ship in a fog bank.

Whatever this object was it did not seem to be very big, though under the circumstances it was difficult to judge its size. In relation to the cars on the road below us, it appeared to be as large as an automobile or perhaps a bit larger, but it was definitely a solid object with a somewhat reflective surface. (Later, Joan told me that she thought it was much farther away and therefore quite a bit larger.)

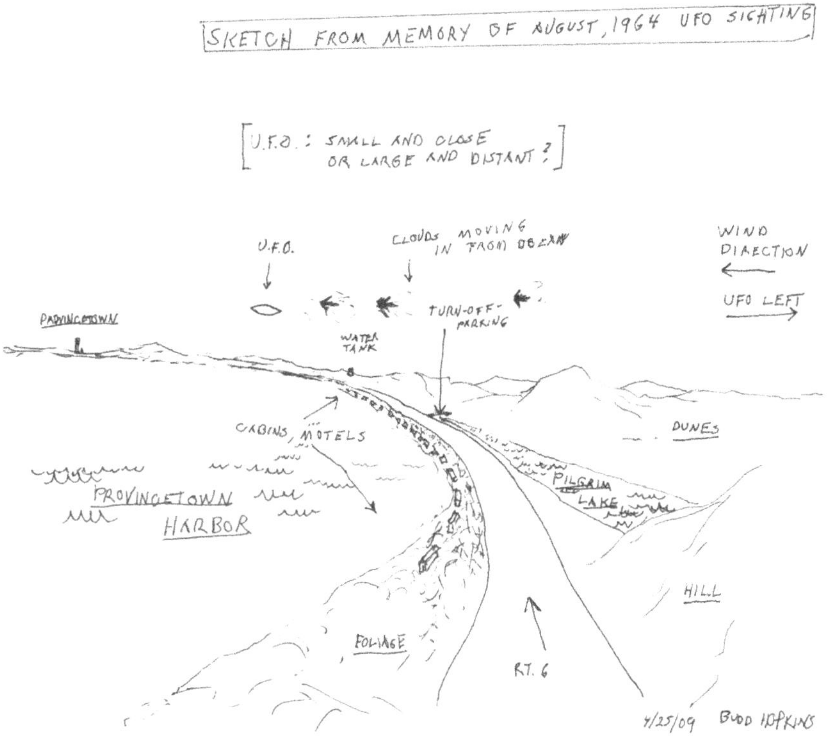

My sketch of the landscape where the August, 1964, UFO sighting took place.

As we drove slowly down the hill to the lower ground, I was looking out of the left window as Joan and Ted, to my right, strained to see what this odd thing might be. From below, viewing it from a steeper, more nearly vertical angle, it appeared to be circular and utterly without details – no lights, wings, doors, windows, or protuberances of any kind.

Then, suddenly, it began to move in a straight horizontal line, flying directly *into* the wind. Whatever it was, it was certainly not a balloon, and it was now traveling at the speed of a small airplane.

I stopped the car, and the three of us jumped out and watched it fly into the cloudbank that hovered over the ocean. At this point, one of us – I'm not certain who – said, "Do you suppose that was one of those flying saucers you used to read about?" In fact, none of us had ever actually read anything substantive about "flying saucers," though by 1964 it was impossible for any literate American not to have at least heard the term.

By the time we arrived at the Walker's home about ten minutes later, we were keyed up and eager to talk about what we thought of as a unique experience, but it was here that things became even stranger. The first person we met as we entered the crowded room was the painter Giorgio Cavallon. He looked at us, and said, "What happened to you? You look as if you've seen a ghost." We told him about our sighting, and he replied rather calmly that he'd seen things like that a number of times over the years, "lights, at night, moving erratically." What we described, of course, was a metallic disc in broad daylight, not a moving light, but nevertheless, Giorgio's report added to the mystery.

Next we approached two friends of ours, Molly Cook, a photographer and gallery owner, and her partner, the poet Mary Oliver (who would eventually win a Pulitzer Prize), and told them about the object we had just seen. They were immediately interested because, they said, a few years before, as they drove along Route 6, they had noticed a similar craft just above the trees, again in the daylight but apparently much closer than the object we sighted. They described it as looking metallic with what appeared to be a row of windows along its side. I was astounded. The two women were obviously sincere and had no reason to invent such a story, yet neither had ever mentioned their strange experience to me. Later in the evening, under similar circumstances, still another friend told me about his similar UFO sighting. *What is going on?* I thought. Were these experiences actually widespread, an underground phenomenon that no one discussed, even though they might be of potentially great importance?

After the party we returned home, still talking about the sighting, but the next day we went about our usual patterns of work and pleasure. The question of the nature of this odd object seemed to linger in my mind more tenaciously than in Joan's or Ted's, though the following summer, when Ted came to visit us again, virtually his first question to me when he came down the ramp from his plane was: "Do you remember that thing we saw in the sky last summer? What do you think it was?" Obviously it had been preying on his mind, too.

Ever since our sighting of whatever it was, I was feeling more and more intrigued. Within the year, I sought out several serious books on UFOs, and the more I read about the phenomenon the more I became persuaded that these craft-like objects, which behaved as if they were under intelligent control, could be extraterrestrial in nature. However, when I brought up the subject with my friends and fellow painters, I discovered that most had no trouble dismissing UFO reports as explainable by one mundane cause or another, even if they were clear, daylight sightings by Air Force personnel or experienced commercial pilots and had also been detected on radar. Such accounts, my friends said, had no bearing on their lives, so why worry about them? For me, however, these reports constituted a disturbing mystery that I could not leave alone.

From the vantage of the present, I can easily see an analogy with my continuing interest in UFOs in 1964 and the indifference almost everyone else displayed – particularly those colleagues of mine in the art world. In my analogy, a biologist in the 1980s comes across some statistics that suggest the average temperatures near the surface of our planet are rising very slightly each year. He realizes that these tiny, incremental increases may have simple explanations and are possibly temporary, but he also understands that these data might mean something quite important, a process of steady global warming, year after year. When he mentions the subject, he finds that most of his fellow scientists dismiss his data, ascribing the rising temperatures to various accidental, unimportant factors. And yet, as the biologist reads about the changes in temperature and their possible connection to greenhouse gas emissions, he becomes even uneasier, and so begins to carry out his own scientific study of the phenomenon. We know, now, how global warming finally came to be seen as truly important, even dangerous, by mainstream science. Though no similar widespread realization has occurred with the UFO phenomenon, as time passes more scientists and laymen are recognizing its potential significance for our planet, and objective investigations have long ago been undertaken in many different countries.

But more than 40 years ago – after the assassination of President Kennedy, the Cold War, the escalating Vietnam morass, the Beatles, Elvis, Lyndon Johnson, Nixon, and a national mood of deepening social unrest – the UFO issue was easily pushed aside by many people in much the same way that twenty years later, ominous signs of global warming could be conveniently overlooked by scientists and the public alike.

I often recall the various uneasy thoughts and peculiar images that the August sighting stimulated in my mind immediately after its occurrence. I had little to go on then, having as yet read nothing about the UFO phenomenon, but I know that from the first moments after it flew out towards the ocean, I began to question the idea that this round, metallic thing was man made. It seemed to be soundless; it could apparently hover and then speed away at will; it had no identifying characteristics; and yet it appeared to be under intelligent control. The central image I formed in my mind in the first few days after the sighting was this: that the object was some kind of probe from "elsewhere," a piece of advanced observational equipment that I thought of as functioning like a diving bell, which had been lowered on an (invisible) cable to examine the "seabed" – the dunes and roads and structures at the end of the Cape – and had then been retracted up and away after the survey was complete. I could even picture how our "seabed" must have appeared from above: a hard-surfaced strip on which tiny machines passed up and down, a rolling expanse of light brown "soil" and green plant life on one side and the blue sea on the other. Stretched along the edge near the water was a row of small, identical, "Monopoly" houses

– one of the many motel complexes on Beach Point. My homely conception, then, was of a virtually magical, disc-shaped object that did not require intelligent beings – "aliens" – inside, steering it. No Beebe or Cousteau in this image, or little green men; in fact, no living things of any sort. I saw it as an unmanned futuristic wonder, a space-age, exploratory vehicle of extraordinary efficiency.

Though my brain was obviously tying itself into knots in an effort to make sense of such a new and utterly puzzling experience, I tried to theorize as parsimoniously as possible about its nature. Nevertheless, as time passed and I began to read about the numerous UFO occupant reports, my ideas began to change. Perhaps, I decided, these craft might contain sentient beings after all. At any rate, it was abundantly clear that the metallic disc we saw that August afternoon had opened a big door in my thinking about the limits of our known world, a portal that remains ever more ajar.

But this is not the whole story of the events associated with our sighting that August afternoon in 1964. A few days later, a friend mentioned that the night before he had watched a strange light maneuvering erratically in the sky over Cape Cod Bay. Had "our" UFO come back? I began to think that perhaps Joan and I should go out to the beach at night, spread a blanket, and watch the sky, just in case whatever it was might return a third time. Amazingly, an unlikely pair of friends surprised us by asking if they could join our vigil, because they, too, had had an unusual recent sighting.

The Provincetown-Truro-Wellfleet area is the summer work and playground for many academics, psychiatrists, writers, and intellectuals, as well as the artists I've mentioned before. In 1964, all of us were pretty well intermixed, with warm friendships flourishing amongst a range of professionals. The interaction was stimulating, with the artists providing the paintings and sculptures and the intellectuals doing the talking, except in those cases when certain artists tried to talk too pompously and certain intellectuals tried to paint too gaudily.

Among my intellectual friends were the psychohistorian Robert J. Lifton and his wife Betty Jean, a therapist and expert on issues of adoption; the composer Arthur Berger; the art historian Eleanor

Munro and her husband, *New Yorker* writer E.J. Kahn, Jr.; the poet Stanley Kunitz; and the Columbia University professor, Richard Hofstadter and his wife, "Beatie." I suppose I had mentioned my UFO sighting to all of these friends shortly after its occurrence, but I was taken aback by the response from two of them.

Richard Hofstadter, one of America's leading historians, said that he and Beatie had once had a strange recent encounter with a blue light as they drove home from a dinner party at the Wellfleet home of their friend, the historian Stuart Hughes and his wife Suzanne. The Hughes' house was located at the edge of Long Pond, and their winding, unpaved driveway curved around through fairly dense woods before it joined the two-lane macadam road that led to Route 6. Dick Hofstadter explained that as they drove away from the Hughes' summerhouse, they noticed a small blue light in among the trees near their car. It seemed to move slowly and erratically, suddenly darting behind the foliage and then reappearing nearby, as if it were following them. Both he and Beatie said that the light seemed small, perhaps the size of an orange or a grapefruit, but it behaved in an intelligent, controlled manner. At one point, Dick stopped and tried to see what might be supporting this bright blue light, which he felt was only a matter of yards away from his car. It seemed to disappear, but then, as he resumed the drive, it reappeared, always staying fairly close, weaving in and out of the shrubbery. When they finally emerged onto the macadam road, the light was gone, but the experience continued to puzzle them.

Though this was not exactly a UFO sighting, it was certainly strange. The blue orb never rose above the trees, and it moved far too quickly to be some kind of hand-held flashlight. Interestingly, a year or so later another friend of mine, aware of my interest in UFOs but knowing nothing of the Hofstadter's "blue light," told me that a neighbor of his on Long Pond (who lived some distance from the Hughes) had occasionally seen a mysterious blue light across the water, moving in and out of the trees. One night when it reappeared he became so curious that he got out of bed, dressed, and rowed his boat across the pond to investigate. Apparently, once he was on the other side, the light vanished, so we still have no idea as to the nature of this intriguing phenomenon.

When the Hofstadters told me their story of the blue light, I asked if they would like to come with Joan and me to the beach one night soon to sky-watch, and they immediately accepted. Though ultimately our August vigil failed to spot any UFOs, it was the time of meteor showers so we were lucky enough to witness many spectacular, split-second false alarms. Dick and I had brought some good cognac to "help keep us warm" on the beach, and, as I recall, Joan and Beatie had fixed some hors d'oeuvres. With our binoculars at the ready, the four of us lay on our beach blankets and passed around our goodies, feeling both a bit foolish and a tad apprehensive. Though we saw nothing but shooting stars and were finally driven away by the mosquitoes, the company, the cognac, and the cheese made the evening a definite success.

In 1964 it was inconceivable to think that my vibrant, creative friend Richard Hofstadter had only six more years to live. During his brief lifetime he received many honors, including two Pulitzer Prizes and is still regarded as one of the most brilliant American historians of the twentieth century, but he died tragically at the age of 54, of leukemia. The last time I saw him was about a year before his death, sitting with his wife in an improvised, folding-chair-16mm-movie theater in Wellfleet, part of the audience for a Buster Keaton film. Dick was a couple of rows behind us, and, sick and emaciated as he was, he was laughing uproariously at Keaton's inventive pratfalls. Humor, it seemed, was yet another of life's great pleasures that this kind, civilized man obviously relished, right up to the very end.

Aftermath

As one might expect, my life shifted a bit after the August UFO sighting. Outwardly, my ingrained habits hadn't changed. I was still the same person, the same committed artist I had been before the sighting, working every day, preparing for my next show, trying to sell my work, getting ready for our 1965 trip to Europe, and pleased that my paintings were becoming better known and appreciated.

In the fall of 1964, a few months after our UFO sighting, I had a one-person exhibition at the Obelisk Gallery on Newbury Street in Boston, and, in New York, a two-man show of drawings and collages with Herman Somberg at the Poindexter Gallery. In May of 1965 my work was included in the inaugural exhibition of the Gertrude Kasle Gallery in Detroit, so, in the light of all this activity and our forthcoming trip to Europe, the UFO issue was barely visible.

Down inside, however, it was still needling my sense of calm. I continued to read anything I could find about it, to watch any TV documentary dealing with the subject, and, I'm afraid, to talk too much about it to my friends. I still could not understand how anyone could ignore an issue so intriguing and

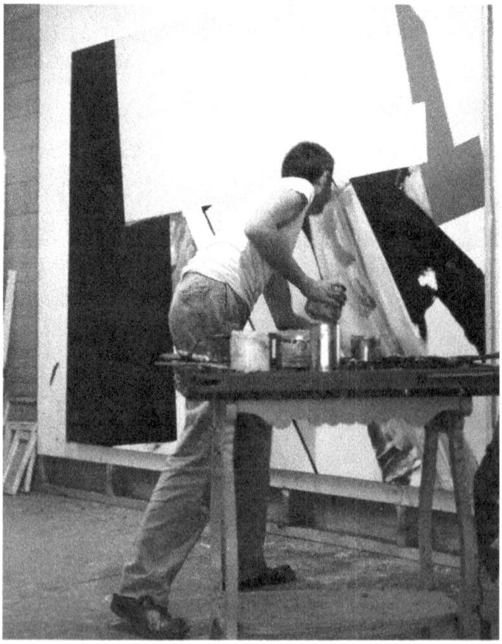

In my new studio, working on Granada, summer, 1965. Photo: Bernard Gottfryd.

potentially important to our future, and though I kept the thought to myself, I viewed my friends' shrugs and cynical comments as signs of a massive and disheartening lack of curiosity and imagination.

On a trip back to Wheeling, I decided to tell my father about our UFO sighting and was pleased that he took it very seriously, even urging me to report it to the Air Force. Having by now read about the official policy of debunking such accounts, I was hesitant to file any kind of formal statement, but by the time I returned to Truro in 1965,1 decided to test the waters. I sent a detailed account of our sighting to Otis Air Force Base, an installation on Cape Cod. In short order I received a brief but intriguing response. The first paragraph was pure boilerplate: the Air Force is charged with the security of the U.S., there is no evidence that the UFO phenomenon represents a security threat, etc., etc. Then came a scold, which I deserved: the Air Force investigates such reports when they are reported in a timely manner, but you have waited for almost a year to report the incident. Therefore... But this reprimand was followed by a surprising final sentence. The spokesman wrote that should I ever have another such sighting, *I was requested to report it immediately to the nearest Air Force installation.*

I thought about that request. If, I reasoned, the Air Force believed there was nothing to any UFO report, and that those who "imagined" such things were like so many nervous Nellies who call the police about hearing strange bumps in the attic, the Air Force was letting itself in for an endless siege of time-wasting false reports. By that interpretation, such an official request was utterly foolish. But if they thought that UFOs, unknown metallic craft of some sort, really existed, this desire to be notified made very real sense. Taken as a whole, then, this official response to my letter only left me with greater suspicion of the Air Force's much ballyhooed skepticism.

Meanwhile, my paintings were beginning to change in a particular way. Artists usually don't like to admit they're influenced either by other artists or by outside events, and for years I insisted that the 1964 UFO sighting had no lasting effect on my work. And yet, admit it or not, we always know that many things can cause changes in our imagery: she/he sells some work and can afford to hire an assistant; a close friend dies; a long- term relationship ends; she becomes a mother; he rents a new studio with a higher ceiling; she travels to Europe; and on and on, all of these things inevitably causing subtle, and sometimes drastic, changes in the art one makes.

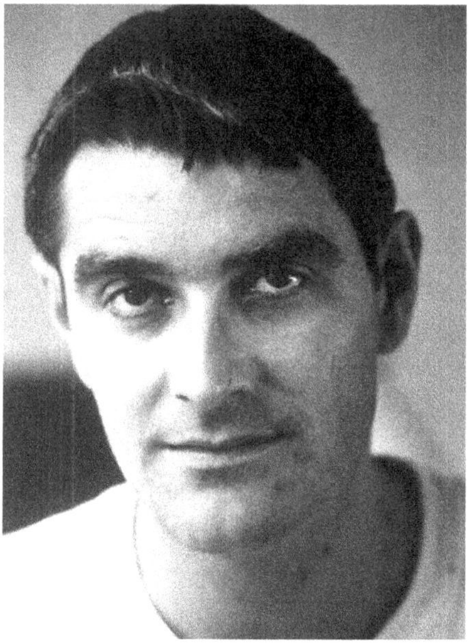

In 1965, taking a moment away from my painting to contemplate the newfound complexity of my world. Photo: Bernard Gottfryd.

Looking back, I realize that in almost all of my paintings prior to 1965 I had used a compositional structure in which a number of large, somewhat equivalent elements came together, often with a degree of violence, to fight it out on the canvas surface. This was the compositional method underlying Franz Kline's smashing, clashing black bars, for example, and De Kooning's powerhouse abstractions of the later 1950s. But in my case, after 1965 I began to employ what might be called a more hierarchical structure in which one central image dominated and controlled the other forms. The central image I used again and again was a geometrically pure circle, usually black, and sometimes invaded by loosely painted streaks of gray and white. One of the earliest of these "hierarchical" paintings I titled *Sun Black*, its black "sun" appearing simultaneously as a disc overlapping the other forms and as a hole in the uniform surface of the work.

In other words, I used the circle as both an imperious, controlling solid and as a mysterious void. Strange as it may seem, it was not until several years later that I first became aware of the possible formal and philosophical links between my *Sun Black* paintings and my 1964 UFO sighting. As I've said, artists ritually try to deny any such influences in a fruitless attempt to make their work seem virginally pure, and I admit now, years later, that at the tine I was as susceptible as anyone to that hopeless effort.

As I look back over the decades following *Sun Black 1*, I can see that virtually everything I painted for the next twenty years contained a large, dominating circle of some sort: black, colored, divided into pie-slice sections, banded, repeated in fragmentary form, and varied in every way I could think of. In fact, one critic remarked that I seemed to be "painting portraits of circles," a canny observation in that I usually located the circle above the mid-point of the canvas and to the left or right, in exactly the kind of off-center area where a portraitist might place a sitter's head. And, like the infinitely varied human face, I wanted my geometrically regular "circle portraits" to seem almost as different from one another.

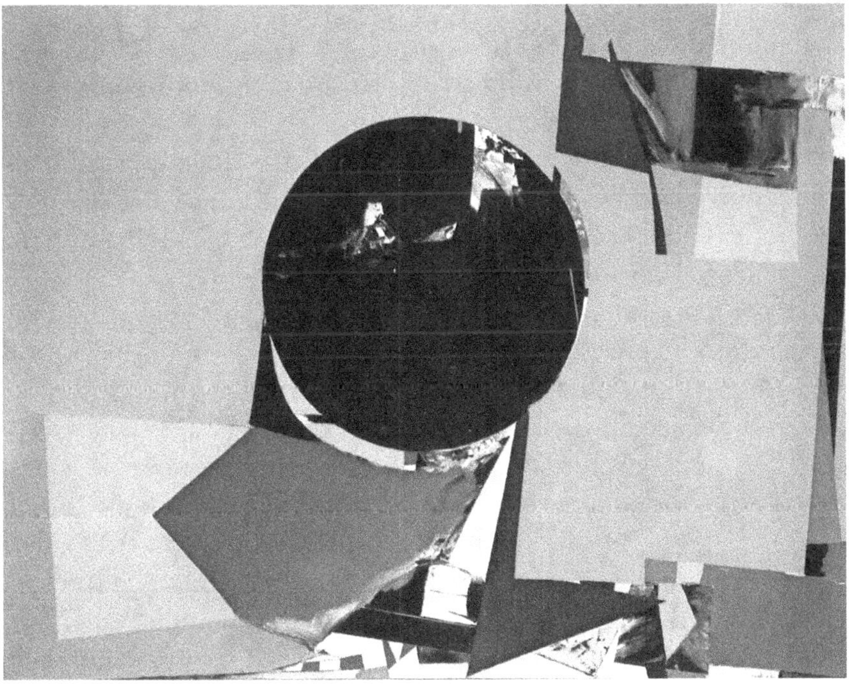

Sun Black I, oil on canvas, 40" x 52", 1966.

Apparently this similarity to classic "flying discs" – circular UFOs – did not go unnoticed. In 1968, when the actor/director Maximilian Schell bought several of my paintings, he made the connection and suggested I see Stanley Kubrick's *2001: A Space Odyssey* because he felt some sort of resonance between my work and Kubrick's film. Joan and I saw *2001* but I felt no personal connection and, in fact, continued to play down any relationship between my paintings and the UFO sighting. As I've said, it takes me years, sometimes, to grasp the obvious.

EVER SINCE 1958, Joan and I had been living illegally in the scruffy, unglamorous second floor loft of a typical nineteenth century brick building in Chelsea. The floor below us, also zoned for commercial use only, was occupied by an antiquated print shop, a veritable Museum of Printing, which featured hand-set type and two of the few remaining gas-powered linotype machines still in current use. (An *homage* to Gutenberg, perhaps?) I had worked to humanize our spartan quarters by installing a tin shower stall, a used refrigerator, a two-burner hotplate and a noisy rotisserie, and in this primitive kitchen Joan still managed to prepare some terrific meals. The area at the back of the loft was taken up by my commodious, sky-lit but low-ceilinged studio, so we slept, lived, ate, and entertained up near the front. The rent for all this, as I recall, was about $150 a month.

Above us, the building's smaller third floor contained one actual apartment, occupied at the time by a large Basque family, while the fourth (top) floor was rented to an elderly woman from Madrid and her two genteel, middle-aged, unmarried daughters who still wore mourning black for their long-dead father. The Basque paterfamilias often hosted Saturday night get-togethers with other Basques, the distorted noise of which descended through our porous ceiling and included what I thought at the time were recordings of Adolf Hitler's ranting speeches. Since the sound was garbled and I don't speak either Basque or German, I can't be sure about the language, but I remember that these soirees also featured a great deal of lockstep marching and tramping about through the Basques' crowded rooms. In the mornings after these wingdings, there was always a lineup of empty gallon wine jugs in the hall outside their door, the fuel of the evening's merriment.

Sociologically speaking, it was clear that the top floor Castilian ladies looked upon the Basques as doltish peasants, while the Basques regarded them as insufferable snobs. Their only point of agreement seemed to be a mutual bias against Puerto Ricans, but ironically, this small-scale class struggle between the third and fourth floors led, very circuitously, to my eventually buying the building. In 1965, after a short trip to Washington, Joan and I returned late one night to find that the house had suffered a serious fire.

The top two apartments had been badly damaged and were boarded up, though our floor, underneath the fire, had received only a deluge of water. Luckily for us, the Fire Patrol had spread tarpaulins over our furniture, so after we bailed out the pools of filthy water they contained, we were able to sleep in our bed. Most of our electrical system still worked, and my studio, located in the building's rear extension, was untouched. All in all, we were extremely fortunate.

In the days afterward, I learned of the bizarre circumstances of the fire. The Basque had started to cook something on the gas stove but had then gone into the living room to watch television. Evidently the grease in the frying pan ignited, and the kitchen began to blaze while the careless cook sat, TV-immersed, in the front room. When he finally became aware that the house was on fire, he regressed to his village days and, instead of calling the Fire Department, he rushed back to the living room, threw open the window, and yelled for the neighbors to bring water.

Meanwhile, the Castilian ladies upstairs smelled smoke and bustled nervously about, but since they were not speaking to the Basque, they said nothing. Not until they finally saw flames coming up the back wall and across their kitchen windows did they pick up the phone. Meanwhile, the fire raged unchecked, and ultimately, when the fire trucks arrived, the halls were so filled with choking smoke that the Castilian women had to be carried down an aerial ladder. The Basque had earlier made his escape down the front stairs.

As a result of all this morbid confusion, the owner put the partially wrecked building up for sale, but since my loft and the print shop below were the only intact areas, real estate agents began showing my floor to prospective buyers, billing it as "ideal for artists." I knew, of course, that if a painter were to purchase the building, I would be evicted because I had the only studio space with a skylight, so I hit upon a plan to prevent its sale. Whenever a couple showed up with a broker, at some point I would take the would-be buyers aside for a private conversation and would present the following sales pitch: "It's really a great buy," I would say. "It's got many advantages, and it's probably a good investment. The studio has excellent light. The only disadvantage to the building is the extreme infestation of rats. They run all over, and at night sometimes they climb up and race across the bed and we almost have to fight them off." At that point in my sales pitch the interested buyers would find themselves no longer interested.

The miracle of my dishonest, self-serving device was that it worked—just long enough for me to find a prospective couple desirous of living in a (renovated) top floor apartment and sharing the rest with me. In the end, we each put up $5,000, and with a modest mortgage, took ownership. I've lived in the building ever since, occupying the gutted and nicely renovated apartment floor that the Basque had burned himself out of, and retaining my studio on the lower floor. They say crime doesn't pay, but in my case, Hispanic bigotry and false rat infestation stories seem to have come together propitiously, providing me with what ever since has been my permanent home.

October 31, 1966

THE TELEPHONE CALL came early in the morning. It was my brother, Stewart, with the sad news that my father was dead of a heart attack. Apparently he passed away in seconds without regaining consciousness. Despite Dad's age, 76, and history of heart disease, nothing had prepared me for the reality of such a sudden, shocking event. One moment he was alive and active, and the next he had disappeared from life, as if a trapdoor had dropped open and swallowed him up. Had he been bedridden, suffering from a long, terminal illness, family members, seeing his slow decline and the worsening of his disease, might have been able to brace themselves emotionally against the inevitable. Our loss would have been the same in either case, but the unbelievable shock I felt when Stewart called me was something for which I had no previous warning. As he relayed the sparse and uncomplicated details of my father's sudden death, I found myself slipping into a kind of self-protective numbness in order to keep the reality of his passing at a safe distance. The tears came later, when I was able to bear them.

My last phone conversation with my father had been only a few days earlier, when, among other things, we discussed my then still ongoing negotiations about the purchase of my building in Chelsea. I sensed that he was rather proud that I might actually own a New York townhouse, but that he was also nervous about my ability to keep up the mortgage payments on both the Chelsea place and my studio on Cape Cod. He knew as well as I that I was not much of a businessman and urged caution, particularly because he doubted that I could continue to make a living from my art. He had little or no understanding of my painting or the art market, and yet he knew that having passed the age of 35, I was both realistic enough, and successful enough, to make my own independent way.

Our last political altercation, one that dealt with the Vietnam

War, took place a few months earlier when I came to Wheeling for what turned out to be my last visit with my father. As a staunch, right-wing anti-Communist, he strongly supported Lyndon Johnson's Asian adventure, while I just as strongly opposed it. An ironic incident punctuated the ongoing argument when Dad asked me to meet him for lunch one day at a club he belonged to in downtown Wheeling. When I entered the room where we were to meet, he was standing at the bar with his back to the door, talking to several friends, all men of his generation. He seemed a bit worked up and said something like this: "I've always believed it would be a terrible mistake for us to wage a land war in Asia. This Vietnam War should never have happened. It's a major mistake…" but he was cut off when one of the men with him noticed me and nudged him.

Dad turned, embarrassed as I approached, greeting him and his friends but saying nothing about their conversation. He must have known that I had overheard him, though neither of us ever referred to the incident. I had learned that he had one attitude to the Vietnam War for his hawkish fellow Republicans and another, diametrically opposed opinion, for his anti-war, New York artist son. Since I was certain he knew that I had overheard him, I had no need ever to mention it. I write these words at the height of the ongoing Iraq debacle, and I suspect that members of my unreconstructed Republican family might be just as willfully concealing from me their condemnation of Bush's disastrous Iraq invasion as Dad was in hiding his real attitude about Vietnam. At least, I hope so, and lately I've deliberately avoided the issue whenever I talk to my right-wing sister or my brother's equally conservative widow. I recall the wisdom of Franz Kline's quip that "being right is the most terrific personal state that nobody else is interested in." In other words, don't gloat, keep it to yourself, and don't rock the family boat.

Toward the end of my father's life, I had suggested that he and my mother visit Frank Lloyd Wright's most famous house, Fallingwater, which was open to the public and only a few hours drive from Wheeling. Knowing that they enjoyed seeing other people's homes, and hoping that they might find the Kaufman house as glorious as Joan and I had when we were there, I recommended that they make the trip. They took my advice and visited Fallingwater, reporting later that they had found it beautiful. I felt a great, warm pleasure in the excitement we had all experienced, wandering separately through Wright's masterpiece. It was the only abiding esthetic experience that I believe my parents and I truly shared; they could enjoy a great work of domestic architecture but not necessarily a modern painting or sculpture.

All of these recent incidents, the rewarding and the depressing, ran together among my memories and thoughts in the hours immediately after I learned of Dad's death. But my sense of gratitude and loss went back many years before, to my early childhood, when I was a sickly boy with a paralyzed leg, and my parents were, in many ways, my rescuers. They praised my scrawly drawings and crude, modeling clay efforts and assured me that someday I would be able to walk like other children. The special love and nurturance they freely gave were greater than any child could expect, and put me well along the road to a happy, productive life. They managed to turn a handicapped boy into an optimist.

As time has passed, I see in how many ways my father's imprint is still upon me, and I am aware of the many other things about him that I have come to recognize and miss. It's perhaps an odd fact, given Dad's usually serious demeanor, but I realize that he wept easily, and though he tried to conceal his tears, they came often, particularly when we said goodbye or met after a long absence. I must have inherited his tear gene, and though I'm ashamed to admit it, I am even more of an easy weeper than Dad was.

Recently, as I sat alone listening to a Joan Sutherland recording of an aria from *Norma*, I found my eyes tearing at its unsurpassable beauty. And after 1976, when I first began working with UFO abductees, I was usually able, with commendable self-control, to keep them calm and relaxed as they relived their traumatic experiences. Yet later, if I should decide to recount to a colleague what they had gone through, I might find myself suddenly choked up and unable to continue. Stranger still, upon occasion, merely hearing a burst of good news from a dear friend might be enough to bring joyful tears to my eyes, as if my natural empathy had spontaneously decided to go over the top. I surprised no one when on November 4, 2008, an uncontrollable salty flood rolled down my cheeks for many minutes at the miraculous news of Barack Obama's election.

I HAVE ALSO COME TO FEEL that my father's natural ethical sense and his open-handed generosity set a high life standard for me and gave me an excuse to pass over his moments of irrational bigotry. (The horrible deaths of his parents provided, as I've described, extenuating circumstances that I used to circumvent the hateful things I sometimes heard him say.) But there was also lodged in my memory the physical affection he expressed for me as a very young child, the gentle scratch of his whiskery stubble against my cheek when he said goodbye in the morning and left to go to the office, and the joyful hugs and elevated swirls of our afternoon play when he returned. As I grew older I became ever more aware of the many intellectual and spiritual gaps between us, and I understood with sadness that they were inevitable but not crippling. What remains, the steadfast love Dad felt for his family, for all of us, is perhaps more powerful for me today, when I've reached the age at which he died, than it was back in October 1966, when he so suddenly left us with only his spirit and our memories.

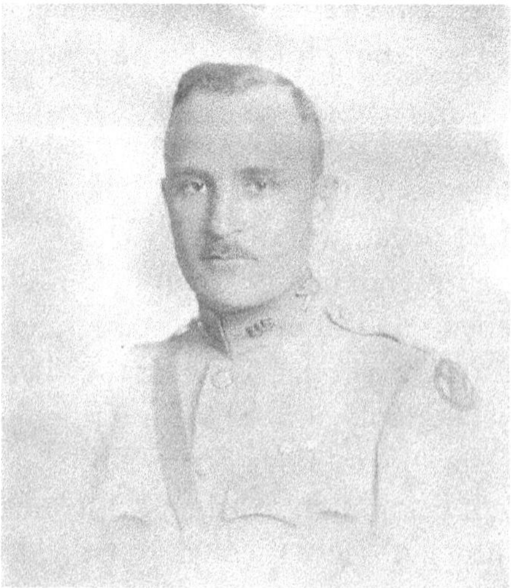

My father in uniform at the end of World War I.

Navigating Some Turbulent Times

THE PERIOD FOLLOWING KENNEDY'S ASSASSINATION and my father's death in 1966 was a time of tumultuous change for me, for the art world, and for the entire country. I was exhibiting more widely than ever, in large one-man shows at New York's Poindexter Gallery in 1967 and 1969, as well as at Reed College, the Philips-Exeter Academy, and annually at the Tirca Karlis Gallery in Provincetown. Individual works were shown at the Whitney, the Yale University Art Gallery, the Cincinnati Art Museum, and elsewhere, while New York's Guggenheim Museum and the San Francisco Art Museum acquired paintings of mine for their collections.

I was busy. My life seemed to contain more and more people and events, and as a result was becoming less under my control than I wished. All of these changes were particularly difficult for Joan, who relished peace and quiet, and enjoyed being as far from the madding crowd as possible. But we were also having problems of a more personal nature. The late 1960s were famously an anti-bourgeois time of social rebellion, drug use, the Beatles, and the Vietnam War, accompanied by the struggling Civil Rights movement and the tragic assassinations of Martin Luther King and Robert Kennedy. In that long ago, freewheeling Woodstock era, friendships between individuals and couples often led to sexual experimentation. Though neither Joan nor I were drawn to the burgeoning drug culture, I was attracted by the lures of unconventional erotic situations and what was then referred to as "open marriage." I was in my middle 30s but I had probably never gotten over the easy-going climate of casual sex so rampant during the Cedar Bar days, so, as one might expect, the issue began to have its effect on my marriage. For her part, Joan often showed a tolerance for, and sometimes a definite interest in, this aspect of our complex 1960s existence, but over time the increased noise of my life, and my desire to explore outside the traditional boundaries, were eroding what we once had shared.

In the meantime Joan and I went south for the famous "March on Washington" protest, in which the hippies tried but failed to levitate the Pentagon, and consoled themselves by sticking the stems of daisies down the gun barrels of the National Guard. We joined a number of other anti-war demonstrations in New York and Washington, cacophonous events that did nothing to answer Joan's desire for greater serenity in her life. One 1968 incident was truly harrowing. During an anti-war moratorium I lettered an old bed sheet with the words, "End the war – bring the boys home now," and hung it outside, across several of my second floor apartment windows. That day I was painting in my rear studio when I heard a terrible crash from the front of the building and ran down to see what was going on. Moments later there was a louder crash of splintered wood and broken glass as a second heavy steel garbage can came smashing through another window in my partner, Bess Schuyler's, studio. Heading for the street to stop the carnage, I ran into the vestibule just as a man outside was lifting yet another heavy can, which he heaved through the glass of the front door, only a few feet from me. I was able to keep it from hitting me, and in the seconds which all of this took, I assumed I was dealing with someone who had gone completely crazy. But as the shattered glass settled, the lunatic reached through the broken front door and opened it, trapping me between him and the inner glass door, which had locked shut behind me. As he came snarling at me, fists clenched, I had to face his rage armed only with my paintbrush.

"Commie bastard," he muttered as he swung at me, and I managed, more or less, to duck his blow. I was desperately yelling for Joan to buzz me in, thinking that if she didn't I would break the inner glass door, run into the house, and maybe find a weapon to defend myself. Whoever he was, he acted as if he wanted to kill me, and I had no idea if he had a knife or a gun, but I knew now that his violent rampage was his idea of a political protest.

Luckily for me, a small, astonished crowd had begun to form outside, so, glancing over his shoulder, the young thug decided to cut and run rather than stay the course. Trembling with shock, I found my keys to the inner door and went upstairs to see if Joan was safe. She was sitting on the floor, shaking, and crying. Having tried again and again to call for help in those pre 911 times, she was unable to get through and was almost paralyzed with helpless fear.

When I calmed down, I ran outside and flagged down a passing police car. The sergeant in charge listened to my account and took down my description of the nut who had attacked my building and me. I pointed out the doorway down the block where he apparently disappeared after the finale, and amazingly, the cop seemed to know who he was.

"That kid," he said, "is bad news. He's a longshoreman like his father. He runs with a tough crowd and he's known to sometimes carry a gun, though I don't think he has a criminal record yet. If you pursue this, he'll be up before a judge and he'll tell the court that he has a buddy in Vietnam, and that he saw your banner and just lost it and now he's sorry. He'll get a short suspended sentence and a police record, and then he'll come after you. In the meantime you have to live on the same block with him and his pals. It's my advice to drop it and not to press charges. I know his father, and he'll probably beat the shit out of him for doing what he did to your house."

I considered the fact that if I did press charges, not only Joan and I, but also my partners in the building, Bess and David Lind, would be targeted by this frenzied, pro-Nixon nitwit, so I swallowed my anger and dropped the idea of having him arrested.

Forty years later he still lives in the neighborhood, if my original identification of him is correct. He has a bony, bitter face and the few strands of hair his scalp still manages to support are long and stringy and gray. Whenever we pass on the street as he walks his dog, an over-fanged, overfed Doberman, he avoids looking at me. But I suspect he's still busy at his brand of right-wing politics, because, in the 2004 presidential election, my car, which he has often seen me driving, was parked on the street, bearing both a Kerry/Edwards bumper sticker and a Massachusetts license plate. When I went out in the morning to shift it to the opposite side in accordance with the street cleaning rules, I found that all four tires had been thoroughly slashed. No other car on the street was damaged, though a few also had Kerry for President bumper stickers. Obviously, I'd been singled out. The total bill for the flatbed truck that hauled my car to a tire dealer, and for the four new replacements, was more than the bill for the carpentry and repairs of the large plate glass windows and the front door after his original rampage.

Apparently, like elephants, right-wing fanatics never forget.

IN THE ART WORLD during the late 1960s the center had moved away from Abstract Expressionism as Color Field Painting, and Pop Art in particular, moved in to take the stage. Color Field works were large, emotionally bland, decorative offshoots of Abstract Expressionism, while Pop Art was resolutely representational, borrowing heavily from commercial advertising in both technique and subject matter. Campbell's soup labels, Elvis Presley film stills, and mocking satires of Picasso and Mondrian all made their appearances. The main thing Pop shared with Color Field was a rejection of the high seriousness and expressive intensity of Abstract Expressionism. Many collectors and museum curators across the country accepted these new movements with an apparent sense of relief, as satire, camp, and decoration replaced the emotional authenticity of AbEx painting.

The central personage of Pop Art was, of course, Andy Warhol, who methodically went about the business of becoming a celebrity. Now Celebrity, in the sense I mean it, deserves the capital letter... or maybe all caps: CELEBRITY. When I came to New York in 1953, there was only one true national celebrity in the New York art world: Salvador Dali. Jackson Pollock, as I have said, was well known among *Life* subscribers and the cognoscenti, and a few of the other AbEx painters were also familiar to many, but Dali had systematically made himself famous across the entire country. His success was due to his extreme mustache and his carefully constructed paranoid persona, as well as the bizarre, confessional books he wrote, the store windows and jewelry he designed, the films he co-directed and contributed to, and, oh, yes, the paintings he did.

Apparently Dali understood that since art was important to only a small percentage of the population, he had to do lots of other things to keep himself in the public eye. Celebrity was something you had to work at, day and night, because mere art-making was never enough. As *people*, Matisse, and even Vermeer in his day, were still virtually unknown entities next to their work. During their lifetimes, neither could be called celebrities. Nor was Van Gogh a celebrity, at least until Kirk Douglas played him in a film and everyone seemed to learn that he had once cut off part of his ear. But in his lifetime he was virtually unknown outside the Paris art world.

Andy Warhol obviously understood all of this and took Dali as his model. He produced silk-screen paintings, many of them depicting familiar celebrities, cultivated a weirdly vacuous personality, wrote books, designed wallpaper, took thousands of bland photographs, wore a platinum fright wig, directed movies, ran with a druggie, fashionista crowd, and generally worked every possible celebrity handle. He easily became as famous as Dali had been and was constantly written about in gossip columns. Apparently he loved every minute of it, even though he was once shot and badly wounded in what turned out to be a perfect tabloid story, an involuntary, but ear-cutting-like episode with an angry, gun-toting feminist.

For the rest of us non-celebrity painters it was depressing to see collectors and museum officials moving towards glitz, camp, and irony, and away from what we felt was emotionally authentic work. Mark Rothko, painting "that grave" all his life, and Andy Warhol, adding color to familiar photographic images of Elizabeth Taylor and Marilyn Monroe, were, by any standard, worlds apart.

Though by now the AbEx cohort was smaller, the kind of painting we believed in persevered and even prospered. By the end of the 1960s, though Rothko had committed suicide, Franz Kline was dead of heart failure, and both Pollock and David Smith had been killed in suicide-like automobile accidents, Bill De Kooning continued to work productively, as did Robert Motherwell, James Brooks, Philip Guston, Clyfford Still, and many other senior AbEx artists. These were difficult times for everyone, yet in some ways the philosophic controversy was also exhilarating. I was moving ahead and in the early 1970s would do some of my best work, often on a very large scale.

However, by that time my marriage to Joan was over. In a relatively amicable settlement, I ceded her complete ownership of the Cape house in Truro while I took full ownership of my half of the New York building. We split up a number of older art works I had acquired, drawings by Delacroix, Cezanne, Klimt, Grosz, and others, and went our separate ways. She remarried after our divorce became final, and with her businessman husband, Arthur "Bugs" Baer, has led a calm, productive, and relatively noise-free life. I am grateful that after all of this Joan and I have remained close friends… as if neither of us was ready to dismiss our thirteen memorable, mostly happy, and crucially formative early years together.

If during the later 1960s there were major political upheavals and significant personal and professional changes in my life, the public's attitude toward the UFO phenomenon was also shifting dramatically. A widely viewed, debunking CBS special on the subject, anchored by the much revered Walter Cronkite, included a sequence in which Air Force officials tell him that their technicians have never picked up anything on radar they could not explain. I was stunned by this claim because I knew that Project Bluebook, the Air Force's ongoing study of UFO reports, listed many radar-visual reports as officially unidentified. These are UFO sightings in which the object is simultaneously seen visually and tracked as a clear target on one or more radar screens. In other words, *something unknown* is up there, flying around. I was also aware that most of these radar-visual cases in the official files were military reports, *made by Air Force pilots and radar operators*. What was going on? Who was lying: the Air Force officers speaking on CBS or the Air Force's Project Bluebook staff?

Nineteen-sixty-six was also the year of the crucial Dexter and Hillsdale, Michigan, sightings, in which 87 frightened college students and adults saw a domed, football-shaped, glowing object hovering and moving about over a swampy area a few hundred yards from their dormitory. The next day, five witnesses, including two police officers, saw a large glowing object rise from a swampy area on a farm nearby. All in all, there were over a hundred witnesses to these sightings, two of whom were close enough to observe its solid-looking, pitted surface.

In the wake of the ensuing uproar, the Air Force sent its scientific consultant, astronomer J. Allen Hynek, to investigate the reports, a task he later described as virtually impossible under the nearly hysterical local conditions. A press conference was hastily arranged, but Dr. Hynek, given the job of defusing the situation, was a virtual neophyte before such a large, contentious gathering of suspicious reporters. He stumbled badly, suggesting to the overflow crowd that the sightings might have been caused by "swamp gas." As an explanation for a domed, maneuvering object with bright, steady lights and a pitted, metallic surface, it was immediately called laughable, particularly by scientists who actually knew a bit about the actual characteristics of swamp gas, a rare, flickering, methane-fueled phenomenon. With the pronouncement of his jerrybuilt theory, Dr. Hynek became a villain to many UFO researchers, who saw him as an Air Force toady willing to go to any outrageous lengths to explain away the UFO phenomenon.

The uproar over the Michigan sightings grew in volume, eventually leading Congressman Gerald Ford, the House minority leader, to convene a Congressional hearing on the subject. In retrospect, the irony for me is that in 1966, I was one of those who, from the sidelines, felt betrayed by Dr. Hynek, viewing him with his cockeyed theory as the enemy of scientific research. And yet in the early 1980s, when I had become deeply involved in examining UFO abduction reports, Allen Hynek and I became warm friends and mutually respected colleagues. In those later years he worked tirelessly and effectively to persuade other scientists to examine, seriously and objectively, the vast amount of UFO data that researchers had accumulated. From time to time Allen and I visited one another's homes and shared the results of our ongoing research, occasionally even working together on various TV and radio programs. But in 1966, all of this lay in the future. Then, for me, Allen Hynek was the enemy with the poisonous swamp gas.

My 1964 UFO experience, so similar to hundreds of other such sightings, left me hesitant to think that these craft might actually have *occupants*, sentient beings, crewmembers, or whatever one wished to call them. Nevertheless, the more I read of the many outwardly credible and similarly described occupant accounts – Close Encounters of the Third Kind, in Allen Hynek's taxonomy – the more I doubted the validity of my dug-in emotional resistance. The one thing I remained absolutely certain of was the belief that if "they" existed, they were at least leaving us alone. But then, in 1966, I read about the Betty and Barney Hill case, the first detailed account of an actual abduction in which the witnesses described the aliens taking them against their will into their craft for a series of quasi-medical procedures.

Despite the fact that the Hills, an interracial couple, were people of sterling character, their frightening experience was something I just could not believe because… because… because it was so unacceptable, that's why. If I could go so far as to accept the idea that the UFO phenomenon represented an extraterrestrial incursion, and that just maybe there were sentient beings aboard, I still felt that this abduction business was too much to take.

Excerpts from John Fuller's fascinating book-length study of the case, *The Interrupted Journey*, had appeared in *Look* magazine, an otherwise respectable publication, but it was still just too much for me to handle. Too unpleasant. Too science-fictionish. Too scary. I had no rational reason to doubt such a harrowing account by two otherwise credible people, except to say that their story exceeded my willing suspension of disbelief.

Eventually I bought and read Fuller's book, which detailed how the UFO occupants had virtually paralyzed the Hills, taken them aboard and placed them on examination tables where, among other things, a long needle was inserted in Betty's navel, as a "pregnancy test," according to one of the aliens. Nonsense, the skeptics said. There is no such thing as any kind of pregnancy test administered through the navel, a cogent objection in 1966 since Betty's ordeal took place before laparoscopy was developed by our own medical fraternity as a way to determine, through the navel, the status of a developing fetus.

For quite some time I was comfortable scoffing at the Hill's account, despite the case's participation of a well-known skeptical psychiatrist who was surprised by the synchronicity of details elicited separately from Betty and Barney Hill. They both described a disturbing period of missing time between seeing the UFO at treetop height, and then driving down the highway much later, with no conscious memory of what had happened in between. It took me a year or two of careful pondering before I began, reluctantly, to feel that their encounter might have happened exactly as they both recalled. But by then I was deeper into the UFO mystery than I had ever wanted to be.

The Hill case – originally a kind of "anomalous anomaly" – was gradually accepted by most researchers as a hallmark account in which many subsequently reported abduction patterns first came to national attention. Since 1966, the year it became publicly known (it actually occurred in 1961), the saga of Betty and Barney Hill has become famous, not only in the UFO literature but also as a familiar event in popular culture. In 1977, a low budget but supremely well-acted, made-for-TV movie was produced on the Hills' abduction, with James Earl Jones as Barney and Estelle Parsons as Betty. Unfortunately, Barney Hill died a few years after their UFO experience, but Betty lived on into her old age. In another irony, similar to that of my altered relationship with Allen Hynek, I eventually became friends with Betty Hill, a woman whose story I had once resisted. Over the years we shared meals and extended conversations at various UFO conferences where we were both speaking. In the 1980s, Betty visited me at my home in New York, and we once appeared together on a Boston television show.

Betty Hill and Allen Hynek are but two of many such rewarding later friendships that in the 1960s seemed as unlikely as my becoming, as I eventually did, an experienced hypnotist, an author of four UFO books, and an abduction specialist. I've come to feel that life is what has already happened, not what comes at us, gradually and unexpectedly, from an unpredictable future.

April, Grace, and *Mahler's Castle*

Apparently I possess a quality that goes by many different names: stoicism, fatalism, or a dissociative ability to numb myself in the face of bad news. Whatever it is, this quality usually allows me to accept an unfortunate turn of events without any obvious reaction, though I'm not sure whether it's a beneficial, self-protective asset or the mark of a deep-seated, neurotic need to avoid reality.

I recall my thoughts and feelings at a time of crisis in 1992 as I lay on a gurney outside the operating room, waiting to be rolled in, anesthetized, and operated on to remove my cancerous right kidney. I was weirdly calm and quiet – even serene – as I thought, *Well, I'm either going to live or die. Whatever happens, happens.* I had drawn up my will and had even written a note about the memorial service I would like arranged if I didn't pull through. It included a brief list of possible speakers, a slide review of some of my key paintings that I wanted shown, and a recording to be played at the very end of the service: the triumphant final choral movement of Mahler's Second Symphony, one of my favorite works.

As I lay there absolutely still, three tired young doctors, wearing their OR greens and obviously assuming I had been anesthetized and was unconscious, came walking up and stopped by my gurney to talk shop. One of them, leaning on the gurney's arm rail, told the others that he had "only one old bag – the woman over there – left to do," and then he could go home. I think he mentioned the OR procedure the old bag was there for, but I've forgotten what he said.

As I write this sixteen years have passed, so the operation was obviously successful, and I've survived both kidney cancer and a depressingly thoughtless remark by my surgeon. When I returned to have the staples removed from my incision, I asked him about my prognosis. "Oh, I don't know," he replied. "I don't want to say anything to get your hopes up." And all this time I thought doctors were, to some extent, at least, supposed to offer hope to their patients on the grounds that optimism can contribute to the healing process. It makes me wonder what kind of bedside manner they teach in medical school nowadays.

These thoughts about fatalism and calm in the face of bad news popped into my mind when I recalled Joan telling me, years ago, that our thirteen-year marriage was over. Her decision was not unexpected, which helped cushion the emotional fallout, but I remember just feeling empty, like a deflated tire. No tears or recriminations, just an old habit of resignation and acceptance of whatever comes my way. I phoned my close friends, the artists Sideo Fromboluti and his wife, Nora Speyer, and asked: if I come over, would you give me a drink? I needn't have asked. I went to their studio and they gave me, as I recall, three or four drinks, as I told them the whole story. Then I walked home and went to bed, reflecting calmly, almost blankly, on the coming changes in my life.

I was now living alone, working and dating various young women and feeling as if I were starting my early years all over again – except that in 1971, I turned 40. In the summer on the Cape I met an attractive twenty-something young woman in a local club, and we sat together, having a friendly drink and chatting about movies, her college experience, and my being a recently divorced painter. Though I probably looked younger than my age, at one point in our casual chitchat I slipped and mentioned having taken my ex-wife to see a certain film just after it premiered, a movie my young companion had seen when she was six. As she slowly did the math, her eyes widened and then narrowed. Very coolly she asked how old I was, and I coughed uncontrollably, trying to (mis)pronounce the word "forty."

"Forty!" she said, gasping. "Forty! But you don't seem mature!" Not knowing if this was an insult or a compliment, I took it to be the latter and leaned across the table to kiss her cheek. The damage, however, had been done. A few minutes later, she politely thanked me for the drink, excused herself, and went back to the bar, on the prowl for younger stuff. I drained my glass, paid the tab, and left.

Around this time an artist friend and his wife introduced me to April Kingsley, a young assistant curator at the Museum of Modern Art. We liked each other and began to date, feeling compatible from the start, partly because April's profession and mine dovetailed so nicely. She introduced me to a lively group of younger artists and critics, and she was herself very interested in the older AbEx painters with whom I was connected. In fact, she later wrote an excellent book, *The Turning Point*, about the Abstract Expressionist movement as it came to public attention in 1950, historically the "turning point."

At the time I met April, I knew almost no one from the Museum of Modern Art. In the early 1950s, when I was first hired to sell admission tickets, books, and the rest, I was friendly with a few guards and my fellow workers at the front desk, but I was not yet acquainted with any of the curatorial staff. I had never met either Alfred Barr, the fabled founder of the Museum, or Rene d'Harnoncourt, the current director, though occasionally I saw them pass by my station on the main floor.

The aristocratic Rene d'Harnoncourt was a giant of a man, perhaps six feet six inches, and far from slender. One afternoon I boarded an elevator and found myself standing next to him and his rather petite guest, the painter Marc Chagall, who was in the U.S. on a visit. They were speaking French and were absorbed in intense conversation. Chagall, his eyes sparkling and his curly mop of gray hair bobbing around, was addressing his extremely tall companion, but since his head came up only a bit past d'Harnoncourt's belt buckle, he had had to raise his arms to gesture upwards, palms outward, as if in supplication. D'Harnoncourt, in turn, gesturing with a bit more patrician grace, aimed his arms downwards as he made his points so that the two speakers' active hands almost touched in a Gallic, dance-like dialogue. I watched them, fascinated, until the elevator stopped at an upper floor and they got off, still conversing with quick, nasal sounds and frantically darting gestures.

When I met April in the early 1970s, the Museum of Modern Art was well on its way from its founding in 1929 as a kind of intimate, Mom and Pop art store to its present status as an institutional behemoth with a payroll rivaling that of the Belgian Army. In its post-renovation avatar, the Modern now resembles a vast corporation of the Arts, delivering culture by the ton to masses of uncomprehending tourists, slyly interested New Yorkers, and artists who temperamentally feel the need to grouse about it. It has always been fashionable for painters to denigrate the Modern: "I don't like it because I'm not in its collection," or "I hate the Modern because they never hang the work of mine they own," or, "I can't stand to go there because I don't like what they show," and on and on, down to "It's too crowded, too glitzy, too commercial, too big, too... whatever."

When the Modern caught fire – literally – in 1958, one painter friend of mine said that he'd always wished the place would burn down someday, but now that it might actually be happening he was having second thoughts. At the time of the fire, I was at home and Joan was working at the front desk of the Whitney Museum, then on 54th Street, with its main floor connecting with the Museum of Modern Art near its garden entrance. I had just turned on the radio when I heard a rather hysterical news bulletin claiming that the Modern was in flames and that people were trapped on the roof, the kind of false, hyperbolic report that always seems to appear at such critical times. I rushed out, took the subway, and in about fifteen minutes was part of the crowds on 53rd Street, watching a fireman on an aerial ladder chop through some closed-off windows on the second floor, behind which, unfortunately, some large art works were stored. A beautiful Monet water lily painting was destroyed and other works were damaged by the fire and the firemen, but there was also a major human cost: two workmen who had been repainting one of the galleries died of smoke inhalation. The cause of the fire was thought to be an errant blowtorch they were using.

I worked my way through the crowds and went around the corner to the Whitney, joining Joan and some of her co-workers at the glass doors that led into the Museum of Modern Art sculpture garden. Many of us were concerned about the Georges Seurat exhibition on the floor above the fire, because the great bulk of his paintings were on display there. Seurat, who was not overly prolific, had died at the age of 31, so the fire could have conceivably wiped out most of the work of his short lifetime. From our vantage point, we could see harried curators, guards, and executives carrying Seurat paintings out of the building, while firemen were lugging hoses, ladders, and other equipment into the sculpture garden from the street in case water would be needed from that location.

At one point, an older, gray haired fireman hurried into the garden with a thick coil of unattached hose around his shoulder. He stooped to drop the bundle on the ground just behind Gaston Lachaise's bronze sculpture of a standing nude, an Amazonian woman. When he straightened up, he found himself staring at the figure's firm but very large ass, only a few feet away and exactly at his eye level. We watched him as he gazed at her muscular rear and then broke into a lewd, very happy grin. He cupped his hand and, reaching up under one of her bronze ass-cheeks, patted it gently. Then he turned and raced back to the street, as if he just remembered that he was at a fire and that it had to be put out. I had the sudden fantasy that when the Modern reopened, he would be one of the first in line at the ticket booth, hoping to discover still more erotic marvels in this previously strange and unfamiliar place.

The Museum of Modern Art fire took place about twelve years before I met April, who had been a teenager at the time and was now barely aware of the 1958 near disaster. But shortly after we started going together, she received a tempting job offer from a museum in California, and after months of weighing the matter, finally decided to leave the Modern and move to the West Coast. Though I very much liked being with her, I knew that professionally the new, more responsible position would be a step up for her, so I urged her to take it. And because I had no intention of settling down so soon after my divorce, it seemed the right thing to do.

April's fellow workers at the Modern gave her a going away party, and when I saw her off at Kennedy Airport, her immediate future seemed set. We talked often by phone after that, and I learned that evidently her life in California and the new job both had their drawbacks. She began making fairly regular return trips back to New

York to see me and the New York art world she knew best, and as we became closer, she independently decided to give up her West Coast position and move in with me.

I was working well during these years, and in 1972 I painted a large, almost symmetrical three-panel work that I called *Mahler's Castle*. It represented something very new in my work, as its stable, hieratic composition suggested the façade of a building, most specifically that of a classical temple. How this seminal painting came about was almost magical. Weeks before, in the middle of the night, I had awakened from a dream in which I clearly saw this compelling, architectural image. Not willing to lose it, I sleepily fumbled around on my night table until I found a pencil and a scrap of paper and made a sketch of it from memory. The next day, relying on my shaky little drawing, I put together a largish collage of the image, trying to recall the colors I had seen in my dream. I used the collage as the basis of a medium-sized canvas in which I altered some of the colors before I felt able to move up to the eleven-foot wide final version. Because of its hieratic, near symmetrical composition and its three-panel, triptych construction, some viewers have said that *Mahler's Castle* reminded them of an altarpiece, with the centered and intensely colored tripartite circle taking on the role of an abstract icon.

In retrospect, I see that the basic change that *Mahler's Castle* presaged was a change of emotional content. The paintings I finished immediately before, such as my 17½-foot-wide *Homage To Franz Kline* (1971) have more expressionist energy and deliberate coloristic discord than *Mahler's Castle*, which seems, by contrast, more inward and serene. I'm not sure what caused this shift in my thinking and feeling, but it would lead a few years later to my Guardian and Temple paintings and the Altar sculptures.

I am extremely pleased that the large version of *Mahler's Castle* was eventually purchased by the Boston Museum of Fine Arts as part of its extraordinary permanent collection. But years before it went to the Boston Museum, it was included in a large retrospective exhibition – my first – at the Huntington Galleries, a museum in Huntington, W.Va. The museum's director contacted me as a result of a feature article in the April issue of *The Art Gallery Guide*, which mentioned that I had been born in West Virginia, so the Huntington Galleries, with financial support from the State Arts and Humanities Council, arranged a large exhibition and a handsome catalogue. The show not only included *Mahler's Castle*, but also my *Homage to Franz Kline* and nearly 50 other works, many of them also quite large, dating from 1957-1972. That same year *Homage to Kline* was shown in New York in *Large Works*, a seven-person group show that included Donald Judd and Edward Clark.

I had left the Poindexter Gallery and was now represented by the William Zierler Gallery on Madison Avenue, when another major change in my life occurred: April informed me that she was pregnant. I was completely shocked and confused. We had been taking precautions, but obviously one very sly sperm had somehow found its way around the various barriers we'd erected and had gone straight to an expectant ovum and that was that. Just for starters I had no desire to remarry so soon, and 42 – my age when the baby was due – seemed ominously close to my father's age when I was born. I did not want to risk being as philosophically and chronologically distant from my child as my father had been from me, so long ago I had given up the idea of ever producing offspring.

What to do? April was desperate to have the baby, and I was filled with doubts, reasons, arguments, and hesitations about the idea. I knew that I would be a good father once the baby was born, but I was utterly unprepared for the reality of its arrival in my life. So one evening, with April in one room, weeping, and I in another, worrying, I began, finally, to produce rationalizations in favor of fatherhood. I realized that I spent all day bringing new objects – art works – into the world, so why should I object to co-producing an actual human being? As an artist, I was a reluctant father, but other artists had become parents and survived. Picasso had had several children, and De Kooning had had a daughter and was still painting. David Smith, Jack Tworkov, and Tony Vevers, all friends of mine, had each had two daughters, while Mark Rothko and the Frombolutis, Sideo and Nora, had each produced a boy and a girl. They seemed to keep on going as strongly as ever.

O.K., I finally decided, I'll become a dad. I went into the front room, and as I told April my decision we embraced, and she wept tears of joyous relief on my shoulder. And by the way, I added, we'll get married, just to keep everything kosher.

And so we did, and in September, at Cape Cod Hospital, my daughter Grace came into the world, named after her grandmother and her aunt: three Graces, a neat package. At the same time I had three Grace friends – Paley, the writer; Hartigan, the painter; and Borgenicht, the dealer – so the name had a certain additional resonance in my own life.

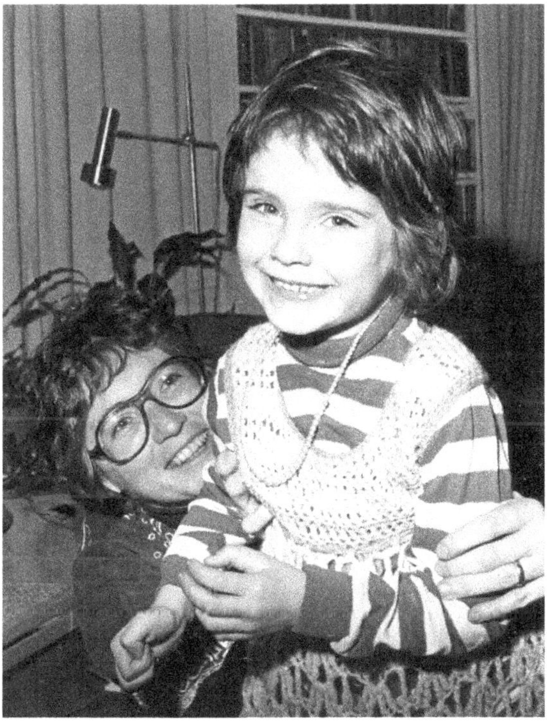

April Kingsley and our daughter, Grace, about 1979.

Our baby was, of course, adorable, and April, slinging her in various carrying rigs, took her to one opening after another, where the little one silently beat the drums for the idea of children within a largely older group of artist friends well past child-bearing age. I had to admit that Grace vastly widened the joys and concerns of my life, as she still does now, at 35, a brilliant photographer and the mother of yet another Grace, my delicious little grandchild who goes by the nickname GiGi.

So my life went on, dramatically augmented, and in 1974, as my work took yet another direction, I had my first one-man show in Europe, at the Gallerie Liatowitsch, in Bern, Switzerland. But I could never have known what lurked around the corner – or actually, across the street – a year later, when I became personally embroiled in the UFO phenomenon and its press coverage.

Part Three: UFOs

One Mile From Broadway

IN THE FALL OF 1975, Grace, having just had her second birthday, was now officially a so-called Terrible-Two, but she was quickly disproving that grim stereotype by showing herself to be a calm, non-terrible, and unusually loving child. April, for her part, had been busy teaching a course in art history at New York's School of Visual Arts and writing reviews of art exhibitions for various magazines – at one later period, *Newsweek* – and taking care of Grace. Meanwhile, I was continuing to explore a series of what could be called "'assembled' paintings," works made up of several rectangular canvases of various sizes, bolted together to form a single composition. These compositions, which approached Mondrian's geometrical esthetic, had come partially from the triptych structure of *Mahler's Castle*, but in their new, irregular silhouette, suggested a kind of urban landscape. Collectively, I referred to these recent works as "City Paintings" and exhibited them with my new dealer in New York, the William Zierler Gallery. Thus April and I worked and played that fall, watching Grace as she blossomed into a fascinating little girl with a distinctive, rather fastidious personality. But an unnerving discovery was waiting in the wings.

It was approaching suppertime that evening in late November 1975, when I left my apartment and crossed the street to the liquor store for a bottle of dinner wine. George O'Barski, the proprietor, was, as usual, the sole occupant of his tiny, scrungy shop, and I noticed when I came in that he was pacing uneasily back and forth behind the counter. An aging, grouchy man who had seen it all and resented most of it, George was grumbling about a number of disparate things, such as crime in the neighborhood, the inept Ford Administration, and his bothersome, arthritic knee. As I put my chilled bottle of Soave down on the counter and fished around in my wallet for money, he continued his half-muttered complaints:

"And you don't know any more what might happen. A man can be driving home, minding his own business, and something can come down out of the sky and scare you half to death..."

My mind went to full attention. "What do you mean, 'Something can come down out of the sky?'" I asked. Slowly and reluctantly he began to tell me about what I soon recognized as an extraordinary UFO encounter. I'd been a patron of George's store for nearly twenty years, buying my wine there and cashing an occasional check, and though I had often chatted with him about politics and listened to his bitching about many other mundane things, this was something entirely new. Unfortunately, as his story unfolded, other customers came and went, interrupting the flow. I told him that I would come back right after supper to hear the rest of his account when there would be more privacy and fewer interruptions. Until that moment he had no idea that I was interested in "things that come down out of the sky" – I had never mentioned either abstract art or the UFO phenomenon – so his initial hesitation was quite understandable. In fact, he was so unfamiliar with the subject that eventually he had to ask me what the letters "UFO" stood for.

An hour or so later, I was back with my little cassette tape recorder, and George began to unburden himself. I asked him to give me a chronological account of the events that night, and he first explained that the incident had happened the previous January, so for the past ten months he had been hesitant to tell anyone about it. It began, he said, when he closed the store as usual at midnight, walked his guard dog, Cognac, and then did a little bookkeeping and shelf restocking. Around one or two a.m., in his black Chevrolet, he began the drive home to his apartment in North Bergen, New Jersey, passing through the Lincoln Tunnel and then exiting onto Boulevard East, a road that runs roughly north, parallel to the Hudson River. To avoid some of the traffic lights on that artery, he turned, as was his habit, into North Hudson Park, a large, wooded and well-tended area roughly opposite West 86th Street in Manhattan. He was on his way to an all-night diner in Fort Lee at the western end of the George Washington Bridge for a late-night meal.

It was in the park that his radio began to pick up static and "sound tinny," and as he fumbled with the dial, he said he was grousing to himself at the prospect of another costly repair: "They always have to take the whole damn dashboard apart to fix the radio." Suddenly a low, brightly lit object, traveling in the same direction, passed his car a hundred feet or so on his left. It was a warm night, George remembered. The window was partly down on the driver's side, and he heard a quiet humming or droning sound coming from the craft, which stopped in a playing field a short distance ahead of his car. Proceeding very slowly and bewildered by what he was seeing, he drew closer to the roundish, 30-foot-long craft, which was now hovering about ten feet above the ground. It was circumscribed by a series of regularly-spaced, vertical, window-like rectangles, roughly a foot wide and four feet tall. George said he looked on in disbelief as a narrow panel opened between two of these "windows" and a ladder-like apparatus appeared. The ship settled to within about four feet above the playing field, and immediately a group of small figures emerged, one after another, descending to the ground.

In answer to my question, he told me that they seemed to be about three-and-a-half to four feet tall and were wearing identical helmeted, or hooded, one-piece, light colored garments. "They looked like kids in snow suits," George said, using one of his typically simple, direct images. I had always found his conversation clear and often surprisingly vivid, but as he described the small figures, his eyes were round, startled again by the memory of his terror. "There were at least nine or ten of them, but I couldn't see their faces. I've been held up in the store lots of times by men with pistols and knives, and I've been plenty scared, *but nothing like this, ever.*" He accented and repeated the last phrase.

George kept his car moving slowly but the strange little beings paid no attention to him. Each one carried a large, spoon-like tool and a little bag with a handle. They were quick, and in George's words, "They came down this ladder thing like kids coming down a fire escape. Fast. No wasted motion." Then they dug in the ground, spooning the soil into their bags, and in a few moments they were back inside the UFO. It ascended quietly and smoothly, moving north. George, at his closest, estimated that he had been 60 feet away from the craft and the digging figures, and that the entire incident took place in less than four minutes.

I asked him what he did when he got home. "Hey... I was sweating," he said. "I immediately made some tea." Usually he switched on the TV and watched a late movie, but this time he said he was too frightened to turn on any lights in the apartment. "I went to bed. I went to bed, I was that scared. I pulled the covers over my head because I didn't want them to know where I lived. I got up and took two aspirin. You know, I was scared. I figured the whole damn world had come to an end. I didn't know what the hell to think... I thought, either I'm going crazy or there's something awfully wrong down there."

After a fitful night, George went back to the park. He walked over to the spot where the UFO had landed, and there, in a small area, were about fifteen little holes, four or five inches deep. "You know, when I went there and saw those holes, I got even more scared... I'll tell you something. I even felt those holes. I didn't believe it looking at them. I put my hand in one."

It was obvious that George simply did not want to accept what his eyes were seeing. Anything that could explain away the craft and its busy little occupants was welcome. He told me that he'd wanted to believe he'd dreamed the whole thing, or that "maybe I'd slipped a gear," but after he saw and felt the holes, he said that he had to go home and make some more tea and take two more aspirin.

In the years since that time in 1975, I've talked to thousands of possible UFO witnesses, who tend to fall into two basic groups. In the first are those who report *distant* phenomena, mostly lights at night but sometimes "daylight disks," in astronomer J. Allen Hynek's classification system for UFOs. Many, if not most of the people who seek me out to describe these incidents strongly desire to believe that they observed a "real" unidentified flying object, "probably a spaceship," and yet most reports of this kind have mundane explanations: odd weather phenomena, sunlight glinting off an airplane's fuselage, unusually bright planets, and so on. In this class of reports, the great distances between the observers and the observed mitigate fear, so it is safe for them to become excited and hopeful that they've seen the real thing.

However, the second, very different group of reports, like that of George O'Barski, are deeply disturbing to the witnesses because the objects observed are much too close for comfort and all but impossible to explain away. These are, of course, precisely the kinds of traumatic incidents that demand investigation, though the witnesses involved will often try anything to make them seem mundane. Sometime after George told me his story of that night in North Hudson Park, he half-heartedly offered the theory that the government or the CIA or "perhaps a foundation somewhere" had developed a secret method of propulsion to power unconventional craft like the one he saw.

"But then," he mused, "it makes no sense. Why couldn't they just send up for soil samples? And how could they recruit all those little guys? A normal run would have guys all heights. It doesn't make sense." Such was the internal argument George was having between his reluctance to believe that such non-terrestrial things as UFOs and their occupants might actually exist, and the clear evidence that he had seen just such astounding phenomena, 60 feet away, with his own eyes. "Confirmation anxiety" is my term for the unsettling confusion witnesses typically feel when confronted by compelling evidence for the reality of their UFO experiences. Meeting additional witnesses to their sighting and discovering various kinds of physical evidence often cause anything but reassurance, and for George, the little holes in the ground he saw and felt the morning after his encounter served to create a classic case of confirmation anxiety.

For my part, I went home with my tape recording of his account, stunned by what I had heard, and undergoing, it must be said, my own kind of confirmation anxiety. I had absolutely no reason to doubt George's truthfulness. I'd known him for too many years as a skeptical, astute, no-nonsense type who was, like so many other working-class New Yorkers, intelligent but poorly educated. He was also a teetotaler who had come to look with pity and a degree of moral condescension upon many of his poor but regular customers, some of whom were hopeless alcoholics. (He was not proud that his clientele mostly bought a lot of Thunderbird, Wild Turkey, and the cheapest vodka on the shelf, but very little champagne or cognac.)

I also knew George as a reflective person who mulled over many things while he manned his cramped and seedy little store. He had far too gloomy a view of life to permit a sense of humor, or to play a complex practical joke on one of his customers – on me, who regularly bought fairly expensive Scotch rather than cheap rotgut. In addition, as I thought about his story, I noticed certain details that reinforced his veracity. First of all, probably no one making up a story like this – and for what reason – would in effect leave himself out of the ongoing events. George's role is strictly passive. Never once does he say that a small figure notices him, turns toward him, threatens him, or hands him a "message from on high." George merely drives by, stunned, observing the incredible events as they unfold.

Second, it seems to me that in 1975, anyone inventing a sensational encounter with "space beings" would begin by creating a weird, memorable face: huge eyes, pointed ears, protruding antennas, or whatever, and then work down to trivial details. George's "snowsuited kids" wore helmets or hoods that obscured their faces, yet he noticed that their boots were of one piece with their trouser legs. And far from giving himself a heroic role in the encounter, George underlined how terrified he had been. "You just stop functioning," he said, and went on to admit that he, a man in his seventies, had gone to bed like a frightened child, with the covers pulled over his head.

When the UFO took off, it flew north extremely quickly and lightly, he recalled, as if it were metal and somewhere high up there was a giant magnet attracting it. Listening to George's homely but vivid choice of images, I had the inescapable impression that an intelligent, careful, but ill-educated man was trying his best to find words to describe an unbelievable experience. "When it took off," he said, "I looked underneath, you know. I said, 'There must be a big fan in there or something that runs this thing… But I can't see nothin'!'"

Later he returned to this theme. "You know, when I was a kid I saw everything. I saw the dirigibles, and they made noise. The little biplanes used to come to the towns and you'd have to pay a quarter to watch them land and take off, and they made more noise. And then they had airliners with twin engines and they made a terrible racket. After the war there were the jets and they practically deafened you. Each time they made somethin' go faster, it was harder on the ears. Now they have the Concorde and it's the fastest of all and nobody wants it around because when it takes off it shakes all the shingles off the houses. But this thing I saw that night in the park! It made only a little hum, just like a refrigerator starting up. And it went away almost before you could blink an eye! I'll tell you! I've never seen or heard anything like it. It was awesome."

One of the first things I did in the next few days was to find a seasoned investigator, someone who knew how to proceed in a case such as this. With a little research I located Ted Bloecher, a fellow New Yorker who had been carrying out UFO investigations for more than 25 years and was currently the state director for MUFON (the Mutual UFO Network). Ted showed instant interest when I told him some of the details of George's encounter, and when he came to my studio and listened to the cassette tape of his account, he was fascinated. This UFO landing, if such it was, had taken place only one mile from Broadway directly across the Hudson River, and about four miles from the headquarters of *The New York Times*.

But I was not prepared for certain more personal coincidences that I would soon discover about the January 1975 incident. I had no precise idea of the location of North Hudson Park because the topography of New Jersey, I am ashamed to admit, was as obscure to me as that of Estonia. Not only was I unfamiliar with what happens on the opposite bank of the Hudson River, but I had only once been inside a New Jersey apartment house, a tall, round building that sits atop the Palisades and is called, ironically, Stonehenge Apartments. An art collector lived in the building, and I had made several visits there in 1968 because he had commissioned me to create a very large painting for his living room – my own version of Matisse's great *Moroccans* – and I wanted to make sure it would fit.

Now, seven years later, in 1975, I was driving on Boulevard East, following George O'Barski's directions to the landing site, when I saw, up ahead, the Stonehenge Apartments. There were two others in the car with me: Ted Bloecher and a young friend of his, a budding UFO investigator named Gerald Stoehrer. Our plan was to meet George in the park, and as I swung off Boulevard East, heading toward his parked black Chevy, I stared at the Stonehenge. "I know this place," I said, feeling quite astonished. "I've been here before."

We stopped near George's car as he pointed to the flat playing field where the craft had landed, only a few hundred yards away from the apartment building's main entrance. It was uncanny to realize that the landing had taken place so close to the only apartment building in New Jersey that I had ever been in. Even odder was the fact that in 1968, having just missed the bus that would take me back to Manhattan, I had another fifteen minutes to kill, so I strolled a bit in the very playing field where, seven years later, the craft would come down, apparently on a mission to collect soil samples.

I parked the car, and with George leading us, we walked to the area where he said the little figures had been digging. The site lies within a large, grassy area rimmed by trees and used for both football and softball. At the precise area where George saw the little holes, the thick mat of coarse grass contained a series of about fifteen or so bare places, roughly six inches in diameter, where the grass was entirely missing. There were no actual holes remaining, but the dirt in each little grassless circle contained no traces of roots, a fact discovered by Ted Bloecher when he took soil samples for possible future examination. Several weeks later I located the park custodian whose job included packing any holes he finds on the playing field to prevent accidents. He recalled that, in the early summer, he had filled a cluster of small holes in that general vicinity, and though he had no idea what had caused them, he guessed that they might have been dug by unleashed dogs.

On this sunny afternoon, Ted stationed himself at the precise landing spot while Stoehrer and I got into George's car. George took the wheel to retrace his route that January night. With the tape recorder running and Stoehrer timing each incident as George recalled it, we rode along through the park listening to his story. From the moment the radio began to misbehave until the UFO lifted off, slightly less than four minutes elapsed. The drive established a plausible time frame, and we had a new, more detailed account to compare with the earlier one.

But the nearby Stonehenge Apartments still occupied my attention. Anyone inside the main entrance would have had an excellent view of anything coming to earth in the spot George had pointed out to us, and I was aware, from my visits there in 1968, that the building employs a 24-hour doorman. I decided to walk down the hill and see what I could find out.

The doorman then on duty was a large, hearty, helpful man named Eddie Oberterbussing. I told him that I was investigating an incident that had occurred in the park the previous January, very late at night, that might have involved a UFO. I deliberately withheld any other details, such as precise date, location, description of the object, and so on. Eddie told me that the two night men who worked at the Stonehenge that January had both since left for other jobs. However, one of them, Bill Pawlowski by name, had reported an odd incident: sometime in January, during the wee hours, one of the huge plate glass windows was badly cracked under rather unclear circumstances. Eddie had not been in touch with Pawlowski for many months, but he was kind enough to find his new address for me.

Pawlowski turned out to be difficult to reach because he had taken a nighttime security job and unplugged his phone in the daytime so he could sleep. I got to him, finally, on December 5th and explained that I was looking into an (unspecified) incident that occurred in the park opposite the Stonehenge Apartments the previous January. I simply asked him if he remembered anything odd. His answer was immediate. He said that he did recall an incident, and that it was frightening. Around two or three in the morning, he said he looked up into the park because he had suddenly noticed some extremely bright lights shining down the hill towards him. The lights, he said, were in a horizontal row, ten to fifteen of them, regularly spaced. He had never seen anything like it. For a moment he wondered if it couldn't be an evenly parked row of automobiles shining their headlights towards him, but then he realized the lights appeared to be about ten feet off the ground. He could also make out a continuous dark mass surrounding the lights, and knew, then, that he was seeing something very unusual.

Pawlowski told me that he walked over to the window for a better view, and then decided to call a tenant friend of his in the building to alert him to the strange object in the park. When he turned away to dial the number and began to speak, he heard a high-pitched vibration and a sudden crack. The lobby window had broken at a low point near his feet. He hung up and crouched down to look at the break, and when he glanced up a moment later, the lights were gone.

He immediately called the police, and when they arrived, he showed them the cracked window but declined to tell them about the object in the park. "The lights had disappeared," he said, "and I thought they'd never believe me anyway." When I asked him if he had told anyone else at the time about the object in the park, he said that he had told another friend, a police lieutenant who also lived in the building and often worked nights. A few days later I was able to reach Lieutenant Al Del Gaudio who confirmed Pawlowski's account: "I came in about six-thirty that morning, and he had some wild story about this big thing with lights on it that came down in the park. He thought it was involved with the broken window, but you can't believe a story like that." Naturally. Unless you've seen it with your own eyes.

I ended my calls to Pawlowski and the police lieutenant quite shaken. The whole business was getting far too conclusive to allow for cool, half-skeptical detachment. But the next step in the investigation was to prove even more personally disturbing to me. We needed to meet Pawlowski face to face in order to question him about that night, and to bring him back to the Stonehenge so that he could show us exactly where he saw the row of lights. So far, he knew none of the details George had given us, and most important, he had no idea of the location that had been pointed out to us. But after he generously agreed to make the hour-long drive from his new home, we arranged to meet him in the park, directly across from the Stonehenge.

Ted Bloecher, Gerry Stoehrer, and I were parked and waiting when the former doorman drove up. After he got out of his car and we started to introduce ourselves, he looked at me and said, "Hey! I remember you. You're the artist with the big painting that I helped you bring into the building some years back. Remember? We had trouble getting it into the elevator." I did remember. He had helped me maneuver my ten-foot-wide canvas, partially unfastened from its folding stretcher, into the elevator and then down the hall into the collector's apartment.

If the North Hudson Park UFO landing case had been unnerving before, the shock I felt now had doubled. What were the odds that I would have known *both* witnesses to this bizarre incident long before it took place? Neither had ever met the other, but I knew them both. In advance! So upsetting to me was this micro-coincidence, that I have never before made it public, even though I wrote a long account of the case for a New York newspaper, covered it at length in my first book, and have since discussed it many times in various media appearances. Unsettling coincidences such as this have a way of breeding paranoia, and since I pride myself on my rationalism, I've preferred, in the three decades since, to keep it to myself.

Later on, during that unforgettable Sunday in the park, and to no one's surprise, Bill Pawloski led us up the hill to exactly the same spot that George had previously identified as the landing site. Thus the former doorman gave us yet another crucial corroboration.

In the weeks which followed, I continued my investigation in which, for one thing, I learned that the temperature at the hour of the landing was in the high fifties; five hours earlier, when the UFO was seen by several additional witnesses as it made a tree-top high pass over the area, the temperature had been a balmy 63 degrees. These oddly warmish temperatures for January explained why George had the car window partly rolled down, and why the UFO occupants apparently had no trouble digging soil samples in non-frozen ground.

I dealt with the FAA, the North Bergen Police Department, the glass company that had replaced Stonehenge's broken front window, and together with Ted and Jerry we located a few more witnesses to aspects of the case. Park personnel also pointed out a split right through the trunk of a tree that stood on a line between the lights in the park and the cracked glass in the Stonehenge building. This major damage was apparently noticed the morning after the broken window, and thus might be connected with the "shot" that shattered the glass. So, as one might expect, there is much more to this remarkable event than I have related here. I wrote about it in depth in *Missing Time* (Richard Marek/Putnam, 1981, the source of much of the present account), and in an article I had published in *The Village Voice* in early 1976.

In yet another unlikely twist, *Cosmopolitan* magazine bought and reprinted my *Voice* article, where it appeared a few months later (sandwiched in between one article on how to have an orgasm and another on what to wear on your first date – or so I like to tell it). As a result of the original *Village Voice* piece, the case became well known and created a great deal of media interest. George O'Barski had allowed me to use his name in my article but disdained to get involved in the media flurry that followed. Several days in a row there were TV vans, cameras, and eager reporters laying siege outside his squalid liquor store, and occasionally George, refusing to be interviewed, came out and tried to chase them all away.

The cumulative effect of all this on my life was inescapable. In response to the genuine public interest in this important, well-documented case, I began doing interviews and speaking out on the reality of the UFO phenomenon. I remember that when I walked into a gallery opening shortly after my *Voice* article appeared, several friends came over, eyes wide, and told me they had seen me on the local TV news the night before. TV was not the place anyone expected to see a painter in 1976, unless he had committed some kind of heinous crime and was doing the perp walk in an orange jumpsuit. Naturally my friends at the opening wanted to hear more about both the landing in North Hudson Park and the UFO phenomenon in general.

"Is there really something to it?" they asked, a question I've heard so many times since that I feel I should carry around a pre-recorded CD packed with case material and designed to fully answer such questions. Such a CD would be wonderfully efficient – an automatic recitation that would do the job, leaving me free to chat about whatever other things I might prefer to discuss at the moment. In a way, this basic question about the UFO phenomenon is a bit like the hoary old chestnut, "What is Abstract Art all about?" Or, more personally, "What do *your* paintings mean?" Try answering any of this in 25 words or less.

April had been supportive of my interest in UFO research, but she remained quite focused on her own critical art writing and teaching. Among her many colleagues and friends, she introduced me to Max Kozloff and John Coplans, co-editors of *Artforum*, the most influential art magazine of its day. Early in 1975 I sent them a short article I'd written outlining a proposal for the Museum of Modern Art in which I suggested that the curators set aside a room in the permanent collection area for a changing series of one-person exhibitions displaying *every work in every medium that the Museum owns by that particular artist.* These more intimate one-person shows would co-exist with the Modern's usual display of the canonical march of movements and masterpieces. Kozloff and Coplans published my proposal and it was well received by the artists but ignored by the Modern's staff; apparently curators dislike taking suggestions from people whose works they are charged with exhibiting.

But the *Artforum* editors seemed to like my article well enough to commission me to do occasional pieces for the magazine, and between 1975 and 1979, they printed seven more. During these years I was also asked to contribute to *Art in America* and *Arts* magazines, but it was centrally my *Artforum* pieces on, among others, Richard Diebenkorn, Ad Reinhardt, Franz Kline, and Frank Stella, that caused further confusion in the art world as to what it was that I did in life: was Hopkins a painter, an art-writer, a UFO investigator, a journalist, a teacher, or what? Because in the 1960s and 1970s, teaching, in the form of short gigs as a visiting artist, was yet another avenue I found myself wandering down. Lasting anywhere from a day to a week, these teaching jobs involved colleges and universities such as Brown, LSU, the University of Texas at Austin, the Rhode Island School of Design, the University of Minnesota, Kent State, and a number of others. I enjoyed teaching – it also paid well – and I possessed enough objectivity and a good enough eye to be helpful to my temporary students. As a matter of fact, I still teach five-day workshops on the Cape every summer and have yet to find them less than worthwhile.

But however complex things were during those years – and through it all I was also occupied by my bright little daughter – life was to become even more multi-leveled in the early 1980s when I began to make sculpture. These works, which I'll return to anon, weren't small, decorative things but instead were large wood pieces, which in 1982 included a 70-foot-long outdoor work, *Ritual Bridge*, displayed during the summer in Brooklyn's Fort Greene Park. I situated *Bridge* so that it pointed directly at the distant World Trade Center, whose silhouetted twin towers were framed by an opening in the shape of the Minoan bull's horns, located in a vertical stele at the sculpture's far end.

Nineteen years later, in September 2001, the shocks and ironies of time would bring me to a place on the bank of the Hudson River where I watched in disbelieving horror as the one remaining tower of the World Trade Center slowly imploded and collapsed into a cloud of obliterating smoke and dust. I stood transfixed, unable to deal with the nightmare of all those who must have been trapped inside. But on the wide bicycle path a few yards to my left, a seemingly endless column of people from the devastated area was trudging by, heading north, away from the carnage. The image brought to mind bleak World War II newsreels of silent refugees on narrow country roads, carrying their meager belongings and plodding slowly, mile by mile, away from the advancing Germans. But here, in lower Manhattan, instead of farm wagons and frightened children, there were thousands upon thousands of expensively tailored, traumatized businessmen clutching attaché cases; pale, carefully coiffed female executives moving unsteadily in fashionable high heels; blue-uniformed maintenance workers; and unsteady, dust-covered survivors who had barely made it to safety in time. All were walking north in eerie, robotic silence.

While emergency vehicles – fire trucks, ambulances, and police cars – screamed by in the opposite direction, heading down into the maelstrom, this ceaseless column of mute refugees moved slowly north as if determined not to pause, even for a moment, lest they look back and see behind them even more senseless destruction and death.

Catching Up

THOUGH OBERLIN COLLEGE had given me a good education and I had subsequently audited Meyer Schapiro's inspiring post-graduate courses at Columbia, I still thought of myself as more of an autodidact than a formally educated man. In the long run, I guess, we're all basically self-educated, but in my case, for a number of reasons, the description seems particularly fitting. I was now beginning to make sculpture, a complex medium in which I'd had no previous experience, and in my *Village Voice* piece I tried to emulate a well-written newspaper article, even though journalism was yet another demanding profession in which I'd not been trained. In my new UFO work, I was intuitively using police-type investigatory techniques, having never taken a correspondence course for budding private investigators, let alone spent an hour hanging out at the Police Academy. Obviously, I had a great deal of catching up to do in many different disciplines, but despite my lowly beginner's status, I plugged away, using whatever smarts I had and hoping for the best.

One thing I understood when I wrote my *Village Voice* article was that I should withhold certain details of the case as a way of checking the veracity of anyone who might come forward after reading the piece. I was aware that this was a standard police tactic, one that made a great deal of sense. In the North Hudson Park case, George O'Barski had described the color of the landed UFO as being "dark, almost black." This detail is quite unusual, since such craft are generally described as being shiny, reflective, light gray, or a metallic, aluminum-like color. Since I had never before heard of anyone describing a UFO as nearly black, I decided to keep that telling detail out of my article. I also decided not to mention the exact January date of the incident, nor anything about the unusually warm weather that evening, omissions which turned out to be useful.

Shortly after the *Voice* ran my article, a new group of witnesses, members of the Joseph Wamsley family who lived near North Hudson Park, approached Gerry Stoehrer when he gave a talk on the case before a local PTA group. Mrs. Wamsley told him that at about 9:30 the evening of the incident – they remembered the time because they were watching *The Bob Newhart Show* on TV – she, her husband and their four teenage children all saw the UFO make a slow pass over their street at tree-top height. It was so low, Mrs. Wamsley said, that "it could have been looking in people's windows." All six ran outside, where they watched it leave in the direction of the Stonehenge Apartments, a few blocks away. Not only were they able, when asked, to correctly describe its color, but Mrs. Wamsley casually mentioned to Gerry that she was in her bare feet when it passed by outside their house, and she wasted no time putting on her shoes. Luckily she wasn't cold, she said, as she ran down the street, following the UFO as it flew away, because it was "an unusually warm night." Thus, two crucial details I'd omitted from my article were nicely confirmed.

Since 1975, when I began looking into UFO reports, I've developed a number of other methods to test the credibility of witnesses. And since I had to invent these techniques as I went along, I think of my work as a prime example of on-the-job training, but ironically in this case the trainee was by necessity also the instructor.

The media attention stirred up by my *Voice* article plunged me into yet another arena in which I had very little prior experience: the contentious world of polemics, specifically the argument for the reality of the UFO phenomenon versus the debunkers' *a priori* insistence that such intelligently controlled objects do not and can not exist. Once or twice before I'd discussed the pros and cons of particular *esthetic* issues in a more formal way, such as a 1972 debate I had with the conceptual artist, Douglas Huebler, which later appeared in *Arts* magazine under the title "Concept versus Object." April Kingsley, to whom I was not yet married, moderated and edited the tape-recorded transcript of our discussion, and though it was resolutely abstract, the debate was originally recorded as the three of us lay naked on a nude beach in Truro, arguing a blue streak and tanning our fannies beneath a radiant yellow sun.

This kind of defensive art discussion was easy for me because it proceeded from decades of creating and valuing emotionally rich *objects*, oil paintings, drawings, and sculpture. By contrast, I had come to regard the typewritten sheets, diagrams, informational photographs, and the other paraphernalia of Conceptual Art as more properly in the province of academia and philosophy than in that of an art gallery or museum. April, being more broadminded and younger than I, admired Conceptual Art. I said to her one day: "The reason I'm not interested in Conceptual Art, and dislike having to go into an art gallery to read all that typewritten stuff, is that it reminds me of school, and I hated school."

"Oh, but I *loved* school!" she replied, our differing tastes thereby explained.

The issues I had to face as a result of my *Village Voice* piece were entirely different from anything I'd had to face before in the more placid realm of esthetics. So, when I was asked to go on various local radio programs to discuss the subject of UFOs and the North Hudson Park incident, I discovered that I was in for a grilling by generally cynical, or at least highly skeptical, interlocutors. Once again I had to learn a new technique: how to deal with such people and occasionally to come up with effective rejoinders to sarcastic questions. On one program, the interviewer, a self-described skeptic, went on and on, saying: UFOs can't exist, because you can't get here from there, wherever "there" is. And even if spacecraft existed, they wouldn't be round like you say these are, and if there's intelligent life elsewhere in the universe, it wouldn't look like those little figures O'Barski claimed he saw. And on top of everything, they would never land and take soil samples. That's a ridiculous idea!

Whew!

Suddenly I flashed on a response, and answered him this way: You say you're a skeptic and I'm a "believer." Well, I see it the other way around. You've stated not skepticism but a complicated personal belief system. You *know* what is and what is not possible. You *know* that an extraterrestrial spaceship can't get here from there, and that it wouldn't be round. You *know* that intelligent beings from elsewhere would never be humanoid in appearance, and you *know* that they'd never need to take earthly soil samples. Now, I don't *know* any of those things. I have no long list of absolute beliefs like you seem to have. I'm the skeptic here, a true one, since I have to investigate, gather data, and do a little science to find out, if I can, which things seem to be true and which seem false. But you believe in a fixed list of absolutes that precludes any investigation.

I almost said, but declined to do so at the last minute, that this true-believer radio host was more like a Catholic Archbishop insisting on the immutable truth of the virgin birth than a scientifically-inclined skeptic who felt the need to actually investigate something unusual before announcing the results.

These first few broadcast situations in the mid-1970s helped prepare me for what have become, over the years, hundreds of print, TV, and radio interviews in which I am asked to present the case for UFO reality. These programs sometimes include a designated "skeptic" who presents the same point of view as the bishop-like true-believer I've just described, but most often the host on such broadcasts acts in the place of an invited skeptic, asking what he or she considers to be powerfully damaging questions. Naturally, these interviewers come in all shapes, sizes, and degrees of open- or closed-mindedness. In the past decades I've been interviewed on the air by a wide range of people including Charlie Rose (archly condescending), Bryant Gumble and Scott Simon (both, excellent and extremely fair interviewers), Regis Philbin (trivializing), Oprah Winfrey (even-handed), Matt Lauer (businesslike), Larry King (supportive on two interviews and rather detached on two others), and many, many others, but it's fair to say that almost all interviewers, astute or not, have been woefully uninformed about the UFO phenomenon. As educators, we've got our work cut out for us.

Shortly after my *Voice* and *Cosmo* articles appeared, I became involved in a strange media experience that included the "most trusted man in America," as the polls then described Walter Cronkite, the legendary anchor at CBS News. One day I happened to pass a newsstand and noticed the headline on the current issue of the *National Enquirer:* "WALTER CRONKITE: WHY I BELIEVE

IN UFOs." In 1976, the *Enquirer* was an even more suspect tabloid than it is now, but I was curious enough to buy a copy. The writer of the article described his conversation with the great man in specific, detailed quotes. The interview, which he said took place in Cronkite's "elegant office" on an upper floor of CBS headquarters, included a reference to a fascinating UFO sighting which Cronkite and several network executives supposedly made, while they were all on a short vacation. I was intrigued because it sounded a bit like a little known UFO case that my friend Ted Bloecher had told me about.

Though I was still dubious of the so-called interview, I called the *National Enquirer* for more details. I was told that the article was written by a freelancer, not someone from the regular staff, and I was given the man's name and phone number. When I contacted him, he said, in an unfamiliar, quasi-English accent, that he stood by his story. It was true, all of it.

That led me to call CBS News to find out if Cronkite had made any public comment on his so-called interview, and, after being shunted around to various assistants, I was told by a woman on Cronkite's staff that so far, no one at CBS seemed to know anything about it. (Evidently, not a bunch of *National Enquirer* readers up there at CBS.) Then, to my surprise, the assistant asked if I wanted to speak to Mr. Cronkite, who, she said, was currently out of the office. I told her that all I needed from him was a statement of some kind about the truth of the article. "You know the *National Enquirer*," I added, winking stupidly over the telephone.

Almost as an afterthought, she asked me whom I was representing. I gulped, feeling every inch the impostor, and replied that I was a freelance writer on the subject of UFOs, and that I'd written on it for, uh, places like the *Village Voice* and, uh, *Cosmopolitan* magazine. (One article, two claims: a semi-fraud.)

I signed off after leaving my phone number, and still a bit unnerved by the tempest in the teapot I'd unleashed, I went uptown to look at some current art shows. When I came back a few hours later, April glanced up from her work and said, rather coolly, "Walter Cronkite called you. I have his number." I smiled weakly and said it must have been his secretary. "No," she said, "the woman said for you to call Walter Cronkite. Himself."

I dialed the number, disbelieving and trembling a bit, as his secretary said, "One moment please."

Then came the unmistakable voice that I had listened to every evening for the past twenty years: "Hello, Mr. Hopkins."

I was talking to the Pope, to the President, to God himself. The great man told me that he had found and read the article, and then, in a gentle tone of voice, said, "I'm afraid, Mr. Hopkins, that the article is made up of the whole cloth. I never met the writer, and he was never in my office." He gave his denial softly, as if, afraid of disappointing me, he was letting me down easy. Walter Cronkite must really be the most trusted man in America, I thought, and the most caring. I told him that I had suspected the article from the start; otherwise, why would a newsman like himself choose the *National Enquirer*, of all places, to make such a dramatic personal announcement?

But what followed next was startling. In a different, quieter voice – he had an amazing number of subtle and soothing inflections – he said, "I'm curious, Mr. Hopkins, how you became interested in the subject of UFOs?" He asked about my *Voice* piece when I described its content to him, and that question was followed by another and then still others. Astute, probing questions. April, listening to my end of the conversation, later remarked that he interviewed me; I didn't interview him. It was true. I felt foolish, but then I was filled with admiration for his low-keyed effectiveness. Cronkite had seemed so casual and un-interviewer-like that I hadn't known what he was doing.

I did manage, in our roughly twenty-minute conversation, to ask him what he actually thought about the UFO phenomenon, and I received a typically equivocal Walter Cronkite kind of answer. On the one hand, he said, he was skeptical because it was hard to believe that such a thing could be going on, largely undetected, etc., but on the other hand, he said that several Air Force officers whom he knew and respected, as well as other people of integrity, had told him that they had, themselves, seen such craft. On the one hand, this, and on the other hand that – an ideological tie – but still significant to me because he had left open the door to the UFO problem, rather than slamming it shut.

After I hung up, I called the author of the *Enquirer* piece and repeated what Cronkite had told me. Okay, okay, he said, nervously. To paraphrase our conversation, he admitted that he had never been in Cronkite's office and had never done a formal interview with him, but he insisted that the rest of what he wrote was essentially true! He explained that when Cronkite and some of his broadcast friends were having drinks at Elaine's – Manhattan's best known literary bar and grill – he had joined their table a couple of times and had "overheard" Cronkite say the things he wrote in his *Enquirer* article. The embarrassed author made a few toothless threats to sue Cronkite – it seemed to me that he had it the wrong way around – and then I ended the call.

So, according to his own description, the writer turned out to be a kind of *paparazzo* sans camera, an eavesdropper, a listener-in on celebrity conversations, who tried to remember what he'd overheard in order to have material for yet another "exclusive interview." This writer's name, virtually anonymous at the time, was Robin Leach (is that spelled "ea" or "ee"?) and his odd accent was Australian. Leach has, of course, gone on to fame and fortune by formalizing his celebrity eavesdropping on TV's *The Lives of the Rich and Famous*, his profound contribution to higher culture in the United States of America. But I suppose I should be grateful to him for helping to provide the phone call in which I was able to tell "the most trusted man in America" all about George O'Barski's extraordinary adventure in North Hudson Park.

The Erosion of Doubt

I HADN'T EXPECTED THE RAIN of letters and phone calls that followed the media coverage of the North Hudson Park incident, but since both my name and George O'Barski's appeared in the *Voice* article, we were easy to reach. Because there were few if any other O'Barskis listed in the phone book and his approximate address was given in the press accounts, poor George was inundated with calls and even visits from people who wanted to ask questions about what he saw, to tell him about their own sightings, or to offer their opinions about "what it all means." But apart from what he had experienced that January night, George still knew almost nothing about the UFO phenomenon and could add little to the discussion.

In his store one afternoon shortly after the *Voice* article appeared, he began to tell me about some of the "crazy" or sincere phone calls he'd received, and as usual I had my tape recorder with me. One call was from someone who identified himself as a Catholic bishop, asking George how the UFO experience had affected his religious beliefs. (Since O'Barski is a Polish name, the bishop assumed, quite rightly, that George had been

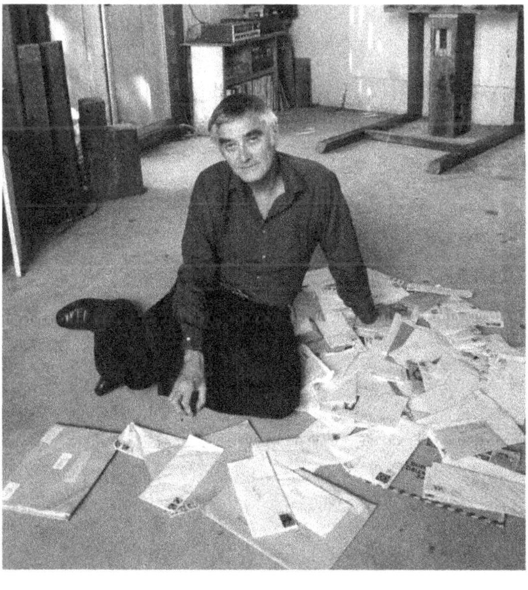

My Cape studio with a recent sculpture and a week's sample of mail, circa 1987.

raised as a Catholic.) And as he described the bishop's call, he began to muse over the possible intersections of UFOs and religion.

"You know, Budd," he said, "I'm not a religious man. My wife was religious. But I'm getting on and I figure I haven't got a lot of time left, so I think about it. I figure if there is a God, and I face him sometime, I'll just say, Lord, you didn't give me all the brains in the world or all the advantages, but I done the best I could with what you gave me. And I figure he'll have to accept that. And if he does, I'm gonna say, O.K. Lord, here's one I want to ask you. Who were those little guys I saw in the park that night? Where are they from? Are you their God, too, or what?"

He described another phone call from a man who, at a different time and place, saw through the window of his stalled automobile a similar landed vehicle and small figures taking soil samples. He said that the craft just "disappeared," and he somehow "lost" two hours on the drive home. There were more such intriguing calls, George related, including one from a "nut" who said he was driving along a local Long Island road one night when he saw a UFO resting on tripod landing gear in a field fairly close to the road.

"You know what this guy told me?" George asked, angry and incredulous. "He told me he got out of his car and just went walking up to where this thing had settled down. There was a ramp or something, and he saw these little people inside looking at him. He said he just walked up the ramp, and went inside, and lay down on a table, and they did something to his eye. Imagine that!"

"Did the man leave his name or phone number?" I asked.

"Hell, no!" George bellowed. "I hung up before he could say anything more. Who could believe a crazy story like that! I wasn't going to listen to him any more. I hung up on him. Just one more nut."

Whatever the caller's ultimate credibility, O'Barski's appalled reaction to the possibility that the man hoped for some kind of sympathy or understanding – after all, he was phoning not the police or the press, but someone who apparently had also had a traumatic UFO experience – demonstrates all too well the innate skepticism of the average person when faced with such seemingly unbelievable accounts. Several times George had said that if I had come into his store that November evening and told him about my having seen the object that landed in the park and the "little guys who dug the holes," he would never have believed me, either. But since he was the witness that night, he was stuck with what he had seen with his own eyes.

And yet… despite the outrageously "unbelievable" sight that he'd observed in North Hudson Park and its solid confirmation by a second witness, George could go only so far as accepting what he had seen, and not one inch farther. A man getting out of his car, walking over to a landed craft, and *going inside* – even lying down on a table for some kind of quasi-medical procedure – that was beyond the pale, and George firmly, self-righteously, rejected it.

My feelings about the caller's story were different. As I related earlier, two years after my Cape Cod sighting, *Look* magazine published, in 1966, a pair of articles about Betty and Barney Hill's alleged UFO abduction experience, the first such case ever to become widely known. Even though I had seen a UFO myself, and in broad daylight, when I first read about the Hills' "abduction," I probably said something about it reminiscent of George O'Barski's angry comments about the "nut case caller" who told of finding himself inside a UFO, lying on some kind of examination table. Within a year or two of reading the *Look* articles and then Fuller's substantial book on the case my skepticism about the Hills' encounter had become less certain. I could find no obvious holes in their account. Their personal integrity seemed to be beyond question, and their traumatic recollections matched in disturbing detail. Also I came to see that their account had nothing brave or self-glamorizing about it; they did not paint themselves as heroes, and in fact the very believable terror each described implied the opposite. Over the years, the more I thought about the abduction phenomenon, the more plausible and disturbing it seemed. And for the first time a report suggested a *purpose* for UFO incursions: considering the quasi-medical procedures carried out on the Hills, one could imagine that the UFO occupants were here to study… us! And in uncomfortably intimate ways, too.

As my skepticism of the Hills' abduction case continued to erode, in 1973 another incident accelerated that erosion. A second compelling UFO abduction account surfaced and was covered extensively in the national press. Two shipyard workers in Pascagoula, Mississippi, Charles Hickson and Calvin Parker, were fishing one night, when an oval UFO alit near them and they found themselves unable to move. Three strange robotic figures emerged and floated the terror-stricken men inside. (Parker, the younger of the two, fainted.)

Like the Hills, they described being placed on examination tables where they were apparently scanned by a large piece of equipment suspended from the ceiling. Despite the fact that other witnesses reported seeing the bright blue light of the UFO near the site of Hickson and Parker's abduction, their account was so fantastic that it would have been easily rejected with O'Barskian contempt – except for what happened later.

When they were returned to the pier where they had been fishing and the craft left suddenly, the panicked pair knew that something had to be done. They telephoned the nearest Air Force base and reported what had happened, but they were rebuffed: "The Air Force does not investigate flying saucers," they were told. As the night wore on and they became even more alarmed, they decided they should take matters into their own hands and go to the local police station to report their experience.

There they were taken into the interrogation room where they sat down with a pair of skeptical police officers who listened to their story. A concealed tape recorder was switched on, and shortly after, the officers left the room, ostensibly to get the frightened men some coffee. Hickson and Parker were left alone for a few minutes so the police interrogators would have time to secretly record what the men said to each other when they thought they could speak freely. But instead of hearing them whispering conspiratorially, the police heard a fatherly Charlie Hickson trying to calm his frantic companion, who finally began to weep, in a kind of prayer of desperation.

Parker: "I got to get home and get to bed or get some nerve pills or see the doctor or something. I can't stand it. I'm about to go half crazy."

Hickson: "I tell you when we [get] through, I'll get you something to settle you down so you can get some damn sleep."

Parker: "I can't sleep yet like it is. I'm just damn near crazy… I passed out. I expect I never passed out in my whole life."

Hickson: "I've never seen nothin' like that before in my life. You can't make people believe."

Parker: "I don't want to keep sittin' here. I want to see a doctor."

Hickson: "They better wake up and start believin'… they better start believin'…"

Parker: "You see how that damn door come right up?"

Hickson: "I don't know how it opened, son. Don't know."

Parker: "It just laid up and just like that those son' bitches – just like they just came out."

Hickson: "I know. Can't believe it. You just can't make people believe it."

Parker: "I [was] paralyzed. Right then. I couldn't move."

Hickson: "They won't believe it. They gonna believe it one of these days. Might be too late. I knew all along they was people from other worlds up there. I knew all along. I never thought it would happen to me…"

Soon Hickson left the room. All alone, Parker began to pray. "It's hard to believe… Oh, God, it's awful… I know there's a God up there…"

Later, after the police interrogators reviewed the secret tape, they said that they had no doubt that these two men were terrified by what they had experienced and were absolutely not shamming. Ralph Blum, in his book *Beyond Earth*, describes what took place as he joined the men in the police station the following day:

"I sat in one corner across from Calvin [Parker]… a handsome country boy with dark hair and sideburns. He didn't smile at all and looked as though he expected to have to run for it any moment. Charlie is balding, quiet. He has a good face, an open face, somehow naïve and wise at the same time. But sitting there in an armchair, he looked like a man just coming out of anesthesia…

"'Boy, I need sleep,' Calvin said. 'We ain't had no sleep since it happened'

"'Tell you one thing,' said [Police Captain] Willis… 'if either of these boys had a bad heart, he'd a gone.'

"'That's the truth,' said Calvin. 'My arms just froze solid… I don't remember nothin' else. That's how scared I was.'

"Charlie hadn't moved. His hands lay slack in his lap… 'I just keep thinking,' he said at last, 'what if they'd carried us off? You'd a dragged the river and then forgot about us.'"

After the two traumatized men left the room to get some air, Blum writes, he said that Captain Willis began to muse over the incredible and detailed event that Hickson and Parker had described to him and other police officers the night before. After a long pause, he made this simple, common sense evaluation: "They're just country boys. Neither of them has enough imagination to concoct such a tale, or enough guile to carry it off. They never read a science story in their life. All they meant to do was go fishing."

Dr. J. Allen Hynek, for twenty years the Air Force's official scientific UFO consultant, had also flown to Pascagoula to interview Hickson and Parker and to carry out a further investigation. At a press conference he made this statement: "There's simply no question in my mind that these men have had a very real, frightening experience, the physical nature of which I am not certain about – and I don't think we have any answers to that. But I think we should definitely point out that under no circumstances should these men be ridiculed. They are absolutely honest. They have had a fantastic experience, and also I think it should be taken in context with experiences that others have had elsewhere in this country and the world."

And so, fifteen months later, when George O'Barski related his "nut" phone call from a man who, like Hickson and Parker, and Betty and Barney Hill, described being inside a landed UFO, on an examination table, I had a very different attitude. George was contemptuous, but I was intrigued and disappointed that I had no way to follow up the man's report and see if it was possibly credible.

In later years I became friendly with Charlie Hickson and Calvin Parker and came to feel a deep respect for both men: for their integrity and for the bravery they exhibited by going to the police and risking ridicule and worse in their small southern community. It's fair to say that eventually they paid dearly for their testimony, Calvin spending some time in Laurel's Community Hospital after suffering an emotional breakdown a few weeks after the event. He would eventually withdraw from making any public appearances or statements about his abduction experience and has had a difficult time dealing with it through the ensuing years. Hickson, however, seems to have handled the trauma a bit more successfully.

There are many other aspects to this important case, which Jerome Clark covers admirably in his scholarly and invaluable *UFO Encyclopedia*, but as far as I know, everyone who ever met and interviewed Charlie Hickson believes he is a man of truthfulness and integrity who asked for, and passed, a polygraph test about his abduction.

It struck me that George O'Barski was, in several ways, a kind of New York City version of Charlie Hickson. Both were poorly educated but intelligent men from working-class backgrounds, and though they thought things through rather carefully, neither seemed to be either imaginative or readers of lurid fiction. Both men had the same drastic reactions to their UFO experiences. George told me that, as the sole clerk in his liquor store, he had several times faced robbers with guns or knives, and, though frightened, he forced himself to remain calm. But at the time of his UFO experience, he was so terrified that when he got into bed he pulled the covers over his head because he thought that maybe the world was coming to an end.

Like George, Charlie Hickson is normally hard to intimidate; he was awarded two Purple Hearts and a medal for bravery for his service in the Korean War. But the night of his abduction he asked a policeman, "What if those sons of bitches got mad? What if they came back?" The officer said he thought Charlie was deeply afraid for what might happen to his family. It's safe to say that, in a sense, the world did come to an end for all three of these confused and frightened men. Before their respective UFO experiences they knew only that the world was made up of work and marriage and friends and family, as well as happiness, accidents, disease, and all the other vicissitudes of normal, day-to-day adult life. One lived, loved, produced offspring, toiled, and finally died. But in that stable, age-old context, what did these new experiences mean? Who were these "others," these apparently non-human beings who had temporarily invaded their lives? Would they come back? Did they mean us well or ill? In addition to all of life's usual uncertainties, there was now another, even bigger and potentially more dangerous uncertainty. For Calvin Parker, Charlie Hickson, and George O'Barski, the world would never be the same. It would never be the same for me, either.

I realize that an infinite number of things can suddenly alter the trajectory of one's life: a diagnosis of cancer, a winning lottery ticket, the death of a loved one, a tornado, a fire, or the unexpected birth of triplets, yet these kinds of intrusions are, in a way, *local* and do not affect mankind in any large, global sense. For me, the birth of my daughter in 1973 had been a beautiful "local" event in my life, as was a positive change in the imagery of my painting, and in each case I believed I had had a degree of control. But now, with evidence accumulating for the reality of UFOs and their non-human occupants, I felt that the firm, supportive floor I had always taken for granted was riddled with ominous cracks and fissures I had never noticed before. Worse, as I began a series of investigations into the many abduction reports that came my way, I felt increasingly isolated. So few people seemed to have curiosity or courage enough to demand what was urgently required: an objective, scientific investigation into these vastly troubling accounts.

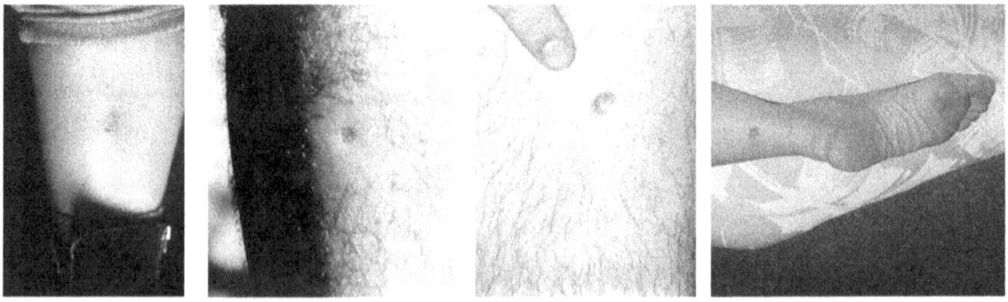

Scoop marks on abductees from Australia , Turkey, and the United States.

In the following decades I would discover ever more powerful evidence for the reality of UFOs and the abduction phenomenon: hundreds upon hundreds of disturbingly similar witness accounts; a series of distinct, round, "scoop-mark" scars inflicted by the aliens on many of their captives; and an unmistakable pattern of ground traces at UFO landing sites. Perhaps most inarguable of all, some 45 different men and women have sketched for me sets of extraordinarily similar – often *identical* – "notational symbols" they observed inside the crafts during their traumatic encounters. Though the astounding congruence of these symbols stands as solid evidence for the physical reality of UFO abductions, I have never published them because they are extremely helpful to me in determining the credibility of individual abduction reports. But back in 1975, at the very beginning of what would be decades of investigations, I was on my own, swimming against a powerful tide of ignorance and ridicule that was inevitably bound to descend on me.

The Case of the Connecticut Hikers

By the summer of 1977 our new house in Wellfleet, Massachusetts, begun the previous fall, was almost finished. The three-story, reinforced concrete walls had been poured, the floors, plumbing, and wiring were in, and the house was almost livable; but though it was well hidden by thick, dense foliage, some of our neighbors were uneasy about its bare cement exterior. When one curious couple from next door dropped in for a look, they asked me what we were going to put on the outside of the building. "Aluminum siding," I said, "to protect the concrete." They were not amused.

Though some major interior work remained to be done, there was no money left to pay the contractor. Naturally the job fell to April and me, and I was glad to busy myself in something a million miles away from the gnawing issue of the UFO phenomenon. Like most painters, I was a self-taught carpenter anyway, having had to build storage racks, palette tables, room partitions, and even, sometimes, my own furniture. Over time I developed my own personal style of improvised construction, which could best be described as "fast and dirty." That meant I got the work done in record time, buying as little new lumber as possible and cobbling together whatever materials I had lying around. The results were usually serviceable but often clunky-looking, especially when I was forced to use heavy two-by-fours instead of the requisite and more graceful one-by-twos just because I had lots of the thicker boards on hand and not enough of the thinner ones.

In the early summer, April, wielding a very heavy brush, painted the interior walls with white Portland cement, while I was busy dividing the top floor of the house into rooms, erecting partitions and installing pre-fabricated doors. I still found time to work on some paintings in my spacious new ground floor studio and even managed to teach a workshop at the Rhode Island School of Design's summer school in Provincetown.

One night in August, April and I were invited to a party at a fellow artist's studio, and after a search we had been lucky enough to find a reliable teenage babysitter for Grace, then closing in on her fourth birthday. The evening with colleagues was fun, but as often happened, some friends who were familiar with my 1976 *Village Voice* article asked me if there were any new developments in the UFO landing case. I related an incident from the previous winter when a security guard and a doorman at the Stonehenge Apartments told me that they'd noticed, late one chilly night, a tall, thin man standing coatless in the park near the site where the UFO had landed. He moved oddly, they said, holding his arms stiffly at his sides when he walked, but even stranger was the fact that he was wearing something on his head like an extremely bright miner's lamp. At one point the man tipped his head back and the light beamed straight up into the sky. Despite their curiosity, the two security men felt uneasy and decided not to leave the building for a closer look, but eventually, they said, the thin man moved away and they lost sight of him. The story was unusual, I told my friends, but I had no idea what to make of it, or if it was connected in any way with George O'Barski's sighting the previous year.

The party was winding down when we realized we had told "Mary," the babysitter, that we'd return by 11:30 to take her home and it was now midnight. We arrived an hour late, and as she got into the car, I was full of apologies. I explained that we had been gabbing about art, art-world politics, and UFOs, and had not been watching the time.

"You know," Mary said. "I saw some funny lights one night a couple of years ago. I don't know if they were UFOs or not, but there were a lot of them, coming down the side of the mountain near where we live in Connecticut."

She explained that it was summer and she and two girlfriends were camping in a tent in their front yard when they saw the lights descending erratically down the steep face of a mountain slope across the river from her house. "They were moving too fast to be hikers with bright flashlights," she continued, "and they seemed to be above the trees. But they couldn't be hikers, anyway. Nobody hikes on the mountain at night. There's no path where we saw them, and there are lots of rattlesnakes."

Then came the shocker. "My older sister, 'Beth,' and her boyfriend were out together that night, and they did see a bunch of hikers, though. She said that they were marching along the road at the bottom of the mountain and were really weird. They were all wearing lights on their heads, like miners' lights."

I gasped at that detail – another disturbing coincidence – but her story became even more interesting. "Beth said she and her boyfriend were driving back from a club they belonged to, and they saw this huge UFO rise up from behind the mountain. They stopped to watch it, and some friends of theirs in another car coming back from the same meeting stopped, too, and they all saw it. And they said that when lights came out of it and moved along the mountain ridge, they decided to follow them. That's all before they saw the hikers marching past their cars with lights on their heads."

I asked Mary whether her sister said she'd been close enough to the hikers to ask where they were going or why they were walking along at night – it was after eleven – with lamps on their heads. "That's one of the weird things," she replied. "Beth told me they never said a word, even though they walked right by her boyfriend's car. She said they acted strange."

I was able to get Beth's phone number, and within a few weeks I had a much more complete – and far more complex – account of the events that night. Though issues of confidentiality mean that I've altered names and places, this is what I learned: Beth and her boyfriend were driving home on a two-lane road that ran along the Housatonic River when they saw a very large UFO, with blue, red, and white lights on it, rising up from behind the mountain ridge just across the river, about a quarter of a mile away. Awed, they stopped to look at it when the two other club members pulled up behind them. Beth said that as the UFO hovered, a series of small lights dropped out of its underside, one after another, and circled around just above the trees. One of the boys was so excited that he wanted to alert more witnesses, so he drove a short distance to a local pizza parlor and picked up the owner and an employee who were both friends of his. Returning to the scene, he had now added two more witnesses to the original four.

Meanwhile, at a nearby hilltop on their side of the river, a young Vietnam vet was driving along when he saw the UFO and the circling lights from his higher vantage point. He immediately stopped at the home of some friends, a young married couple, and shouted for them to come and see the UFO. They hurried out, joined the vet in his car, and sped down the hill for a closer look. They pulled up behind the two other cars, so there now were *nine* witnesses – seven from the three cars and two from the pizza parlor – watching this spectacle from a quarter of a mile away.

Across the river the individual lights formed a loose, irregular line above the trees and were moving away from the large UFO, following the ridge as the ship once more slipped down behind the mountain. The two pizza men were alarmed enough to want to go back to their restaurant, and after they were delivered there, the seven young people in their three cars drove off in the direction the irregular row of lights had been heading.

By now they had lost sight of them, but the three cars, staying together, crossed the bridge over the Housatonic and drove along the main road, turning off onto a narrow lane at the base of the mountain. Feeling excited and a bit apprehensive, they were now in the general area where they expected to see the moving lights. But after driving up this deserted road and seeing nothing, the drivers turned their cars around and came back to a wider parking area where they stopped to confer about the situation.

A moment later the hikers came marching down the same narrow road that the three cars had just traversed, though the young people had not passed them on the way. "They just appeared," one of the witnesses later told me. They described the hikers as having bright lights, like miner's lamps, on their heads and were "muttering or chanting" as they walked by. Two of the boys who had stepped out on the roadway were only *a few feet* from the marching figures while those in the cars were only a matter of yards away.

When I later interviewed six of the seven young people, they all agreed on the eerie behavior of the roughly *two-dozen* hikers, who neither spoke to them nor even glanced in their direction; they merely marched by with neither a greeting nor a sign of recognition. Despite their unfriendly behavior, one of the witnesses later told me that she felt "at ease" when they came by and was without even a trace of the momentary fear that one might have expected under these peculiar circumstances, in such an isolated spot.

Suddenly the seven baffled friends were aware that the band of hikers had vanished, presumably having marched just around the bend. Starting their cars, they drove the short distance to the main road where they fully expected to find the hikers walking along towards town, but they were astonished to see no sign of them anywhere in the surrounding wide, flat fields. In just a moment or two the marchers had simply vanished as suddenly as they had appeared.

Now, with Beth and her boyfriend in one car and the two other boys following closely behind, they drove into the small, conservative Connecticut town and parked in a well-lit area to compare impressions and try to understand what had happened. A few minutes later, Beth told me, a police car pulled up, and the officers asked them what they were doing out so late, since it was now after two a.m. The four were astonished because it had been only about 11:30 a few minutes earlier, when the hikers first approached.

After I heard all of this from Beth, I called Ted Bloecher and he agreed that the situation demanded an investigation. There were many intriguing anomalies in the "hikers" part of the case, and yet, according to Beth, all seven witnesses apparently described the same details and sequence of events. In addition there were the three girls, Beth's sister, Mary, and her young friends, who separately watched the mysterious lights come down the mountainside, and the two witnesses from the pizza parlor who saw both the UFO over the ridge and the lights that emerged from it. My babysitter's casual story was turning out to be a remarkable UFO encounter with twelve different witnesses to its various aspects. And on top of everything, it contained at its heart an inexplicable period of missing time. None of the four who drove into town together could understand what happened between approximately 11:30, when they last saw the hikers, and 2:00 a.m., when they were questioned by the police. They felt that at most perhaps five minutes had elapsed between the two incidents, though it had actually been more than two hours.

I left the Cape and returned to Manhattan at the end of September, and made a preliminary trip with Gerry Stoehrer and another investigator to "Center Falls," as I'll call the little New England town where the incident took place. We interviewed several of the witnesses, including both Beth and Mary, who showed us the spot in their front yard where she and her two friends were camping when they saw the lights coming down the mountainside, apparently *above* the trees. I was also able to talk to the girls' mother, who said that her daughters had excitedly told her the next morning all about the peculiar incidents of the night before. But most important for us, she agreed to host a gathering at her house so that we could meet and interview the seven who witnessed both the UFO and the strange hikers. As it happened, Beth's boyfriend was unable to attend, but Ted and I were ultimately able to interview the remaining six in what turned out to be a disturbing afternoon.

The six main witnesses ranged in age from seventeen to 25. The married couple and the Vietnam vet were a bit older than the rest, but since it was a small town, they were all acquainted with one another and some were close friends. Apart from Beth and her sister Mary (a marginal witness), most of the others seemed to be from working class backgrounds, though all of them had graduated from high school. Beth's family was obviously prosperous and well educated, and we were grateful that her mother was entirely supportive of our investigation.

We proceeded this way: I took each witness in turn into another room for a private interview, while Ted sat with the rest to make sure there was no communication about the case, especially after those I'd interviewed rejoined their fellow witnesses. I was particularly intent upon getting exact descriptions of the hikers from each of the six who had seen them as they marched by, close to their cars.

I asked the first witness how the marchers were dressed. After a long pause, he replied, somewhat tentatively, "They were dressed... like hikers."

"How was that?" I asked.

"You know... in jeans and shirts," he replied.

"Were they wearing backpacks?"

There was another long pause: "Well, yes, I guess so..." Even though some twenty hikers had passed within a few feet of him, it was clear that the first witness could give very few specific details of their appearance.

The next witness was equally hard to pin down, though in both cases their recollections of the UFO itself, the moving lights, the missing time problem, and the other details of that night matched exactly. When I asked this second young man what the hikers were wearing, he paused like the first. "They were wearing, you know, hikers' clothes."

I asked what kind of hikers' clothes and again he seemed to be searching his memory. "I think it was shorts, and shirts... and boots," he replied at last.

"And were they wearing backpacks?" I asked.

"I don't remember exactly," he said. "I don't think so."

And on it went. There was no real agreement about the marchers' clothing, other than the vague statement that they were wearing hikers' clothes, a remark which, of course, told me nothing. The backpack question especially seemed to baffle the witnesses, and I received a range of apparent guesses about what, if anything, the strangers carried on their backs. It was in the last interview – the one with Beth, as it happened – when a response to the backpack question suddenly began to make the puzzle pieces fit together.

"You know," she said, "I don't think I ever saw them from the back."

I separately re-interviewed the other five, asking each if they could describe how the procession looked as it passed them by on its way to the main road. I suggested that perhaps some of the hikers might have glanced back at them or even called out a goodbye, and all agreed that they hadn't. But in answer to my questions, one by one, the young people admitted that they couldn't clearly picture how the marchers looked from the back.

So here was the crux of the problem. The seven young people recalled in clear detail the UFO, its location, and the colors of its illumination, the appearance of the small, individual lights that came out of it, and the direction they took as they moved along the mountain ridge. All of these highly specific and congruent observations, it should be remembered, were of objects roughly a quarter of a mile away. The witnesses also described the sudden appearance of the marching figures, "muttering or chanting," with something like "miners' lamps" on their heads. But from that point on, as the hikers approached them, no one was able to clearly describe what kinds of clothing they were wearing, whether or not they carried backpacks, or what they really looked like as they passed by, *only a few feet away*. The memories of all six seemed to fail simultaneously at the very moment when they should have been most acute.

To further test their degree of suggestibility, I separately asked each of them many leading questions: Were the hikers all dressed alike? Were they perhaps wearing uniforms, like a Boy Scout troop or an army detachment, or were they wearing civilian clothes? Did they seem to be of different ages – adults, children, teenagers? Did they seem to be all males, or were there some females intermixed? Were they all the same general height, or were some taller than others? Despite the fact that the witnesses said they were extremely close to the procession, not one was able to answer these questions with any degree of certainty, though a few made tentative guesses. Their previously lucid memories all seemed to melt into vagueness just as the marchers approached.

One byproduct of these interviews was that, for the first time, the young people themselves began to wonder why they recalled so little about the hikers, other than their sudden appearance on the scene and the lights on their heads. This realization was obviously deepened by their lingering concern about the two-hour period of missing time and the sudden, inexplicable disappearance of the marching figures. Gradually all of them were becoming aware that, instead of remembering an odd but consistent UFO sighting, their recollections were grossly incomplete. It was as if they were accurately recalling A, B, and C, when, in the next instant, their memories suddenly jumped to Y and Z, leaving them with no idea of what may have taken place in between.

When the gathering ended and I was having a private chat with Beth and Mary's mother, she asked me what I thought may have happened to the seven young people during the two-hour period of missing time. I stalled as best I could and said I wasn't sure yet, but to find out we must continue looking into the case. And then this sensible, down-to-earth mother gave me her opinion. "Do you know what I think?" she asked. "I think they were abducted that night. And the idea frightens me."

When Ted and I began this investigation in the fall of 1977, neither of us still knew very much about the UFO abduction phenomenon, and its details were almost entirely absent from popular culture. A few such cases had been reported to me as a result of my 1976 *Voice* article and the ensuing media coverage, but for various reasons I had not been able to go very deeply into any of them. At the time I was not aware of one key aspect of the phenomenon: the fact that abductees' memories can apparently be effectively altered so that they recall the UFO occupants as relatively benign presences of one sort or another. The actual, unsettling alien appearance is thereby screened out and replaced by a more palatable image in a change that not only helps reduce potential shock, but also maintains their activities' covert nature.

This ability to at least partly control abductees' memories is so effective that they naturally accept whatever images the aliens have installed in their minds, no matter how bizarre. In a later case, for example, a woman told me that she was driving along a country road when a huge owl landed in front of her car. She stopped and was amazed to see that the owl, apparently standing on the ground, was staring intently at her over the hood of her car. "That's a really big owl," I said. "It must have been about three or four feet tall." She agreed that it was extremely big, the biggest owl she'd ever seen. It stared at her for several minutes, she said, and then it suddenly flew away. I remarked that for such a big bird, it must have had enormous wings. "Oh, it didn't have any wings," she replied.

It took her a few moments before she realized the ludicrous impossibility of a four-foot-tall, wingless owl. And it was only then, when she thought over her seemingly outrageous statements, that she began to wonder just what it was that had stared at her so intently over the hood of her car and why she thought it was an owl. Later investigation and the effective use of hypnotic regression revealed exactly what had stopped her car, and why.

So the existence of twenty-some nighttime hikers who apparently and effortlessly descended a steep, pathless mountainside infested with rattlesnakes, who marched, "muttering and chanting," past a group of young people without speaking to them or even glancing in their direction and then suddenly disappeared – the existence of these so-called hikers seemed exactly as plausible to me as that of a four-foot-tall, wingless owl. And were the individually moving lights that all twelve witnesses thought were *above* the trees – were these in some way the marchers who approached the seven young people in their cars?

Ted and I agreed that the next steps in our investigation were, first, to have at least some of the witnesses interviewed by a mental health professional, and then, if all seemed well, to use hypnotic regression to learn what may have happened during the missing two hours. As I've mentioned earlier, among the artists, physicians, and intellectuals whom I'd met on the Cape, I was particularly friendly with the psychohistorian and social critic Robert J. Lifton and his wife, the psychotherapist and writer Betty Jean Lifton. I met the Liftons in the mid 1960s when we discovered that we shared not only the same liberal politics but many other interests as well. We saw each other often during the summer and again in New York, where the Liftons also lived during the rest of the year.

I was aware that Bob Lifton, with a heavy teaching and writing schedule, was easing away from an active clinical practice, but his superb psychiatric skills led me to tell him about the Connecticut UFO case. I asked if he would do me the immense favor of meeting with some of the witnesses for informal psychiatric interviews since I needed to make sure that they weren't suffering from any obvious psychopathology. In his role as a social critic with a particular interest in the issue of the "survivor syndrome," Bob was curious about people claiming UFO experiences, and as a friend he was generous enough to agree to do the interviews.

Because of the relative youth of some of the witnesses, I asked the two older men, "Carl," the Vietnam vet, and his married friend "Tim," to come to New York for an exploratory meeting with Dr. Lifton. During the session, which I attended as an observer, I realized that Bob's low, even baritone voice has an undertone, a soothing, very masculine rumble, and the combination of his reassuring voice and his relaxed manner quickly put the two nervous men at ease. They told him in detail what had begun to seem, even to them, a more unsettling story than any of us had previously assumed. As the discussion proceeded, I was amazed at the subtlety of Bob's disarmingly casual but highly effective questions and comments, and the suggestive insights contained in the men's ingenuous responses.

After the meeting was over and the two had left for the return trip to Connecticut, Bob told me that in his opinion they seemed credible and emotionally stable, though both showed signs of having undergone some kind of trauma. Nevertheless, he said, he was not ready, himself, to embrace UFOs and UFO abductions as the source of the traumas. But he had given me exactly what I needed, and I thanked him profusely, feeling reassured that hypnotic regression was something the two would be able to deal with successfully.

Our next step was to find a qualified professional to conduct the hypnosis session, in what would be, for me, the first time I'd observed such a therapeutic procedure. Through the Liftons I had recently met another psychiatrist, Dr. Robert Naiman, and his wife, Lee, a private art dealer who handled several painting sales for me. Bob Naiman is a robust, jovial, highly intelligent man who savors life enough to enjoy traveling around Manhattan on his bicycle, but he is also an expert hypnotherapist. I phoned him to describe the Connecticut case, and asked, finally, if he would be interested in working with the two young men. Like Bob Lifton, he was also intrigued by such a new and exotic situation, so we eventually made an appointment with him for Carl, the Vietnam vet and the oldest of the group, who had previously agreed to be our first hypnotic subject.

A successful hypnosis session, I would learn, begins with a normal, fully conscious interview with the subject about his or her recollections. In this case, Dr. Naiman heard Carl's account of the moment he sighted the UFO, summoned his friends, and saw the moving lights. He related the unproductive drive on the road at the foot of the mountain and then described the approaching hikers and their sudden, inexplicable disappearance. Finally, he told us about his and his friends' dawning realization that more than two hours had elapsed between the 11:30 arrival of the hikers and the five minute drive into town, when they discovered that, impossibly, it was about 2:00 a.m.

The mystery of that period of missing time was the central issue we hoped to explore, along with a more exact description of the hikers' appearance. Bob Naiman, in his warm and relaxing manner, explained to Carl some of the basic characteristics of hypnosis, and answered any questions he might have about the process. After these preliminaries, the young man agreeably stretched out on the office couch as Bob began the slow, gradually deepening process of induction. Once he was sure that Carl was in a suitably relaxed trance state, he asked him to tell us about the beginning of the night's events. Carl described where he was when he first saw the UFO, then his rush to his friends' house, their drive down the hill to the river where they found the other cars, and so on. He spoke slowly, as if he was drowsy, but his phrasing, punctuated by several long pauses, was clear and exact. Speaking in the present tense, his narrative moved along until the point when the three cars finally stopped on the roadside at the base of the mountain. Then his pauses grew longer and he became more apprehensive. Several times Bob had to ask him the basic question one asks in such slow-moving hypnosis sessions: "What's happening now?"

In an increasingly tense and hesitant voice, Carl said that "hikers are coming… they have lights on their heads…" His body went rigid and he gasped. "They're stopping… they're stopping… the lights are shining on us…" He seemed to be struggling to escape something, and, moaning and shivering, he suddenly sat up, opening his eyes and bringing himself out of the trance state.

Bob reached over to comfort him, speaking softly and calmly reminding him that he was safe, that he had only been remembering something from the past, and that he was here, now, with friends. Carl worked for a few moments to control his panic, and when he relaxed back onto the couch, his chest was still agitated and he was breathing irregularly. Bob glanced over to me, as if to say, that's enough for today. I guessed that an abreaction powerful enough to bring a subject out of a deep trance state must have been unusual in his long experience with hypnosis. And, I was equally sure, quite unsettling.

When Carl had gained sufficient control of himself, he told us that the hikers all looked alike, and that they didn't march by. They stopped in a line and simultaneously turned to face the young people, bombarding them with light. He had felt paralyzed with fear or possibly with the effect of the light. He wasn't sure what happened next, but he knew he didn't want to think about it any more. He just wanted to go home.

Inevitably, the dramatic, truncated outcome of Carl's hypnosis session had a negative affect on the remaining five witnesses. (Two of the original seven, including Beth's boyfriend, had by now moved away.) Having heard of Carl's experience, they were wary of undergoing hypnotic regression themselves and thus possibly having to face frightening memories of their own. Even worse for our investigation, the father of one of the boys heard that we had discussed hypnosis with some of the witnesses, a process which he regarded as the work of the devil. We were told that this man regarded Ted and me as virtual demons, and that he had put out the word that if either of us ever showed our faces in Center Falls, he had a loaded shotgun ready. He added that if he ever caught his boy speaking to us, son or no son, he would throw him out of the house. Even though his threats were probably nothing more than macho blather, we knew they spelled the end of any further visits to Center Falls. Neither Ted nor I wanted to cause any more problems for the already troubled young people who, having encountered the so-called hikers, might have to deal with an enraged parent. For that matter, we were not eager to go back to that town either, as long as it contained someone on the lookout for us with hatred in his heart and a shotgun in his hand.

And so this important and intriguing case, one with so many young and credible witnesses, had to be put aside when we were at the very brink of learning the details of what happened when they encountered the strange, light-bearing procession and "lost" two hours. But there was to be one final incident that suggested what might have taken place that fateful night.

The other two young people in Carl's car were the married couple, Tim and his wife, "Jody," and Tim called me some weeks after Carl's hypnosis session to tell me what had just happened. He said that he and Jody were starting their own modest little service business, and in some way the regulations required them to purchase insurance policies. To qualify for the insurance they had to have physical exams administered by a local doctor, a person they both knew and liked. The problem, Tim said, was that Jody had begun to dread her visit to the doctor's office. She cancelled one appointment and then another as her fears increased. He tried to calm her down, pointing out that such examinations were simple: no needles, nothing invasive or painful, no undressing, and so on, but she was adamant.

Tim said that she had never been this way before, and that her fear was now extreme. The day came when the choice was either to get the examinations or to forfeit their plans for the new business. Under these circumstances, Jody agreed to see the doctor, but as the day approached, her behavior became even more edgy and bizarre. They drove to the medical office in virtual silence, and once inside the waiting room, Tim told her that he would go in first so he could explain to her just how harmless the procedures were. Earlier, the physician had explained that he would check their blood pressure, weigh them and measure their height, check their pulses and so on, and that the entire business would take only a few minutes. It was all *pro forma*. Tim repeated this to his wife, but to no avail.

He went into the doctor's office first as he had promised, but when he came out, Jody was not in the waiting room. Growing increasingly alarmed, he began searching for her and noticed that the door to the restroom was closed and locked. He called to her, but there was no answer. He alerted the physician who came out of the examination room, and he, too, tried calling to her through the locked door. There was still no response.

Luckily, the lock on the restroom door had a small slot on the outside of the knob, a set-up designed for just such emergencies. Using a narrow, key-like instrument, the doctor was finally able to open the door. Together, he and Tim found Jody crouched on the floor inside, sitting with her knees drawn up into a fetal position and utterly silent. Both men tried to talk to her, but she was obviously in a near-catatonic state.

Jody was given an injection so that Tim was able to get her up and into the car to drive her home. His question to me was, "What could have happened to her to cause this? Do you think it was connected with the UFO experience? She was never like this before."

As I was to learn, this kind of intense phobic reaction to medical settings is not uncommon in women who have been subjected to certain invasive gynecological procedures during their abductions. I eventually came to understand the reproductive aspect of the phenomenon far more completely, and I made this the central theme of *Intruders*, my second book, which appeared ten years later, in 1987.

In the meantime, despite the congruent reports of nine witnesses to the large UFO, seven of whom watched the arrival of the enigmatic "hikers," and the three girls at another location who saw the lights float down the mountainside, Ted and I reluctantly had to suspend our investigation of what increasingly appeared to be the possible mass abduction of the seven young people. Though we were forced to leave this compelling mystery largely unsolved, I would soon learn enough about the repetitive patterns of the abduction phenomenon to guess the nature of the traumatic events that took place that night, in the woods near the calmly flowing Housatonic River.

Guardians, Temples, and Altars

In the art world of the late 1960s and early 1970s, the quasi-dictatorial critic Clement Greenberg held sway over a new movement that became known as Color Field painting. I had met Greenberg – "Clem" to his friends – in the mid-1950s and was aware of his fabled intellect and fierce need to dominate, but in our various brief encounters over the years we managed to get along. He was a tall, bald man with intense eyes and a sharp, inquisitive nose, and in 1956, as we chatted at an artists' party, I introduced him to Joan, my new wife. Clem said that he had also recently been married and pointed out a very tall young woman talking to some friends. "That's my wife over there," he said, pointing discreetly. "You can tell because we're both mouth breathers." I naturally glanced down and realized that between sentences Clem's mouth was slightly agape and that his bride, across the room, listening to a friend's conversation, stood with her mouth also a bit ajar. His comment was both strange and funny, revealing a pleasant sense of self-awareness, but then no one who read his articles on particular paintings would ever doubt his powers of observation.

Clement Greenberg's had earned his formidable reputation by his incisive critical writings in *The Nation* and *Partisan Review*, and by his dramatic assertion, published by *Life* magazine in 1949, that Jackson Pollock was America's greatest living artist. Since Pollock's decline and death, Clem had moved on to seemingly invent a new movement, Color Field painting, based on his bizarre idea that painting was becoming ever more *simplified*, narrowing itself down to what he considered its two essential elements: color and flatness. He developed a long list of things that artists should eliminate from their work if they wanted to belong to what he claimed was the new avant-garde: no more lines, no more representational imagery, no more thick brushstrokes, no more drawing, no strong dark and light contrasts, and so on. On top of those proscriptions he said that, ideally, the color artists used should be applied thinly, *staining* the canvas rather than lying upon it as a thick impasto. The resulting Color Field paintings were generally bright in color, physically thin, pleasantly decorative, and emotionally undernourished. But again, after the *Sturm und Drang* of De Kooning's and Kline's Abstract Expressionism, many collectors and curators, feeling a sense of relief, began to buy them.

This new style rejected almost everything that I had been doing in my work. I found myself increasingly isolated and angry at what I saw as Greenberg's impoverishment of the rich resources of abstract art, just as my paintings were becoming increasingly complex, both esthetically and emotionally. I finally faced Greenberg's cult of radical simplifications and wrote an article in opposition for a journal called *Communiculture* in which I argued that the defining theme of Modernism in all the arts was not simplification but its opposite, complexity, the result of what I called the "Collage Esthetic." I didn't mean the *physical technique* of collage, but rather its *philosophical* presence: the combination of disparate, even contradictory, emotional areas, materials, references, techniques, and so on in the same poem, painting, building, or other modern work of art. As examples, I cited many familiar twentieth century artworks, from T.S. Eliot's multi-voiced poem *The Wasteland*, through Frank Lloyd Wright's complex architecture to Picasso's Cubism, and movements such as Surrealism and Constructivism. I described film – an inherently collage-like medium – as the ultimate example of the Collage Esthetic. To make this point as clear as possible in the realm of painting, I posited the comforting, old-world unity and harmony of a Renoir nude as the polar *opposite* of the Collage Esthetic.

In everyday terms, Modernity in the Western world means that in each individual life there is a surprising array of coexistent but different roles and personal relationships. We travel frequently and widely, we consume unbelievably varied products, and through technologies like electric lighting, air conditioning, the telephone, and the internet we can have day or night, summer or winter, distance or intimacy virtually at will, with no concern for the actual conditions of the outside world. Since these increasingly disjunctive habits and possibilities define our existence, the Renoir nude seems psychologically foreign because its placid uniformity of subject, color, space, and technique is so unlike our own multi-leveled experience. Now, in the twenty-first century, our response to the Renoir nude is one of nostalgia for its lost simplicity.

A revised version of my article, "Modernism and the Collage Esthetic," was published in the spring 1997, edition of the *New England Review*, but its central theme described my own complex life as it was twenty years earlier, in the summer of 1977. As I've explained, my art had recently become a mix of sculpture and painting, and though still very much an artifact of the late twentieth century, it was now concerned with the ancient themes of Temple, Guardian, and Altar. Also, by 1977, I had become deeply committed to research in the arcane and ultra-modern area of UFO abductions, and within a few years I would not only write several books on the subject but also become adept in using hypnosis as an effective tool of investigation. On a more personal level, I was a new father, had been married twice, and over the years had been involved in a number of brief relationships. I was also an occasional art teacher, lecturer, and writer on art, an experienced traveler, and a resident of two entirely different locales: rural Cape Cod and hyper-urban New York City. I maintained many good friendships in a wide variety of professions other than my own and was about to become a partner in a business venture – a co-operative art gallery in Provincetown. By any standard, my life in 1977, like that of millions of others, can best be described as an "existential collage," so to simplify my painting as Greenberg insisted would have been to dissociate my art from my life.

In painting as in science, and indeed, as in life itself, you sometimes make important discoveries while just fooling around. Noodling. In the summer of 1977, as I was sitting at the worktable in my new studio, I glued together, almost by accident, my first Guardian collage. This little work turned out to be the seed for the 70 or 80 shaped paintings that I made in the next decades of my art.

I stumbled upon this new sentinel-like image without intending much of anything. Before, in the process of making collage studies for my assembled paintings, I always had many small pieces of colored paper left over: discards, junk, it would seem. Some of them were clean, pie-slice sections of circles, so, with nothing better on my mind, I decided to try to make a collage out of these remnants just as they were, with no cutting or shaping. It was a project that, at the time, seemed almost frivolous, a real time-waster.

I partially overlapped several of these incomplete circular fragments to create interesting color contrasts. I liked the resulting unit: a kind of multicolored paper pie with a big slice missing. Next, I glued together several long stripes of different hues and fastened them underneath the partial circle, pointing downward. Where these vertical stripes passed under the incomplete, multicolored circle, I attached a few more irregular shapes, creating an active transition between curved top and striped, rectilinear bottom. When I held the little collage upright in my hand, it suggested an abstract figure, with a head and supporting legs. A standing personage of some kind. A sentinel.

I'd originally intended to work outward from this sentinel-like unit, using other colored paper as background until the whole grew to be a traditional rectangle, but I decided I liked the odd, curved-top image just as it was – as a standing, oddly-shaped presence. Years before, I had seen, in a show of David Smith's sculpture, a group of tall, thin, forged-steel pieces that he called Sentinels. The idea stayed with me. If David Smith could make vaguely figural abstract sculptures with active silhouettes and call them Sentinels, why couldn't I make abstract, vertical, eccentrically-shaped paintings and call them Guardians?

My fooling around was yielding something. I plunged ahead and turned out a few more small, six- or seven-inch-tall, curved-headed collages and then began to think of how to enlarge them into human-size paintings. Since canvas couldn't be stretched around the projections of such erratic silhouettes, I realized that the images would have to be painted on reinforced wood panels, and my next step was to plan that rather complex process. No matter how difficult it might be to transfer these collages into large paintings, I knew that day that I had discovered something new and important. The accidental seed had fallen into very rich soil.

Apart from a few small, atypical landscape and figure works I'd made over time, just to keep my hand in, the tall Guardians, and the Temples and Altars which soon accompanied them comprised the clearest, most consistent set of references to specific objects I'd ever attempted within the abstract mode. Still, I'd always taken it for granted that abstract paintings usually brought to mind real-world places or objects of some sort, even if the connections were tenuous. For example, my assembled City Paintings from the mid-1970s suggested urban landscapes of rectangular buildings, even though they were fully abstract and contained no specific architectural references. My loosely painted expressionist works of the 1950s and early 1960s had distinct landscape overtones, though again they used no identifiable images from nature. In both cases, they suggested real-life *emotional territories* without conjuring up particular real-world objects.

The Guardians, however, were different. By giving these slender, vertical, eccentrically-shaped paintings that title, I was making a far more specific connection with the world of living, sentient beings. Their collective title suggested Warriors, Angels, Dragons, or whatever. And the Temples which followed, though purely geometrical constructions, established, by their generic name, a direct link with the universal world of sacred architecture. And so, too, did the later free-standing works I called Altars.

I soon worked out a way to measure and mathematically expand each collage to produce a full-scale pencil drawing of its silhouette. A cabinet-maker/carpenter would then have a template to use in fabricating a wooden chassis for each large-scale Guardian. Then, when the flat, reinforced panel was delivered to me, I would follow the colors and internal structure of the collage study so that the finished work would greatly resemble it. If this seems a complicated, even tedious way of working, it was. I was sometimes almost crazy with impatience. But then, as the work finally began to cohere, I felt a kind of elation, as I saw how strange and powerful the results could be.

But aside from being painted on irregularly-shaped wooden panels instead of stretched canvas, the Guardians contained another major stylistic change for me. Virtually all my prior work, from the 1950s on, contained at least one loose, painterly area, even in my hard-edged City Paintings. I thought of these free, spontaneous passages as suggesting unformed nature, and therefore as a necessary contrast to the rigor of manmade, architectural forms. For me, their presence created a nice emotional mix, as if the rigidities of printing and the casualness of handwriting had been forced into a coexistent harmony. (A shotgun marriage in some cases, perhaps, but a marriage nevertheless.) In the Guardians, I abandoned these flowing, painterly areas altogether. It seemed to me that the sharp projections of their silhouettes, the intensity of their color, and their personage-like presence made any hint of urban or rural landscape completely beside the point.

In 1978, when I first exhibited the Guardians, two on each side of a geometric but asymmetrical Temple, I included, in front of it, a free-standing wood and plaster Altar. I called the six-part ensemble *Hera's Wall*, intending a clear connection between the energy of twentieth century abstract art and the mythic, classical order of the past. The reviews of the show were positive, as were the comments of friends and colleagues who nevertheless interpreted the Guardians in surprisingly personal ways. "They remind me of helmeted Greek warriors," one said, but another, with perhaps a more placid disposition, thought they resembled tropical birds. Someone else told me that a Guardian's shape, upright posture, and curved top were definitely phallic, while another said they reminded him of Native American art. Huge Kachina dolls, perhaps?

And so it went, but almost everyone used terms redolent of some kind of literal, figurative image. These different interpretations pleased me because I realized that if the Guardians, abstract and precisely ordered as they were, could reach out in so many directions, stoking so many different imaginative responses, then I'd created an image of unusual generic power. As against the currently popular decorative style of Color Field painting – Muzak for the eyes – the Guardians had a way of compelling attention and demanding emotional responses. They constituted the first series of paintings I'd made in decades that can be called, in some way, psychological.

ONE AREA IN WHICH THESE CLEAN, hard-edged works connected with the paintings of my Abstract Expressionist past had to do with the presence of a similar energy, though in the Guardians it was expressed by strong color, active silhouettes, and thrusting, discontinuous interior shapes instead of by loose, agitated swaths of paint. The "architectural" Temple that I placed at the center of *Hera's Wall* was painted a clean, even white with a few discrete black lines, but its center was a large, open square framing a section of the gallery wall. The inner sides of this opening were a brilliant yellow, so when the Temple was hung and the lighting properly adjusted, the yellow color was reflected onto the wall. Thus, the open center of the entire *Hera* ensemble was a golden void, a perfect square of subtle, glowing color into which viewers could project their own thoughts and emotions.

In its separate parts, *Hera's Wall* successfully brought together the two aspects of my esthetic thinking that had been present ever since I was an art student at Oberlin College. If the Temples had their roots in my early hunger for Mondrian's purity and spirituality, the Guardians' energy and emotion flowed from my years as an Abstract Expressionist. A classical scholar might say that *Hera's Wall* attempted to marry the Apollonian and the Dionysian, though I prefer to say that this new complexity was simply more human and more representative of the multifaceted lives all of us lead.

Longpoint Gallery

My first art dealer in Provincetown was the Tirca Karlis Gallery where I showed almost every summer from 1958 to 1975. Tirca herself, a Russian émigré who had fled Stalin's anti-Semitism, was a small, generous, formidable woman who was loved by all of us for her boundless respect for art and her delightfully quirky personality. She loved Jewish humor, but sometimes, with her distinct accent and theatrical flair, it was hard to tell if she was telling a joke or subtly acting one out. One afternoon, for example, she called to say that she was sending an interested couple to my Truro studio. "They're art collectors, but I don't like them very much. Too stuck up. Let me know what you think of them."

They came and bought a small painting, and after they left, I called Tirca to tell her about the sale. "But what did you think of them?" she asked, and I replied that I didn't like the wife very much – definitely too stuck up – but that I thought the low-keyed husband seemed O.K. "He's innocuous," I said, and she gasped: "He's an oculist? I didn't know!" I corrected the raise in rank she'd just awarded him, and together we demoted him from specialist back to garden-variety guy. It was a real life Borscht Belt joke of the Henny Youngman or Jackie Mason genre, and I wasn't sure whether Tirca was in on it or not. But at the ends of the phone line we were both laughing.

Tirca was devoted to her hero, John F. Kennedy, and shortly after his election but before his inauguration, she happened to phone another man named Kennedy who was interested in a Milton Avery painting she had for sale. What she didn't know was that this Kennedy was a cousin of the president-elect, nor did she, or anyone else, know that JFK was staying with this cousin for a few days to escape the devouring attention of the press. By chance, when Tirca called about the Avery, it was the president-elect and not his cousin who answered the phone in his unmistakable Kennedy accent.

Upset that his cover was blown, he demanded to know who Tirca was and how she had gotten his number. After her tremulous, tongue-tied explanation, Kennedy asked her not to tell anyone and she swore that she would never, ever say a word until after he had been inaugurated and was living in the White House. She told the new president how much she admired him, that she had voted for him, that he was the best hope for America, and then she God-Blessed-him abundantly. She told me that when she said goodbye she was weeping with joy and amazement, and true to her word, she never told me or anyone else about this remarkable conversation until the Kennedys were safely ensconced in the White House. I never thought to ask her if the Kennedy cousin bought the Avery.

I last saw Tirca in the mid-1970s when she was dying of cancer and I visited her hospital room. She was lying comatose, pale, drained, with almost no flesh on her once graceful dancer's body. This tragic image has stayed with me for years, almost obliterating many warm, lively recollections I have of her in her active prime. Unfortunately, the memory of her drugged and almost lifeless body has several times prevented me from visiting other very ill friends in the hospital, depriving me of a chance to say a final goodbye.

Tirca's death and the closing of her gallery meant the end of a special time for me in the history of the Provincetown art colony. My friends, the painters Nora Speyer, Sideo Fromboluti, Leo Manso, and the sculptor Sidney Simon, had also shown with Tirca and were now, like me, without a Cape dealer. So one day the five of us began to talk about starting our own artist-run gallery. One thing led to another, and soon we gathered together an enthusiastic group of future colleagues. We rented the second floor of an old, barn-like wooden building that had housed Provincetown's nearly moribund American Legion Post, and the twelve-member Longpoint Gallery was born.

Our spacious, artist-run co-op lasted twenty seasons, a season being roughly two months – July and August – and almost from the start was regarded as Cape Cod's leading gallery. We were a variegated collection of mostly older artists, and, apart from several

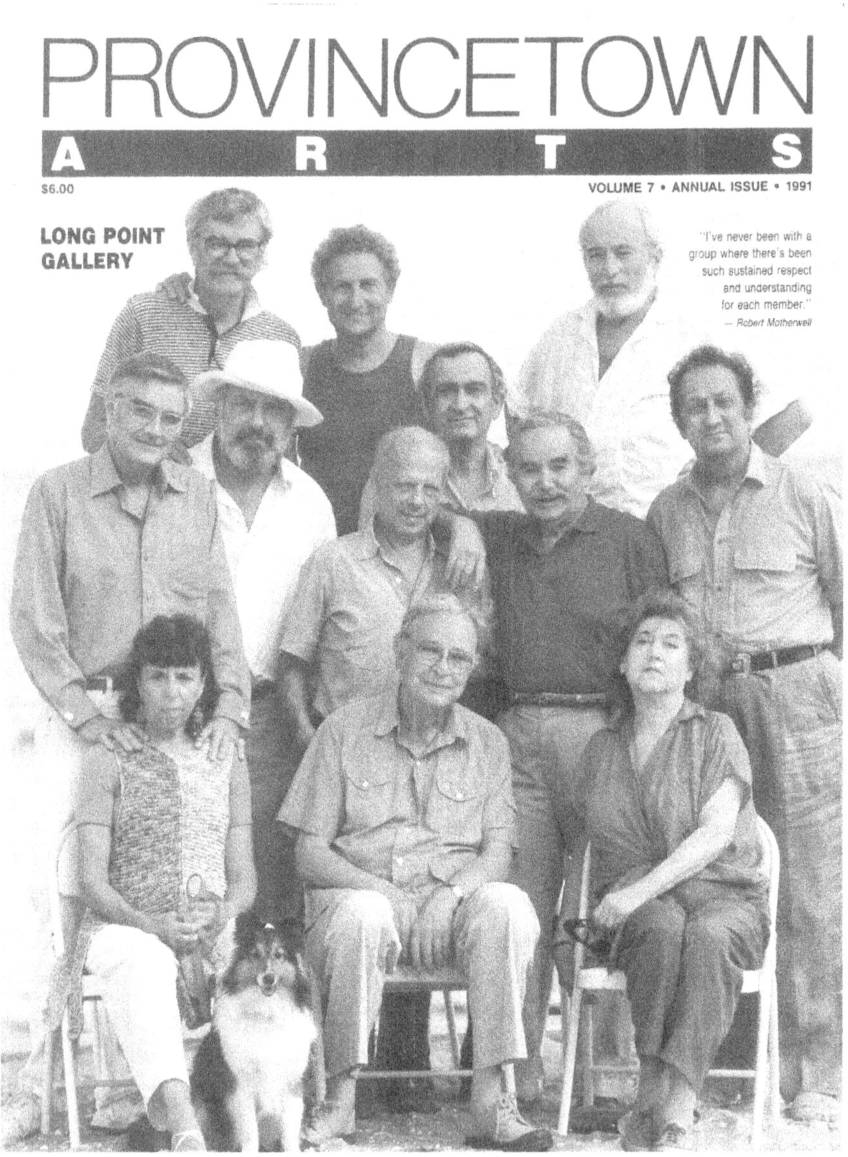

PROVINCETOWN
A R T S
$6.00
VOLUME 7 • ANNUAL ISSUE • 1991
LONG POINT GALLERY
"I've never been with a group where there's been such sustained respect and understanding for each member."
— Robert Motherwell

Longpoint Gallery members on the cover of Provincetown Arts, summer, 1991. Front row, from left: Nora Speyer, Robert Motherwell, Judith Rothschild; second row, Budd Hopkins, Edward Giobbi, Leo Manso, Sideo Fromboluti; third row, Paul Resika, Varujan Boghosian; top row, Tony Vevers, Carmen Cicero, Sidney Simon. 1990 photo by Joel Meyrowitz, courtesy Provincetown Arts.

seasons with the temporary presence of twenty-something Rick Klauber, our token kid, I was, at 46, the youngest member of the group. Robert Motherwell, the veteran Abstract Expressionist, was our best-known painter, and figure-sculptor Sidney Simon was another senior member who had enjoyed a national reputation ever since the end of World War II. Sidney was a marvelous storyteller and regularly enlivened the gallery's boring meetings with tales of long-ago art-world arguments.

Sidney had been a soldier-artist during the war, part of an official group of combat-painters who were sent to the front lines with the infantry to sketch, for the historical record, the ensuing carnage. It was a truly bizarre idea – art-making in a quiet studio is difficult enough – but at the time Sidney defended it and was proud of his dangerous calling, even though the explosions he endured left him nearly deaf. He had a rare, self-deprecating wit, and at a Longpoint meeting one day he told us of participating in a panel discussion shortly after the war, at the Museum of Modern Art. He was making the case for the superior authenticity of combat-art, claiming that you had to be there in person, dodging the bullets, smelling the powder, seeing the blood, and so on in order to make authentic wartime artworks. Waxing ever more eloquent, he said that unless you personally faced the machinegun fire and felt the shells bursting around you, your paintings of the war would be shallow and inauthentic. At the peak of his peroration, his friend the painter Ben Shahn stood up in the audience and said, "Aw, come off it, Sidney. Was Leonardo at the Last Supper?"

Longpoint's exhibitions interspersed group and one-person shows, and my suggestions of themes for our collective exhibitions were often accepted. I saw the gallery as providing a unique chance to display the more personal and revealing aspects of our art making. Knowing that most artists have wall areas near their work tables where we pin up postcards of favorite paintings, ephemeral photographs clipped from magazines or newspapers, and miscellaneous images of various kinds that interest us, I proposed a group show based on this idea: each of us would have a recent work along with a personal selection of his or her favorite images transferred from our studio walls and pinned up nearby. In this way the viewers could see the finished blossoms next to some of their nourishing roots.

Another of my proposals was for each of us to display a recent work along with that artist's choice of a painting, drawing, or sculpture by someone else. The stipulation was that the chosen work was one the selector admired and respected but regarded as emotionally *opposite* from his or her concerns. Both shows were highly successful, giving viewers unusual insights into the artists' creative thinking and the ways in which we saw our own work. To sell the often dubious gallery members on these self-revelatory shows, I said that if we didn't do it our way, sooner or later the art historians would try the same kind of thing and probably misrepresent our work altogether. I think this argument clinched the deal, and these theme shows turned out to be among the most popular exhibitions we presented – even among ourselves.

But we were contentious. At a meeting one summer, Paul Resika, a figurative and landscape painter in our group, asked me what new ideas I had for future shows. "You always come up with these great ideas," he said, "and I always think at first that they're terrible. Awful. But then we put on the shows and everybody loves them, and they really look good, and I realize I was wrong. So what do you suggest for next season?"

I outlined another project I'd thought of, and he responded quickly. "But that's a *terrible* idea!" he said. "*Awful*! Ridiculous! It will never work!"

History repeats itself in amusing ways.

So we were twelve experienced but very dissimilar painters and sculptors, each of us absorbed in our own esthetic worlds, each of us with healthy egos, and all of us of a certain age. Some of us were figurative, others abstract, and we worked in various different mediums: painting, sculpture, collage, assemblage, drawing, printmaking, etc. All of us knew, without saying so out loud, that an artist doesn't just think he or she is *good* – better than "the others" – but also that he or she is *right* and the others are *wrong*. Historically, it's well known, for example, that Picasso denigrated Bonnard's work because his own skills as a draughtsman so far exceeded Bonnard's. But for his part, Bonnard's mastery of subtle color and painterly touch lay outside Picasso's collection of extraordinary talents. Each probably thought he was not only better than the other but also more *correct* in his view of how a painting should properly be created. In the same way, Cezanne famously disliked Van Gogh's canvases because of his sense that Van Gogh "painted dark lines around everything." That was not the way Cezanne thought that art should be made. In his view, Vincent's approach was *wrong*.

Each of the members of Longpoint Gallery undoubtedly held similarly contentious personal views of the other eleven members, but in the interest of diplomacy, we kept these views to ourselves. One incident, however, let us glimpse the hidden truth in a fiendishly clever way. During our financially successful second season, we published a collective poster to which each of us had contributed a small, signed, individual work. These personal images were ganged up together on one sheet and reproduced closely together beneath the Longpoint name and date. At the end of August we held a celebratory banquet for ourselves at the Flagship, one of Provincetown's best restaurants. The seafood was delicious, the wine flowed generously, and we began making self-congratulatory speeches, especially praising Edys Hunter, our director. We crowed about what a great, cohesive group we were, how we truly loved and respected one another's art, and so on, the bonhomie growing ever thicker and more outlandish with every fresh bottle of wine. Finally, when gifts were being presented to Edys, Varujan Boghosian, a sly maker of poetic assemblages, handed her his, a beautifully wrapped tubular object. When she unfurled it, we saw that it was our Longpoint poster, but Varujan had taken a precision knife to it and carefully excised every single artwork and signature but his own. The sheet looked like a piece of white lace, or a slab of Swiss cheese with very little cheese left in it. The sole remaining artwork was a graceful little Boghosian watercolor standing alone down in one corner. It was a hilarious demonstration of the boundless ego that we all possessed but were temporarily denying, and it set off gales of laughter. He'd caught us all, himself included, in a subtle, mischievous net.

Our lengthy, disorganized meetings were occasions for serious future planning as well as the exchange of new jokes, art world gossip, ideological arguments, and the passing around of the ever-present bottles of white wine and plates of cheese. (Artists always seem to be either celebratory or depressed, and at our meetings we chose to be celebratory.) The fiercely bearded Paul Resika always arrived late in his paint spattered work clothes and broad-brimmed, nineteenth century white hat, looking (intentionally?) like a cross between Monet and Pissarro. I suspected that his dramatic entrances were designed to present himself as the one hard-working *real* painter of the group, unlike the rest of us cheese eating, wine-swilling sybarites. But we were all pretty much on to him anyway, so no one was insulted.

The Longpoint Gallery openings became a kind of social event in Provincetown, regularly bringing out most of the painters, writers, and collectors in town and many of the academics and psychiatrists who summered in Wellfleet and Truro. Several of our theme shows were planned to do honor to particular local residents, friends of the members, like the poet Stanley Kunitz and the composer Arthur Berger. We also presented a few readings and one or two musical evenings, but the center, of course, was our program of first-rate, one-person exhibitions and memorable group shows. Apart from the chance to show our own current work, an unstated benefit for all of us was the rich, intimate, and abundant give and take we shared. We listened, looked around, and, without admitting it, learned from one another. Our easy mutual support helped all of us through a few rough patches at one time or another.

And, of course, when we got together, we cherished the playful side of things, because humor is an essential antidote to the rigors, loneliness, and inevitable disappointments of an artist's isolated life. As an example, one of the senior sculptors in the gallery told us about an exhibition he had once had in a Sun Belt state. He was on tenterhooks because the blond, glamorous young wife of a local millionaire was toying with the idea of buying one of his largest, priciest works. Would she or wouldn't she, he worried, because the sale would mean a lot. She told him how much she loved the work, but because of its high price she said she would have to call her husband at his office and confer with him. It would take a bit of persuasion. The sculptor paced nervously back and forth and after a while the young woman returned, beaming. "He told me I could buy it," she said, smiling gaily. "Looks like I'll have to fuck him tonight."

One of the most colorful members of Longpoint was the painter/sculptor/draftsman/collagist Fritz Bultman, who was not only a multi-talented artist but a man who had led an extraordinary life. Fritz was born and raised in New Orleans, the scion of a well-to-do family that owned the largest funeral parlor business in that funeral-obsessed city. He was a good friend of Tennessee Williams, whose play *The Glass Menagerie* referred to a collection of small glass figurines Fritz's sister collected. In the 1940s, in Provincetown, Fritz introduced Tennessee Williams to another friend, the painter Jackson Pollock, and, as one might have expected, they didn't get along well. In later years, however, some people suggested that the character of Stanley Kowalski in *Streetcar Named Desire* was partly based on Pollock's macho, sullen personality.

Shortly after he graduated from high school in 1936, Fritz, already a budding painter, decided to go to Germany to study at the Bauhaus, the famous *avant-garde* art school. When he arrived in Munich, he discovered that the Nazis had closed the school, but he found a place to live with several other American boys in a rooming house run by "Miz" Hofmann, the semi-estranged wife of the early AbEx painter Hans Hofmann who was living in the United States. A few years later Fritz was able to arrange an exit visa for Miz Hofmann, and she made it to the U.S. just before the war, to be reunited with her husband. The Hofmanns went on to become summer residents of Provincetown and Fritz Bultman's very close friends.

But one of Fritz's youthful adventures in Germany was remarkable in a very different way. As a seventeen-year-old art student living in Munich, he knew that the Nazis ruled Germany, though he was ill informed about local politics. In the winter, he and some of his young friends, having decided to go skiing, traveled to Berchtesgaden unaware that Hitler's mountain retreat was nearby. Shortly after their arrival, as Fritz recalled, the boys were in their hotel lobby when an English-speaking German approached them and began to chat. He introduced himself as Dr. Ernst Hanfstaengl – "Putzi" to his friends – an American-born Harvard graduate, a lightweight, piano-playing party animal, and an intimate of Der Fuhrer. Though Fritz did not know it at the time, one of Hanfstaengl's unofficial tasks was to improve the image of the Nazi government in the eyes of English-speaking nations. He must have seen these obviously well-to-do American boys as PR propaganda targets and asked if they would like to meet Chancellor Hitler. The boys said yes, of course, knowing that Hitler was the biggest celebrity in Germany and meeting him would be an adventure to write home about.

An appointment was set up, and the next day Hanfstaengl arrived promptly in an impressive-looking, chauffeur-driven car. The boys piled in, and as they drove up the winding mountain road, Putzi explained that since Der Fuhrer spoke no English, he would translate for everyone. Fritz said that they passed several checkpoints where armed, helmeted SS guards waved them though. By the time they arrived at Hitler's chalet, they were all rather intimidated and very quiet. With Putzi leading the way, they mounted the steps past more armed guards and were led into the formal entry hall where they were asked to form a straight line at the base of a wide stairway. Then they waited. And waited. The SS guards stood at attention. Minutes passed and finally Hitler appeared at the top of the stairs, dressed in his brown uniform. It was, Fritz said, a superbly stage-managed piece of theater. Hitler came down the steps slowly – haste would have been unseemly in such a royal personage – and approached the line of quaking boys. He came close to each in turn, saying nothing, but staring intensely into their eyes and firmly shaking hands with each as if he were gravely welcoming a troop of Luftwaffe aces. Then he turned and went back up the stairs. The solemn colloquy, if it can be called that, was over. The boys were led out, back to the car, relieved, dazzled, and still frightened. The next day, Fritz said, he and his friends went skiing, but they now had quite a story to tell back home.

In retrospect, there is something vaguely comical about the uniformed, hypnotically staring dictator reviewing a line of trembling American kids, and I think Fritz appreciated this aspect of his adventure. He was a great raconteur, telling his stories in a soft southern accent, and he appreciated irony whenever it reared its seductive head. How much energy must Hitler have uselessly exerted during those pre-war years in his efforts to overpower irrelevant young people, dimwitted British countesses, and powerless Slavic potentates. To turn one's life into a relentless theatrical performance is, I guess, the price a soulless politician has to pay. After all, Hitler, a failed artist, a mass murderer, and the world's most hated man, ended up in abject defeat, marrying, at the last minute, an empty vessel like Eva Braun, and then, in a dank basement room, in dread fear of the Russians, forcing himself to stick a gun in his mouth to blow himself away. But he had had his moments, from the satanic to the ludicrous. One of the latter was in 1936, when, for ten minutes or so, he managed to intimidate a seventeen-year-old boy named Fritz Bultman, who soon forgot all about it and went on to become a major American artist.

In retrospect, it seems to me that the painters and sculptors who organized and exhibited at the Longpoint Gallery were a colorful bunch. One of us, the painter Carmen Cicero, had a second busy career as a jazz saxophonist, and I was, of course, doing research into the UFO phenomenon and writing books about it. Surely these are among the more unusual extra-curricular activities indulged in by professional painters. Some of our members were, like me, struggling to make a living, while a few others, particularly Judith Rothschild, were wealthy. I remember my dazzling first visit to her Park Avenue townhouse along with most of the gallery members. We sipped cocktails and sampled her caviar while we chatted about Longpoint affairs and tried not to gape too obviously at her major Picasso, her Brancusi sculpture, and her seven or eight Mondrians.

The other female member of the gallery, Nora Speyer, usually came to our meetings with her small dog on a leash. Slender, petite, and quietly flamboyant, Nora was always beautifully dressed and wearing her trademark long, exotic earrings. During the meetings, she and her husband, Sideo Fromboluti, were given to frequent sharp-edged arguments with each other, tense altercations that alarmed those unaware of this feature of the Fromboluti's long and happy marriage, a union that has now lasted more than 60 years.

After our twenty-year run as a gallery, we finally lost our lease, and the 1997 season was Longpoint's last. I had had eight one-man shows there and was bereft when it was all over. Even worse was the fact that by the end of those two decades, five of our original group of twelve artists had passed away. Sidney Simon, Leo Manso, Robert Motherwell, Fritz Bultman, and Judith Rothschild were gone and sadly missed. We had been comrades, colleagues, and good friends for too many years for me not to be filled with grief and helpless anger at the inevitable losses that the passing of time had inflicted.

But at the very beginning, when the Longpoint Gallery was still in the planning stage, I experienced moments of… I almost wrote "youthful" elation but since I was in my forties, "youthful" isn't the right adjective, but it's close. In one of those high moments I was notified that I'd received a Guggenheim Fellowship for Painting, an award that is not only prestigious but comes with a generous financial grant. It helped me, my wife, and our three-year-old daughter through yet another year of modest sales and was a welcome sign of art world support for my work.

When the list of the other 1976 Guggenheim Fellows was released, I was happy to see that one of my jazz idols, Thelonious Monk, had also received a fellowship for his music. I liked to say, that though we'd never met, Thelonious and I had something in common: we were fellow Fellows. Apart from its pretentiousness, the sentence had a nice, mellifluous ring to it, and I'm afraid I've repeated it far too many times.

Missing Time

In the middle and later 1970s, while we artist-members were busy organizing exhibitions at the Longpoint Gallery, I was also becoming more deeply involved in UFO research. Working with my colleague Ted Bloecher, I found myself looking into ever stranger reports, some of which, like the case of the Connecticut "hikers," suggested hidden UFO abductions, a phenomenon that was still extremely controversial, even among long-time UFO investigators. In the Connecticut case and a few others like it, the witness reports of inexplicable periods of "missing time" were especially intriguing to me because we'd learned that hypnosis could unlock the mysterious gaps in the witnesses' otherwise normal recall. So far, based on the handful of published accounts like those of Betty and Barney Hill and the two Pascagoula fishermen, I assumed that abductees would consciously remember at least having seen both the UFO and its alien occupants, even if the rest was a blank. If, as seems likely, the so-called Connecticut hikers were actually occupants of the UFO that the young people had sighted earlier, then that case fits the same template as these others. But I was soon forced to narrow my notion of what abductees should recall *consciously* about their encounters, a change in thinking that opened the door to a far more widespread and thus more disturbing phenomenon.

In 1978, Ted Bloecher introduced me to Steven Kilburn, a strikingly handsome, dark haired young man he had met at a Fortean conference a few years before. Charles Fort was an eccentric writer who, in the early twentieth century, had obsessively dedicated himself to collecting reports of unusual occurrences of many kinds, ranging from mysterious rains of frogs (a bizarre image later used in the film *Magnolia*) to unexplained flying objects. Today his work is still enthusiastically carried on by many followers who occasionally hold conferences like the one that young Steven, a college student at the time, found compelling enough to attend. When I first met him, I saw that he knew a little about the UFO phenomenon in general but was only slightly aware of what then were the extremely rare reports of UFO abductions.

Every so often Ted and I held, at my apartment, informal gatherings for those interested in UFO case reports, and Steven came to one of them in which abduction accounts were discussed. He seemed a bit uneasy, and after the meeting broke up and we were saying goodbye in the downstairs hall, he stopped me. He has a way of shifting about nervously, his eyes fixed in middle distance, and then suddenly raising them to meet yours in a steady, pleading gaze. The effect is riveting. "There's probably nothing to it," he said, "but something may have happened to me when I was in college. I can't remember anything specific, but something has always bothered me about a certain stretch of road I used to pass through whenever I left my girlfriend's house in Maryland. I don't know if there's anything to it, but I think there may be."

I asked if he recalled anything unusual that night, a strange light, an odd sound or… whatever… but he said he remembered nothing, just the feeling that something had happened to him. However, his fear of that particular stretch of highway – Route 40 – was so intense that a number of times he had driven miles out of his way to avoid it. When I asked about the issue of time (had he checked his watch or a clock when he came home?), he replied that he hadn't, but it did seem rather late. Finally he said that he would be willing to try hypnosis to see if anything more happened that night that he wasn't remembering.

For a number of reasons, I was interested enough in the situation to consider his offer. First, he seemed sincere in his need to understand the source of his intense fear and honest in relating what he could and could not recall. If he were just an abductee-wannabe trying to get attention, he could certainly have made up a few juicy details to regale us with. Wannabes are all too obvious. For example, one morning, after I had done a radio interview about abductions, a sixteen-year-old boy called me (I was listed in the Manhattan phone book) and went on and on about his "UFO experience." He said that on his way home from school this huge UFO landed on the road near him, and tall, beautiful people with long golden hair came out and invited him into their ship. He said that they were so nice and friendly and they showed him the cockpit area where they controlled their ship and their sleeping quarters and everything, and even took him for a ride, allowing him to steer for a minute or two. It was all so neat and exciting, he said, and he would like to tell his story on the radio if I could arrange it for him. I thanked him for sharing, as they say, interminably, in twelve-step programs, and suggested that he write it up as a story and hand it in to his English teacher. I assured him that it was very imaginative and that she would like it very much.

By contrast, the very paucity of details in Steven Kilburn's account supported his credibility, as did the obvious fear that he displayed. *Something* seemed to have happened to him on that stretch of highway, I thought, something that definitely had had a traumatizing result. But since he did not remember seeing either a UFO or its occupants, or even a strange light, how could this have been a UFO abduction? I wondered if he might have been involved in some other kind of traumatic accident that night, something that caused enough shock that he had entirely blocked it out of his mind. I was aware that shock-induced amnesia sometimes occurs in victims of violent crimes or serious automobile accidents, but he told me that his car was not damaged and that he was physically uninjured. So what had caused his intense fear of that stretch of highway?

My final reason for considering hypnosis in this very sketchy case was my deepening curiosity about the patterns within the abduction phenomenon, and where their boundaries might be. If Steven Kilburn had had a UFO encounter that night without remembering any of it, then almost anyone could undergo such an experience and have no memory of it, not even the recall of seeing a UFO. If this were true, the only sign that such a thing had happened to someone would be its powerful but unexplained traumatic aftereffects – like Steven's fear of a certain stretch of highway.

After a few more conversations with Steven and Ted Bloecher, we decided to arrange a hypnosis session as a kind of exploratory experiment. Dr. Naiman was extremely busy and had been overly generous with his time, but he referred me to a psychologist, Dr. Girard Franklin, whom he was training in the use of hypnosis. When I spoke to Dr. Franklin, he explained that he was skeptical about UFO reality, but would be willing to work with Steven as part of his ongoing experience with the process. Dr. Franklin's skepticism was fine by me, since I knew that Dr. Benjamin Simon, who had hypnotized Betty and Barney Hill, was a skeptic, and my friend Bob Naiman, who had dealt with several people who recalled abduction experiences, had also not given up his basically skeptical position either. Yet despite this skepticism their hypnotic subjects recalled often highly detailed abduction experiences. So much for the debunkers' oft-stated claim that hypnotists are deliberately implanting false abduction memories in their subjects.

In my first book on UFO abductions, *Missing Time* (1981) I presented a full transcript of the fascinating Kilburn hypnosis session conducted by Dr. Franklin. Ted Bloecher and I attended as witnesses, as Steven, in the pre-hypnosis interview, described the night in question: "I felt very strange for some reason. I didn't know why. It was that feeling someone is watching you as you wake up, that sort of thing… I felt that something maybe had happened to me, or was going to happen… Every time I [later] passed that approximate area I felt for some reason something right there had happened…

"I can't be sure but I believe I was a little bit confused about the time… It's possible, of course, that I'm mistaken, but there's something about it that I've never quite understood, and I don't even know what – what questions to ask to find the answer I'm looking for, if that makes any sense."

He then said, shyly, to Dr. Franklin, something that I've since heard hundreds of times from other self-doubting, possible abductees: "I hope I'm not [wasting your time]."

Dr. Franklin's response was exactly appropriate: "It isn't a waste of time, because if nothing happened, that's as informative as if something did happen, so don't worry about that. It's not a waste of time. Either way we would be okay."

Under hypnosis, Steven, deeply relaxed and speaking slowly in a slightly slurred voice, described driving home, his car suddenly stopping at the side of the road, and his confusion as to what was happening. Without repeating here more of the long transcript I published in *Missing Time*, it is enough to say he got out of his car and stood beside it, watching and listening in great fear, and that when several small, huge-eyed figures began to approach him he became terrified. Haltingly, he described the one closest to him as "… very white… neck, head, face… no hair… ugly. He doesn't have regular skin. It's, uh, funny skin… it looks like putty or something… like you could move it with your hand…"

He was asked about its color: "Whitish, like chalkish, whitish… a little tint of gray in it." As the figures approached more closely, he became even more frightened, and seeing his state of near panic, Dr. Franklin calmed him and began the process of ending the trance state. It had been almost as harrowing an experience for Dr. Franklin, Ted, and me as it had been for Steven. There were moments when his fear was so great that tears coursed down his cheeks.

It is important to keep in mind the rarity in 1978 of such close-up, detailed descriptions of UFO occupants, but Steven's account of their appearance would be repeated again and again over the years in the descriptions of thousands of others. Some time after this session, Travis Walton's book about his 1975 abduction was published, and in it he described the aliens this way: "Their thin bones were covered with white, marshmallowy-looking flesh. When they extended their hands towards me I noticed they had no nails… their hands were small, delicate, and without hair on the backs of them. Their thin round fingers looked smooth and unwrinkled."

In light of this description, Steven Kilburn's earlier and rather cryptic comment about their hands took on meaning: "All the fingers are perfect," he had said, near the end of the hypnosis, and he would expand on this remark in a later session.

In October of 1975, in a less well-known incident, two young men from Norway, Maine, had a similar encounter, and under hypnosis one of them described their captors' appearance this way: "It looked like skin, but you know how somebody was indoors, say, a year, a year and a half, how it would look? It looked really white… like a mushroom." In another abduction that occurred in 1978 but was, like the Maine case, little known at the time, Bill Herrmann described the UFO occupants as "the color of marshmallow." Later examples of similarly unexotic alien descriptions are almost endless in number, but early accounts such as Steven Kilburn's, from a time when the abduction phenomenon was hardly known and rarely reported, are all amazingly consonant. In these reports we heard nothing about little green-skinned figures with antennas sticking out of their heads, or any of the other exotic or monstrous science fiction images that saturated popular culture. Instead, as we have seen, these abductees used the simplest and most homely words at their disposal to describe, for example, the aliens' skin as the color and texture of putty, or a mushroom, or a marshmallow. This consistency of the unusual tone and texture of the aliens' skin supports the credibility and the accuracy of observation in these very early abductee accounts.

But so far we had only a few, admittedly subjective reasons to accept Steven Kilburn's report of his encounter with UFO occupants. The first was his apparently unfeigned fear about that particular stretch of highway; the second was his obvious psychological stability; the third was the intensity of his reactions under hypnosis; and the fourth was the way his detailed description of the aliens dovetailed with the accounts of a number of other abductees, several of which only came to light *after* Steven's testimony. But we still lacked a fuller account of what transpired that night, or any kind of physical evidence of his encounter.

The first gap, at least, was partially closed some months later when Steven finally decided to undergo further hypnosis, though, for his part, Dr. Franklin was disinclined to venture again into such disturbing territory. After his unnerving session, Steven he told me that though he was calm about his experience, he was trying to put it out of his mind. It was already the end of May, however, and about time for me to leave New York to take my family back to Wellfleet for the summer, so further explorations had to be tabled. Ted Bloecher continued to talk to Steven from time to time, but deliberately, neither brought up the subject of the hypnotic regression. In fact, Ted had custody of the tape recording of the session and Steven had never asked to hear it. This meant that when we resumed the hypnosis we were in an ideal position to see if any new material that might surface would dovetail with what we already knew, or instead might in some way contradict it and thereby cast doubt on the accuracy of his recall. One of my favorite comments of Mark Twain is his statement that "always telling the truth means never having to remember anything." For a deliberate liar or an emotionally confused confabulator to avoid mistakes in later testimony, he must first memorize many irksome, even trivial details from what he has claimed so far; thus Steven's forthcoming hypnosis sessions would be extremely important, either substantiating or undermining his credibility.

In the meantime, my psychiatrist friend, Bob Naiman, had referred me to yet another psychologist skilled in hypnosis, a woman of Greek parentage named Aphrodite Clamar. In his first of three sessions with Dr. Clamar, Steven begins by describing the uneventful drive home on Route 40, but suddenly he cries out, "Oh, what's happening? No! I don't want this to happen!" He said the car jerked violently to the right: "It's like a huge magnet just sucked it over to the right!"

He gets out of the car, the aliens approach, but now he uses a few new images to describe them. With great fear, he says, "I see the faces... and they look like they're made of rubber... ah, not rubber... what do you call it? Putty or something. Like an artist's eraser." He describes their hands: "I see these fingers... They're... like tubes. That's exactly... they're tubes. White plastic tubes..." (Travis Walton later said about his alien captors that "Their thin round fingers looked smooth and unwrinkled.")

Steven goes on to say that the being closest to him is small. "Below my shoulder... He's skinny... really skinny... I don't think he'd weigh... not even 50 pounds... His head is not round, it's like, uh, an inverted teardrop..." But it is the alien's eyes that he finds most compelling, particularly in the way they reflect the bright light source that he senses behind him. "His eyes are really shiny… black… and they're big… like they're black and endless. Like they're liquid or something… I keep looking at these eyes looking at me. God… I feel like under a microscope."

He describes the alien's odd movements: "…When he walked, it was almost like he had two really bad knees… He was hobbling almost… shifting his weight to the left and right. Almost rocking back and forth. And he drags his feet a little bit… I don't know whether they're feet or boots… They're… almond-shaped. I don't see any toes or anything, but the almond shapes are pointed in the front and the back so that, ah, they're kind of [like] clubfeet… Yeah. Skinny ankles, legs. Really skinny… He's so little… I'm really afraid to look at him. I don't want him to think I'm being aggressive… I want it to be over. I want the whole thing to be over. I'm not sure… I'm not believing what I'm seeing at all… ah… there's no way to explain it away… I can't do what I want to. They've really got something on me… and I don't know what it is…"

There is more to this session, but as Steven continued with his descriptions of the beings and his sense that they were communicating with one another in total silence, Ted and I decided that he was, perhaps unconsciously, expressing his fear of moving on to the next stage of the narrative. And because the well-being of the subject is foremost, we signaled Dr. Clamar to bring him out of the trance state.

There was obviously more to his experience that night, but we were not to find out about it until his fourth and final hypnosis, in January 1980. Steven had always been nervous about these explorations, and what had begun in May of 1978 he was only willing to complete some twenty months later. Evidently he felt it was time to move ahead, and in this session, after briefly going over the earlier events of that night, he finally allows himself to look directly at the UFO, apparently the source of the bright light that had reflected off the alien's black, glittering eyes. He describes the craft this way: "It looks like a saucer… It's whitish. And it's sitting on something… a kind of platform… some kind of girders, crisscross… latticework…

Like an egg sitting on it…"

After a long pause, he continues: "They want me to come in. [There's] a ramp… a little ramp. He wants me to walk up before him…

"…I think there's some kind of noise… it's coming from this thing, whatever it is, the saucer… It's like a very quiet hum…

"And now he's beside me at my left, and there's a passageway… almost like a tube we're walking through… I'm very relaxed. They're not going to hurt me… I feel like I'm almost paralyzed. It doesn't hurt, though. I'm just very relaxed, very calm…"

Steven's unexpected comment about feeling calm and relaxed is one I would hear hundreds of times in the future, from witnesses who also seem to have been artificially tranquilized at a similar stage of the abduction process. In what follows, he describes finding himself on an examination table, virtually naked, but with no memory of having undressed. This gap in recall is also typical of thousands of later abduction reports, suggesting that the UFO occupants, aware of the terror a human might feel at being stripped of his clothes in such a situation, apparently render the abductees unconscious while the undressing is carried out. This may also explain why more than a few abductees have been returned to their normal surroundings wearing someone else's clothes. This confusion is apparently caused by the aliens mixing up their subjects' clothing in the re-dressing part of the process.

Again, without repeating the lengthy and detailed transcript of Steven's hypnosis published in *Missing Time*, it is important to mention what seems to be the aliens' examination of his central nervous system in a complex and mysterious set of procedures, which frequently inflicted excruciating pain. But something else occurred that he did not mention under hypnosis, perhaps because he found it too embarrassing to describe to a female hypnotist. Just as hypnosis does not guarantee absolute truth, it does not compel the subject to helplessly report everything he or she is experiencing. And so, two days after this final hypnosis session, during a phone conversation, Steven had something to tell me.

At the end of his "examination," he said that a set of metal loops encircled his thighs very high up, almost at the level of his hip sockets, and his legs were forced apart. Ultimately, he was in a posture not unlike that of obstetrical stirrups. He said that he felt "like a frog" and that as he remembered this under hypnosis, he deliberately concealed it from Dr. Clamar. He said he "felt embarrassed, somehow ashamed… the way you would feel if you had flunked a test or something and tried to conceal it from your parents." To me, there was an edge of sexual shame in the way he described this embarrassment. He went on to say that when he came home that fateful morning, he felt physically dirty and wanted very much to shower, though he was so tired he gave up on the idea and just went to bed.

I was not aware of it at the time of this conversation, but I was eventually to learn from Betty Hill that her late husband, Barney, said that the aliens had taken a sperm sample from him, as he lay helpless on the examination table. It was an experience so humiliating to him at the time that it was deleted from all published accounts of his, and Betty's, abduction experience. However, I was soon to hear similar reports from other equally humiliated male abductees, in a pattern that suggested consistent alien interest in the processes of human reproduction.

There was to be an interesting coda to Steven Kilburn's lengthy testimony about his UFO experience. Under hypnosis, he had described in great detail how the aliens had apparently stimulated various nerves in his body, causing his leg to jump involuntarily, or one of his arms to suddenly go numb, or to feel excruciating back pain, and so on, as his body was touched in various places. A few months before this final hypnosis session, I met a young neurosurgeon who was also an art collector interested in my work. A conversation in my studio one day came around to the subject of UFOs, and he became curious about my investigations, though he remained neutral in his judgment of the reality of the phenomenon. I told him about cases I had investigated involving scars on the bodies of UFO abductees, and, screwing up my courage, I asked him if he would ever do me the favor of examining one or two people, just to see what could be deduced from the character and location of the wound traces. He agreed out of a mixture of friendship and curiosity.

Steven Kilburn's final hypnosis had been so connected with the recall of what seemed to be a neurological examination that he became an obvious candidate for the first appointment with Dr. Paul Cooper. He received Steven at his Brooklyn Hospital office about ten days after this last hypnosis. I was not present, but a few hours after Steven's appointment, Dr. Cooper called me.

"I've just had the spookiest two-and-a-half hours of my life," he told me. "Steven is a remarkable young man. He's extremely bright, an excellent observer, and totally believable. And very, very decent… a nice human being. I was spellbound. Everything he told me about what they did to him and how his body reacted accorded exactly with what should have happened if they stimulated the different nerves he said they touched.

"I tried to mislead him," Dr. Cooper added. "He said when they pressed here, and he indicated his femoral nerve, his thigh moved. I said, 'Are you sure it wasn't elsewhere?' He said, 'No, it was right here, I'm sure of it.' I'd insist it couldn't have been where he said, just to mislead him, but he would always stick by his memory of it. He exactly described the motor reaction that happens when the femoral nerve is stimulated. And he has no particular knowledge of the nervous system. He'd have to know a great deal to make it all up, and I'm certain he's not the type to lie. He's a very decent guy, and I'm really impressed with him. It's remarkable, the whole thing…

"I don't know what it all means," he said, "but it's remarkable. Fascinating! Really fascinating!"

SO WHERE DID ALL OF THIS LEAVE ME? There was, first of all, my personal, three-witness daylight UFO sighting on Cape Cod in 1964; then, George O'Barski's account of the UFO landing in North Hudson Park, and the numerous witnesses and physical evidence we uncovered there; the fascinating Connecticut hikers case, involving twelve witnesses at several different locations; Steven Kilburn's account and the supporting testimony of a neurosurgeon; plus a group of other credible abduction reports I'd investigated by

1979 but which I haven't discussed in these pages. So there was all of this, plus compelling earlier cases I had read about, such as that of the Hills and the Pascagoula fishermen, and the striking internal consistency of detail I noticed in virtually all of them. Even worse for the skeptical position, I had found no *disconfirming* evidence in any of them.

To be sure, the phenomenon seemed, on its face, unbelievable, but I had found no way to effectively undermine its reality. The only way I knew to reject it was just that, to reject it as a matter of sheer belief, and to insist that such things just cannot happen. Years later someone asked me a basic question: did I believe that UFOs – extraterrestrial spacecraft – really existed, and that the thousands of abductee accounts were possibly true? I recall answering that I found, sadly, I no longer had the luxury of *dis*belief. Even back in the 1970s I felt that sense of being helpless in the face of the accumulating evidence, and aware that the UFO phenomenon made the future seem increasingly ominous.

NBC News – The Catalyst

THE THREE YEARS THAT FOLLOWED the publication of my article in the *Village Voice* were for me a period of intense activity on many fronts. Between 1976 and 1979, I was given six one-man exhibitions of my work in places like New York, Houston, Provincetown, and Vermont's Middlebury College, and I had begun making and showing my complex Guardian paintings. In the summers on the Cape I was deeply committed to the evolving affairs of our new co-op gallery, and then partying in the evenings with artist friends. Since April and I both loved to dance, we gave a number of noisy, sweaty dance parties in my Wellfleet studio after we cleared out the easel and some unnecessary furniture and rugs, stashing everything in the yard and praying it wouldn't rain.

Turning host-as-control-freak, I took over as DJ and played great danceable numbers by an increasingly dated list of groups like the *Supremes*, the *Stones*, the *Beatles*, and Ray Charles with his various bands. However, since most of our friends were in their forties or older, only a sprinkling of younger people complained and asked for something more up to date. But I was stubborn. After all, it was *my* house and *my* party, so occasionally I revisited my teenage years by slipping in a Big Band classic from the 1940s, Vaughn Monroe's "There, I Said it Again," an absolute favorite of mine. Sometimes I went even farther back, all the way to the 1930s, and played a ballad by Fred Astaire, but these breaks from the pounding rock-and-roll menu we'd been dancing to always drew a chorus of boos and I had to guard the record player against outright rebellion.

In my more sedate home life I was relishing each new step my little daughter Grace took on her way to more active childhood. I took her to the Wellfleet ponds and began to teach her how to swim, and she, April, and I spent many lovely afternoons basking on the ocean beaches of Wellfleet and Truro. I'd become adept at body surfing and, with a number of fellow surfing addicts, often rode the waves at Longnook Beach.

But it was not all fun and games and art making. There was no way to escape the plausible UFO abduction cases I had uncovered, often as a result of the media attention I'd received. Many of the local radio shows I'd been on featured call-ins, and I asked the more responsible-sounding callers to leave their phone numbers with the station so I could return their calls; many interesting but necessarily brief on-air accounts cried out for more extensive interviews.

During all of this I was beginning what would be, in effect, a seven-year apprenticeship in the art of regressive hypnosis. Whenever a missing time report like Steven Kilburn's seemed appropriate for regressive hypnosis, I took the person to a psychologist – most often Aphrodite Clamar – who conducted the regression. I sat in on one such case after another, taking notes, listening, learning the language of hypnosis and the required verbal skills, but also teaching myself how to recognize significant clues in the subject's responses. At the end of what I call my seven year apprenticeship, I had observed the techniques of eight or nine different hypnotherapists, so when I finally began doing hypnosis myself in 1983, I was well equipped.

In January 1979, I received a phone call from Harry Lynn, a producer for New York City's "Channel 4 News," asking me about the UFO abduction phenomenon. One thing led to another, and eventually Channel 4 presented three successive ten-minute segments on the subject, an NBC series for which Ted Bloecher and I supplied most of the case material. The result was an extremely fair-minded and informative piece, with anchorman Chuck Scarborough doing the voice-over narration. We were immensely relieved that at the finale he avoided the usual smarmy grins and winks at the camera that anchormen often indulge in after presenting UFO material. (Apparently they feel they must reassure their public that everything they've just viewed is really a joke that they don't take seriously.) Sometimes, however, we get lucky, and Harry Lynn's three-part series was straightforward, clear, and persuasive, three qualities too often absent from such efforts.

The NBC program examined several different abduction accounts, including supporting interviews with Rockland County police officers and testimony from eyewitnesses, as well as relevant police department records and footage of the original locations. Steven Kilburn, despite his strong initial hesitation, appeared on camera. Harry wanted to film him undergoing hypnosis, and after days of back-and-forth soul-searching, Steven finally agreed to have another go at it with Dr. Clamar. He insisted on two conditions: that his face not appear on camera and that his name be kept confidential. Harry said later: "Usually when I do a story, everybody seems eager to be on TV. But not here, not with UFOs. No one wants his name used. I had to shoot everyone so that their faces were not visible, and so on. It's really strange. They want to tell their stories, they want the information out, but they are afraid of ridicule. Afraid to be recognized."

A few days after the final segment aired, Aphrodite Clamar received a phone call from a woman I will call "Virginia Horton." Virginia had not seen the NBC program, but a woman friend told her about it, and mentioned the hypnosis session with Dr. Clamar and the theory that many people may have had UFO abduction experiences without any conscious recall. Later, when we met in Dr. Clamar's office, Virginia explained how she'd responded at first to her friend's comment: "I told her I thought that was really unbelievable. I can't think of a single person who…" And then, she said, a disturbing memory began to emerge. Something connected in her mind, something that had happened to her as a child. And later, she told us, she remembered a second incident that also fit the pattern because both experiences seemed to involve inexplicable memory loss. She explained that ever since she was six years old she had been keeping the first event in the back of her mind, thinking, "There's something odd about this, and when I grow up I'm going to understand it."

Virginia Horton was a tall, striking-looking lawyer, 35 years old and happily married. She had an excellent position with an important company and thus was extremely anxious about protecting her anonymity. We gave her our assurances that any investigation we carried out would remain absolutely confidential, so eventually she relaxed and told us her story. (As in the case of Steven Kilburn, a full account of Virginia Horton's experiences and those of the abductees included in the NBC series were covered in depth in *Missing Time*. The material presented here borrows from those longer accounts.)

Virginia explained that at the age of six she was living at her grandfather's farm in southern Manitoba. She went into the barn to collect the eggs from the chickens, a chore she enjoyed, and then, she said, "All of a sudden I was in the yard and I didn't remember going from the barn into the yard, toward the house. I had an itch on my leg and I reached down to scratch it. I pulled up my blue jeans and when I scratched my leg I realized it was wet. I was covered with blood, from a cut on the back of my leg. It was a large and clean cut... no dirt or anything. It must have been at least a half-inch deep and an inch long. It was bleeding but there was no pain."

She told us that she and her family were all extraordinarily pain-sensitive, but despite the blood pouring out, she felt no pain. It was doubly strange because she had no idea how she'd cut herself or how she arrived in the yard. One second she had been in the barn gathering eggs, and the next second she was standing in the yard with a bleeding leg. On top of everything, she discovered that there was no rip or tear in her blue jeans, despite the fact that the cut was far up her leg, near her calf's maximum thickness. She told us that she went into the house, and when her alarmed mother saw the bloody wound, she cleaned and bandaged it carefully. Virginia, her mother, and grandfather then searched the barn, but they found no apparent sharp object that could have caused the cut.

"The only natural way I could have gotten cut," she said, "would have required that I somehow catch myself on the jeans hard enough to pull them up, and then get cut on something different, or else my jeans would have been cut, too. Even at age six I was clever enough to figure that out.

"We went back in and they told me not to worry about it... [the cut] was clean. There wasn't any dirt in it. It wasn't ragged, and the kinds of things you can cut yourself on on a farm are ragged and dirty."

She told us that her curiosity about the wound would not abate.

And so later, "I ripped the bandage off and I said to myself, 'I want to see this wound. There's something fascinating, completely fascinating about it.'"

But Virginia had yet another odd experience to describe, an incident she had forgotten about until her mother mentioned it when she called to ask what her mother recalled about the cut-on-the-leg incident. "…There was that time later on when we were at the picnic," her mother said, "and you showed up out of the woods covered with blood."

Virginia explained it this way: "It happened when we were on a family picnic, and my father was taking movies of all the kids, and my brother and I came running out of the woods. I had been separated from my brother and I didn't remember where I had been, and I was talking when somebody said 'You have blood on your blouse.' I was horrified and I started feeling the tip of my nose, if I had a bloody nose or something. There was nothing, no wound, but I had blood on my blouse from somewhere, as though I had been splattered.

"I said the only thing I could remember is that I saw a beautiful deer in the woods. It was almost like a mystical deer… it's very strange. It's all on film… me with blood on my blouse and feeling all horrified and kind of yucky. I've always hated that film because it looks so awful. But my mother just reminded me about it because she said that was a time when I was missing and no one knew where I was… I just went on and on about that deer, though, this beautiful deer I had seen."

In our interview with Virginia we learned, among other things, that since childhood she had been fascinated with space travel, had had many vivid flying dreams, and as a teenager wanted to be an astronaut. She knew very little about the UFO phenomenon, and we cautioned her against reading anything about it as long as we were looking into her experiences. We also learned that, during her disappearance from the picnic, her brother said he had been searching for her for over a half-hour, but it seemed possible that the missing time period might have lasted as long as a full hour.

I was interested in pursuing her two odd experiences for a number of reasons. Virginia Horton was extremely intelligent and articulate, and, as I was beginning to learn, when someone stubbornly clings to such fragmentary and innocuous recollections – like Steven Kilburn's gnawing sense that something had happened to him on a certain stretch of highway – these memories may turn out to be the proverbial tip of a traumatic iceberg. I was also impressed by Virginia's absolute refusal to expand upon or embellish her recollections, and I was particularly curious about the origin of both the cut on her leg and, later, the blood spatter on her blouse.

There is, of course, far more to our pre-hypnosis interviews and preliminary investigation than I can detail here, but eventually Dr. Aphrodite Clamar set up a hypnosis session that Ted and I attended, along with Virginia's husband, Mark, who came along to offer his support. Both Dr. Clamar and I explained that it was highly likely that nothing exotic or unusual had happened to her on either occasion, and that each might have a very simple, mundane explanation.

Aphrodite began a long, careful induction and set the scene of the incident of the leg wound Virginia experienced on her grandfather's farm. When she started speaking, I found it touching to hear this articulate, 35-year-old lawyer speaking in the voice and vocabulary of a six-year-old child. She described going into the barn to collect the chickens' eggs. "I remember the feeling of those nice, warm tummies, and putting my hand under each tummy. They don't always have eggs under them… and so you have to poke around… I gather them. I think there are eight or nine of them and they were brown…"

She says that on her way back to the house, her leg itches, and as she reaches down to scratch, her hand feels wet. When she sees the blood, she can't figure out how she cut herself, and assumes at first that the blood might somehow have come from the chickens. She describes in great detail her mother's alarm and the discussion she and her grandfather have about how she may have cut herself. "The wound itself doesn't have any feeling at all. Like it isn't even part of me. Like I'm looking at somebody else's leg…"

Next, Dr. Clamar makes a request: "Ask your mind to help

you recall how you got the cut." Virginia asks her how to do that, and Aphrodite explains. Then she says, "Well, I'm kind of afraid to watch myself get cut. That will bother me."

This exchange is followed by a five-minute period in which Virginia discusses pain, her fear of it, and her fear of remembering the incident. It's clear that she is resisting any further recall. Finally, after another long pause, she says, "I think my leg was cut by a scalpel. It was just sharp and clean… as if somebody made a nice, quick incision… and I don't think it hurt, but I expected it to hurt."

Again, she is hesitant to recall anything more, but then she resumes her narrative: "They took a little cut. They didn't mean to hurt me… I was just lying on a… bed or almost like a medical thing… It doesn't have the quality of a doctor's office. It's not chromey and white and the light's bright. There's plenty of light but I think maybe – it might be pale gray or a real soft gray. It's pearly…"

When Dr. Clamar asks how she's feeling, she says that she's "really relaxed and almost at home. Comfortable. Curious. Like you feel when you're a guest of somebody and you're glad to be there…"

Then Virginia begins to recall more about the purpose of the incision: "I was told about the cut, that it wouldn't hurt and that there was a reason for it, but I don't think the reason was one that was too clear to me… whatever the explanation I didn't really understand…"

A few minutes later she said, "…It was as though they had a puzzle that they were working on and it was very important to them… They just said, '[We will] take a little teeny piece of you home'… the way they described it to me, it's like a combination of a souvenir and a way of getting to know me better. It was as though somebody was doing the explaining and someone else was the one who did it [the cutting]."

In answer to Dr. Clamar's questions, she said she didn't recall an actual voice, nor did she remember what the "they" looked like, "It's as though they said, 'You can't see us because you wouldn't understand how we look. It would scare you…' I think he says that they are a little grayer than we are in color and he says that it would take me quite a while to get used to how he looks."

Virginia had many more recollections of her little, six-year-old self, chatting, apparently telepathically, with an alien being who seems able to communicate effectively with such a young child. Often during her hypnotic recall I had the feeling that this particular alien's psychological powers were so acute that he was able to control Virginia's fear and to establish a sense of warm comradeship – even though the little girl was not only his prisoner but also the recipient of a bloody wound on her leg. I was also reminded of Steven Kilburn's unnatural calmness when he was finally taken inside the landed UFO. As in Virginia's case, it seemed to me that being inside an alien craft would make anyone feel far from relaxed, but instead would cause even more panic about what might happen next: *Am I about to be taken away for good so I will never see my family again? Who are these beings? Do they plan to hurt me in here, or even kill me?* In the apparent absence of such instinctive fears, I theorized that the abductees' emotions must have been somehow controlled, anesthetized, or whatever.

After the long hypnosis session ended, Virginia looked relieved and even a bit excited. We talked at length about what she had recalled and eventually began to discuss the possibility of a second session to explore her experience when she was lost in the woods and emerged with blood splattered on her blouse. Her meeting with a "mystical deer" had earlier caught my attention because I was beginning to think that the deer might be a kind of imposed (pleasant) screen memory that concealed the alien's actual (frightening) appearance. She had, after all, described feeling that she was told their real appearance might frighten her, and that it would take some time for her to get used to how they look. And since we were becoming aware of the aliens' apparent ability to impose thoughts and images upon their captives, perhaps Virginia's "mystical deer" was yet another example of this kind of control.

We met at Dr. Clamar's office for a second session ten weeks after the first, and in our pre-hypnosis conversation I once more brought up the issue of the mystical deer. Virginia said that she still remembered "the sense of wonder that I had at the time, at the beautiful, beautiful deer that I saw… it was as though I had walked out of the woods and claimed I saw a unicorn… And when I think about the visual memories that I had, there wasn't anything unusual about the deer, except that it was looking at me… in a very conscious way, but it could just as easily have been that I was hypnotized and thought I saw a deer…"

I reminded her that she mentioned that possibility the very first time we discussed it: "You said that the more you talked about the deer to your parents, the less sure you [were that you] had even seen a deer…"

Virginia was certain, at least, of one thing: "I don't have any doubts that I saw something that moved me. Something real. It may have been a hypnotic cover, but it looked like a deer to my memory…"

This second hypnosis session was long, fascinating, and filled with a great deal of speculation on Virginia's part as to what it all meant. But at the beginning, to no one's surprise, the deer metamorphosed into a small gray alien whom she regarded as a friend she was hesitant to leave. She recalled an earlier moment when she was separated from her brother and wandered in the woods alone where she encountered a landed UFO. She heard, "in her head," her name being called and entered the craft via an extended ramp. Inside the ship there was, in her words, a kind of "celebration" going on, as if an alien "scientific project" that involved her had been very successful. Ultimately, she recalled a long instrument being inserted in her left nostril, apparently causing the bleeding that soiled her blouse.

Again, I suggest that anyone interested in reading more about this complex case should consult the relevant chapters in *Missing Time.* But what I learned from this case and the others discussed here and in *Missing Time* dramatically altered my earlier views about the UFO abduction phenomenon. First, I learned that an abductee might consciously remember virtually nothing – neither the UFO itself nor its occupants – about such a traumatic experience. This means that the phenomenon must be more widespread than any of us had previously believed… an ominous thought. Many years and many investigations later I would conclude that classic cases like those of the Hills and Hickson and Parker, in which the abductees consciously recalled seeing both the UFO and the alien beings, are actually in the *minority*.

Second, I learned that an abduction is not necessarily a once-in-a-lifetime event, and that as the Virginia Horton case shows, it may begin in childhood and be repeated later, as if particular individuals are being deliberately tracked. Another unnerving thought, replicated again and again in later cases, even across generations of the same family.

Third, I learned that specific scars and marks of unknown, unremembered origin might turn up on abductees, as if an aspect of the aliens' interest in us is our physical makeup. Why? This was one issue that I would come to understand far more completely in the next decade. But as time passed and my database expanded, I have collected scores of photos of extremely similar scars, apparently caused by physical sampling procedures during abductions. The so-called "scoop marks," of which I have seen perhaps a hundred, form a very large subgroup, though cases involving bloody cuts like Virginia's are quite rare. Apparently the aliens employ some unknown means to cauterize the wounds and radically speed their healing.

Fourth, I learned that the UFO occupants are able to partially conceal their presence by imposing screen memories on their abductees, as they did with Virginia Horton's "mystical deer" and the Connecticut "hikers." Therefore, abductees cannot trust their conscious recollections to be accurate about how things looked and felt during their encounters, though, as we have seen, hypnosis offers a way to pierce through such illusions. Since the Virginia Horton case was published, screen memories have appeared as virtual staples in UFO abduction accounts – yet another portentous realization.

Prior to their elucidation in 1981, in *Missing Time*, none of these points were either known or accepted by veteran UFO researchers. When I mulled over the gap I felt between my work and the somewhat indifferent air of the more mainstream UFO research community, I saw myself in an extraordinary position. I was a little like the proverbial man who had the tiger by the tail, or, in another apt but trite cliché from sci-fi movies, I was the poor soul who knows the monstrous perils the world faces, but no matter how loudly he shouts, can find no one to listen to him.

Little by little, however, researchers who read my book began to accept these discoveries as distinct, repeated aspects of the abduction phenomenon, and because the presence of these patterns can be tested by future case investigations, trial by replication, a basic method of science, is possible. In the meantime, I felt both a sense of pride and excitement as well as an overtone of dread in what I had discovered. The modern world was turning out to be very different from the calmer, safer, more provincial place where I grew up, and I began to worry more about the place my little daughter Grace would one day inhabit.

Straddling Two Lives

IN THE SUMMER OF 1981 I TURNED 50. Like most people in their forties I thought of myself as young and frisky, but the half-century mark hit me like a pail of ice water. So as my birthday neared, I decided I couldn't sit around home and let my younger friends watch me undergo the humiliation of approaching geezerdom. I would flee. Leave the country. Go to Greece and hide out. Perhaps, I thought, wandering among twenty-five-century-old artworks would make me feel young again. Maybe they would help me get my frisk back.

Missing Time had just been published and was being well received by the UFO research community, but more immediately important, the publisher's advance provided a little extra money for the trip. April arranged for a babysitter to come and stay with Grace the first week of our absence, and for another woman and her daughter, a close friend of Grace, to stay for the second week. In June we were off, temporarily childless for the first time in seven years.

Because I had been painting Temples and Guardians since 1978, I felt a definite connection with the stateliness and order of classical Greek art, a fact that lent the trip a very specific purpose, in addition to giving me a place to hide during the fateful birthday. I knew I needed to see the Acropolis in Athens, the remains of the temples in Olympia and Delphi, the great bronzes of Zeus in Athens, and the Charioteer in Delphi. The entire experience was overwhelming, but during my visit to Crete, while walking on the "Sacred Way," an eerie, marbled Minoan path below ground level, I began to imagine something specific: a *raised*, bridge-like structure, built above ground but carrying a similar mystical charge. The idea led me to make a series of sketches and models after I came home, and eventually, in 1982, after winning a competition from Pratt Institute, I built and temporarily installed my 75-foot-long *Ritual Bridge* sculpture in Brooklyn's Fort Greene Park, my first monumental sculpture.

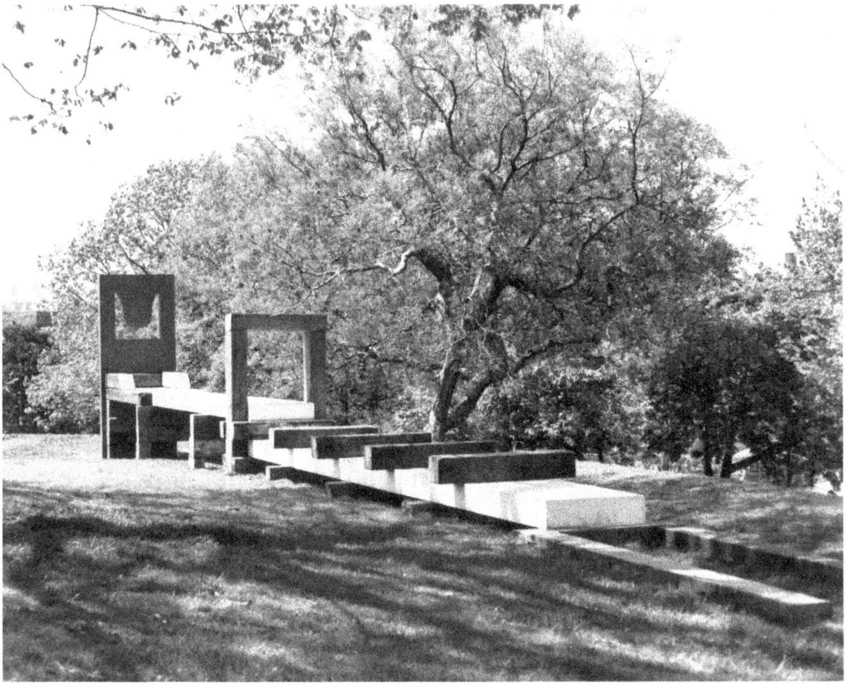

Ritual Bridge, 1982, Fort Greene Park, Brooklyn, N.Y. 70' x 11' x 54".

One entered the *Ritual Bridge* by mounting its pure white platform and then traversing it by stepping across a series of low, regular barriers. At the halfway point the visitor had to crouch beneath a low arch and then continue onto a higher platform until a vertical stele was reached. This gray plinth bore, in a negative, cutout shape, the sacred symbol of the Horns of the Bull from the Minoan culture. One summer afternoon while visiting the park, I heard some haunting music and came upon a tall, thin African-American man standing on the sculpture and improvising a slow, beautiful, hymn-like melody on his flute. I waited nearby and listened, thrilled by his soft, pagan song and feeling for a moment, and with his help, that I had brought Greece home with me.

When April and I returned the week after my birthday, we found a note from seven-year-old Grace who was temporarily out visiting a friend. It went something like this: "Dear Mom and Dad: I had a good time. I missed you. I had fun with Mary. I threw up eleven times. Love, Grace."

Since this was the first time we'd both left her alone with someone else for more than a few hours, her note naturally gave us pangs of guilt. Until now I've never dared ask Grace how she handled our leaving her for two weeks, or what made her throw up so many times, but now that she has a daughter of her own I finally did. To my surprise she seems to have recalled very little about it, other than a disappointing mix-up in plans with one of the babysitters; the throwing-up part was no longer in her memory bank.

As if the roles of attentive father and good husband were not energy-consuming enough, I found myself, since the publication of *Missing Time*, straddling two very active careers, two entirely different styles of work. Luckily, good things were happening in both areas. Between 1975 and 1981, I was awarded a National Endowment for the Arts Fellowship for Painting, the Guggenheim Museum acquired a Guardian (one of four major works of mine currently in their collection), and *The New York Times* and other media were favorably reviewing my exhibitions. More of my paintings were being bought by collectors, and at somewhat higher prices. All in all, I was enjoying the mix of pleasure and pain, the worry and freedom of being a 50-year-old experimental artist with no regular source of income.

The art world is small, but in the even smaller world of serious UFO research my book was being widely read and the new patterns I had discovered within the abduction phenomenon were gradually being tested and then accepted as firmly established. In fact, the term "Missing Time" was beginning to be used generically to describe many abduction accounts, and as such was taking its place alongside Allen Hynek's famous formulation, "Close Encounters," as common parlance.

Despite all of this, I was keenly aware that few people in the UFO research community had any knowledge of abstract art, mine included, and very few artists cared a fig for the idea of UFOs. I was pained by the disconnect between two groups with which I was so deeply involved, but there was a major difference in what I felt in each case. Naturally, I hoped that people in and out of the UFO research world would accept and be moved by my paintings and sculptures, but personal taste is personal taste and if someone dislikes what I paint, or is indifferent, it's their problem, not mine. That's life.

But the discoveries I was making about the reality of the UFO phenomenon were a different matter. I thought that everyone, potentially, should be informed about what *all* of us may be facing. As I've said before, I can easily identify with the later concerns of a scientist desperately trying to warn an indifferent public about the perils of global warming. Like me, trying to alert the public to the UFO phenomenon, the global-warming climatologist was like the poor guy I've described who, at the end of the sci-fi movie, is yelling "Wake up!" to a public that couldn't be bothered to pay attention.

This situation made things difficult for me, particularly with other artists and my friends within the intellectual community. Some, I'm sure, began to regard me as a Cassandra, or at least as an occasional bore, even though I'd tried to contain my remarks on the subject. Nevertheless, a few artists were quite interested in the abduction phenomenon, none more so than James Turrell, the internationally respected artist and perceptual magician. I met Jim in the late 1970s, and, together with my wife and daughter, we visited his vast sculptural/perceptual undertaking at Roden Crater in Arizona. Also, in his museum shows, the otherworldly ambient light in various room-size installation pieces had reminded me of descriptions I'd heard from UFO witnesses of the generalized but "sourceless" light they'd seen inside the craft. I found Turrell's 1983 piece, *Hover*, particularly unsettling in this way.

In 1996, Jim invited me, in my role as a UFO investigator, to speak at an important international Futurist conference he convened in Fribourg, Switzerland, and in the years since then he has continued to show a strong interest in my abduction research. As an indication of the importance accorded his work as an artist,

James Turrell was awarded a coveted, no-strings-attached MacArthur Grant. He is one of two recipients of this munificent "genius grant" who have contacted me about their interest in UFOs and the abduction phenomenon. (The other MacArthur recipient, a self-described possible abductee, wishes to remain anonymous.) So, contrary to the stand-up comics' snide little UFO jokes, it's not just "yokels in pick-up trucks" who take such reports seriously. And in this context it is worth noting that within the ultra sophisticated New York art world, two esteemed art dealers, Sidney Janis and Alan Stone, were also extremely interested in the UFO phenomenon and, having read my books, would ask me about the latest developments in the field whenever we met. Unfortunately, though, most of my art-world colleagues were either dubious or indifferent and, as one might expect, woefully ignorant of the supporting evidence.

Some writers, however, were refreshingly curious, though I was disappointed to find two prominent science-fiction novelists almost completely uninformed about a subject I thought should have interested them. Through a mutual friend I had met the novelist Kurt Vonnegut in the late 1960s, and though he visited my studio and we had a pleasant dinner together, we didn't discuss UFOs. At the time he seemed friendly, casual and open, but a few years later, when we met again at a party in Bob and B.J. Lifton's New York apartment, someone brought up the subject of UFOs and to my surprise Vonnegut coldly dismissed it as ridiculous. I had assumed that imaginative writers – and he was certainly that – would at least be curious about the phenomenon, but I could not have been more wrong.

In the late 1980s, I was a guest on a TV talk show along with the noted sci-fi novelist Ray Bradbury, and as if to assert his eccentricity Bradbury wore lederhosen and hiking shoes to the studio. A short, stocky man with hairy legs, Bradbury's odd ensemble clearly made its point to the TV audience. Since I'd brought along some good UFO photographs to display, as well as a sequence of pictures taken over a several year period to illustrate the changes in the soil at a reported UFO landing site, during the commercial breaks I showed them to him. As Bradbury and I chatted, I was surprised to learn that he had no idea such photos existed, or that there were ever any physical traces left at reputed UFO landing sites. In fact, he seemed totally uninformed and almost shocked that such material existed.

Thinking about it later, I theorized that sci-fi writers might like to have total control over their literary inventions, and thus anything like physical evidence for the UFO phenomenon might present an obstacle rather than a creative opportunity.

Among the writers on Cape Cod I had a few supporters and a few absolute, self-assured opponents. One example of the latter was Norman Mailer, whom I saw occasionally at Longpoint Gallery openings, cocktail parties, and elsewhere. He used to enjoy making sly, needling remarks to me, such as, "Well, Budd, are you still seeing those *things* flying around the sky at night?" while grinning with pleasure at his own sarcastic putdown. Some writers, however, were not so subtly teasing. Once, at a small Truro dinner party the painter Peter Watts gave for his friend, Dwight Macdonald, a guest asked me about my UFO work. Macdonald, a renowned, widely published, and self-important critic, had been dominating the conversation, and as it shifted over to my subject I could see that he was miffed to have temporarily lost the guests' attention. I tried to mutter a few things about my work and then gracefully extricate myself, but evidently I was not fast enough to suit him. Peter told me later that Macdonald had turned to him and in a stage whisper, heard by those seated near him, exclaimed, "UFOs are bullshit!"

With regard to Norman Mailer, I wondered if his wife, Norris Church, might have inadvertently stirred things up because she once told me she'd read all my books and had been particularly frightened by *Witnessed*, a later account of a UFO abduction near the Brooklyn Bridge in Manhattan. "I can see the area where that happened from our place in Brooklyn Heights," she said, "and I sometimes go out to look across the East River, just in case the UFO might come back." Maybe Norman didn't like her serious interest in what he regarded as a joke.

A major supporter of mine on the Cape was a marvelous man who was once our national poet laureate, Stanley Kunitz. Stanley had written a poem entitled "The Abduction," using an image from the Virginia Horton case in *Missing Time*, and in an article he included in his 1985 book, *Next To Last Things: New Poems and Essays*, he described the genesis of the poem: "[T]he scenario of her fantastic adventure clearly derived from a book I had been reading, written by a friend, about UFO abductions. One of the documents in the book is the transcript of an hypnotic session with a subject named Virginia, detailing her encounter in a glade with a 'beautiful deer… a mystical deer.'" It was this image and others from *Missing Time* that Stanley adopted and used in his poem.

Over the years I spent several evenings with Stanley and his artist wife, Elise Asher, bringing them up to date on recent UFO reports. Stanley Kunitz was a warm, highly intelligent man and a great poet, and remarkably, he lived to be 100 years old, tending his glorious botanical and poetical gardens almost to the end.

In my experience, musicians as a group are often more receptive than others to the idea of extraterrestrial visitors ("too much pot," a debunker would undoubtedly claim), and some musicians I've known were extremely interested. For example, the singer Phoebe Snow, with whom I've had many conversations about the UFO phenomenon, is intensely curious about, and well read on, the subject, while the classic big band drummer Buddy Rich said that next to music, UFOs were the thing that he cared about the most. He told me this as he sat exhausted in his dressing room after finishing a frantic set, a towel wound around his sweat-drenched neck and a robe clutched around him. He said that he had had a copy of *Missing Time* with him when he took his band on tour in the U.K., and the book kept getting passed around on the band bus until someone finally copped it for good. I gave him a replacement.

Buddy Rich also told of a strange personal encounter, later confirmed to me by his wife, during a late night trip from Las Vegas to Los Angeles. He said they were driving across the desert with the top down on his convertible, when something going very fast passed soundlessly over his car, only a hundred feet or so above it. In amazement, he stopped to look as it flew away, when another object suddenly zoomed over, and then another, all very low and making no effort to avoid him. It struck me as a curious story, and I wondered if there might not have been more to it that neither he nor his wife were recalling.

I met Buddy Rich's great friend, the masterful jazz singer Mel Tormé, in 1981, through his son, Tracy. After *Missing Time* appeared, Tracy called to introduce himself and say that he liked the book and was interested in taking an option on it for a possible film. But first, he said, he wanted me to meet with his father at the St. Regis Hotel to discuss things. I assumed that since Tracy was quite young and inexperienced he probably wanted his father to look me over and decide if I could be trusted, so I quickly agreed to go to the hotel and have a chat.

Mel Tormé was a short, friendly, cherubic man, and as he ushered me into his sitting room and we seated ourselves, he offered me a chocolate from an open Godiva box. He explained that because he was trying to diet, he always kept the tempting candy box in sight to strengthen his willpower. As I sampled a delicious piece, he watched me so carefully that I began to think his willpower-testing system was probably counterproductive.

As we talked, Mel told me about a UFO sighting he had had in New York in the early 1950s. At the time he was hosting an afternoon TV music and talk show and regarded the admission on his program of a personal UFO sighting as a kind of television first. The incident took place when he went out one evening to walk his dog and noticed that the dog had stopped and was staring up into the sky. Usually when a dog is outside being walked, his nose is about an inch off of the pavement; he is certainly not gazing skyward because that is not where the interesting smells are. Mel glanced up in the general direction that the dog was staring and noticed a bright light high above them, bigger than a star and apparently rather distant. He said it suddenly started to move and flew quickly downtown toward the Empire State Building where it stopped for a moment. Then it made a sharp right turn and flew across the Hudson River and out over New Jersey where he lost sight of it. He said the dog's gaze followed the light when it moved downtown, something which, for an animal, he found amazing. And that, he said, was the story of his brief but very unusual UFO sighting.

Though Mel approved of Tracy's idea of basing a film on *Miss-*

ing Time, nothing came of it, but some years later Tracy and I reconnected when he wrote the screenplay for *Intruders*, the 1992 CBS miniseries based on my second book. Underlining his continuing interest in the subject, Tracy also produced the screenplay for the film *Fire in the Sky*, about the spectacular 1975 Travis Walton abduction case.

Over the decades I've been contacted by many thousands of people who feel they may have themselves experienced UFO abductions, and I've dealt with scientists, police officers, high-ranking military personnel, psychiatrists (eight of them), pilots, physicians, business executives, lawyers, musicians, artists, writers – people from virtually all walks of life, even including a few admitted prostitutes and convicted felons. Some of these people are well known in their fields, and virtually all of them have requested anonymity. Recently, I saw on a network TV news program an interview with a prominent physician whose area of scientific research is currently receiving international attention. I recognized the scientist as an abductee whose UFO experiences I once helped to explore and whose name I have kept confidential ever since.

The one professional group most helpful to people reporting traumatic UFO abductions has been the mental health community: psychiatrists, psychologists, and psychotherapists. Together, their training and levels of education provide them with the ability to deal with people suffering from post-traumatic stress disorder (PTSD), a common problem for UFO abductees, and in addition they are skilled (ideally) in telling the difference between those with mental illnesses of some kind – delusional states, paranoia, etc. – and those suffering from the shock of genuine experiences. Fortunately, many practitioners are able to work effectively with clients despite their personal uncertainty about UFO reality. For example, psychiatrist Robert J. Lifton, who as I have recounted met and interviewed several probable abductees, told me that while he could not accept the reality of UFOs and the abduction phenomenon, he knew of no psychological theory that could comfortably explain the classical PTSD symptoms they were evincing.

From my point of view, that's fair enough.

Calming The Tremors

I'll return later to the subject of my second book, *Intruders*, but in 1987 the press attention caused by its nearly simultaneous appearance with two other books about UFO abductions – Gary Kinder's *Light Years* and Whitley Strieber's *Communion* – had a major effect on my life, dispatching me off to almost as many exotic climes as Marco Polo. Because artists are generally not devoted travelers, I would never have visited these unfamiliar places except for the nearly global interest in the UFO phenomenon and my contribution to its understanding. Painters, in fact, are more like nesters than nomads, and since we require our studios to be nicely set up and our tools ready to hand, bunking temporarily in strange countries is not an agreeable business. In his long life, Picasso, for example, never once came to the United States where he was wildly popular, and even in Europe he rarely traveled. Cezanne made his home in Aix-en-Provence and for a time in Paris, but otherwise saw very little of the rest of France, to say nothing of the rest of the world. Many prominent American artists, like Jackson Pollock, never made it to Europe, and De Kooning only returned to his native Holland very late in life. For most of us, New York has been a fixed and steady home, and when one Cedar Bar habitué, a painter, mentioned to Earl Kerkam that he was going to Chicago for a couple of weeks, Earl shot back, "Oh, so you're camping out?" as if the Second City was a remote forest dotted with tents and campfires.

Though I'd traveled several times to Europe, those earlier trips marked the limits of my modest geographical explorations, and even when I was in France or Italy I spent much of the time in museums or sightseeing or off sketching somewhere. But in the years after the publication of *Intruders* I began to receive invitations to speak at UFO conferences in places like Germany, the U.K., Mexico, France, the Netherlands, Switzerland, and in other, more exotic locations such as Brazil and Turkey. On two successive years I was in Istanbul, a place I never imagined I would visit, and I made three trips to Australia where, after lecturing, I was taken to a petting zoo where I could pat the flanks of resting kangaroos and gaze at stoned koalas, asleep in their eucalyptus trees. I learned that these poor little animals, which really do look like rubber-nosed toys, spend some twenty hours a day sleeping… dozing through most of their short lifetimes. What a sad thought.

The 1992 airing of the CBS miniseries based on *Intruders* led to yet another wave of promotional tours and international speaking engagements, which were abetted four years later with the publication of *Witnessed*, my third book, a four-hundred-page compendium of the evidence in a spectacular abduction case I shall also return to anon. The most important perk these expense-free trips provided was the opportunity, in my off time, to explore great art museums and historical monuments around the world. In one case, a single hour's TV appearance in a Spanish city gave me the chance to stay for a few days in Madrid where was I able to revisit the Prado and to see once more, at the Reina Sofia, Picasso's *Guernica*, along with most of the great studies he did in its preparation. For years *Guernica* had been exiled to New York's Museum of Modern Art where Picasso left it while he, and most of world, awaited the death of Francisco Franco and the end of Spanish fascism. Without doubt the twentieth-century's most powerful anti-war painting, *Guernica* commemorated in horrifying, symbolic detail the Nazi bombing of that small, defenseless city during the Spanish Civil War. Years later, Picasso's intense hatred for fascism led to a famous incident when, during the Nazi occupation of France, some German officers visited his studio. Silently he gave each of them a small reproduction of *Guernica*, and when one German asked, "Did you do this?" Picasso answered, "No. You did."

Though I was rarely able to spend much time drawing during these short overseas junkets, I accomplished something else that was, in its own way, equally valuable. Though my lectures and media appearances about the UFO phenomenon were often emotionally fraught – I was dealing, after all, with an unpleasant subject

– the next day I could usually calm the tremors by visiting an art museum or a cathedral or a great work of architecture to allow the serenity of past centuries to seep into me and erase the sense of impermanence I'd been feeling. In the context of the dread I felt about the UFO phenomenon, I could bathe in the stable glories of the past and return home refreshed and even hopeful.

I began to think in the broadest emotional terms about the art I was seeing, and, as I've described before, I became adept at sorting out what most nourished me. The Egyptian art I saw in the British Museum and the Louvre, though sculpturally powerful and enduring, was not what I needed. Its eternal rigidities, its rejection of actual life in favor of a belief in a grandiose hereafter, bothered me, as did the knowledge that all of it had been produced on the backs of thousands of slaves for the sole glory of the priests and pharaohs.

Greek art, on the other hand, embraced daily life – physical, sensual existence – and I was increasingly drawn to it. Unlike Egyptian art, in which the figures stand bolt upright in a military posture, arms stiffly at their sides, and eyes straight ahead, in Greek art the athletes and goddesses slouch casually, one leg stiff and one relaxed, much the way we stand around waiting for a bus. The Greeks rendered female figures as softly seductive and appealing, their delicate hands simultaneously hiding and calling attention to their breasts and pudenda, while the ancient art of Egypt barely differentiates between genders. In another, almost unconscious reaction, I saw the static, hieratic, sexless world of Egyptian art as uncomfortably close to that of the fixed, emotionless world of the UFO occupants. By contrast, the culture of the Greeks, with their amorous, jealous, sometimes petty gods, and their realistically carved images of muscular warrior-heroes and sensuous maidens, seemed both familiar and admirable. Its life-affirming values offered me an emotional antidote to the UFO abductees' descriptions of their non-human, technocratic captors.

On one of my trips to Mexico I was exposed to Mayan art and architecture, and I was struck, despite its monumentality, by how death-oriented it was. At Chichen Itza there is a formal, walled-in ball court where a ritual game was played, the losing team members receiving the honor of being sacrificed to the gods. The surrounding walls, platforms, and raised reviewing stand reminded me of Albert Speer's equally merciless design for Hitler's vast Nazi parade ground at Nuremburg, the setting for Leni Riefenstahl's infamous Nazi propaganda film, *Triumph of the Will*. At heart, Mayan art and architecture seems as death oriented as its Egyptian counterpart, the difference being that the ancient Mexicans probably slaughtered more innocent people in their bloody rituals than any ten Pharaohs ever dreamt of doing.

I've noticed and find rather curious that many people holding New Age beliefs invariably show far more interest in the ancient Egyptians and Mayans – inherently enigmatic, death-centered cultures – than in the earthier Greeks or Romans, or even in the more "primitive" but once-vital cultures of tribal Oceania and Africa. I've thought that this preference may be due to the New Agers' profound hunger for mystery, and a belief, if not in the afterlife, then in a kind of spiritual Golden Age in which the foibles and weaknesses of mere humans such as ourselves are somehow replaced by a greater spiritual polity. Greek art is probably too physical and "normal" and its gods too much like errant human beings for New Age adherents to accept it as sufficiently mystical and enigmatic. But then, of course, maybe I'm wrong.

Another thing I've noticed as I've grown older, and that I may also be wrong about, is that no group seems as set in its tastes, even to the point of esthetic bigotry, as young, beginning painters in art school: "I hate Picasso. He's flashy and Matisse is far greater," or "Ingres is a bore and I can't stand his work," or "Rembrandt is just too dark for me. Why can't he lighten up?" and on and on. Happily for artists, age and experience broaden us, and to paraphrase Mark Twain, eventually the once-certain young student is now surprised by how much better Picasso's early work has gotten in the past few years, or how the light in Rembrandt' paintings seems to be far more interesting and varied than it used to be.

But the irony here is that in our middle years that hard-won ecumenical flexibility begins to melt away and we become rigid again, not exactly in the way of the intolerant, ignorant beginner, but because art has now become even more essential, and thus, like a shelf full of tonics, some of it works for us and some of it doesn't. Brancusi, for example, gives me far more spiritual nourishment than, say, Henry Moore, who, despite his sculptural skills, has become a bore. In fact, to my perhaps bigoted eyes and ears, English sculpture of the 1950s and 1960s is strained, mannered, and unnatural in the same way that Episcopalian stand-up comedy would be if such a peculiar thing existed.

In my later years my own work has been animated by a deepening desire for order and serenity, an emotional chord that I believe to be a source of its own kind of spirituality. The Guardian image remains my central preoccupation, though age and ill-health have affected both my rate of production and the scale of the work I can easily handle. It's still hard to imagine just how much time has passed since my first show in New York in 1956, but I had a vivid reminder in 2002 when I was given a one-man exhibition in Andre Zarre's Chelsea gallery. At the opening, a handsome older man with salt-and-pepper hair approached and congratulated me on my new work.

"I own a few things of yours," he said. "I bought them some years ago at the Poindexter Gallery." Not recognizing him, I asked his name, and when he said "Edward Albee" I gasped and recalled that he had bought two or three collages in, I believe, 1964, almost 40 years earlier. At that time, his hit play, *Who's Afraid of Virginia Woolf,* was playing on Broadway, and when my dealer told me that its author had bought my work, I was as thrilled as if the purchaser had been the Metropolitan Museum. So, four decades later he was here again at a show of mine, looking grayer and older like me, but once again I felt the rush of excitement I had when I was young and new at the game and had just been told that the famous playwright had bought my work. The vast gap of years between then and now melted for a moment but then quickly re-ossified, leaving me alternately sad yet very happy.

Age was definitely becoming an issue for me. As I write these words I have already passed the legendary life span of three score years and ten, and my thoughts continue to wander to the question of how many more there might be. Apart from helping to slow down the rush of time, writing this memoir has offered a way of firming up the many disparate parts of my complicated and unconventional life, as if I were sorting through boxes of old photographs and gluing the significant ones down into an album in vaguely chronological order. It's a forced, rather artificial, but gratifying business that has its rewards. The inherent strangeness of memoir writing is nicely revealed in the cynical but not inaccurate title that Preston Sturges, the great 1940s comedy filmmaker, gave to his still unpublished autobiography: *Events Leading Up To My Death.*

Unavoidably, though, mortality has insisted upon casting its shadows. In 1990, my mother passed away at the age of 88 after a series of illnesses. To place her life in a rough chronological context, she came into the world three years after the birth of Ernest Hemingway, three years before the arrival of Greta Garbo, and two years before the birth of Willem De Kooning and the British writer Nancy Mitford, and aside from the virtually indestructible De Kooning, she managed to outlive them all. Throughout her long life she lived almost entirely for her family and had few other outside interests – certainly not those of painting, writing, or film acting. To me she was always a loving, even doting mother and grandmother, and after my father's death in 1966 she lived alone and continued to involve herself mainly in the lives of her children and their offspring.

My family was not comprised of people who cherished the life of the mind, and I can't recall ever seeing my mother reading a book. But late in life she told me she liked to re-read Agatha Christie's whodunits; they were still suspenseful the second or third time around because, she said, she could never recall who the killers were. When *Missing Time* and *Intruders* first appeared, I sent her copies of each but she shyly confessed that they scared her so badly she never finished either one.

My mother was, in fact, a mass of fears, and I have never known anyone as helplessly phobic as she. Her claustrophobia was so crippling that she could scarcely bring herself to ride in an elevator. She also had a peculiar avian problem: she was terrified if a bird flew near her head, and if she came across a dead bird – to her, an even more unspeakable horror – she would close her eyes and flee blindly. She regarded mice, bats, and rats as so ghastly that even a photograph of one of these little animals could send her racing out of the room. One of the classic, much-repeated family stories involves a phone conversation between my mother and Mary Jane Hopkins, my brother's wife, in their respective homes located in different neighborhoods. As they chatted, Mary Jane suddenly remarked that a mouse had just run across the floor in her living room. A half mile away, in her own house, my mother screamed and frantically climbed up on a chair, almost weeping with fright and unwilling to move until Mary Jane drove up to assure her that it was safe to climb back down.

I have no idea what lay behind my mother's vast bundle of phobias, and I'm grateful my siblings and I inherited none of them. But for her, her otherwise pleasant visits to New York were fraught with imaginary danger – naturally, she was afraid of flying – and I sometimes found it difficult to walk the streets with her because she sensed muggers lurking everywhere. Luckily for me, however, she had a great sense of humor about her fears, and when I gently teased her about them I usually made her laugh. It seemed for the moment to make them a bit less lethal for her, and it reminded me that a sense of fun was one of her most abiding qualities.

My mother's conversational agenda did not permit discussions of sex, religion, or politics, and since art, music, and literature were not subjects with which she was familiar, whenever I saw her in Wheeling, we chatted almost exclusively about family affairs. I can recall only one brief political statement she made, sometime back in the late 1970s, and it was a pure reflection of her values. President Jimmy Carter and his wife had just returned from a state visit to Japan, and my mother was outraged. She had read somewhere that in official Japanese motorcades the husband being honored always rode in one car and the wife followed humbly behind in a second car. She was furious because the President insisted that he and his wife *ride in the same car!* This, she felt, was an inexcusable breach of etiquette and that Carter had done something unforgivable. Obviously, in the 1970s, Women's Lib had not yet swept through the slumberous lanes of Wheeling, W. Va., and for my mother's generation, the idea of equal rights for women was just one more step toward perdition.

But despite her fears and general lack of curiosity about the world, she was always a warm and loving presence in my life, especially during my earliest, disease-ridden years when her nurturance and unconditional love kept me going. Later, whenever I gave her a painting or a drawing for her birthday or as a Christmas gift, she always hung it on her wall immediately, though some of my work must have seemed a bit strange to her and her circle of friends. Still, her uncritical pride in my work was another sign of the love that she never hesitated to offer, and which was so important throughout our life together. It's a sad truism that if we're lucky, we live long enough to become orphans. But then we have plenty of time left to miss our parents.

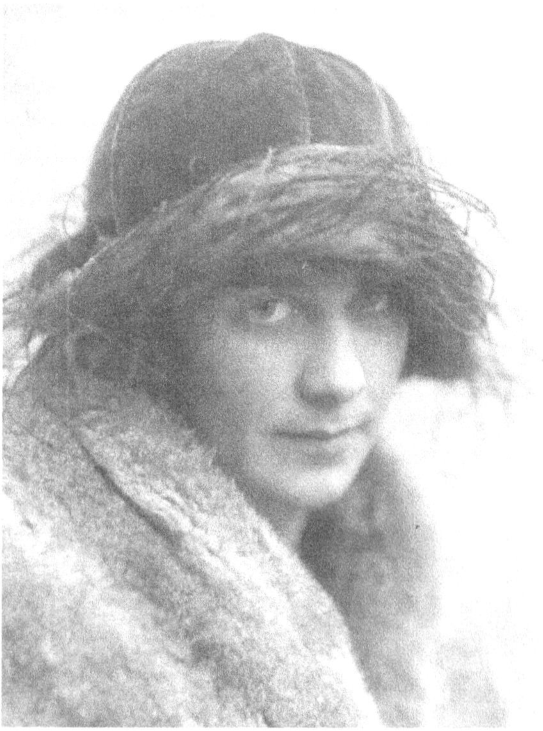

My beautiful mother, circa 1920, the year of her marriage.

Robert Motherwell and the Sculpture Years

In 1983, in addition to producing more Guardian paintings, I found myself making large, three-dimensional wooden Altars and Gates. Apart from my 1981 trip to Greece, I had no clear idea of what led me to take up a medium I was unfamiliar with, especially since for years I'd hardly thought about sculpture. In 1953, when I first came to New York, I shared the smug, condescending attitude many painters had toward the medium, and agreed with Ad Reinhardt's cutting definition of a sculpture as something a painter backs into while looking at a painting. Also, at that early time it seemed to me that "Abstract Expressionist Sculpture" was an oxymoron because the liquid, gestural qualities of AbEx paint handling, such as De Kooning's or Pollock's, could not possibly be translated into a vocabulary of heavy, three-dimensional materials like metal or stone or wood. Nevertheless, between 1982, the year of *Ritual Bridge*, and the early 1990s, I found myself obsessively making large, evocative Altars and Gates from old wooden structural members that I salvaged from dumpsters, recycling yards, and the remains of decaying barns. It had taken me 30 years to decide that sculpture was a viable option after all, and when I made that decision I plunged in headfirst.

In retrospect, this intense period of sculpture making is another example of the way my life would suddenly take another turn without my seeming to will it or understand how the new "whatever" was connected to the old. The trip to Greece was, of course, a crucial element in my attraction to sculpture, but I've only recently understood another, perhaps deeper, reason why the Altars and their kin came into being. Since all of these new sculptures were made of aged, unpainted wooden beams, they suggest objects that might have been used centuries ago by worshippers in an unknown, primitive cult of some sort. Resolutely symmetrical and designed to

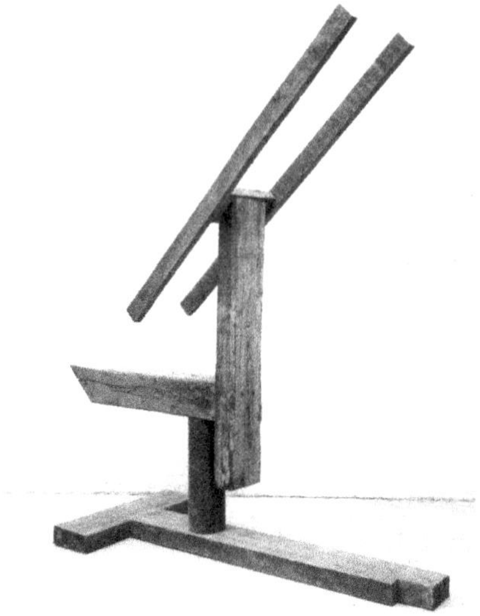

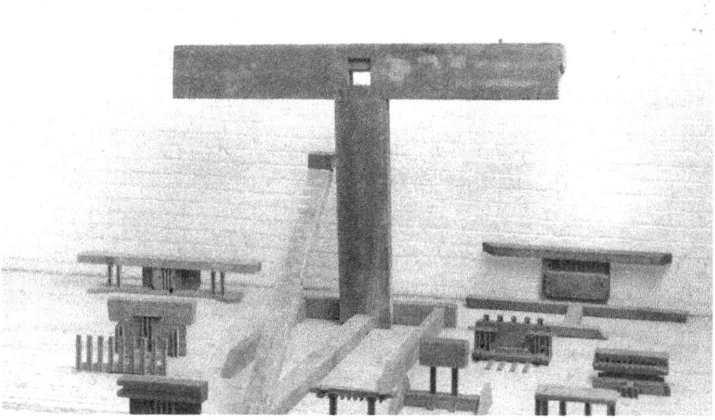

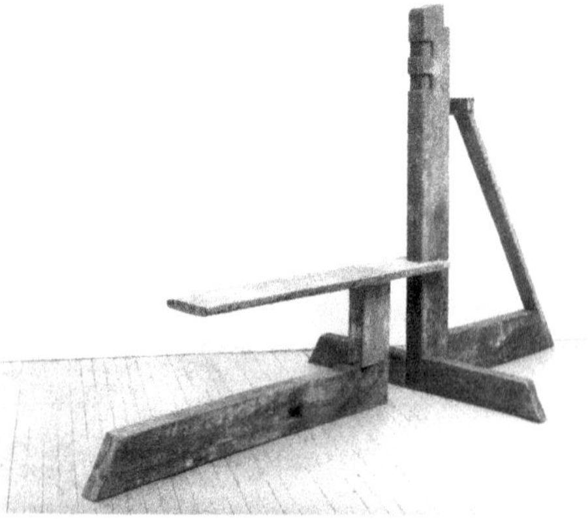

Top to bottom: *Sky Altar, 1986, 105"x 36"x 93"; Altar and Small Temples, 1990; Altar, 1985, 80"x 60"x 139".*

stand on the floor without a base, these table-like Altars look as if they had once been functional pieces of ritualistic furniture.

I now can see that, in the 1980s, as I became more deeply involved in the enigmatic UFO phenomenon with its corollary of an uncertain future, I felt an unconscious need *to go back in time* and to invent objects from a mythical past that evoked their own earthbound mystery. If UFOs, with their unearthly lights and gravity-defying movements, were amazing pieces of slick, quasi-"spiritual" technology, my wooden Altars and Gates were exactly the opposite: old, weathered, and fixed, and emitting a very different kind of implied spirituality. And since these ancient-seeming objects were also things I could make by hand, they were under my complete control – something, God knows, that UFOs never were.

If the Guardians and the white, wall-mounted Temples they flanked were clean, brightly painted modernist works, the worn, monochrome Altars invoked another era altogether, creating a juxtaposition that I found deeply satisfying. In my 1988 show at the Marilyn Pearl Gallery in Soho, I exhibited a series of active, coloristic Guardian paintings interspersed with large, wood-brown, self-contained Altars. This abrupt pairing of the energetic with the serene seemed to create its own Sacred Space, and the critic Michael Brenson, reviewing my show for *The New York Times*, stated that "Budd Hopkins is one of the very few artists whose work argues for the necessity of measuring current artistic achievements against the great art of the past." Robert Motherwell, in a short piece he wrote about my work, mentioned its "ritualistic sense," and added that it suggested "a sacred place where holy personages may be lurking..." So, it seems, as I wandered into uncharted, futuristic waters in my UFO investigations, in my art I was doing the opposite: I was traveling back in time to a mysteriously mythic age that was, paradoxically, completely of my own invention.

I have written elsewhere that through my paintings, particularly the intensely colored Guardians, I hoped to add energy to the world, but the stolid, enigmatic character of the Altars seemed to do the opposite, drawing the viewers' energy out to be absorbed in their weathered presence. If, as a maker of altars, I might appear to be interested in the religious or the spiritual, I remained outside any fixed dogma or spiritual practice; it might be said that I was drawn to the *religious* but not to *religion*. In a short piece I wrote for the catalogue of my 1988 show at Marilyn Pearl, I summed it up this way: "Over the centuries, from Lascaux to Athens to the present, what has changed in art is endlessly fascinating, but what has remained the same is even more important. We can no longer easily accept the answers provided by the traditional religions, but artists, as we have done for centuries, can still raise the same transcendental questions. Because we are, at heart, mediators, making objects that begin in our own physicality and yet ultimately point outside ourselves to all the final mysteries."

Important as I thought these sculptures were, the practical aspects of their making were both time-consuming and space-devouring. Some of my Altars were eight or nine feet long and up to seven feet tall. Working on these large, heavy pieces was difficult enough, but problems of storage soon became acute. Unfortunately there was only a small market in New York for large sculptures, and I was still new enough in the field to have difficulty in selling what I was turning out. One Altar was acquired by the Guggenheim Museum, and a few years later, Joan and Bugs Baer commissioned me to make a large outdoor sculpture for their Connecticut home. *Table and Gate* was installed there in the early 1990s; it is still the only permanent outdoor sculpture for which I've been commissioned.

In 1982 I received a Special Projects Grant from the New York State Council on the Arts that enabled me to put together a small artist's book entitled *Sacred Spaces: The Book of Temples, Guardians and Altars*. It is essentially a picture book of many art works from across the ages, among them, Stonehenge and the Parthenon (Temples), an Assyrian relief and a Piero della Francesca painting (Guardians), and the Inti-Huatana at Peru's Machu Piccu (an Altar). These classic images are interspersed with relevant modern paintings and sculptures, my own and others, by such artists as Constantin Brancusi, Piet Mondrian, Josef Albers, and Robert Morris. The short texts, reproduced in my handwriting, comment upon each of the three major components in *Sacred Spaces*, and end with a story – one of my favorites – that gives an ironic edge to the whole enterprise: A kindergarten teacher asked the children in her class to paint whatever they wished. Later, she inquired of each child what he or she was painting. "A picture of Mommy" or "My cat" were typical answers.

One child, however, said, "I'm painting a picture of God."

"But how can you paint God?" the teacher asked. "No one knows what God looks like."

"Wait till I finish the painting," the child replied.

It's a statement that Fra Angelico could possibly have made – he seemed to know what God looked like – but it would have made Mark Rothko blush. It makes me a bit uncomfortable, too, which is why I included it in my little book.

My choice of material for the Altars – notched, antique wooden beams – had to do with my desire to convey great age. Nothing modern, no paint, no fancy carving – just a range of brown and gray colors and splintery surfaces was what I wanted. I had taken to heart Gustave Flaubert's famous dictum that "an artist should be in his work like God in nature – present everywhere but visible nowhere," so I tried to conceal the saw cuts I made in the wood as well as the modern hardware I used to fasten the beams together. I came to feel a deep affection for the notches and bevels that skilled, unknown carpenters had made in them years ago, visual testimony to the heavy timbers' one-time functions as floor beams and wall supports. It was all a far cry from my clean, color-drenched abstract paintings that so clearly belonged to the ethos of the twentieth century, but somehow, in my heart, I needed both to feel complete.

During a conversation I had one day with Robert Motherwell, we talked about Frank Lloyd Wright and the magnificent house, Fallingwater, he built in Pennsylvania for the Kaufman family. I told him of my interest in the structure's collage quality, in which clean, reinforced concrete units were interspersed with native stone-and-mortar sections. One dramatically cantilevered "modern" section overhung another, more traditional post-and-lintel area, creating a modern/ancient contrast not unlike my own Guardian/Altar combination. I mentioned that this structural system also reminded me of the way, as a child, I played with rough wooden blocks of unequal lengths, which often forced me to use cantilevered projections in my little forts and houses. I admitted that the dramatic cantilevers I used in my recent Altars and Gates might have come from my having built things in a similar way as a child.

Robert seemed interested, and a few days later he called me to say that he had been reading about Frank Lloyd Wright and had learned that Wright's mother had given him, as a child, a set of Froebel blocks, a special educational toy developed by the man who initiated the idea of pre-school kindergarten classes ("kindergarten" is a German word). He told me that Wright always said that building things with these toy blocks profoundly influenced his eventual decision to become an architect. A few days after this phone call, a UPS truck drove up to my Wellfleet house with a package from Robert: a complete set of the famous, newly reissued Froebel blocks that he had ordered for me as a result of our conversation. It was a thoughtful and generous gift, and it provided Grace and me many happy afternoons together building tabletop altars, fortresses, and *faux* Frank Lloyd Wright houses.

During the twenty years we were colleagues at the Longpoint Gallery, Robert and I became friends, and despite his seniority in years, his greater experience, and art-world success, I sensed that in some way he felt there were similarities in our creative lives. This manifested itself in an odd duality of closeness and distance that appeared in the way I instinctively addressed him. In any formal or public situation – a gallery opening, Cape cocktail party, panel discussion, or the like, he was "Robert," the senior artist; but in our talks together, in visits to one another's studios, or in more intimate dinners, I always called him "Bob," as if we were equals. It seemed to me that he liked my two-tiered system of address and appreciated its tactfulness.

I was, of course, aware that he had come from a wealthy, upper-class family, and that he alone of the early Abstract Expressionists had never had to worry about his daily bread. He was resented for his affluence by many of his struggling colleagues, and his educational advantages, including years at Harvard University, only created envy among those who had never been to any college, let alone such a prestigious one. Just as damaging to his chance of being regarded as "one of the boys" in those years was the fact that he was exceptionally articulate, and as I've mentioned, he acted in the 1950s as a kind of informal spokesman for the Abstract Expressionist movement. Though his colleagues benefited from his ability to eloquently discuss both his and their paintings with relatively uncomprehending critics and collectors, even this contribution was held against him; "Art should be seen and not talked about" was the general objection (or perhaps rationalization).

In those early years Robert read compulsively, taught frequently, and wrote and lectured widely, acting as a kind of artist/writer/intellectual hybrid. It is in some of these areas, I believe, that he saw me to some extent as a younger version of himself, even asking me, as I've written earlier, to take his place as editor of the prestigious series *Documents of Modern Art.* As I think about it, if I subtract his money and replace his Harvard years with mine at Oberlin, there are some similarities. For years Robert had been a sought-after writer and editor on art subjects, and though I was infinitely less prolific than he, I had also been commissioned to write a number of articles for major art magazines. And here I am now, writing a longish memoir after having published four books on the UFO phenomenon (a subject we never discussed because I sensed he was uninterested). All things considered, it's fair to say that we both enjoyed a kind of literary sideline.

Also, like him I have taught fairly frequently in visiting artist venues and have lectured here and there about modern painting. In 1979, when the Carnegie Institute in Pittsburgh organized a De Kooning retrospective, Robert was invited to give a talk on the exhibition. For some reason, he declined and called to ask me to speak in his place. I gratefully accepted and had a fine time at the Carnegie (which owns a large painting of mine), though I have a hunch that the honorarium I received was a bit less than the one Robert had been offered. Under the circumstances, I was Billy Crudup going in for Tom Cruise.

One afternoon Bob visited my New York apartment and saw on my walls some older drawings I'd collected: a Cezanne, a Corot, a Delacroix, and a Mondrian, among others, along with works of my contemporaries, like Robert Beauchamp, Sideo Fromboluti, Robert Henry, Nora Speyer, and many others. He studied each drawing in turn and then said with a smile: "Another thing we have in common, Budd, is that we're both art buffs. Not all artists are art buffs." He, too, had collected other artists' work over the years – including, I'm pleased to say, a few Hopkins. At his home in Greenwich, Connecticut, he showed me a Miro oil that, he proudly said, he'd exchanged with a dealer for a Motherwell painting. He also owned first-rate works by Franz Kline, Joseph Cornell, Henri Matisse, and many others. I'm always happy to see artists collecting other artists' work, though it was rare within the early AbEx group. Bob's term, "art buffs," was a casual, off-the-cuff name for serious artists collecting serious art, a rubric that includes Degas and Picasso, each of whom had a distinguished art collection.

A crucial aspect of our friendship had to do with his trust in my response to his work. I once told him that I had seen a show of his Spanish Elegy paintings, and though I praised them highly – they are, I believe, his finest works – I said that I thought one large painting in the series was a failure. Circumstances suggested that he was about to donate it to a major museum, and I told him I thought it would be a mistake to do so. We had been having drinks on his deck in Provincetown and he asked me to come inside and show him, in a catalogue, which painting I meant. I felt very conflicted about doing so, but I cared too much about his work not to respond. I turned to the reproduction of this questionable Elegy and explained in detail my reservations about it. He thanked me, very sincerely I thought, and the painting was subsequently withdrawn. It had been reproduced in an earlier monograph on his work, and when the book was reissued in a revised edition, the image was dropped.

The incident is important to me for two reasons: it demonstrated Robert's trust in my judgment, and showed his determination to make sure his work in public venues represented him at his best.

He understood, I think, that presenting this particular painting to a major museum would lower the esteem his Spanish Elegy series had always enjoyed.

Despite a certain Olympian manner that Robert adapted from time to time – a pose that irritated many of his contemporaries – he was not a superman. In many respects he was just like the rest of us in that he could be very unsure of the success of particular paintings and eager for a critical analysis by a colleague's different pair of eyes. I was astonished once by a remark he made while looking through a catalogue of my work: "Budd, you paint with such assurance." I was flattered, of course, but surprised by what seemed to be a personally revealing remark. After all, I feel that I'm just like so many of my fellow painters, working away, hoping to turn out something good, and ultimately far from certain of the results, just as Bob was about his errant Elegy painting. (For that matter, I've recently destroyed eleven of my older paintings that I came to regard as failures.)

By common consent, Robert Motherwell was a complicated, extraordinarily intelligent and often difficult man. He once remarked to me that in his view, all artists are monsters, but as I found, he could also be an affectionate and generous friend. Many of his paintings, like his Spanish Elegies in museums such as Buffalo's Albright-Knox and New York's Metropolitan, are twentieth century masterpieces, but he also produced too many smaller paintings and collages that now seem overly seductive, elegant, and a bit self-indulgent. He was probably America's finest translator of French modernist painting – of Matisse in particular – into an AbEx, American idiom, a fact that partly accounts for his great success with collectors. But this ability also provided a reason why he was looked down upon by some of his early colleagues, men who were opposed to classic French modernism and wanted to replace it rather than expand upon it. I also noticed that Robert seemed to have no real interest in sculpture, though he and David Smith had been close friends, and I don't recall any extended conversation we ever had about my large Altars and Gates. Paintings, yes, sculpture, no.

Robert Motherwell was a complex, truly remarkable man, and at his best a great painter. In July 1991, he suffered a heart attack in his Provincetown studio, and when help arrived, he asked to be placed so he could look out towards his beloved harbor. He died there at the age of 76. His widow, the photographer Renate Ponsold, arranged a memorial service for him on the beach behind his studio, in the place he had taken his final look at the sea. I had written a short poem about him, a kind of homage, and she asked me to read it during the service. I am not a poet, but what I said that day was heartfelt.

Intruders

In real life, time seems to sweep by in one wide, unstoppable current, but in retrospect I know that many individual brooks and streams have, year by year, coursed together to form this restless flow. Looking back to 1983, I can see that the composite branches in my life were many and disparate, beginning with the period in which sculpture-making temporarily overcame my painting.

But 1983 was also the year that I began to practice hypnosis in my work with UFO abductees. Hypnosis had proved to be extremely helpful in overcoming the memory blocks that are apparently imposed by the UFO occupants, though in a sizeable number of abduction cases the abductees remember their traumatic experiences through normal, conscious recall. However, for the prior seven years, I had availed myself of the time and skills of various psychologists – Aphrodite Clamar, in particular – and psychiatrists like Robert Naiman and Donald Klein, as well as that of other hypnotherapists in New York and Cape Cod who agreed to conduct sessions with possible abductees. These mental health professionals were variously intrigued by the subject of UFOs, skeptical of it, mildly curious, or simply willing to contribute their time out of generosity and friendship. During those seven years, I observed a range of different hypnotic styles and techniques, and, as I have said, I essentially underwent what may be one of the longest apprenticeships anyone has yet served in mastering this useful art. By necessity, my earlier work with abductees had included more than a hint of the therapeutic, but when I began to use hypnosis to help people revisit often traumatic UFO encounters, I found myself, like it or not, practicing a kind of *de facto* therapy. And this somber new role required changes in my usual lifestyle.

From the time April Kingsley and I first met, we had shared an almost identical spirit of personal freedom and erotic exploration.

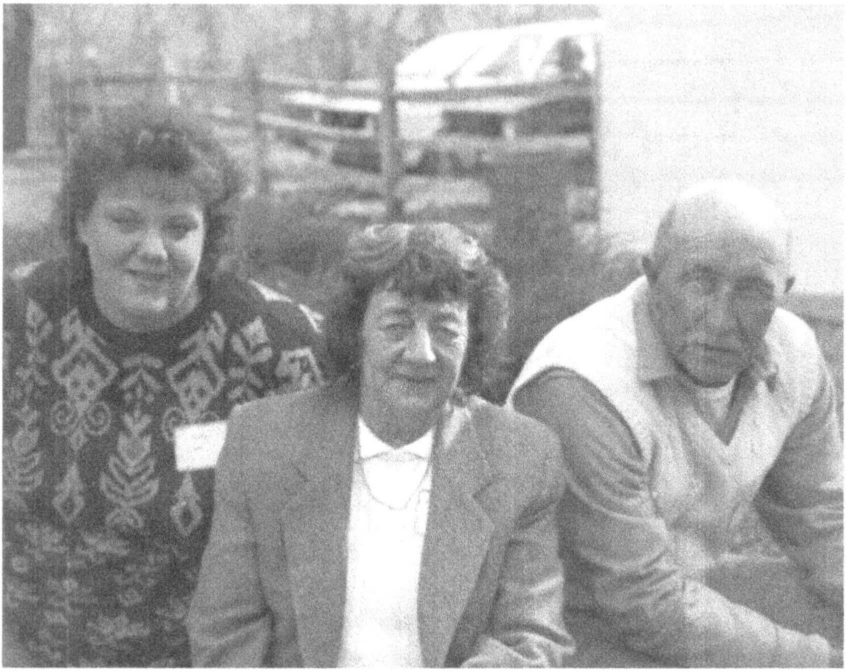

Three of the most important figures in the literature of UFO abductions: left to right, Debbie Kauble, (aka "Kathie Davis"), Betty Hill, Charles Hickson. Photo courtesy of Rosemary Osnato.

Though our relationship was not a formally proclaimed "open marriage," it was something very much like it, particularly during the first few years we were together. Old habits and hungers die slowly, and it was difficult for me to shake off the casual, relatively free-wheeling existence I'd enjoyed off and on since my arrival in New York 30 years before. But now, in 1983, as I began to understand my complex new responsibilities in working with abductees, I realized that I had to accept a much stricter lifestyle. So, in its placid way, another, quieter stream joined, and calmed, some of the swirling older currents of my life.

Also in 1983, and crowning the events of that seminal year, I received, in September, an extraordinary letter from a young woman in Indiana who was writing in response to my book *Missing Time*. "Kathie Davis" enclosed a series of photographs of dramatic changes in the soil and vegetation within a circular area on her family's property where a UFO had apparently landed a few weeks before. She also described an intriguing missing time episode her sister, "Laura," had experienced. Laura, she wrote, had been driving home late one afternoon, when for some reason she found herself compelled to pull off the main road and turn into a parking lot behind a local church. When she stopped the car and looked up, she saw a large UFO with multicolored lights hovering at telephone-pole height. Her next memory was that it was nighttime, she was once more driving down the street, and the church, the UFO, and the parking lot were gone. She was aware that she had "lost" several hours.

Kathie's handwritten letter went on to describe the "missing time" experiences of several of her family members, and she admitted having had some disturbing "dreams" of her own. I called her in response, and, partly because of the dramatic ground traces in the photographs she'd sent, I began an investigation. The next few years of intensive research led to the discovery of what might be called the Rosetta Stone of the UFO phenomenon: the apparent purpose of the aliens' program of human abductions.

But before that became clear I learned that the Kathie Davis case involved two witnesses who attested to Kathie's own period of missing time at the UFO landing site; a history of UFO abduction memories across three generations of her family; and a series of "scoop marks" – small, virtually identical scars that seem to result from alien sampling procedures – on Kathie, her mother, and her next-door neighbor, "Joyce Lloyd." (Subsequently I've seen scoop marks on the bodies of roughly one hundred different abductees, but these three were the first.)

At the hour we believe the landed UFO took off from behind Kathie's house, Joyce Lloyd, idly watching TV at home about 100 yards away, was terrified by a sudden flash of blinding light, earthquake-like tremors, and a complete but temporary power outage. Her husband, generally skeptical of the UFO phenomenon, admitted to me that when he returned home that night his wife was extraordinarily frightened by these events in her normally placid house. And there was more. At various times, two of Kathie's women friends, her sister, Laura, and members of her sister's family seemed to have had additional abduction experiences. All in all there were nearly two dozen witnesses to one or more aspects of this complex, many-leveled saga, and its dramatic central discovery would eventually be documented in detail in 1987 in my second book, *Intruders: The Incredible Visitations at Copley Woods.*

There was another life-altering current that flowed into my life in the early 1980s: I met David Jacobs, the man who would eventually become my closest colleague in the field of abduction research as well as one of my dearest friends. David was a professor of history at Temple University and had become interested in the UFO phenomenon when he was a graduate student. He went on to write a pioneering Ph.D. thesis on the subject, and even more significant for an aspiring young academic, his paper was reworked into book form and published by the prestigious Indiana University Press in 1975. It was reissued the following year as a Signet paperback entitled *The UFO Controversy in America,* with an introduction by Dr. J. Allen Hynek and a supportive jacket blurb by the normally

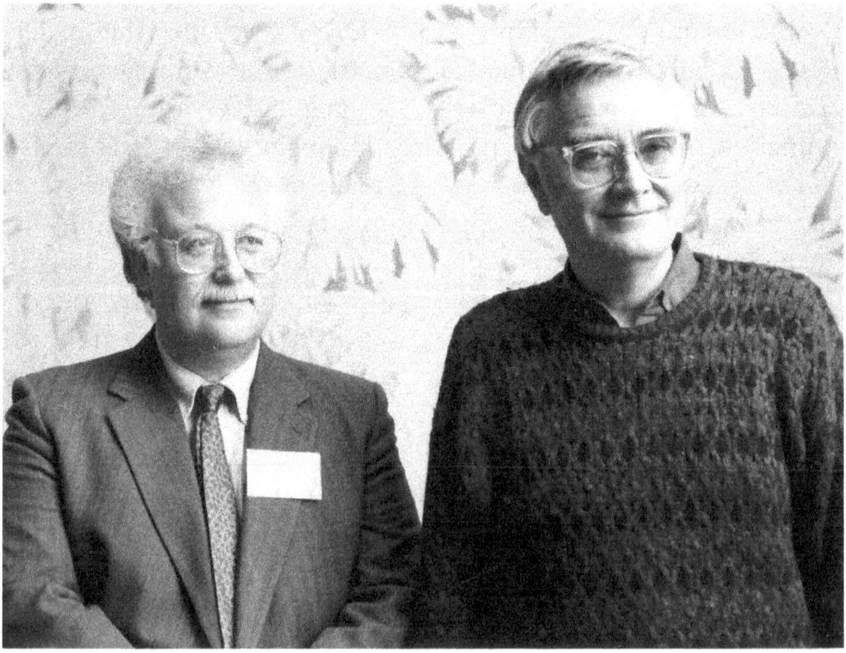

Dr. David M. Jacobs and I, circa 1998.

skeptical Arthur C. Clarke.

The way David and I met is not without irony. In 1981, a short time after *Missing Time* appeared, we were both speaking at a UFO conference in Chicago. During a lull, David introduced himself and, with a certain air of suspicion, mentioned an odd contradiction in my new book. Just before it was published, Virginia Horton, checking the galleys, had asked me to make several changes to place-names in her chapter that she felt might somehow identify her. Since she was extraordinarily concerned about maintaining her anonymity, I altered one reference to a specific location but overlooked the second, thus placing an important incident in two different European countries. As I nervously tried to explain the problem, David kept looking at me with narrowed, distrustful eyes. Finally, I decided to skip the politicians' passive locution, "mistakes were made," and admit my grievous error like a man. (I plan to have "The Errata Stop Here" etched into a bronze plaque to sit facing me at my work desk.) David finally relented and accepted my explanation of the mistake and we've been friends ever since.

However, the real problem about that first meeting had to do with his early discomfort with the UFO abduction phenomenon *per se*. Like many mainstream UFO researchers – and David Jacobs was very mainstream in 1981 – he had doubts about the whole abduction business. That might seem strange at the present time to those who think of him as being out on the cutting edge of research, running the risks, taking the hits, and doing the work the debunkers most love to denounce. I see him, however, as the bravest of the brave, because his rational, highly intelligent abduction investigations and his seminal books, *Secret Life* and *The Threat*, have changed the face and content of UFO research.

But there are the other sides to this remarkable man. He is an extremely popular history professor whom the Temple students have voted "teacher of the year," and, another time, "advisor of the year." He is an astute photography collector, who, with modest means, has assembled a noteworthy group of classic photographs, as well as a number of fine paintings and drawings (some of which, in the interest of full disclosure, I admit I made myself). And then there is David Jacobs, the consummate speaker and self-deprecating wit, who always protests during his talks that his brains are fried and his memory shot, even while he cites his sources precisely, chapter and verse. In his funny, disarming way he manages to have his audience at his feet, every trace of resistance gone.

So David entered my life in 1981 and I entered his, perhaps to his detriment, because he was soon as hooked as I was on the most arcane aspects of the UFO phenomenon. He became fascinated with the use of hypnosis as an investigative tool in missing time cases and plunged headfirst into the literature on the subject. He devoured books on technique, consulted frequently with a psychiatrist friend, and within a year or so had become a first-rate hypnotist.

Meanwhile, I was looking into the Kathie Davis case, telephoning several of the central witnesses, talking at length with Kathie and her family members, and finally arranging for her to visit me in New York. During the next three years I twice visited her at her Indianapolis home to meet with the many people involved in the case, while Kathie made three trips to Manhattan where I was able to further explore her experiences with the help of hypnotic regressions. It is impossible, here, to summarize an investigation that took more than 300 pages in the final book to document, but some details must be mentioned.

First was the issue of the ground traces in the photographs. We took samples of the extraordinarily hard, grayish, desiccated soil that constituted the entire affected area, along with control samples of the dark, moist, normal soil a few feet away. Crystallographic and spectrographic analysis showed no apparent difference between the two; nevertheless, it was necessary for the technicians to heat the control sample in an oven at 800 degrees Fahrenheit for six hours to achieve the same color as the affected soil. Remarkably, the intense heat was unable to duplicate its solidified appearance. Clearly the amount of energy emitted by *something* in the Davis' backyard that night was enormous, though we have no idea of its source.

On my first trip to Indianapolis I was able to establish Kathie's movements the night of the incident. She had supper, put her boys to bed, and then about nine o'clock drove to the home of a friend of hers – "Dee Anne" – who lived only five minutes away. (I knew from my early years in Wheeling that people who live in suburbia, unlike us New Yorkers, just don't like to walk.) Just before she left, however, Kathie noticed a "funny-colored light... more like a fluorescent light than the usual yellowish bulb we had there..." glowing inside the pool house in the back yard. When she investigated further, the light had disappeared, so she left for Dee Anne's, assuming that everything was normal at home.

A few minutes later, Mary, Kathie's mother who was babysitting the boys, noticed a strange, basketball-size ball of light in the backyard. Feeling uneasy, she phoned her daughter, suggesting she should come back and take a look around. Kathie left immediately, sometime before 9:30. When she arrived, she went straight to the closet and took out her father's rifle to provide herself with a little spiritual edge over any possible intruders. Her mother reminded her that the gun was unloaded, but Kathie said that was all right, she'd take it anyway. Mary chuckled and said, "What are you going to do with it – beat 'em to death?"

Both Kathie and her mother were certain that she was outside, looking around, for no more than ten minutes. Since everything once again seemed normal, she left and returned to Dee Anne's, assuming that it was now sometime between 9:45 and 10:00 p.m. But when she arrived, she discovered that it was about *11:00 p.m.* Dee Anne and her daughter, both of whom I later interviewed, testified to Kathie's inexplicably late arrival, a fact that suggested over an hour of missing time. Kathie told Dee Anne that she had begun to feel nauseated and uneasy, and in the ensuing weeks she experienced some hair loss, a rarely reported detail in UFO abductions.

Again, as in so many similar missing time cases involving memories of unusual light phenomena, physical aftereffects, and a general sense of witness uneasiness, hypnosis helped to unlock the mystery of Kathie's experiences that night. We learned what the object looked like, the smallish UFO that landed on the Davis' property. The evidence strongly suggested that the object had simultaneously caused both the extraordinary changes in the Davis' soil, and the vibrations, the frightening flash of light, and the temporary power outage at the Lloyd's house next door. The accounts of the five participants in this remarkable incident are mutually corroborative, and in my dealings with those of Kathie's friends and relatives involved in related incidents – some of whom were children – I never found any reason to doubt their credibility or personal integrity. These folks seemed to me to be simple, law-abiding, Middle-Western Americans, neither highly-educated nor overly-sophisticated, but plainly honest and reliable.

Kathie's memory of the night of the incident in her yard – an abduction in which she recalled being taken into the small, landed craft – is only the beginning of a much more important story. In 1983, during our first face-to-face meeting, she mentioned that five years before, early in 1978, she discovered she was pregnant, a fact confirmed by positive urinalysis and blood tests. She and her fiancé were both pleased by this unexpected turn of events and moved the date of the wedding forward.

Things were proceeding happily and her body was beginning its inevitable changes, but one day in March Kathie awoke with what seemed to be a normal menstrual flow. Her mother assured her that such things sometimes happened and that she shouldn't be too alarmed, but a visit to her doctor confirmed her fears: she was no longer pregnant. There had been no apparent miscarriage, no physical traces that would attest to a natural abortion. She just wasn't pregnant anymore. Her doctor was perplexed, but for Kathie the experience was shattering.

She and her fiancé were married in April according to plan, and she went on to have two sons, one born in July 1979, and the other in September 1980, two months prematurely. When Kathie told me about the loss of her first pregnancy, I saw it as a personal tragedy for her but never connected it with the UFO phenomenon in any way. It was not until my second trip to Indianapolis that I began to put the pieces together, as we looked into what she had described as an unnerving, low-level UFO sighting in late 1977 as she "was driving around" one night with two young women friends. She recalled a suspicious period of missing time after this original sighting, a recollection later confirmed in an interview I conducted with her friend "Dorothy," the driver that night. According to both Kathie and Dorothy, the third young woman in the car, "Roberta," was so frightened by the UFO that she hid on the floor of the back-seat and apparently missed most of what happened after the craft first appeared, its lights flashing ominously.

Under hypnosis, Kathie described an abduction that night during which she underwent a painful, quasi-gynecological procedure of some sort carried out as she lies unable to move on the examination table. She doesn't want to look down to see what the aliens are doing to her: "If I don't look I won't be scared… I feel like I'm getting one of those gyno… I've got the cramps really bad… where my uterus is, down low, like I'm gonna have my period… it hurts… like someone's pushing on me *real hard*… wiggling and pushing, right in there…"

Eventually the pain stops and she feels relief: "They just told me to rest. I'm done." She had no idea of the purpose of the UFO occupants' gynecological procedure but was immensely relieved when it was over. It had been extremely painful and demeaning.

But though she was "done" for the time being, the worst was yet to come. It was shortly after this abduction in early 1978 that Kathie discovered she was pregnant, and then only a few months later that she had a normal menstrual period and learned, to her sorrow, that she was no longer pregnant. She said that Dorothy, her friend from their as yet unremembered 1978 abduction, had driven her to the doctor's office, and that when she came out with the devastating news, she was in tears: "I couldn't stop crying. I kept saying, 'They took my baby… they took my baby,' and I cried so much they didn't know what to do with me. But I knew somebody took my baby." In retrospect, it was as if unconscious memories were beginning to surface.

I was aware that Kathie had had at least one other UFO experience during this same general time period, but I looked forward to exploring it with a certain amount of dread. She had mentioned that one night she had had some very strange feelings when she was baby-sitting for her sister Laura. As frequently happened with other subjects, once they begin the process of hypnotic regression,

Kathie's buried memories, like theirs, begin coming to the surface consciously, spontaneously, without hypnosis being necessary. Often these memories are only fragmentary, but they nevertheless provide new information and specific areas for later, more in-depth hypnotic exploration. It was not until October 1985, however, during Kathie's third visit to New York, that we decided to act on her intuitive feelings and explore the possibility that something had happened to her one night early in 1978 while she was at Laura's house.

Setting the scene, Kathie described being nervous and apprehensive. She was still pregnant at the time and not at her best to begin with, and she said the isolated, rural location of her sister's house always made her uneasy. As we begin the regression, she tells me that the kids are in bed and that she is in Laura's room watching TV. She feels nervous, as if someone (a prowler?) is watching her through the window. She moves into the living room and lies down on the couch where she turns on the TV for the feeling of company, watching reruns of *The Bob Newhart Show* and *Mary Tyler Moore*.

After a long pause she describes someone touching her, but she doesn't look. She keeps her eyes shut. Surprisingly, she says, "After a moment I wasn't afraid anymore. It's real nice." She alternates between feeling calm and frightened as she senses that she is being moved around on the couch. "Feel kinda funny, but not bad. Peaceful, but tingly all over. Real warm and nice... O.K.... My legs feel funny... [She sighs deeply, and after a long pause she suddenly cries out.] I feel like I'm being pulled apart. But it doesn't hurt...

"I can't move my legs... I feel... half numb... I can feel... something... big... too big... but it doesn't hurt..."

I ask her where she feels this "too big" thing. She sighs in obvious discomfort. "I feel like a flower opened up... it's... too weird, it feels wide open... All my female stuff... inside..." She feels something in her, and describes it as "too large..." At one point she says that it's "... sort of... like when the doctor puts the thing [speculum] in and spreads it real far. Only a lot wider... A lot more..."

There is more description of sensations of movement within

her pelvis, but then there is a long pause, and she says, urgently, "Something's not right… My back is starting to hurt…"

I ask if she means her spine.

"No," she groans, suddenly upset, and starts to shake. She begins weeping, the tears flowing down her tense cheeks.

I ask her what's happening, and she says that it's "like I was being squashed… my stomach… even my ribs are sore…" She sighs, then moans softly. "It's… it's… I just want to scream."

"From the pain?" I ask.

"No."

"What makes you want to scream?"

There is a long pause and then suddenly, in a high, wailing voice, she cries out, "NO! It's not right! It's not fair! IT'S NOT FAIR! IT'S *MINE*! I *HATE* YOU! I *HATE* YOU! … IT'S NOT FAIR!"

As her sobbing continued, I began the process to end the hypnosis. Moments later she was able to tell me what I feared – that they had taken her baby. As she continued to sob helplessly, her shoulders shaking and tears flooding down her cheeks, I tried to calm her by speaking about her two little boys, Robbie and Tommy, and what loveable children they were. I reminded her that she would be going home soon and would see them safely resting.

That shattering experience of Kathie's took place in early 1978 and was apparently the cause of her disappearing pregnancy a short time later, when she left the doctor's office in tears, crying to Dorothy, "They took my baby." Even then she must have had subconscious memories of what the aliens had done to her during the abduction we had just explored. But dramatic as this was, there would be another event even more astonishing. In January 1985, during her second trip to New York, Kathie and I were sitting in my living room, chatting about this and that, when I sensed there was something important she wanted to tell me. She seemed nervous and hesitant, and I could see that there were tears glistening in her eyes.

"Budd, you remember when I said that I knew I had a daughter?" She paused and cleared her throat. "Well, they showed her to me. I've seen her."

I was too moved and surprised to think about setting up my tape recorder. Then I remembered that my friend Tracy Tormé planned to drop in to meet Kathie, so I decided that when he came I could ask her to repeat her account and I could record it then. He arrived about an hour later, and by that time she had collected herself somewhat, so the following taped version, now radically reduced, is less emotional and more formal in tone than her unrecorded narrative earlier that evening. As Tracy listened with rapt attention, I heard it for the second time, and experienced, once again, the same amazement and profound sympathy I had felt before.

"It was the ending of some kind of scene," she said. "… Someone had talked to me… I was in this place and it was all white… There was a whole bunch of these… little gray guys… and there were several of them… around me. I was standing up…"

She begins speaking slowly and more softly – almost confessionally – as if the undercurrents of emotion were closer to the surface. "And then… a little girl came into the room, escorted by two more of them. She stood in front of the doorway… She looked to be about four… about Tommy's size. He's four, and she didn't look like them, but she didn't look like us, either. She was real pretty. She looked like an elf… or an… angel. She had really big blue eyes, and a little, teeny-weeny nose, just so perfect. And her mouth was just so perfect and tiny, and she was pale, except her lips were pink and her eyes were blue. And her hair was white and wispy and thin… fine. Her head was a little larger than normal, 'specially the forehead and back here. Her forehead was a bit bigger… but she was just a doll. And they brought her to me… They stood there and looked at me. Everyone was looking at me. And I looked at her, and I wanted to hold her… And I started crying… I was crying when I told Budd earlier tonight. This is the only part of any of these weird things that really gets me emotionally. There's no emotion left for any of the other."

After a thoughtful pause, Tracy asked if she had recalled any of this through hypnosis.

"No. It was almost like they let me remember this part. They held her [the little girl's] hands... She was almost like she was timid, like a little rabbit, and she was almost afraid of me. She turned towards one of them and reached out to her. [Earlier, Kathie said that she thought the two aliens attending the little girl were females.] ... Then she looked at me from the side, and when she did her lip quivered and she almost... it was kind of like a smile, on one side. It was like she was really interested in me but was a little bit afraid of me. And it was so sweet... I think I was even crying, actually, then... I cried when I told Budd. I can almost cry just thinking about it... It wasn't sad, but... I wanted to take her with me.

"...I don't know what any of them said to me, but one of them... told me something that I can't remember... [She later said that she had been told she was the child's mother.] I'm pretty sure somebody said I should be proud. Her eyes were so blue and huge, and her pupils were so blue, and she blinked them at me... it was like a blink, but it wasn't. It was almost as if her eyes rolled up. Her skin was creamy... it wasn't gray... She was pale and soft and creamy..."

The three of us talked for a few minutes about why the aliens had apparently let Kathie consciously remember so much of her experience without the need for hypnosis, and she offered a possible explanation: "It's almost like someone felt sorry for me 'cause I was so emotional over the child... It was like a little piece of her they left with me 'cause they had to take her away.

"I know I'm going to see her again. They told me so. But I wish it was going to be sooner than I think it probably will be..."

Nevertheless Kathie said she wanted to undergo hypnosis about that event just so she might relive the joy she felt with the magical little girl, so a bit later with Tracy Tormé sitting in, I conducted a regression. As the experience unfolds for her in real time, her emotions are far more intense. I ask if she thinks the child knows she is her mother. She replies softly, after a pause: "Yes, but she doesn't understand 'mother.' She's too young."

At another moment she says, in tears, "I want... to hold her... She's mine..."

But the male alien who presented the child to her says that she can't take her, that the child would not be able to live. "You wouldn't be able to feed her. She has to stay with us."

I asked if she thought the child could understand her, and she replied, "Yes, because when I thought to myself that she was beautiful and I wanted to hold her, she smiled at me… I knew she could hear me…"

These short excerpts from the long transcripts I published in *Intruders* can only begin to suggest the intensely emotional tone of Kathie's account. But a day or so later I recalled an earlier incident involving another woman from another city, which at the time I had passed off as an odd, unrelated anomaly. During a phone conversation with "Lisa," who, like Kathie, had reported several experiences suggestive of UFO abductions, I asked what was now a rather routine question: "Is there anything else in your past you may want to mention that seems to you even peripherally connected with UFOs – any odd, dangling, unresolved memories that bother you and just don't make much sense?"

Lisa asked me to hold the phone while she went into another room "for a better connection." She resumed the conversation in what was almost a whisper, explaining that she didn't want her husband, who had been nearby, to hear what she had to tell me. "I know this sounds crazy," she said, "but I think I have another child I think I've lost."

As I listened, I thought, what can this possibly have to do with UFO's? But she went on, "I woke up from a dream one night, absolutely certain I had a little baby and that I had lost it. I got out of bed and searched the house. I know this sounds crazy but it seemed absolutely real. I even looked in the closets and under the bed. I know this doesn't make any sense, and it doesn't even make sense to me, but I *knew* I somehow lost a child. *I thought I had actually seen it.* And I felt this way for weeks after. Sometimes I would just stop what I was doing, put down the vacuum cleaner, and search the house all over again."

This statement seemed so bizarre to me that I didn't know what to make of it. In an attempt to find a mundane explanation, I asked if she had ever had a miscarriage or an abortion or a stillborn child, and she answered that she had not. As a matter of fact, she had already given birth to a daughter before she had the dream, and she produced two sons later on.

Her account of a "missing baby," which now, after Kathie's report, seemed significant, would turn out to be just one of a number of similar reports that I uncovered *before* the publication of *Intruders*. In those years, as I worked with other female abductees, I began to subtly ask a few new questions about their health and any "problems" they may have had around the subject of pregnancy. As more cases like Kathie's came to light, I made certain that none of these women – who generally lived in different parts of the country – knew each other. All of them mentioned "missing pregnancies" and described the children they had later been shown in virtually identical terms: pale, with unusually shaped craniums, very large blue eyes, almost nonexistent ears and blondish white hair that was quite thin and barely covered their scalps. In fact, during hypnotic regressions, two different women remarked sadly that "no one is taking care of their hair... no one is brushing it..." To me, this subtle observation is both a sign of the women's warm, maternal instinct and evidence for the physical reality of the hybrid children they were describing. I have always taken particular note when a cluster of abduction reports appeared congruent in even the smallest details, no matter how bizarre or "unbelievable" they may seem, so now, after Kathie Davis' account and that of a number of other women, I found myself saddled with this latest and most staggering of patterns.

Another test I apply to an individual's possible abduction memories is to determine if they appear self-serving in any way, casting "glory and uniqueness" upon the teller, a wannabe quality found in most fantasies. I noticed in Kathie's case that the opposite was true. Physically, she is a rather heavy, large-framed woman, and she explained to me that one of the most painful aspects of her meeting with the elfin little girl was her sense that the child was afraid of her, of the *way she looked*. Her description of the child's thin, patchy white hair and oddly-shaped cranium matched those of the other women and suggested to me features that might be considered unattractive malformations in a normal child. In fact, "Pam," another of the abductees who was also was shown a younger "daughter" in a similar presentation, told me that at first she was somewhat repelled by the baby's appearance and was hesitant to touch it.

Each of the women in these cases apparently later suffered a range of motions – a sense of love, or loss, or anger, or even guilt – after being shown a child to whom each felt somehow connected and yet blocked from any kind of further relationship. None of this bestowed either glory or happiness upon any of them, and none of it could be interpreted as the product of a pleasant, maternal fantasy of ideal, loving children. In fact, several of these women had already given birth to normal offspring when they first explored their strange "presentation memories" and thus had real, loving children of their own.

All of this, I freely admit, is almost impossible to believe, but there is only one logical conclusion I could draw. Apparently, the central purpose of the systematic alien program of human abductions is the creation of these genetically altered beings – part alien, part human "hybrids." This startling new concept came to light in the mid-1980s, but in the decades since it was first presented in *Intruders*, it has been confirmed in hundreds, perhaps thousands of cases, one after another, by many within the UFO research community. The need to create "hybrid" beings would explain the covert nature of the UFO phenomenon, the pattern of cross-generational abductions within the same family – as if a particular genetic lifeline were being followed – and the thousands of earlier reports of alien interest in the human reproductive system.

Obviously none of this it is what I, or anyone else in the field, wanted to hear. But if we now believe we've uncovered the basic patterns, purposes, and goals of the aliens' systematic abduction of humans, we are still unclear as to what they intend for their genetically engineered "hybrids." After all, hybrids, like humans, grow up, and thus the largest question of all – their eventual role – still eludes us, casting an enormous shadow upon the future of our planet.

The Novelist and the Movie Star

ONE CAN IMAGINE how all of this ominous and revolutionary new information affected me. I had never asked to become enmeshed in such an emotionally draining and ultimately depressing business as UFO abductions, but now, with the publication of *Intruders*, I was in it up to my neck. By comparison with the 1976 mini-publicity blitz I'd undergone after my article in the *Village Voice* and *Cosmopolitan*, and the attention I'd received in 1981 with *Missing Time*, the media coverage this time was extraordinary and relentless. Random House, my publisher, arranged a national book tour that lasted three weeks, taking me to virtually a different city each weekday. There was extensive coverage all the way from local TV and radio stations, to print interviews with major American newspapers (for example, a long, supportive article on one of my abduction cases was published in the Sunday magazine section of the *Washington Post*), to appearances on many national shows such as, *Today*; *Good Morning, America*; *Nightline*; *Oprah Winfrey*; and *Larry King Live*. It was all a dizzy, emotionally draining experience I had not foreseen, but at least it gave me a chance to inform the public about an issue I felt was of extraordinary importance. When I was at home, I kept my balance and protected my sanity by staying close to April and my now teenage daughter Grace, by plunging into my painting and sculpture-making, and by spending hours at the Metropolitan Museum, absorbing the cool serenity of Vermeer and Corot and Cezanne.

But there were also many side trips of one sort or another. In the summer of 1987, Kathie Davis accompanied me to the annual conference of MUFON (the Mutual UFO Network), a large, international organization. Held at The George Washington University in Washington D.C. that year, the conference was very well attended, partly because of the extensive publicity that resulted from the nearly simultaneous publication of three new books on the UFO phenomenon: my *Intruders,* Whitley Strieber's *Communion,* and Gary Kinder's *Light Years,* the latter a serious book about the highly dubious claims of a man named Billy Meier. I was asked to address the meeting on the subject of abduction research and Kathie had agreed to join a Sunday panel of people who, like her, had reported UFO abduction experiences. She was normally a shy woman, hesitant to talk about herself, so this would be the first time she'd ever spoken to a large audience and she was extremely tense about how it would go.

Saturday night, during the *pro forma* banquet, we sat together, and Kathie, who knew almost no one at the conference, was a bit over-awed. As the banquet speaker droned on and we sipped our after-dinner coffee to relieve the boredom, a man I knew as some kind of Hollywood operator (agent, producer, screenwriter?) came up behind us and squatted down to whisper something to me. "Budd," he said," "after dinner, would you like to meet Shirley MacLaine? She's staying in a hotel nearby, and she's a friend of mine, and I think she'd like to meet you and Kathie."

I intended to decline his invitation because I knew that Shirley MacLaine was a committed New Ager who was ill-informed about the phenomenon and had decided that the UFO occupants were our spiritual "Space Brothers," here only to do good for humanity. I was aware that she would certainly have rejected what I'd written in *Intruders* and that an unpleasant argument would probably occur. (Spiritually evolved New Agers can sometimes get nasty when their belief systems are crossed.) But before I had a chance to refuse the man's well-meaning invitation, Kathie, who had heard it, turned to me and said, "Oh, I'd *love* to meet Shirley MacLaine! I've always liked her movies a whole lot. Can we really go and meet her?"

"Of course," the man replied. "Shirley and I are good friends. I'll take you there myself, and I'm sure she'd like to meet you, too, Kathie." With that, unfortunately for me, the die was cast.

My Hollywood acquaintance drove us to the hotel, and when we disembarked and took the elevator up to MacLaine's suite, Kathie was as thrilled and excited as I was worried and apprehensive.

We were ushered into the main room and there before us, as if presiding over a royal court, was Shirley herself, seated in a large armchair and flanked by an array of personages. Standing on one side were Congresswoman Bella Abzug – she of the big hats – and Senator Claiborne Pell of Rhode Island, Chairman of the Senate Foreign Affairs Committee. On the other side was a retired Navy Commander – Pell's Chief of Staff – a high-ranking and influential European political figure, and a few others. I also noticed a huge bowl of delicious looking fruit on a table next to Queen Shirley, but as Kathie and I were introduced, two chairs were brought out and placed about ten feet away, facing the august group. We seated ourselves before the court as if we were defendants on trial, and though I looked hungrily at Shirley's bowl of fruit, none was offered.

MacLaine then asked Kathie to tell the story of her UFO experiences, an extremely complicated endeavor under normal circumstances, and as the shy, intimidated young woman proceeded, all eyes were fixed on her, seemingly with sympathy. Kathie had always hated to retell these sad events, partly because she shunned the spotlight, but also because reliving it was extremely painful. The worst, of course, was the climax – the baby taken from her and then, a few years later, her confrontation inside the white chamber with the little girl who seemed afraid of her... the child she felt was her daughter. She had never before told this part of her experience to a group of strangers, and I well understood the cost of such intimate self-revelation. Her halting attempt to convey all of this personal heartbreak was interrupted from time to time by long pauses, the wiping away of tears, and moments of wrenching emotion. Even though I knew her story well, it was still deeply moving to me and, apparently, to all of the others who were hearing it for the first time. They listened in rapt, sympathetic silence.

When Kathie finished, she looked down at her hands folded in her lap and her eyes held their clouded gaze. It seemed that at that moment she was not there in the room with the rest of us, but rather in her own world, a place where she could still see the young child whom she had wanted so much to hold and to love.

Shirley MacLaine came over to her, offering whatever comfort she could and whispered that she understood what Kathie had been through. We stayed only a short time after that. I answered a few questions and then we left.

For separate reasons Kathie and I were downcast at the way the interview had turned out: she, because her earlier excitement at meeting a movie star she admired had been drained away in the anguish of personal recollection, and I because once again I saw vividly the pain the aliens had caused an innocent, well-meaning young woman of whom I had become fondly protective.

Two days later I ran into the Hollywood go-between who had taken us to meet Shirley MacLaine, and I asked him if he had spoken to her since our interview. He seemed distressed at my question, but then he apparently gathered his courage, looked me straight in the eyes and replied: "Yes, I talked to her at length about Kathie and her experiences and she made me very angry." Taking a deep breath, he continued: "Shirley said, 'That woman is a liar and I don't believe a word she said.'"

I gasped in disbelief, but he went on. "She told me that Kathie is just a great actress, and that she – Shirley MacLaine – has been an actress all her life and *she* can recognize great acting when she sees it, and that Kathie made it all up and is just a great actress."

I said I was astonished, that there was no way that Kathie, a poorly educated young woman from rural Indiana with no training as an actress, could be that convincing as a hoaxer. Besides, all of the people in the room who were listening to her seemed to be genuinely moved by what she was telling them.

"That's exactly the trouble," the man replied. "Everybody *was* moved. And that meant that Shirley temporarily lost her position as queen of the room to Kathie who was, in her view, a little nobody, and for the moment she was insanely jealous of her. I know Shirley. I've known her for years, and she always has to be the center of attention. A lot of actors are like that. She was furious that she lost the spotlight to a woman she looked down upon, especially in front of Senator Pell and Bella Abzug and the others."

As the years passed, I never told Kathie of the disgraceful personal comments by a woman whom she had admired and trusted enough to reveal her most intimate and painful sense of loss. Fortunately, however, in later conversations I had with Senator Pell and his friend, the European political figure (whose desire for anonymity I am respecting), I learned that they had both been deeply touched by Kathie's account, and apparently never accepted the movie star's jealous condemnation. Meanwhile, Shirley MacLaine, the "profoundly spiritual, highly evolved, loving human being," valiantly soldiered on in her self-defined role as New Age guru to thousands upon thousands of admirers apparently unaware of the degree of her narcissism.

Before all of this, in late 1985, another new and complex rivulet had joined the other streams flowing into the ongoing current of my life. I received a phone call from a man named Whitley Strieber who seemed quite nervous as he explained that he had read my book, *Missing Time*, and had had an experience that might have been a UFO abduction. Since he lived nearby, I invited him to my studio to tell me in detail exactly what it was that had so disturbed him, and thus began an involvement of several years with someone I found always to be interesting, "difficult," highly intelligent, and possessed of a vivid but treacherous creative imagination. So vivid, in fact, that he once remarked he sometimes had difficulty telling fantasy from reality.

Whitley Strieber was, by profession, a novelist, particularly adept at the horror and sci-fi genres, a situation that caused the reliability of his abduction stories to be fraught with uncertainty. In addition to this problem, there was another: Strieber seemed emotionally unsteady, far more so than most of the abductees I had worked with up to this time. He described his fear during an abduction experience in this way: "If I had been afraid before, I now became quite simply crazed with terror," so it's safe to say that for months he lived in a constant state of fear. When he came to write about his experiences, however, he referred to the beings who had abducted him and who, he said, had pressed a needle into his brain, as "Visitors." (!)

I've always believed that this mild, even friendly designation of his captors was Strieber's attempt at appeasement, a ploy he hoped might reassure them of his lack of hostility. I was certain of it one day when he telephoned to inform me that his "Visitors" did not like being referred to as "Intruders," the title of the book I was then completing, and as a friend, he thought he should warn me to change my designation. I thanked him for the advice, but said that in my book they were definitely "Intruders" and not innocent "Visitors." His warning was delivered well over twenty years ago, and despite my having ignored it all that time, I still have not been struck down by even a single thunderbolt hurled by a vengeful "Visitor."

Strieber's obvious emotional unsteadiness led me early on to refer him to a well-known psychiatrist, Dr. Donald Klein, whom I had met recently and who seemed open-minded about the UFO phenomenon. I suggested that he visit Dr. Klein both for therapy and for hypnotic regression, a technique in which Dr. Klein was highly skilled. As for myself, having never been trained as a psychotherapist, I was hesitant to use hypnosis with someone like Strieber in his present fragile state, though I continued to interview him about his recollections and to work with two important witnesses to the central incident he wanted to explore. Their hypnotic recall helped me both to clarify the sequence of events and to buttress Strieber's own recollections. Based upon these witnesses' testimony, and a number of previously unpublished details about the abduction phenomenon that Strieber recalled accurately, I came to the conclusion that he had most probably undergone the traumatic "Visitor" experiences he described, despite his suspect and hyperactive imagination.

I had been keeping David Jacobs informed about my progress on the case, and he was as disturbed as I when Strieber announced that after only a few months of the investigation, he was writing a book about his experiences. Several other abductees he had met at my support group added their own cautionary words, suggesting that he should wait a year or so until things became clearer and he had overcome some of the trauma and confusion he had endured, and in that way produce a wiser, more objective account. But as a professional novelist ever hungry for promising material, Whitley would not be deterred and plunged ahead on a manuscript he would eventually publish as *Communion*.

I felt a gnawing uncertainty about the work of a genre writer such as he – his novels dealt with vampires and werewolves, among other things – but I still clung to the hope that the finished account would bring the abduction phenomenon before a wider public. He was, so far, the rare example of an abductee with name recognition in some quarters who was willing to come forward without the protection of a pseudonym.

My own worries and misgivings remained because, to many who knew him, Whitley Strieber was a classic example of the cacophonous old cliché, a loose cannon on a rolling deck. He was "difficult" in every sense of the word and highly unpredictable. When he told me that he would have no objection if I used his name and referred to his experiences in my upcoming book, I thanked him but did not tell him that I found him too generally unreliable to risk using his name. Though I declined to identify him in *Intruders*, I briefly referred to an anonymous abductee "writer" and his family.

As *Communion* was nearing completion, Strieber asked me to go over his manuscript in advance of its submission to a publisher, and I did so, suggesting the deletions of several passages that I thought might damage his credibility because they were too over the top and lacked any persuasive supporting evidence. He agreed, and I was relieved when he made the deletions. I was also flattered that several times in his book Strieber stated his debt to my investigation of his claims, and when he received some advance author's copies of *Communion*, he presented one to me, inscribed, "To Budd, who saved my life."

My *Intruders* was still a few months away from publication when Beech Tree Books, a division of William Morrow, introduced *Communion*. A day or two after I congratulated Whitley on his new book and had gone home with the dedicated copy he'd given me, I received a shocking phone call from my editor, Elizabeth Scharlott. She and another official at Random House had just received personal letters from Whitley Strieber, asking them to postpone the publication of *Intruders* for a period of at least seven months! The reason he gave was that he thought the planned publication date of my book would interfere with the sales of his book and, eventually, mine. His letter was slyly worded to imply that he was asking for the postponement of *Intruders* "as a *favor* for Budd Hopkins," so that *Intruders* would "sell well" after a seven month delay and in the meantime would give his book a clear shot at the same audience. The people at Random House were both astounded and outraged; they had never heard of such a preposterous and self-serving request from a competitor in their many years in publishing, and they responded by *speeding up* the production of my book. They were doubly shocked when I told them that Strieber – supposedly my friend – had never mentioned these letters to me, even though I had just visited him in his apartment.

If the people at Random House were astounded and outraged by his letters, I was in a cold fury. I saw his behavior as an act of selfish treachery to someone who, he said, had "saved his life." He later made the unbelievable claim that he had also written to me about his plan for my book's postponement, but that somehow his letter to me "must have been lost in the mail." (The dog ate his homework.) As might be expected, this event marked the end of my friendship with Whitley Strieber.

Ironically, in his desire to have the field of abduction materials to himself, subsequent events took a surprising turn. Despite his efforts, *Communion*, Gary Kinder's *Light Years*, and *Intruders* all appeared within the same general time period, and the near simultaneity of three books on the UFO phenomenon, backed by three well-known publishers – Random House, William Morrow, and the Atlantic Monthly Press – benefited all three. Each book received far more publicity than it would have if published alone, and the three were often reviewed together.

Strieber's book was regarded as a vividly written, subjective account of one man's experiences with non-human beings, while *Intruders* was seen as an objective study of the abduction phenomenon across a broad spectrum of individual testimony and evidence. Put simply, *Communion* was a *cri de coeur* while *Intruders* was a more scientific brief on the meaning and reality of UFO abductions. If anything, each book complemented the other, and both *Communion* and *Intruders* ended up on *The New York Times* best-seller lists.

Communion was ultimately turned into a motion picture while *Intruders* became a miniseries on CBS television; both books have been translated into many languages, and both are now regarded as classics in the field. It is my belief that if the two publications, along with *Light Years*, had not appeared almost simultaneously, these advantages would not have accrued.

One final point about *Communion* should be made, and it, too, is not without irony. At the time Strieber was completing his manuscript and I was continuing to help him in many ways, he asked me to recommend an artist/illustrator to produce a painting of an alien – I should say "Visitor" – for the cover of his finished book. He would work closely with the artist, he said, instructing him as to his recollections of the alien face so that the image would be as exact as possible, and I referred him to Ted Seth Jacobs, a highly skilled painter and illustrator who had produced an alien image for an insert in my first book, *Missing Time*. When Ted completed the work, Strieber called to tell me that it was incredible, absolutely frightening and *exactly* what he had seen and remembered from his many experiences. He was eager for me to come to his apartment as soon as possible to see it.

When I arrived and he showed it to me, I was shocked. The main feature of the face had, as most abductees describe, huge black eyes, haunting and impenetrable. But above the eyes the cranium was tiny, a virtual pinhead. "Whitley," I said, "the head is wrong! Everybody describes the alien cranium as abnormally large and you've had Ted make it tiny."

He looked at the painting with a rather dejected expression, "Yeah, I guess you're right. The heads are a lot bigger." But it was too late to have Ted do another version; this one was already in the works as the dust jacket illustration for *Communion*. So, despite the head problem, an alien face would appear for the first time on a book cover.

A few weeks later, when I visited the Striebers' apartment for a small party he gave to launch his book, an editor from William Morrow told me proudly, "That's a million dollar book cover!" and he was probably right; the cover illustration – particularly the central feature of the huge black eyes – sold the book. Literally tens of thousands of people recognized, on some half-conscious level, those hypnotically staring black eyes, and, feeling they had seen them somewhere before, bought the book to find out where. Morrow wisely advertised *Communion* mainly through its cover illustration rather than its press reviews, which were, as one might expect, decidedly mixed.

I feel I can safely claim that Ted Jacob's dust jacket illustration on *Communion* is the most famous and effective jacket illustration in the history of publishing. (Just try to think of any competitors.) But here is the irony. I began getting letters from people who wrote that they had bought Strieber's book because of a disturbing sense of familiarity with the alien face on the cover, but who then added that they felt there was something wrong with the head: "The head's not right." And *then*, they wrote, "But the problem is, I wondered how I *knew* that the head's not right, that it's too little? How do I know what the head *should* look like if I can't remember exactly where I saw it before?" I received many letters and comments like that from people who, thanks to the incorrect cover illustration, were beginning to suspect that they had actually seen those huge black eyes before, and that they were somehow familiar with the abduction phenomenon Strieber described. I have no idea how many letters he received pointing out the same unsettling conundrum, but there must have been many.

So, in a felicitous way Whitley's error functioned rather like a control in a scientific experiment. Anyone who felt drawn to the face and sensed that it was somehow familiar, but who, at the same time, spotted the incorrect rendering of the cranium, was troubled by the possibility that he or she actually *was* familiar with this kind of being. That uncanny insight nicely helped to separate the abductees from the wannabes. It was as if they knew something that the writer of the book and the cover artist *didn't* know, and that made their situation truly unnerving.

The wide sales of *Communion* succeeded in bringing thousands upon thousands of people to consider that they, too, like the author, may have had half-remembered UFO experiences, and this realization opened many doors in the previously troubled souls of many people. The credit for this phenomenon is due to Ted Seth Jacobs for his mesmerizing illustration, and to Whitley Strieber for having written his vivid book – and gotten the head wrong.

The Curious Case Of Carl Sagan

IN THE SPRING OF 1987, months after I completed my formal book tour to publicize *Intruders*, media curiosity about the abduction phenomenon continued unabated, and so a late invitation to appear on a Boston TV program was in no way unusual. I was asked to bring along an abductee to discuss his or her experience on the air, though such people are hard to find because of their quite justifiable fear of ridicule. Unfortunately this appalling weapon of the debunkers – almost as effective in silencing witnesses as Mafia death threats – means that very few abductees are willing to go public, but when I asked Rosemary Osnato, an articulate and intelligent young woman with whom I'd worked in the early 1980s, she agreed to brave the odds and appear on the program with me.

A TV station's green room, the traditional off-stage waiting area for performers, guests, and their friends, is a very busy place, particularly before morning interview shows such as the one to which Rosemary and I had been invited. This sort of news and variety program is essentially a local version of established network shows like *Today* and *Good Morning, America*, so one's fellow guests are a miscellany: perhaps another book-touring author accompanied by escorts – called minders, in the business – provided by their publishers, a politician, a local chef preparing to whip up a soufflé before the cameras, and perhaps a hunky young soap opera actor being hyped by the network. One never knows.

But one of my oddest 1987 TV green room experiences had been an evening appearance on *The Late Show* in its post-Joan Rivers, pre-David Letterman phase when various celebrities acted as temporary hosts. On the night in question I was one of four guests, along with the lead sax player in Bruce Springsteen's band, the wry and prolific writer George Plimpton, and Benjy, the Wonder Dog. Each of us, even Benjy, had his own dressing room, and in keeping with its opulent style *The Late Show's* green room was super deluxe. Instead of the usual doughnuts, bagels, and coffee, it housed a bartender minding a full bar stocked with top-of-the-line liquors, a table of elegant *hors d'oeurves,* and even trays of freshly baked chocolate chip cookies carried in, still warm and aromatic, by attractive young female interns.

Plimpton and I, two authors with books to sell, chatted quite amicably while we waited to go on. We found we shared a few friends and acquaintances, and I mentioned that I had once attended a crowded book party at his Sutton Place townhouse. When I explained why I was a guest on the *Late Show,* he seemed curious and told me about a UFO sighting a friend of his had had recently on Long Island, near East Hampton. Things were going swimmingly for an hour or so, but eventually we realized that the combination of easy conversation and free flowing Scotch (Johnny Walker, Black Label) had become overly appealing. Luckily, by the time I went on I had switched to Perrier and so was relatively in control, though when poor Plimpton was introduced he parted the curtains to the stage and strode firmly in the wrong direction, stumbling over a barrier, and almost falling into the house band. As I recall, though, Benjy the Wonder Dog performed flawlessly, and at one point even jumped into Plimpton's lap for a few minutes rest.

In stark contrast, the green room of the Boston television station where Rosemary and I were currently to appear offered only the usual bare bones, doughnuts-and-coffee refreshments, but then this was a morning show on local TV. The green room itself was nevertheless quite a busy place. Along with a miscellany of the guests' friends, relatives, and publicists, young segment producers with clipboards hurried around asking for signatures on releases and explaining the sequence of appearances and the (minimal) time each guest would have on camera. Other interns efficiently shepherded each of us pale, rumpled guests into the makeup room and brought us out with glamorous new false suntans and cemented hairdos. In the meantime everyone waited nervously, eyeing the monitor and sipping lukewarm coffee, while silently trying to compose a few clever sound bites for use in the coming interviews.

Rosemary and I were chatting when our segment producer came over and asked a few last-minute questions. "By the way," she added, avoiding eye contact, "Carl Sagan is here and he'll be on the program, too."

My heart sank. Carl Sagan, the astronomer and prolific writer, was one of the most popular and authoritative figures on television, a kind of Pope of Science to unsophisticated TV viewers, and his highly negative position on the question of UFOs was well known. The idea of Sagan's universal expertise was so widely accepted that I saw myself outranked no matter how effectively I presented a subject I knew well and about which he knew next to nothing. I had a gloomy fantasy of skipping UFOs and just showing my paintings, whereupon Sagan, ignorant of abstract art, would wave his hand and say "They're bad," and the television audience would automatically agree. Against such a popular celebrity scientist, I couldn't win on any issue.

"You didn't tell me Carl Sagan was going to be on the program," I said icily to the producer.

"No," she replied, "but don't worry, you're not going to be on the same segment."

"I bet I go on first, don't I?" I asked, and she nodded a bit sheepishly. As I suspected, Sagan's segment would immediately follow ours. Thus whatever points Rosemary or I might make could be instantly crushed by a celebrity whose influence with a scientifically uninformed public had been buttressed by dozens of appearances with Johnny Carson on the *Tonight* show, and on his own PBS series, *Cosmos*. With this arrangement I would be unable to respond to or correct any misleading statements he might make. I thought of poor Rosemary, an abductee who would inevitably be humiliated if such an august authority insisted her experiences were "imaginary," the debunkers' pet euphemism to imply either lying or mental illness. What had I gotten her into? Feeling we'd been deliberately tricked, I considered asking her to join me in walking out on the program.

But at that moment a dark haired, somewhat frail-looking man approached me and said, "You're Budd Hopkins, aren't you?" I nodded. "I'm Carl Sagan. I'm glad to meet you."

I hadn't recognized him and was surprised he'd sought me out. He seemed far less imposing than he had on TV, but at the time I was unaware of his serious health problems. He introduced me to his wife, I presented Rosemary, and we began a conversation. I was on my guard, but since he seemed relaxed and friendly I felt a little less desperate. To divert the conversation and to create a bond in a non-UFO area I mentioned my regard for a long-time friend of mine, the psychohistorian Robert J. Lifton, who I knew was well acquainted with Sagan through their joint efforts in the anti-nuclear movement. This connection and other remarks cemented a political tie between us that helped establish mutual respect; though we disagreed about the issue of UFOs, it became clear that we shared the same liberal, humanistic worldview.

"I read your book," Carl said, referring, I assumed, to *Missing Time*, which I knew Allen Hynek had sent him. "It was interesting. But you need better evidence. An artifact that you could prove had not originated on Earth."

And thus we were off, the four of us, calmly and civilly discussing a subject that to my surprise seemed to interest him a great deal. At some point he uttered the skeptics' all-purpose sound bite: "Extraordinary claims demand extraordinary evidence." As I tried to think of an effective reply, an idea struck me.

"Carl," I replied, "it seems to me that all the UFO sightings reported by pilots, by astronauts and by other trained observers, all the radar returns and radar-visual sightings, the UFO films and photographs that have stood up under analysis, all the ground traces after UFO landings, all the similar abduction reports and the attendant scars and marks – all of this collectively constitutes an extraordinary phenomenon, no matter what you think may lie behind it."

He nodded in agreement. "And so," I continued, feeling rather proud of myself, "shouldn't we be saying instead that an extraordinary phenomenon such as this *demands an extraordinary investigation*?"

For the moment, as he mulled it over, he had no reply.

Earlier, Sagan had said that I should have run more extensive tests on the affected soil in one of the cases I described to him. I explained that all of our lab work was either volunteered by a few dedicated scientists or was paid for out of our own pockets. I said that I wasn't a scientist, nor was I claiming generalship in this field of research. "I'm not trying to be George Washington," I said, "but I am trying to be Paul Revere. You should be doing this investigation, Carl, not me."

Again he seemed somewhat taken aback.

And so through this half hour of easy conversation I stumbled upon my strategy for the program. I would not try to persuade viewers that the phenomenon is real; instead I would simply insist that the quantity of evidence behind such an extraordinary phenomenon demanded an extraordinary investigation. I knew that very few skeptical, mainstream scientists – Carl Sagan included – showed signs of familiarity with the UFO case material and its supporting literature. Thus it would be intellectually irresponsible, even dishonest, to blindly assert that such things as intelligently controlled, non-human spacecraft simply cannot exist, and then refuse to examine any evidence that suggests they do.

This, in essence, is what I said on the program, with Sagan and his wife just off the set, listening. I was demanding that skeptical scientists do some science – actually investigate in depth – rather than blithely assert that all UFO reports are hoaxes, fantasies, or simple misidentifications.

When Rosemary and I finished our brief segment, I said goodbye to the Sagans since I had to leave immediately for Logan Airport to catch another plane. Carl waved to me and said rather loudly before the TV crew, "Budd, the next really good abduction case you have, let me know and I'll look into it with you."

I felt gratified by this quite public promise, but I resolved to wait until I had a case in the Ithaca-Cornell University area where he lived and taught so that it would be maximally convenient for him to join me in the investigation; potential excuses and evasions were easy to foresee. I left the TV station and was not surprised to be told later that during his segment Sagan downplayed the UFO phenomenon, insisting that he had looked into it thoroughly and found that it was nothing more than a collection of hoaxes and misidentifications.

Then in May I received a letter from "Edward," a 21-year-old student at Cornell University in which he described himself as someone who had always been skeptical about the idea of UFOs until a frightening incident that occurred to him the previous September, on the 10th of the month. At the time it had seemed absolutely real, he wrote, though subsequently he had tried – unsuccessfully – to think of it as a dream. Now he was desperate to have someone help him deal with his very real trauma.

"In the weeks following that night," he wrote, "I became fearful that a gang of little white people about four and a half feet tall would once again decide to enter my room, haul me to a clearing in the woods and into their vehicle. They would do all sorts of tests and literally scare the piss out of me. They would leave a scar above my inner right ankle. They would bring me back to my bed unharmed except for my nerves. The worst thing is, Mr. Hopkins, in time I would realize that it was not the first time that sort of thing has happened. There are many details. I thought and thought and tried to force myself to believe that it was a dream. I just couldn't. I have always reviewed my dreams since I was a child. It was no dream. Dreams don't leave scars."

Edward went on to describe how things became worse when he tried to tell some of his friends about his recollections. He asked me to refer him to someone who could help him make sense of what happened, and thanked me for the work I was doing with people like himself. He ended his letter with this: "I hope that anyone who tries to ridicule you will (someday) find themselves in my place on that night in September."

I called Edward later that evening. He seemed intelligent, genuinely upset about his recollections and eager to explore them, under hypnosis if necessary. He described a few other, similar experiences, including one in which his girlfriend was a witness to a part of the incident. I made a proposal: how would he feel about my investigating his case along with Carl Sagan, who, I explained, had promised to help me look into the next good abduction case that came my way? Edward was willing, and added that his father, like the astronomer, was also a professor at Cornell, and he agreed to let me send Sagan a copy of his letter.

In my cover note to Carl Sagan I recalled how we had met at the TV station and reminded him of his promise to jointly look into my "next good case," suggesting that this was just such an example. I saw that from his point of view it could hardly be more convenient; Edward could come to his office, and in effect, Sagan would not even have to get out of his chair to begin an investigation.

I enclosed Edward's telephone number so that if he wished, Sagan could easily carry out preliminary phone interviews. I explained that I would fly to Ithaca at his convenience so that we could meet the young man together, interview his parents and the former girlfriend involved in one of the incidents, and if time permitted, visit the sites of two of his experiences. I said that if hypnosis were called for, I could carry out a session or two, but if he preferred, Sagan could select a psychologist from Cornell to do the regressions.

"I want this investigation to be fully shared by the two of us," I wrote, "and to remain confidential. Our tentative conclusions may differ or agree, but at least we will have had a chance to evaluate one another's methods and concerns and to study the abduction phenomenon firsthand."

I closed by stating that I was proposing this joint investigation because of my great respect for his scientific accomplishments. "Having your fund of scientific knowledge as a resource can only be helpful to me in this endeavor… I believe that if you are willing to join me in looking into Edward's case you will almost inevitably come to one or another conclusion: that there is a stronger case to be made for the reality of the UFO abduction phenomenon than you had previously thought, or that a disturbing and significant new psychosocial disorder is abroad in the land. Firsthand evidence for either conclusion will justify the hours spent in investigation."

Nearly a month later I received the following reply, which I quote in its entirety: "Thanks for your recent letter. I remember well our discussion in Boston. I'm afraid [Edward's] account does not correspond to what I would call an interesting case. As far as I can see, apart from a scar the evidence is purely anecdotal. Do you know David Hume's little essay 'On Miracles?'"

I was shocked. My disappointment over Sagan's refusal to proceed with even a preliminary interview was matched only by my uncomprehending surprise, since I had made it clear that he could begin the investigation with a local telephone call, and that Edward was willing to come to his office if he so wished. How could anyone who professed a lifelong interest in the idea of extraterrestrial intelligence, and who regularly made public statements on the subject of UFOs, refuse such a modest first step? I chose not to reply to his six-line dismissive note.

I was eventually to be even more surprised and disappointed by his lack of genuine scientific curiosity and his indifference to data gathering when, in 1993, he sent me a manuscript copy of an article he was writing on the UFO abduction phenomenon for – of all places – *Parade* magazine, the well-below-middle-brow Sunday newspaper supplement. The tone of his accompanying note was cordial, beginning with "Dear Budd" and ending with "Best wishes for a Happy New Year," and in it he asked for my critical comments. His article showed that he was at least somewhat familiar with my published research, as well as some of the findings of the Roper Survey on *Unusual Personal Experiences*, a poll that David Jacobs and I had had conducted. But the essence of his piece was that abduction reports are caused by "people experiencing some internal mental state they do not understand." He went on to discuss a seventeenth century case of a woman accused of witchcraft as just one such mental state. Since analogies like this can often turn around and bite their authors, I wondered if the woman might be said to represent the twentieth century abductee while the authorities who burned her at the stake might represent twentieth century scientists – like Sagan himself.

He went on to list a number of different, mutually contradictory "explanations" – hallucinations, sleep paralysis, and so on – for what he admitted were disturbingly similar abduction accounts. He preferred these explanations, he said, because they sounded more reasonable to him than an alien presence. Who could disagree?

They sound not only more reasonable but infinitely more comforting to anyone unfamiliar with the actual data.

This time my anger was stronger than my sense of disappointment. Not only had Sagan reneged on his promise to look into my "next good case" – one right in his own backyard – but now he was using his *Parade* article to imply that he had personally investigated abduction cases like Edward's and found the evidence for their reality to be extremely weak.

I answered his letter politely but said that while his article expressed his *opinion* about the abduction phenomenon, it also suggested that he had no idea of the extent and weight of the evidence, or the range and thoroughness of decades of investigative work. I chided him about his rejection of eyewitness testimony, pointing out how essential that kind of testimony is for the criminal justice system, as well as for the many branches of science that require observations in the field. My anger took over and led me to invent some satirical newspaper headlines, such as: SCIENCE POPE ARGUES BEFORE SUPREME COURT – URGES RELEASE OF TENS OF THOUSANDS OF VIOLENT CRIMINALS, STATING THAT ANYONE CONVICTED ON EYEWITNESS TESTIMONY MUST BE SET FREE.

I ended by inventing a very short piece I wished he had written for *Parade* rather than the long, somewhat rambling skeptical article he sent me, and put into his mouth some of my own words from the TV program we had done a few years before. My "Sagan Statement" ended with these thoughts: "As a scientist devoted to the search for truth, I believe that, whatever lies behind them, the thousands of UFO reports assembled over the years comprise an extraordinary phenomenon, and an extraordinary phenomenon such as this demands an extraordinary *investigation*. It would be intellectually irresponsible simply to ignore such a widespread and potentially important collection of physical evidence and verbal testimony.

"Ridicule and outraged rejection are as out of place as uncritical acceptance," I continued, speaking as Sagan. "The issue must be squarely faced and the case reports thoroughly investigated. Science can be satisfied with nothing less."

In my own voice I added a final observation: "If you had written something like this, Carl, science would have been better served."

I received a short reply, a note probably identical to those he sent to nine other researchers to whom he'd mailed his article. He thanked me for my "timely response" and hoped that "the publication of the *Parade* article is likely to spur useful debate on this curious and tantalizing subject." His choice of words had an ironic accuracy; while I was calling or an investigation of the data, Sagan was asking for nothing more than another (wheel-spinning) verbal *debate.*

There was no further communication between us until the fall of 1995, and by that time I knew that Sagan was quite sick with a rare, leukemia-like disease. Someone sent me a newspaper article about a lecture he had given in which he spoke about his determination to carry on his normal life of teaching and research despite his illness. The piece mentioned that bone-marrow treatments had caused him to show some improvement, but accompanying the article was a recent photograph in which the once handsome young scientist now appeared emaciated, his hair gone, and his gaunt features aged and almost unrecognizable. I was genuinely touched and sent him the following note:

> Dear Carl,
>
> Though we have only met once, on a Boston TV program, I feel I know you somewhat, thanks to our shared interest in UFO phenomena. You will probably remember some of our correspondence. Despite the fact that we have opposing views with regard to this subject, you have unfailingly treated me with friendship and respect.
>
> Unfortunately these qualities are too often missing from a controversy in which civility is ideology's first victim.
>
> But the reason I'm writing you has to do with health issues – yours and mine. I was pleased to read recently about

your gain in strength and was inspired by your brave resolution in the face of a terrible foe. I've also had my struggle, first with kidney cancer and then, after apparently successful surgery, with pre-cancerous polyps in my bladder. I've had my share of chronic pain as a result so I can easily empathize with your ordeal.

You have my friendship, Carl, and my fervent hope that you continue to regain your health and well-being. Your strength and courage are an inspiration to many, many people.

A few days later I received this reply:

Dear Budd,

I want to tell you how touched I was by your extremely kind and thoughtful letter. The older I get, the more such civility means to me – especially between people who disagree as profoundly as you and I do. I was very sorry to hear of your medical problems, and hope they will be resolved soon.

With warm regards,
Carl

He added a postscript, moving us back to the subject of UFOs, by asking, "What's your take on the FOX alien abduction film?" I assume he meant the (hoaxed) alien autopsy footage, but unfortunately I never responded. This was the last communication between us.

Several months after this final exchange of letters we were both featured on *Nova*, a PBS science program in which my work and the abduction accounts themselves were distorted beyond recognition, while Sagan repeated his *Parade* magazine psychological explanations of alien abduction reports: sleep paralysis, hallucinations, etc. "There's *outer* space and then there's *inner* space," he said, thus placing the "blame" for abduction accounts squarely on the abductees themselves. Again he offered no evidence of any kind, no data, no reason to believe he had investigated any of the things he was talking about with such a tone of authority. However, by this time my frustration and anger were mitigated by my realization that Carl Sagan was a very sick man. Though *Nova* had filmed him many months before the disturbing newspaper photo that caused me to write to him, he did not look at all well on the broadcast. It was obvious that since then his condition had declined precipitously.

I was saddened when I heard of Carl Sagan's death just before Christmas in 1996. Though we were opponents in a rancorous controversy, several other things bound us together. We were close in age – I was three years older – and in some ways we had come to represent opposite sides of the same momentous debate. Both of us had received a great deal of media attention – he far more than I – and our disagreements were more apparent on television than anywhere else. Also, at our Boston meeting years before, I had sensed that we genuinely liked each other and shared many of the same liberal values. These are not small things.

I've often pondered exactly what Sagan's private, unspoken attitude was towards the UFO phenomenon, and abduction reports in particular. The subject surely lay heavily on his mind because he returned to it again and again. In fact, several incidents from his younger years suggest that at one time he appeared much more open to the idea that the UFO phenomenon deserved serious study. Nearly 30 years ago, when he was presumably less dependent upon government support for his various research projects, Sagan circulated a petition urging the scientific community to prevent the destruction of the UFO files gathered by the Air Force's recently disbanded Project Blue Book. Together with Thornton Page, he also helped facilitate the somewhat open-minded 1969 UFO Symposium held by the American Association for the Advancement of Science, despite its opposition by many establishment scientists.

And there is something even more intriguing about Sagan's youthful behavior. So far as I know he was the first mainstream scientist to publicly suggest that certain artifacts and works of ancient art provided evidence that Earth may have been visited centuries ago by extraterrestrials. In the last two decades, however, Sagan's public stance was, as we have seen, to firmly repeat the establishment's skeptical position. Despite this apparent commitment, he seemed troubled by the possibility that he might be wrong about UFO reality. He simply could not leave the subject alone, writing and speaking about it again and again, and yet for some reason he apparently could not bring himself to actually investigate specific cases.

Had some of his colleagues in NASA or elsewhere informed him privately (or officially) about the existence of UFOs? Were his denials therefore just a public relations performance to assist an ongoing government cover-up? Or was his uneasiness simply due to the fear that his position on UFOs might turn out to be, in the hindsight of history, a colossal scientific error?

I keep going back in my mind to the way Sagan dealt with me before the television program we shared years before. Rather than indifference or condemnation, he showed curiosity and respect for the subject and for my work in the field. He spoke with an enquiring, interested tone, and his suggestions seemed helpfully intended. At no time in our conversation did he reject UFO abductions with his public voice of scientific certainty. Had he truly believed that the phenomenon was nothing more than a minor popular folly that could be easily explained away, I do not imagine he would have approached me as he did.

My guess is that despite his uneasiness, he felt he must publicly support the side of establishment science, the source of both collegial honors and government funding, though the possibility that he was wrong about UFOs must have been deeply unsettling. Carl Sagan was a passionate believer in the idea that the universe must teem with intelligent life. It's unfortunate that we will probably never know what he really knew or suspected about UFOs or the intelligence of the beings who apparently pilot them.

The March To Seniorhood

Sometime in the late 1980s, a few years after the publication of *Intruders*, I did the math and discovered that in 1991 I would turn 60. Full seniorhood. AARP membership. Cheaper movies. Social Security checks. People standing up and giving me their seats on the subway. Canes and walkers. Well, maybe not the last two items, but all of the rest were definitely lurking on the horizon. I am exaggerating a bit, because 60 would not offer the full, slothful glory of seniorhood that 65 would eventually bestow, but by 1991 I knew it wasn't that far away.

Two major changes were imminent, however. The first was the end of my twenty-year relationship with April, an estrangement that had been coming on gradually for many complex reasons. We had one final trip together, in the summer of 1991, a brief visit to Paris with Grace so that I could show my now grown-up daughter some of the beauties of the place, and in my cowardly way also make the ghastly transition to seniorhood in relative peace and obscurity. Grace would be attending Hampshire College in the fall, so when April and I broke up, the empty nest syndrome was already a reality for both of us.

The second change in my life was less drastic and far more subtle. Without realizing it, I was adopting the hermit-like habits of a typical "older artist," becoming more critical and fixed in my tastes, and much less interested in the current New York gallery scene. In that context I recalled a conversation I had with Franz Kline many years before, when, as a young artist, I asked him what he thought about this contemporary exhibition or that and was surprised, even disappointed, when he said he hadn't seen the shows I mentioned. His shrug and tone of voice implied that he wasn't much interested in seeing them, either. Since he wasn't making the rounds of the galleries as often as I did, I privately felt he was negligent and lacking in a proper degree of youthful curiosity. Years later I came to realize that Franz was in his early fifties at the time and in declining health, so when it came to the current art world and its young, emerging painters, he had already seen enough. He must have felt that his main need now was to stay in his studio and work in the time he had left. Though I didn't know it then, all of us, as we age, get to be like that, and at the present time I am more than 25 years older than Franz was when he died. For me, wisdom and insight take such a long, long time to arrive.

A corollary of my declining interest in the contemporary scene was the ever-narrowing range of the work I went to see at the Met, the Modern, and the Guggenheim. Ever since I began making sculpture, Brancusi had assumed a major place in my personal pantheon, while Mondrian, Vermeer, Corot, Caravaggio, Cezanne, and two periods of Matisse not only held their places but were becoming ever more central. I was also aware that many artists, like Leger and Monet, whose work had once nourished me, were beginning to slip toward the margins. The more I struggled with the darkness and uncertainty of the UFO phenomenon, the more I seemed to need the reassuring clarity and sunlight of the classical images I constantly revisited.

But things were also changing on the more mundane business side of my life as well. After a dispute with my Soho dealer, Marilyn Pearl, I left her gallery and for the first time found myself without a New York representative. The Longpoint Gallery in Provincetown, a summer-only showcase, was now my sole exhibition venue. But the truly bad news was the fact that my press and TV appearances on the UFO abduction phenomenon were apparently having a negative affect on the way that many people – dealers, collectors, and even some fellow painters – viewed my work. This situation flew in the face of the cynical adage that there is no such thing as bad publicity, because I had had plenty of national publicity and yet it seemed to compromise the esteem in which my paintings and sculptures were held. It was as if people had decided that I could not pursue two such different activities and still be a serious, creative artist. There is another old saw – that the test of a first-rate intelligence is the ability to hold two contradictory ideas in mind at the same time – and if it's true, then the general intelligence of the people who make up the mass of the art world is not first-rate. Hardly a surprising observation when you think about it, but discouraging, nevertheless.

In 1992, in another compartment of my life, I received a shock when I was diagnosed with kidney cancer. At the relatively early age of 61, I found myself entering what Gore Vidal sadly named "the hospital years." My right kidney was removed and the cancer was caught early enough to save my life. Now humor has always been a lifeline for me, especially in times of stress, and after I regained semi-consciousness in the recovery room, I murmured to the attending nurses a quip I remembered from Bob and Ray, the marvelous old radio comedians. Ray said that if someone had to have a major, very costly operation such as the one I had just had, he knew of a second hospital where instead, for a much lower fee, they would simply retouch your x-rays. The comment helped me deal with the immediate discomfort of my recovery, but I'm not sure it did anything for the busy nurses.

That same year CBS produced its two-part, fictionalized miniseries based on *Intruders*, and as technical consultant I flew to Los Angeles to meet with the producers, the cast, and Dan Curtis, the director. In Tracy Torme's re-imagined screenplay, the role of Kathie Davis was split into two different characters, marvelously played by Mare Winningham and Daphne Ashbrook. My role was also doubled. Instead of a painter who did UFO research, I became two people: an initially skeptical psychiatrist and an eccentric academic sociologist who ran an abductee support group. As part of my job of advising and consulting I was asked to hypnotically regress a young female abductee I'd previously worked with so that Richard Crenna, who was playing one of the two characters my part had morphed into, could see how hypnosis was done and the two actresses could learn how subjects respond. After the session ended, I decided to play for the cast a slow, dramatic section of the audiotape of my original hypnosis with Kathie Davis as she relived the horror of the aliens taking her baby, her fetus. I've described before, how, in the final anguished moments when she realized what they were doing, she cried out in fury and pain, "It's not right! It's not fair! IT'S NOT FAIR! IT'S *MINE*! I *HATE* YOU! I *HATE* YOU! IT'S NOT FAIR!"

When the tape segment was over, I switched off the recorder and noticed that many of us had tears in our eyes. The heartfelt passion we'd just heard had been so intense that there was a profound, ongoing silence in the room before anyone felt like speaking.

Months later, when I saw the finished production, Daphne Ashbrook, playing one of the two versions of Kathie, cried out these same words with virtually the same helpless fury and pain she'd heard on the tape. For me this was one of the emotional high points of the film, and when I told her so, she made a surprising admission: "Budd, that was not in the script. I was improvising and just added those lines to the scene. I never forgot how enraged and devastated Kathie sounded on the tape. How could anyone forget it? So I just repeated her words and Dan decided to leave it in."

I felt grateful to Daphne for her profound understanding of Kathie's ordeal, and for her skill in recreating it so spontaneously, but I was also appreciative of Dan Curtis for his wisdom in recognizing how Daphne's improvisation heightened the emotional power of the scene.

Years before, when Kurt Vonnegut visited my studio and we went out to dinner with some friends, I asked him what he thought of the motion picture version of his novel, *Slaughterhouse Five*. I expected him to rail and bitch about it – writers, I thought, always hated the way their work was distorted when it was turned into film – but he surprised me. "I liked it!" he said. "The movie version was really good." I remember liking it quite a lot myself, too, but I never dreamed I would be in his position one day of seeing a book of mine made into a movie. Of course not, since I hadn't written anything at the time and had no intention ever to do so. However, here I was, in 1992, viewing just such a translation of *Intruders*.

Looking back, I was not pleased by Tracy Torme's decision to expand the story by including Roswell-like scenes of the recovery of a crashed UFO and an ensuing cold-blooded military cover-up. Those controversial issues do not appear in my book. I was not charmed, either, by Tracy's doubling of the central characters so that Kathie and I became four people in all. Nevertheless, I felt that the miniseries movingly captured the emotional turmoil of the abduction experience, and that on a subtle, psychological level, *Intruders* is by far the most successful of the very few films that have tried to deal fairly with the subject. Though I wasn't as pleased as Vonnegut was by the translation of his book, I still have to give the film version of *Intruders* a B+. Ultimately, after it aired in the United States, it was shown in Europe, South America, Australia, and elsewhere throughout the world where it was seen by many more millions of viewers.

The co-producers of the miniseries, Robert O'Connor and Michael Apted (the distinguished director of *Coalminer's Daughter* and *Gorillas in the Mist*), expressed to me their personal interest in the abduction phenomenon, though both stopped short of saying they wholeheartedly accepted the reality of what they had portrayed in their film. Fair enough. They were, after all, motion picture professionals in a highly competitive field, and had they asked, I could have told them from personal experience how such a public avowal

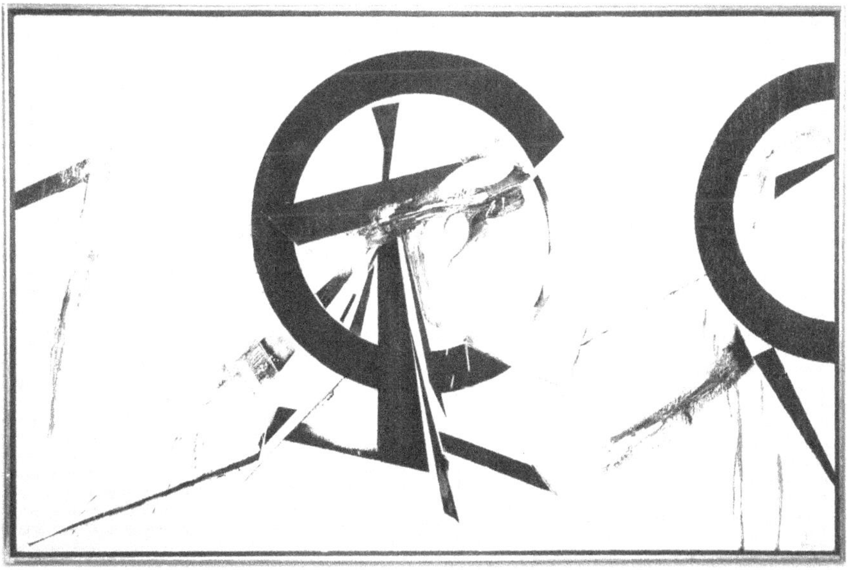

Guardian Procession, oil on canvas, 1992, 32"x 50". Photo: Charles Miller.

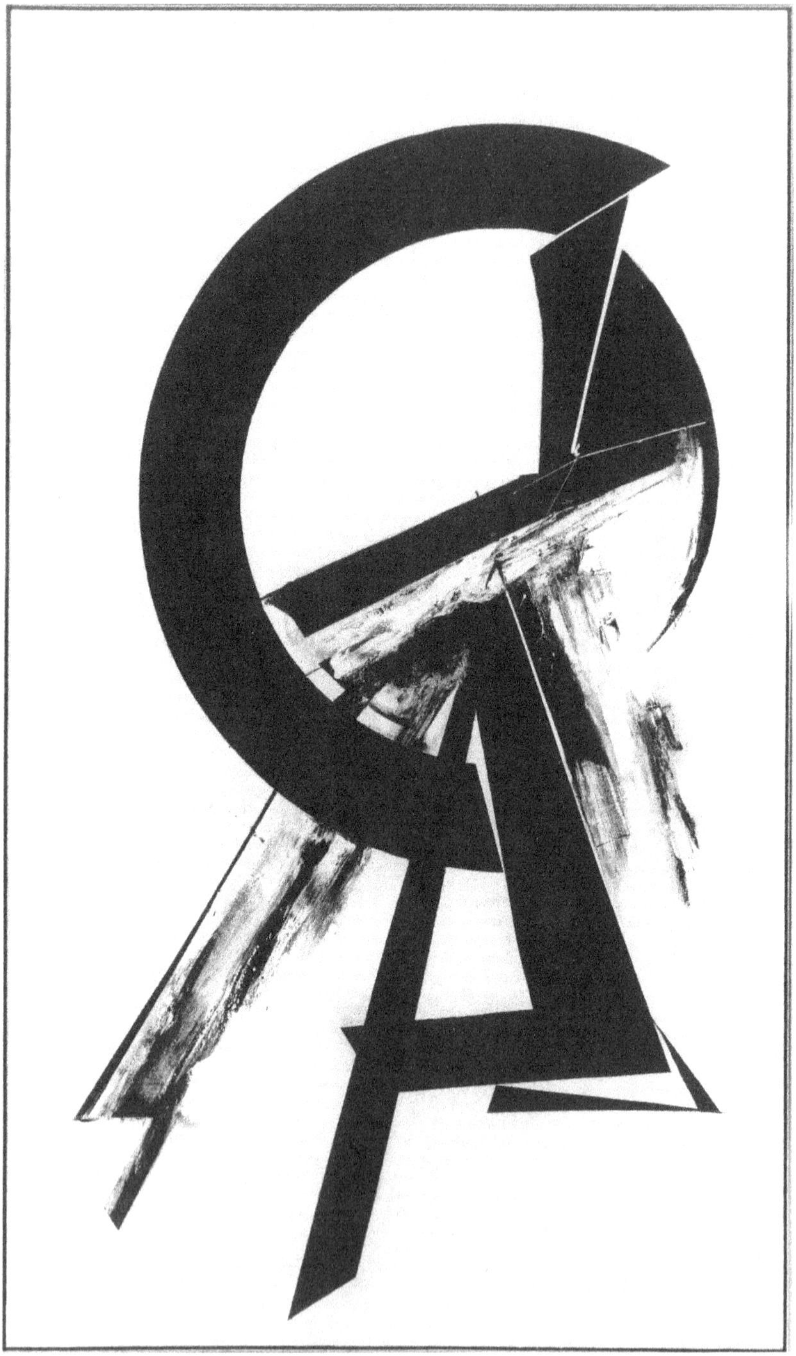

Black and White Guardian, oil, 1990, 87"x 52 ½".

can put a dent in one's career. (And people claim to cut *painters* a little slack because we're expected to have a few wild and unconventional sides to our personality!)

In one of the fortuitous coincidences that seem to happen to me from time to time, some twelve years after *Intruders* had premiered in the United States I was introduced by a friend to a man named Jeff Sagansky. I was told that Jeff had once been head of entertainment programming for CBS TV and that he was interested in the UFO abduction phenomenon. "By the way," he said as we chatted, "I'm the one who bought *Intruders* for CBS and made sure that the miniseries project was carried out."

I did not fall to my knees and kiss his hand, though I felt like it. Since then we have met a few times and he has continued to be supportive of my research, as well as that of my life partner, the journalist Leslie Kean. What goes around, comes around, as they say – even the good things.

But at this time, long before Leslie and I met, I had been seeing an intelligent, attractive young woman named Penny Franklin. Our somewhat intermittent relationship, despite its pleasures, was fraught with too many personal and medical issues to satisfy either of us; the good times were good and the bad times much less so, but nevertheless we continued to go on together for a few years. Looking back, I see that I am the kind of man who is constantly in need of an intimate relationship, no matter what the difficulties. I guess neediness is just another of my inescapable faults, though I hope it's one of the more benign ones.

The changes kept coming. After I was released from the hospital in 1992 with one less kidney than I had when I went in, my art took yet another direction. All of the Guardians I had been painting for the past decade and a half had been hard-edged and intensely colored, but for some reason I found myself wanting to be less classical, less colorful, and more painterly. I embarked on a series of large, loosely austere works that were mostly black and white (echoes of Kline, perhaps?) though still Guardian-like in their basic image. I exhibited them for the first time at Longpoint, and to my surprise and pleasure they were well received. I even sold a few, though a basic art-world cliché had it that collectors don't buy black and white oil paintings – look how long it took Kline to find a market for his work.

A few friends ascribed my new, brushily-worked black-and-whites to the idea that I must be depressed because of my cancer operation or my breakup with April, but instead, I saw them as an affirmation of the joys of a new life and the pleasures of painterliness. Working once more in oil, on stretched, rectangular canvases, I was embracing some of the techniques I had had to set aside in order to make my acrylic, hard-edged, classic Guardians on preconstructed panels. I was having fun again, improvising in an intimate, more physical way, and to me the process was both life enhancing and deliciously sensuous. Renoir once famously remarked that he painted a woman's buttock as if he were caressing it, and though I was not a figure painter, I know exactly what he meant.

Meanwhile, after all I'd been through, I felt closer than ever to my fellow artists and gallery mates like Sideo Fromboluti, Nora Speyer, and Robert Beauchamp, a new member of Longpoint, and to my many old friends from the early AbEx days in New York. It was hard to believe that all of us were now at least in our sixties or seventies, yet we were working with the same creative power and emotional intensity we had decades ago, back in those difficult, partially gilded years – before life had been turned into history.

Three Portrait Sketches

J. Allen Hynek

IT WAS ON THE OCCASION of a 1976 TV program dealing with the New Jersey UFO landing case I had written about in the *Village Voice* that I first met the astronomer J. Allen Hynek, then the most prominent scientist speaking for the reality of the UFO phenomenon. As I've mentioned earlier, Allen had for twenty years been the official scientific consultant to the Air Force on the problem of UFOs and had slowly moved from being an automatic debunker who once suggested that swamp gas (little flickers of burning methane) could be the explanation for the sightings of large structured, maneuvering objects, to his final position as a proponent of UFO reality. It had been a long and essentially heroic voyage of discovery during which his access to official Air Force visual and radar reports gradually persuaded him that people were seeing metallic craft of some sort that could outperform any known aircraft.

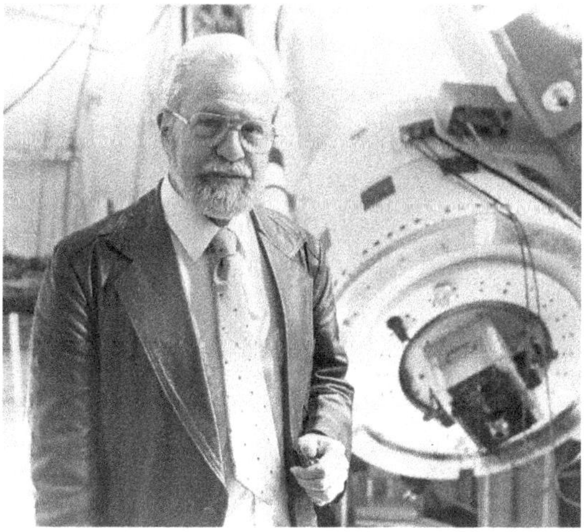

Allen Hynek at work. Photo courtesy of the J. Allen Hynek Center for UFO Studies.

When I first met him, Dr. Hynek had long since left his position with the Air Force and had founded, in Evanston, Illinois, the Center for UFO Studies, which had continued the scientific investigation of UFO reports. On his arrival in New York for the TV broadcast, he came to my apartment and I found him to be open, friendly, and unpretentious, with a rather long, tapering face, rimless glasses, and a neatly-trimmed astronomer's mustache and goatee. His distinctive voice was calm and uninflected, but because of a very subtle burr it suggested the voice of a rather elderly man. (Allen was 66 when we met.) Having spent a great deal of time at an observatory in Arizona, he often dressed in a casual, quasi-western style and was rarely without a rancher's bolo tie, its strings held together by a small clasp of Navajo jewelry.

I was instantly charmed by this understated scientist who eventually became my friend and supporter, and who had about him more than his share of the stereotypical absent-minded professor; in fact I often suspected that he might be suffering from a touch of narcolepsy. One hot summer on the Cape I was asked to drive to Boston to do a radio program with Dr. Hynek who would be flying in that day from Sweden. When we met at the radio station he was tired and rather jet-lagged, adding a new problem to his occasional bouts of drowsiness. The broadcast studio itself was tiny and stifling, but the interviewer was alert and excited and our three-way conversation began very well. Apparently the host had held back the many short advertising tapes he had to play on the air, ganging them up later so as to minimize the interruptions, but during this lengthy commercial break I looked over at Allen and noticed that his eyelids were drooping ominously. As the host busily played one tape after another, ads for used car dealers, Italian restaurants, and so on, I saw that Allen, chin down, was now sound asleep. When the siege of commercials finally ended, the interviewer turned to him, eager to resume our dialogue.

"Dr. Hynek," he said, about to fire another carefully prepared question, but then his eyes widened in horror as he saw that his guest was actually on the verge of snoring. "DR. HYNEK!" he called, almost shouting. No reaction. In a panic he swung around to me and said, "Uh, BUDD… Budd Hopkins… what do *you* think about the Roswell case," or some such question. I answered it and we chatted for a few minutes. I allowed Allen a short restorative nap before I nudged him lightly under the table. His head popped up, he blinked his eyes, and he smiled at me. The broadcast resumed without a hitch.

On my drive back to Wellfleet I had a fantasy of the poor, sweating interviewer talking to his wife at dinner. "You'll never believe this," he would say, "but a guy I was interviewing today actually *fell asleep during the interview*! Sound asleep! I couldn't wake him up! I almost told the engineer to turn off his mike because he looked like he was about to start snoring – *on the air*! My career would have been over. But thank God he finally woke up."

I chuckled to myself all the way home.

During Allen's twenty years of service as Air Force consultant, the unparalleled mass of raw data to which he had access allowed him to develop the first effective classification system for UFO reports. Close Encounters of the Third Kind, his term for nearby sightings of UFO *occupants*, has obviously become part of the popular lexicon, thanks in part to Steven Spielberg's eponymous film in which Allen made a cameo appearance, staring at the sky with his pipe clutched firmly between his teeth. Despite the several abduction cases he investigated, he always had trouble accepting the reality of the abduction phenomenon. At a conference in the early 1980s, I gave a lecture on abductions that included slides of the similar scars and scoop marks that follow the sampling procedures the occupants carry out on abductees during their examinations. I also showed virtually identical abductee drawings of their captors and the crafts' interiors, and photos of the ground traces that remained after UFO landings. After my talk, Allen asked me to come with him back to his hotel room. As we hurried along, he said, "Dammit, Budd, you make a strong case for abductions, and I don't like it, but I'd accept it more easily if I thought the aliens made mistakes… dropped something, or something like that. That would make it more believable." When I asked why we were hurrying back to his room, he replied that he was desperate to make a pit stop. Luckily we made it in time.

But unfortunately, when we had this conversation, I had not yet discovered the wide range of alien "mistakes" that we have since learned about from the accumulation of abduction reports of the last 25 years. For example, because the abductees are stripped of their clothes during these experiences and several people – strangers to one another – might be taken at once, there are many reports of abductees being returned to wherever they had been at the outset of their encounters wearing someone else's clothes, or with their shirts on inside out or backwards, or even, in some cases, having been returned to the wrong house. I have two separate cases in which women were abducted from their cars and when they were returned, each found that her earrings were on backwards, with the clasps on the outside. Apparently the aliens don't understand jewelry.

Sadly, by the time I had accumulated a number of such accounts, Allen Hynek was ill with the cancer that killed him in 1986, at the age of 76. He would have enjoyed the irony that alien beings, in possession of an incredibly advanced technology, apparently lacked the skills to put an abductee's T-shirt on right-side out.

As one might expect, Allen had often been attacked for his open-mindedness on the UFO subject by hard-core debunkers such as Philip Klass and Martin Gardner, and it was an article by the latter in the June 26, 1978 issue of the *New York Review of Books* (*NYRB*) that I once responded to by letter. Like many debunkers, Gardner was slippery and misleading when he wrote against any phenomenon he disliked, and in his *NYRB* piece he implied that Dr. Hynek, at the time chairman of the Department of Astronomy at Northwestern University, was (merely) an astronomer who rather uncritically stressed the importance of the UFO phenomenon, which Gardner stated the Air Force had investigated and rejected. What he left out, of course, was the all-important fact that this very same Air Force investigation, staffed by a constant turnover of inexperienced, lower ranking officers – captains, sergeants, etc. – had had only *one* scientifically trained and credentialed consultant over its twenty-year run, and that scientist was Allen Hynek, who, as a result of these investigations, had come to view the UFO issue as of potentially earth-shaking importance. It is interesting to imagine if the one scientist attached to the Air Force's official investigation for twenty years had come to an *opposite* conclusion, deciding that there was nothing at all to the mass of UFO reports he had looked into. Gardner would have shouted this news from the tops of the highest ivory towers in the land, hailing the man's objectivity and intelligence. But since it didn't turn out that way, he evidently decided that it would be best to conceal Dr. Hynek's twenty-year role in the Air Force study and pretend that he was merely a rather incompetent bystander, a "true believer," who knew nothing about the hated phenomenon that the Air Force investigation had dismissed. I wrote to the *NYRB* and set the record straight.

Many years later a second letter of mine was published in the *NYRB*, this time in my own defense rather than Allen's. The author of this new hit piece was the anti-Freudian fanatic, Frederick Crews, who attacked me partly because of references in my work to the recovery of previously repressed memories. The very notion of repressed memories – an idea that Freud espoused – seems always to set Professor Crews off into a hissy-fit, and in the article his visceral hatred of Freud fused with his contempt for the UFO phenomenon and spilled over in my direction. As a long-time subscriber, I read Crew's piece and responded almost immediately. Unlike other publications which have printed my letters – *Vanity Fair* and *Discover*, among others – the *NYRB* neither edited nor shortened what I wrote either time, a rare and responsible way of handling such submissions.

Along with Allen Hynek's occasional moments of absentmindedness – appropriate, perhaps, to his profession – he had several other endearing habits, one of which I learned about when I stayed overnight at his home in Evanston, Illinois. Evanston is a Chicago suburb that includes Northwestern University, where, as an immensely popular professor, he had been voted teacher of the year. *Chez* Hynek I was assigned the family guest room, which was filled with file cabinets crammed with UFO case reports. When the phone in the room rang several times during the night, I decided I must be sleeping in the headquarters of Allen's Center for UFO Studies.

Earlier that evening, he and I had talked for hours, and in the morning when I came down for breakfast, Mimi Hynek, Allen's charming and efficient wife, informed me of a quirk of her husband's that I was not aware of. "He doesn't like to say much in the morning until he's had his coffee and read the funny papers. He loves the funny papers."

A few minutes later Allen came into the room, gave me a perfunctory greeting, and settled down with what must have been the *Chicago Tribune*. Skipping the front page, he systematically unfolded and refolded the pages until he found what he wanted. Then he leaned back and disappeared behind what I guessed was the comic section. As I ate my breakfast in the ensuing silence, I heard him chuckle from time to time and was amazed that there was still something amusing in what seemed a hopelessly corny genre. As I thought about it, I remembered an example from my childhood, the old comic strip, *Mutt and Jeff*. In one panel, Mutt tells Jeff he wants to sell him his talking dog for five dollars.

"Why are you asking so little?" Jeff asks. "That's a valuable talking dog."

"I know," Mutt replies, "but he lies to me." That seemed the *crème de la crème* of the funny pages when I read it sometime in the late 1930s, and I had laughed then as Allen was doing now, a half-century later, at what was probably an equally naïve and unfunny comic page. The occasional chuckles continued until he finally sighed, refolded his paper, put it back on the table, and then leaned forward as if to say, "Now we can start talking."

On several occasions when he came to New York, Allen spent the night in my studio, and though he seemed to enjoy these visits, he was probably disappointed that my local newspaper, *The New York Times*, was bereft of a comic page. During a memorably serious exchange we had about some depressing UFO cases we were separately investigating, one of us, I don't recall which, said, "You know, I live my life as if none of this were true," and the other immediately replied, "Of course, we have to. If we didn't, how could we get through a day with all of this weighing on us?" But we both knew we would soldier on.

The brain cancer from which Allen Hynek died in 1986 began to manifest itself the year before at a UFO conference in Beverly, Massachusetts. David Jacobs and I, along with Allen and a number of other speakers, attended the weekend meeting, and during several of the morning lectures, Allen and I sat next to one another. I noticed that he was holding a pad and pen but was not taking notes. At one point I saw him write down a single word, "good," and that was that.

At the lunchtime break, Allen asked me to drive him back to his motel, but when he got into my car he admitted that he didn't remember the name of the place he was staying, nor could he recall where it was. I drove around the various motels in the area, and even stopped to ask someone about other places nearby. By the time we finally located his motel I was becoming alarmed, and my worries deepened when Allen said he had no idea what his room number was or if he had been given a key. The management helped us out, and when he was finally settled in, he decided to take a shower. I sat outside, conversing through the bathroom door, and after he came out and dressed he seemed refreshed, so we drove back to the main meeting room for a spot of lunch.

That afternoon, when it came Allen's turn to speak, he began his talk in a halting, almost incoherent way, with long, disconcerting pauses, dismaying to everyone in the room. David Jacobs was the acting introducer of the speakers, and Allen finally turned to him, helplessly handing over his notes and asking David to read his talk for him. He took a seat on the dais while David struggled to make an orderly presentation out of Allen's scattered and very incomplete notes. As Allen sat listening with a dazed expression on his face, it was obvious to all of us that something was terribly wrong. When David finished, I immediately approached the conference organizer and asked that Allen be taken to the hospital. I assumed he was having a stroke and suggested that his family should be notified.

When the ambulance arrived, David had to persuade a reluctant Allen to go along to the hospital, "just for a few hours rest," as he tactfully put it. Sometime later that afternoon Allen returned to the conference, apparently back to his usual self and relieved that the doctors assured him he had not suffered a stroke. That evening during dinner, without realizing it, I saw Allen for the last time. The next day he returned home – he was now living in Arizona – and a few months later, during a visit to a specialist for a prostate problem, he mentioned that he had been experiencing what he called "blackouts." This admission led to more tests and the diagnosis of inoperable brain cancer.

Allen Hynek had been born in 1910, a year that Halley's Comet visited our skies, and he died in 1986, the year it returned once more. He had wanted to witness this rare astronomical sight so his wife and a few friends drove him out into the desert, and there the gravely ill astronomer had his final look. As Halley's Comet marked his arrival in the world, this time it signified his leaving it. Allen passed away a few days later.

John Mack

As MY WORK WITH ABDUCTEES became better known within the psychological community, I began to receive referrals from therapists describing what was to them a new phenomenon in their professional practice: clients who reported post-traumatic symptoms apparently following mysterious periods of missing time and/or the sudden appearance of unusual lights or craft-like objects. In one case a therapist introduced me to a young woman who had described driving to Florida with a friend in a two-car caravan when both stopped on the virtually deserted highway to watch a large, glowing UFO in a nearby field. This disconcerting sight was followed by a shared memory gap, a substantial period of missing time, and a flood of PTSD symptoms. With the therapist sitting in, I interviewed this young woman and ultimately used hypnosis to help her recall the Florida incident as well as several other earlier abductions. Because the process obviously eased the life-long post-traumatic stress from which she'd been suffering, her therapist was impressed and a few months later she told me she was sending a colleague of hers, Dr. John Mack, to talk to me. She thought that this distinguished Harvard psychiatrist would be receptive to the issue of UFO abductions and the therapeutic efficacy of the methods

I'd been using.

One wintry day in January 1990, I received a cautious phone call from Dr. Mack and we arranged a meeting. A few days later he came to my studio, still a bit apprehensive. We talked intensely for an hour or two. I showed him photos of the scars and scoop marks abductees were often left with after their encounters, described their detailed and extremely similar accounts, and ultimately handed him a box of twenty unopened letters from the flood of mail I'd been receiving ever since the publication of *Intruders*.

"*You* open them, John," I said, knowing that as a professional he would keep the identity of the writers confidential. "Read them and let me know what you think. I'm sure you'll be able to tell in at least some cases if the writers are suffering a mental illness or if they seem to be reporting real experiences."

A few days later John called back, clearly amazed by what he'd read. Although he thought that one or two of the writers might be emotionally unstable, the majority seemed to him to be normal, sane people who were reporting a remarkably consistent set of disturbing traumatic experiences. In retrospect John and I both realized that we had become colleagues at that moment and had begun a rich and rewarding friendship that would last until his untimely death in 2007.

Though he lived in the Boston area, we stayed in close touch through letters, phone calls, and visits, just as I had been doing for years with David Jacobs in Philadelphia. John and I talked about our work, about new and challenging cases, and eventually, over drinks and dinner, we even had a few revealing conversations about our rather fraught romantic relationships. Early on, because he hadn't used hypnosis since his student days, he sat in on a few of my sessions to brush up on the techniques involved, and in short order I began referring possible abduction cases in the Boston area to him. By the end of 1990 he was, along with David Jacobs and me, deeply committed to the exploration of the abduction phenomenon, and as a mark of respect for the pioneering work I had done, in 1992 he dedicated his first book, *Abductions*, to me with these generous words: "To Budd Hopkins, who led the way."

John Mack was one of the most charismatic men I have ever known, and his upbeat, optimistic temperament was impossible to resist. Though he was tall, slender, and classically handsome, he walked with short, quick, shuffling steps and a gentle stoop, as if the varied concerns of his abductee clients unconsciously weighed heavily upon him. But if he found these issues upsetting he seemed unwilling to let them disturb his sanguine nature, and in fact his infectious warmth was one of his most appealing traits. Nevertheless, all of us who work with UFO abductees have had to invent ways of keeping our spirits up because we see so much psychic pain in our clients. To get through the day my dear friend David Jacobs relies on the creative teaching of American history and upon his marvelous sense of humor and wry self-denigration. I find solace in making my art and visiting the Metropolitan Museum about every ten days to bask among the Cezannes and Vermeers. But although David and I are sometimes unable to avoid brooding in front of company, John always remained the determined optimist, smiling as he shuffled along, even though his shoulders were hunched and his back was curved uncomfortably. Never in my presence did he seem emotionally down or anything but hopeful about the ultimate intentions of the UFO occupants.

John possessed a marvelously deep, resonant voice, which he used with great effectiveness in his frequent lectures. It was a calming, intelligent voice and helped make his complex presentations both eloquent and seductive. However, like unavoidable nervous tics, all of us have our favorite words and expressions, and "ontological" was his; one could count on hearing it a number of times in each of his talks, an indication of the somewhat abstract level of his usual discourse.

Over coffee or drinks John and I always discussed the fact that though we were both graduates of Oberlin College (two years apart), we had had radically different lives prior to our college years and our later involvement with the UFO phenomenon. Unlike me, John, a native New Yorker, had been born into a wealthy and privileged intellectual environment where, he explained, atheism and cold scientific rationalism prevailed. He had gone on to medical school, had become a psychiatrist, and eventually a strict follower of the teachings of Freud.

In medical school, John had, of course, been trained in science, though to a purist like Carl Sagan, psychiatry did not qualify as one of its branches. Once, in a conversation with the late astronomer, I mentioned that several psychiatrists I knew had become curious about the UFO phenomenon and had admitted they had no adequate explanation for the abductees' detailed and extraordinarily similar accounts. Sagan replied in his high, somewhat pinched and nasal voice, "Well, a *scientist* would say…" followed by a debunking "explanation" and a rote denigration of the methods and standards of those in the field of psychology. Thus, with one condescending verbal flourish the famous astronomer seemed to feel he had not only excommunicated John Mack and all of his colleagues from the halls of science but had also rendered their abduction opinions worthless.

In my discussions with John about our earlier years, I explained that I saw my life trajectory as almost exactly the opposite of his. Unlike the hyper-rationalism of his early, upper-class environment, I was reared in a very conventional, Republican, middle-class home where at least some vague attention was paid to Protestant religious beliefs. Though I would never have described my family as devout, intermittent church attendance was a factor in my childhood. As I've written earlier, I was a bundle of unexamined conservative tenets, political and otherwise, until I attended college, read hungrily, and thus began to achieve a degree of intellectual and ethical maturity.

Science had never been my thing, but art was. I explained to John that as an abstract painter, I was operating in a magic territory where I turned inert physical things, like fabric and pigment and personal marks and strokes, into pure emotion. To me, this creative process has about it more than a whiff of the mystical and is a world away from John's early rationalistic, atheistic background. (His family were non-practicing Jews.) But as his life unfolded, he gradually moved away from these conventionally scientific roots and began to explore what one might describe as more arcane, even mystical realities. He became a follower of EST and a devotee of Werner Erhard, and was soon experimenting with various methods of consciousness expansion, via hallucinogenic drugs and the deep-breathing methods of Stanislav Grof. Eventually, in 1990, when John and I met and I introduced him to the complexities and confusions of the UFO abduction phenomenon, his life took still another radical new direction.

As I've pointed out before, after my 1964 UFO sighting I realized that in order to look more deeply into it I needed to add a rationally grounded scientific curiosity to my normally creative, quasi-mystical life as a painter. From then on, transubstantiation would have to coexist with rigorous, skeptical investigation. But in a case of inverse symmetry, John Mack, a few years after his introduction to the subject, began to view the abduction phenomenon less in the cold, physical light of day – as he had at first – than through the comforting lens of yet another expansive new spiritual framework. While I, the artist, was amassing photographs of abductees' scars and scoop marks and collecting soil samples for analysis, John, the erstwhile scientist, was becoming ever more preoccupied with philosophical speculations about alien reality and developing a nearly sacred regard for the innate truth of witness testimony. So far as I know John never took a photograph of an abductee's abrasions or submitted an object for scientific analysis, and in fact eventually stated that by contrast to witness testimony, he regarded physical evidence as virtually worthless. It is my guess that John took no photographs because he did not like to be reminded of the physical injuries abductees often suffer, while at the same time I did not like to admit that I was too ill-educated to knowledgeably address the complex ontological issues he was used to speaking about at major universities.

Without any doubt, however, one of John's most endearing qualities was a special kind of innocence, an attribute not usually found among university professors and experienced psychiatrists. Around John I always felt like a bit of a cynic in that my view of the innate trustworthiness of my fellow man was always a few notches below his; I insisted upon testing eyewitness testimony in any way I

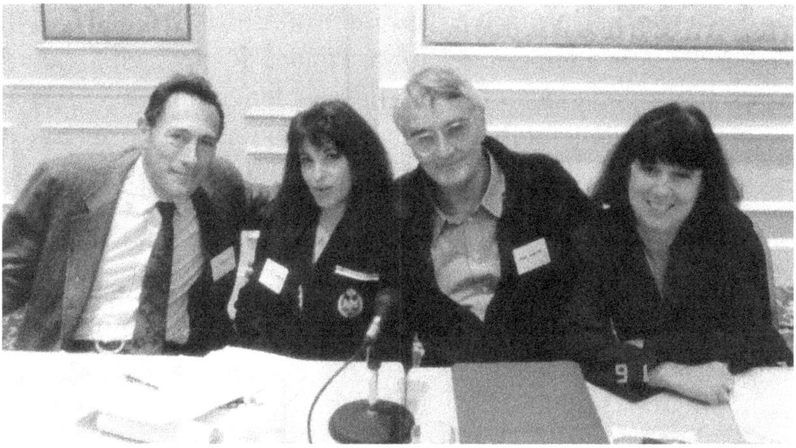

Left to right, psychiatrist John Mack, program coordinator Georgia Flamburis, myself, and psychologist Dr. Susan Fox. We were participating in a Massachusetts Networking Conference in October 1991. John was then very new to the field of UFO abduction research.

could. It was John's innocence that enabled one woman in his support group to carry out an unconscionable deception that eventually caused him enormous difficulties with the Harvard authorities. It was also a measure of John's unruffled sense of trust that, soon after the Harvard crisis, he accepted an invitation to speak before an organization of professional skeptics and committed debunkers. Against my advice, he apparently attended with the naïve idea that he could change a few ironclad minds, only to find, just as he ended his lecture, that these troglodytes had secretly imported this same treacherous woman to denounce him in front of the audience he had just addressed.

As long as I knew him – some fifteen years – John never seemed to lose either his natural, trusting ingenuousness, or his upbeat, chronically hopeful state of mind. These qualities in tandem made him personally irresistible, and many, many people adored him. An abductee who had worked with both John and me once remarked that he went to John to feel uplifted and inspired, and to me to find out what really happened to him during his abduction experiences. Sadly, I realized that though I could deliver truth and accuracy,

I could never deliver enough spiritual uplift to completely satisfy this man's needs. Increasingly, John seemed determined to believe, despite a complete lack of supporting evidence, that the UFO occupants were here to help us humans, and once went so far as to ask an abductee who had been particularly traumatized not to come back to his support group until he understood that the aliens were essentially benevolent.

And so finally John Mack and I, friends and colleagues for the last fifteen years of his life, found ourselves traveling on separate, divergent tracks. His path was the more elevated and hopeful – one might say "religious" – while mine was, I believe, the more grounded and realistic. But despite our differing views of the UFO abduction phenomenon, I miss him terribly and find it almost impossible to believe that someone so real, so vivid, is gone, killed by a drunken driver in a senseless, tragic accident. .

As time has passed, our discordant opinions, once so critical, now seem to have shrunk away, because life, human life and friendship, is finally so much more important than the interpretation of alien intrusions that we are, in any case, helpless to prevent.

Laurence Rockefeller

One of the better-known Willem De Kooning stories describes the time he met Laurence Rockefeller's brother Nelson in the late 1940s, when this major collector of modern art bought a De Kooning abstraction. It was a prestigious sale that marked an enormous breakthrough for the financially struggling painter. He had often talked about how, as a child in Holland living in poverty, his family sometimes referred to "the Rockefellers" as symbolically representing an unattainable peak of wealth and power. And now, he told his friends, he'd even been invited to a party at the Rockefeller's splendid New York apartment where, among other important artworks, a pair of commissioned Matisse panels flanked the fireplace. For Bill it was one of those rare but classic "If my parents could only see me now" events.

Bill was wearing a suit for the occasion, he said, and he remembered to take off his inelegant Dutch seamen's cap and slip into his overcoat pocket before he entered their apartment. When he was ushered into the reception hall, Mrs. Rockefeller, "Happy" as she was known, came over to him smiling gaily and resplendent in a beautiful gown and glittering jewels. Apparently he gazed at her with awe, and then paid her a compliment he'd learned years ago from his artist friends: "Mrs. Rockefeller," he said with feeling, "you look like a million bucks!"

I had that story in mind years later, in 1992, when John Mack arranged for David Jacobs and me to accompany him to Laurence Rockefeller's Pocantico Hills estate for an informal discussion on the subject of UFOs. Laurence – Nelson's older brother – was interested in the phenomenon, and he and John had known one another for years. It seems that John's parents and the Rockefellers moved in some of the same social circles, and that John and Laurence had occasionally played tennis together. Their friendship apparently led Laurence to give financial aid to some of the liberal social organizations John belonged to, and by 1992 he had become interested in his work with UFO abductees. This personal connection was a boon to David and me, who would not otherwise have been able to meet and discuss the phenomenon with someone so able to lend prestige and financial support to its investigation.

Laurence sent a limousine to fetch us in the late afternoon, but because David Jacob's car had broken down on the way to our rendezvous point, we arrived at his stately but rambling mansion rather late. The vast Rockefeller family acreage on the Hudson River includes many large homes as well as an auditorium and a number of other outbuildings, and as we drove through the gate I recalled that it also contained a climate-controlled, underground storage area where the Museum of Modern Art warehoused part of its vast holdings. Picasso underground, one might say.

I had no idea what to expect of our mini-conference, but Laurence greeted us warmly at the door and ushered us into a large, comfortable, quite relaxed living room, which seemed devoid of ostentation; in fact, some of the old furniture looked a bit *too* relaxed.

There were surprisingly few works of art on the walls – his brothers Nelson and David were the family's main collectors – though during a later visit to Laurence's Rockefeller Center office I saw a fine Gauguin on the wall.

From the outset our host insisted that we use his first name, and as David and I adjusted to the notion of addressing this august octogenarian as "Laurence" ("Larry" was clearly out of the question), he offered us drinks from a small recessed bar in the living room. As he poured me a Scotch-on-the-rocks, using a small shot glass to dole out a properly conservative libation, I recalled a remark that a British journalist had made sometime in the late 1950s. For months the man had been in Washington, studying the American political system, and wrote that he was struck by the ideological similarity of our two main political parties at that time. He explained that after chatting with many elected officials, listening to their speeches, and attending numerous political cocktail parties, the only difference he could find between Republicans and Democrats was that at their cocktail parties, Republicans measured and Democrats poured. By this standard Laurence Rockefeller was definitely a Republican.

We were joined at dinner by our host's gracious and elderly wife who told us she had just been watching a TV program about the Rev. Billy Graham. When she brought up the issue of angels, I was reminded that the Rockefellers were, as Garrison Keillor might say, "hopeful Baptists," and therefore Laurence would probably be more predisposed toward John Mack's benign and optimistic view of the (angelic?) UFO occupants than he would be toward the more anguished view David and I shared.

After dinner I was able to brief Laurence about the still unfolding Linda Cortile abduction, and when I asked if I could display two short pieces of videotape dealing with the case he agreed and led John, David, and me up to his bedroom. (The downstairs VCR was apparently broken.) I felt an unexpected, somewhat uncomfortable sense of intimacy in the room as the four of us sat around – and on – Laurence's bed to watch the tape. I suppose that the grandeur of the Rockefeller name, when combined with the courtly manners of this venerable and distinguished gentleman whom I had just met, made it difficult for me to accept the idea that I was merely in someone's bedroom with colleagues, watching a videotape about a UFO case. This odd scene was yet another of the many unexpected little collage moments I've lived through.

Later, in a den-like meeting room downstairs, the four of us discussed the issue that was currently occupying a central place in Laurence's thinking: how to persuade the government to release whatever important information it might be concealing about the UFO phenomenon. He explained that he had met Bill Clinton on several occasions and thought that if he wrote the new president a polite letter and simply asked him to release whatever information the government was withholding, Clinton would agree and the information would automatically be made public.

I saw this hope as unbelievably naïve, though I didn't say so out loud. An official announcement that unknown, possibly extraterrestrial craft, displaying a technology vastly superior to ours, were operating at will on our planet, might well unleash an intolerable degree of social and economic chaos, and no government, I believed, would dare risk it. Neither Clinton nor any other government leader I could think of would publicly admit our utter impotence in the face of such a potential threat. However, Laurence, ever the committed optimist, said he was sure that (a) Clinton would comply with his request to make the UFO issue public, and (b) that this official statement would not cause any real social or economic upheaval. He was clearly determined to write his letter to the new president.

I told him what I thought would happen as a result: Clinton would send Laurence's request on to NASA, the Air Force, or a science advisor and would then be told that there was no secret stash of UFO evidence, that all UFO reports were easily explained away, and that there was nothing to worry about — the decades-long official government policy. Laurence disagreed; Bill Clinton was a fine man and would comply with such a request.

Meanwhile I had thought of a more covert way to find out what the government agency or agencies handling UFO matters might really know and decided to lay it out to the other three. At this time,

1992, I knew that Laurence was acquainted with many prominent government officials, mostly Republicans, who were then either out of office, retired, or working in the private sector – people like Gerald Ford, Jimmy Carter, Barry Goldwater, and Donald Rumsfeld (!); figures from the field of international diplomacy like Perez de Cuellar; and even a few people still holding public office like Senator Claiborne Pell, who I knew from personal conversations was deeply interested in the UFO issue. My plan was simple: I suggested that Laurence invite five or six such people for a private weekend at his home so that David, John, and I could brief them in depth about the evidence, the complexity and the portentousness of the phenomenon. It was possible, I thought, that some of these prominent figures might have retained contacts within the government, perhaps people in lower positions, who might be willing to leak some information to us or provide a few names of those who might. It seemed almost certain to me that some individuals who knew a great deal about hidden UFO evidence might regard it as their duty to the public to release – anonymously, of course – some of that information. It was worth a shot, I said, and I guessed that few of the political figures I'd named would refuse Laurence's invitation to such a confidential and absolutely private gathering.

"No," said Laurence to this proposal. "I'm just going to write my letter to Bill Clinton and ask him directly." And very shortly after, he did – to no effect.

SINCE IT WAS GETTING LATE, Laurence suggested we call it a night and turn in. "We can resume our discussion in the morning," he said. "We'll have breakfast at 7:30 and continue then."

Each of the three of us was assigned a guest room, but when I looked around my quarters I saw there was no alarm clock. I went downstairs to find Laurence and ask if he had an extra one.

"No, I don't think so," he said. "But don't worry. I'll get you up."

And so, at 7:00 a.m., I heard his promised call outside my door: "Budd... Oh, Budd... time to get up!" This was yet another delightfully unexpected and incongruous moment in my complicated life, being awakened, not by a buzzer or a bell or a radio, but by a famous elderly millionaire calling out my name in his gentle, patrician voice.

During and after breakfast we resumed our discussion, but Laurence had already determined that since his request to Bill Clinton would undoubtedly be honored, there would be no need for a Plan B, so we talked about other aspects of the UFO phenomenon. I assumed we would all travel back to Manhattan in Laurence's limousine so that we could continue our discussions on the road, but I was wrong. As David, John, and I climbed into the limo, Laurence waved goodbye and turned away to board a waiting helicopter for the flight to his office. Our visit to Pocantico hills was over.

I SAW LAURENCE ONCE OR TWICE MORE, each time in his Rockefeller Center office, and at one point, after I presented him with some remarkable new evidence supporting the reality of UFO abductions, he said, "Budd, I should be funding your work. What you are doing is quite important." The funding never materialized, however, partly, I think, because Laurence decided not to compromise his optimism about the so-called "benign" nature and goals of the UFO occupants by supporting those of us who were dubious about their ultimate aims. However, during the short period in which I knew him, I saw him as well-meaning and generous, an exemplary product of nineteenth century manners and values. But because Laurence belonged to this rare, nearly obsolescent world of gentility and hopefulness, he was at sea in the rough-and-tumble confusion and complexity of modern life. It is, nevertheless, a tribute to his steady intelligence and humanitarian impulses that he sought ways to end the official censorship of the UFO phenomenon, and I'm pleased that briefly I had a chance to participate with him in this effort.

Life in the New Millennium

SOMETIME IN THE LATE 1930S, on a lazy summer day, I stretched out once again on my favorite grassy spot in the front yard and decided to try a bit of recently mastered arithmetic. Gazing idly up at the delicate leaves of the tall, rather isolated Ginkgo tree that towered nearby, I computed in my head the difference between 1931 – the year of my birth – and the year 2000, the start of the impossibly distant second millennium. So shocked was I to discover that I would be 69 when the new century arrived that I instantly assumed I would be dead by then. No one I knew, except my ancient grandmother and a few doddering relatives, was *that* old.

Well, I made it anyway, though there have been a few times when I thought I wouldn't. Among the goodies that Mother Nature cynically handed me in 1998, two years short of the millennium, were a heart attack – the worst, most continuous pain I'd ever felt – and a diagnosis of non-Hodgkin's lymphoma, a type of leukemia affecting the lymph nodes. Luckily I have a version of this usually fatal disease that develops very slowly, and I've lived with it untreated for ten years. Its distressing outward signs are a series of large, unsightly, goiter-like swellings around my throat and the lower sides of my face, but since I've never been overly vain about my appearance I've mostly been able to ignore my increasing resemblance to the Elephant Man. When I look in the mirror, I try whistling past the impending graveyard to bitch that these ugly bulges on my face merely mean that I've got more acreage to shave each morning.

Still, there are times when I receive unwelcome doses of reality about my appearance. When I was recently interviewed by CNN's science correspondent, Miles O'Brian, and saw myself on TV, I was horrified by the way the swellings around my neck seemed to overpower all of my once-normal face. Nevertheless I dutifully visit Dr. Ian Yudelman, my concerned and highly skilled oncologist, for regular blood tests and examinations, and – fingers crossed – I'm currently beginning the process of chemotherapy. Otherwise I'm alive and painting, writing and working with abductees, though these life-giving activities are fueled from an ever-diminishing energy pool.

A few years before these illnesses occurred, in the lonely and discouraged time preceding the arrival of the new millennium, I met Carol Rainey, a woman whom I enthusiastically began to court. In 1996 we were married, and since each of us had been married twice before, we were both hopeful that this was *It*. Sadly, we eventually came to realize that the marriage had been a major mistake. Harsh arguments and deep-seated emotional problems, which had not been obvious within the initial fog of excitement, soon began to erode what had seemed so promising and led to a series of ever-deepening estrangements. After a number of temporary separations – the first was in 2001 – we began to live apart; I made our separation legal and then filed for divorce, ending the marriage.

But in 2001, and partly with the hope of providing Carol with the start of a new career, I contracted with her to co-write with me another book on the UFO abduction phenomenon. I saw to it that she was given equal authorial credit, but the process of actually creating the book soon became yet another cause of intense friction between us. Nevertheless, in 2003, Atria Books, a division of Simon and Schuster, finally published *Sight Unseen*, my fourth contribution to the subject, and though I regard it as a solid and important piece of work, it unfortunately recalls too many arguments and sad moments for me to relish the memories of its creation and birth.

A few years earlier, however, in 1996, another Simon and Schuster division had published my third book, *Witnessed*, the account of a unique abduction case in which, around three a.m., the UFO occupants apparently decided to reveal their presence for a moment before an audience of important political figures. Its high point came when a helpless protagonist, "Linda Cortile," was abducted through a window of her twelfth story apartment by three diminutive alien beings, who then floated her up into a hovering UFO *in full view of an astounded group of diplomatic figures*. Down below, on nearly deserted South Street, the cars of their official motorcade, as well as nearby vehicles on the Brooklyn Bridge and the FDR Drive, had all simultaneously lost power and come to a stop. One assumes that this mass electrical effect, apparently engineered by the UFO occupants, was to make sure that a particular group of privileged people had a clear look at the unearthly spectacle. Instead of the covert, "invisible" procedures usually followed in urban abductions, this UFO was suddenly and dramatically self-illuminated, even shining a wide beam of light down on Linda Cortile and her three captors as they were levitated up into the craft. Two witnesses at different locations later told me that because of the intensely bright lights and the oddly suspended figures, they thought at first that a special-effects sci-fi movie was being filmed. Amazingly, all of this took place in only two or three minutes, in lower Manhattan near the Brooklyn Bridge, during one of the quietest times of the night!

This unprecedented November 1989, event occurred just as the Cold War was winding down and the Communist Empire was disintegrating. According to what I later learned – off the record – from two security men from the motorcade, the officials who witnessed Linda Cortile's abduction were on their way to a downtown heliport for a flight to yet another emergency meeting. So, in what looked like a carefully orchestrated performance, the aliens apparently chose to reveal their presence and their technological power to a group of world leaders at a critical time in world affairs. Not quite the mythical "landing on the White House lawn," but close.

During a four-year investigation of this smoothly orchestrated 3:00 a.m. abduction, I eventually located a number of still astonished independent eyewitnesses. One had been in her stalled car on the Brooklyn Bridge at the time, while another had been traveling with her companion on the nearby FDR Drive, and several others were standing in various locations even closer to the scene. Eventually I met with officials from a number of organizations, including the United Nations Security Police, the British and Russian delegations to the U.N., the U.S. State Department, the New York Police Department, and the Secret Service. In these years of intense investigation I dealt with over twenty eyewitnesses to one aspect or another of the case, so the work of putting all of this evidence together in coherent form made *Witnessed* by far the most complex of the four books I've written. And because I had to labor over it so intensely and was still pleased by the results, *Witnessed* remains my favorite book, the one closest to my heart.

But as the new millennium moved along I arrived at yet another major turning point. In 2001, three months before 9/11, I turned 70, and my daughter Grace arranged what was inevitably for me a rather ambiguous celebration. Around this time, at another party on the Cape, I greeted a friend and contemporary of mine, the psychiatrist-turned-painter David Sheinberg. "Hi, David," I said. "How've you been? You're looking great."

"I've been fine," he replied, as the ritual decrees. "You're looking great, too," and then we chatted for a bit about how our work was going, etc., typical artist chitchat. "By the way, Budd," he said, "you know there are three ages of man: there's Youth, there's Middle Age, and there's 'You're Looking Great.'"

Sadly, David Sheinberg, a happy, enthusiastic late convert to painting, died a few years later, though I remember him fondly for many reasons apart from his wonderful joke.

In my "Looking Great" later years (the phrase "Old Age" is taboo) I've tried to tie up as many loose ends in my life as possible. I've had a long time to mull over my childhood, and as I wrote earlier, neither my siblings nor I have any glamorous or lurid mistreatments to report. Since all three of us strongly felt our parents' unconditional love and support, they had obviously done a fine job of putting a solid floor under us. None of us grew up emotionally damaged by the occasional toxicity of either my mother's crippling panoply of fears and phobias or my father's racism and anti-Semitism. Looking back, I realize that my parents were extremely conservative in the old-fashioned "clan" sense of the word. Perhaps "tribal" says it better. Essentially they protected their own and had little understanding – and in Dad's case more than a little contempt – for people outside the tribe, such as gays, recent immigrants, African-Americans, and Jews whom, in the 1950s and 1960s, were often referred to as "sissies," "hunkies," or worse – as sometimes in Dad's case, "kikes." It seems to me that, apart from their family units safely ensconced inside their castles, too many conservatives seem to lack the gift of empathy, and xenophobia is as endemic to their beliefs as it is to the right wing of the Republican Party. (The current argument over "illegal aliens" is an excellent example of conservative xenophobia.)

Liberals, on the other hand, generally have a gift of empathy that extends far beyond the tribe into which they were born, and I believe that this special gift is due to their greater aptitude for imaginative thinking of every kind. The simple ability to feel one's way into another's mind and heart is a quality that seems to have become atrophied in many conservatives I've known. In the light of all this I've come to have more insight into my parents than I did in my college years, and I can see that through no fault of their own they were the products of an earlier, narrower, less liberal and therefore less understanding time.

But there is one other aspect of my upbringing that I've recently come to terms with: my father's initial opposition to my becoming an artist. As I look back now, I realize that certain conventional phrases that children often hear from their parents were absent in our home. I never remember hearing either of my parents say, "You should try to be a leader, not a follower," or "Whatever your life goal is, you can achieve it," or "Above all, you should follow your dreams." These and other typically uplifting clichés were never uttered during my childhood, not because my father avoided timeworn clichés but because he preferred us to be obedient rather than independent and to follow *his* dream rather than our own. I'm sure that he thought his plans for his children were superior to anything we could come up with, but I'm saddened that he never once asked me if I *wanted* to work in, and eventually take over, his car dealership. It was automatically assumed that, like my brother, I would also enter the family business, selling Dodge automobiles for the rest of my life, with no other career in mind.

It's a simple observation I've only recently made – another sign of how slowly I catch on to the obvious – but the fact is that Dad was, at heart, an army man, a retired colonel who was used to giving orders and never discussing things with the people under him. It would never have occurred to him to have an intimate talk with me about what I might like to do with my life because he had my life already mapped out. My two siblings more or less followed orders in their life choices, but I was insubordinate and went my own way. Ultimately, I believe that my independence was the real source of the lingering problems between my father and me, far more so than the fact that I held different political views from his.

I remember one characteristic incident in late 1945 or early '46, when Dad had been back only a few months from almost five years of army service. He was sitting downstairs, drink in hand, when he told me to get him something from another room. A few minutes later came another such command – these were not requests – and sometime later he told me to get him something from his upstairs bedroom. I had been trying to read during this flurry of orders and I did not like the way I was being treated. As I ascended the stairs, I turned to him and said, "You know, I'm your son, not your orderly." He looked temporarily chagrined but didn't answer. In the days after this incident however, Dad's commands generally eased off into politer requests, often including the word "please" before spelling out what he wanted.

Interestingly, my brother's wife more than once told me that she had always been afraid of her father-in-law, and it is my guess that my brother, who worked under Dad for years at his car dealership, must have had a rather rough time with his father as his boss. To paraphrase another old cliché, you can take the boy out of the army but you can never take the army out of the boy.

If these were some of the insights into the past that I gained in my "You're looking great years," a mighty change in my life would begin in the new millennium when I met journalist and author Leslie Kean. Leslie had been a producer and on-air host for a leading investigative news program on radio station KPFA in Berkeley, California, but before that she'd spent time in Burma (aka Myanmar to the ruling junta) covering that country's appalling regime and interviewing Aung San Suu Kyi, the Peace Nobelist who had for years been held under house arrest. By 1999 Leslie had become interested in the UFO phenomenon, and since then has become its leading investigative journalist, publishing serious, probing pieces in the *Boston Globe*, the *Providence Journal*, and the *Sacramento Bee*, as well as through her many credited contributions to the broadly distributed national wire services. When we first met at a UFO conference where I was speaking, Leslie, attending as a press observer, told me of her deep interest in the Linda Cortile case I'd written about in *Witnessed.* As we talked, I found her to be extremely intelligent, well informed, intensely focused on the UFO phenomenon in general, and curious to learn more about the physical evidence for UFO abduction reports. Our relationship began as one of colleagues, and continued in that relatively neutral vein for years before it gradually became more romantic for both of us.

Leslie is a trim, attractive, petite woman with a mass of short, curly, dark blonde hair and beautiful, steady blue eyes. She often wears neat black jackets, pants suits, and distinctive, oval-lens glasses that together lend her an official, no-nonsense demeanor and conceal her more adventuresome, unconventional nature. It was this latter side of her that I slowly began to discover.

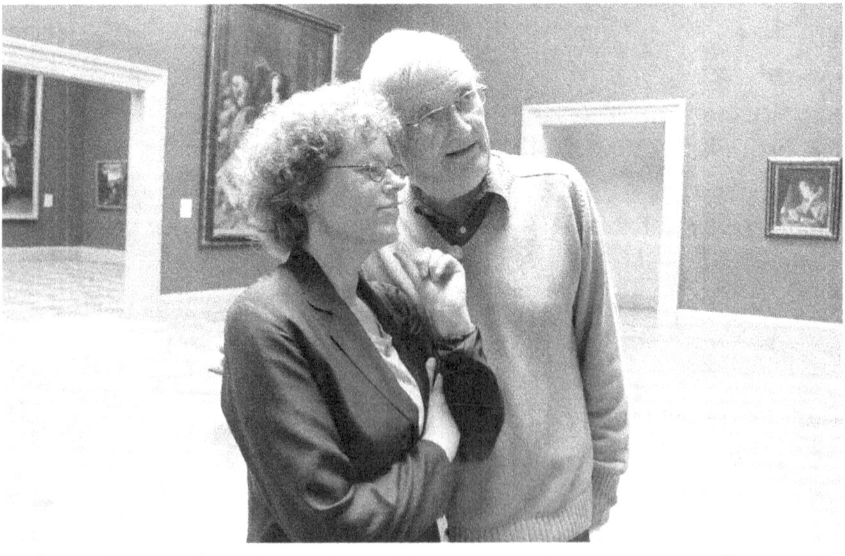

Leslie and I at the Metropolitan Museum, gazing at a great Caravaggio. Photo: Tim Coleman.

One additional fact about Leslie is that she is descended from two historically important American families. On her mother's side, she is the great, great – many greats – granddaughter of the famous abolitionist William Lloyd Garrison, and her grandfather, lawyer Lloyd K. Garrison, represented J. Robert Oppenheimer in the fight over his security clearance during the reign of the bloodthirsty Joseph McCarthy. Family memories include the story of an intimate party at her grandparents' New York apartment when the six guests were Eleanor Roosevelt, J. Robert Oppenheimer, Edward R. Murrow, the president of Sarah Lawrence College, and Leslie's parents. It was one of those times when, if you're sensible, you just sit down, close your mouth, and listen.

On Leslie's father's side, her uncle, Thomas Kean, was a recent governor of New Jersey and later co-chairman of the national 9/11 Commission. Her father, Hamilton Fish Kean is an active environmentalist with the National Resources Defense Council (NRDC), but carries the name of his cousin, Congressman Hamilton Fish, an implacable opponent of Roosevelt's New Deal. I was pleased to learn that today most of Leslie's distinguished family are committed Democrats, and even the most notable exception, former Governor Tom Kean, belongs to the moderate wing of the Republican Party. Ideologically, I felt right at home.

When we first traveled together, Leslie was not experienced in looking at paintings or sculpture, but in a very short time I discovered that she had a remarkable eye and exquisite visual taste. Visiting the museums of Paris and wandering into the Cezanne gallery at the Musee D'Orsay, she instinctively spotted the finest Cezanne in the room (*Le Pont De Maincy*) and bypassed the more routine examples. She did this again and again in room after room. In a museum in Sydney, Australia, she noticed, off in a corner, a modest still life that she told me she thought was especially beautiful. The painting was by Georgio Morandi, a relatively obscure Italian artist whose work only a fine eye and exceptional taste might notice. And so it went. Our years together have been filled with love, and at this late stage in my life I am thankful beyond words that we have become a couple in so many profound ways.

On the larger stage of national life I am also deeply thankful for our country's health and sanity as evinced by the voters' miraculous choice of Barack Obama to be our president. For the first time in many decades we've received the gift of a calm, brilliant, balanced individual as our national leader, and within our historically racist country, we seem to have overcome the past by electing, with a large majority, a man of African-American parentage. Obama's elevation to the presidency, after centuries of bigotry, lynchings, and crushing racism, announces what I see as a new openness and genuine freedom in America, and I wonder, were my father alive today, if he might not gracefully accept the country's rejection of the politics he espoused and some of the social mores by which he lived so many years ago. It's a hope – perhaps a fantasy – that I choose to cling to.

But if the state of our nation is at last on its way to health and sanity, I find the state of the art world in millennium America to be extremely discouraging. The serious kind of painting for which I've lived has taken a distant second place to, among other things, performance art, installations, pop, tongue-in-cheek irony, works made from bizarre materials, and assertive political images beating the drums for causes like gay rights, feminism, and the peace movement. I am not interested in the latter kinds of politically motivated art, not because these causes are no longer worthy but because I believe the fight for them is so much more effectively joined in other venues. Feminist art works made of used menstrual materials can shock or repel, but they hardly help to eliminate the disparity between the wages paid men and women for the same work.

At the present time, the kind of painting I and my fellow artists have made for decades seems not enough to hold the attention of most art reviewers and critics. For example, a work by the fashionable British artist Damian Hirst, consisting of a dead shark suspended in a transparent box of formaldehyde, offers a lot more shocking pizzazz for the art writers' imaginations than does a traditional oil painting, and to prove my point, Hirst's dead shark now floats in a tank at no less august an institution as New York's Metropolitan Museum where it has received a great deal of critical attention while taking up an inordinate amount of space. At the least, I guess, Hirst's piece is breaking new ground because no one has ever before used a dead shark as the centerpiece of an artwork, a situation for which we can all be thankful.

As for me, I continue painting and collaging offshoots of my earlier Guardians and am quite pleased by what I've been producing. Occasionally I even sell something, but for me the commercial art world is not as emotionally rewarding as it used to be, mainly because I have so little interest in most of the competition. However, with Leslie and her discerning eye for the best of my work, I'm assured of both an excellent in-house critic and a genuinely appreciative audience.

The UFO situation is, for me, far healthier at the present time than is the art world. First, it's personally gratifying to know that the information I published in my four books on UFO encounters has made its way around the world and is now accepted by virtually all abduction researchers as comprising the basic scenario of the phenomenon. I'm not so happy, however, about the nature of these ominous discoveries; in fact, the opposite is true, but I'm not alone in this ambivalence about my own work. In a recent magazine article, Malcolm Jones makes this statement about Charles Darwin and his theory of evolution: "As delighted as he was with his discovery, Darwin was equally horrified, because he understood the consequence of his theory. Mankind was no longer the culmination of life but merely part of it; creation was mechanistic and purposeless. In a letter to a fellow scientist, Darwin wrote that confiding his theory was 'like confessing a murder.'" I understand that feeling all too well.

Nevertheless, the discoveries I've made and published over the past 27 years collectively provide the foundation upon which abduction research has been built and I am (ambivalently) proud to have assembled so many substantial timbers for that basic floor. In saying that I'm also aware that patting oneself on the back can easily dislocate a shoulder, but for this book, the telling of my life story, I'm willing to take that risk.

A parallel accomplishment of which I'm proud is the establishment of *IF*, the Intruders Foundation, a not-for-profit organization I founded in 1989, with a four-fold mission statement: to offer support to those who report abduction experiences; to gather more information about UFO abductions through further investigation; to present the public with the mounting evidence for its reality; and to train a cadre of younger people to do the work I've been doing. Because of its all-volunteer make-up, *IF* has only been partially successful in these massive endeavors, but we have tried. Our successes, though not as frequent as we might have wished, have been gratifying to me and to all of our loyal staff members.

As with the New York art world in the 1950s and 1960s, over the years I've met many people in UFO research who have become dear friends and highly respected colleagues. David Jacobs has been foremost among them in both categories, but there are many others, too many to name. Leslie Kean, because of her journalistic skills and her work with a coalition of high level contacts around the world, has shown herself to be a leading participant, and in November 2007, in cooperation with filmmaker James Fox, she put together one of the most significant public events in modern UFO history. She and Fox assembled, in Washington, D.C., a sterling panel of some fourteen retired officials and military men from seven countries for a National Press Club press conference in which each man gave a brief description of his personal UFO encounter or his work in a

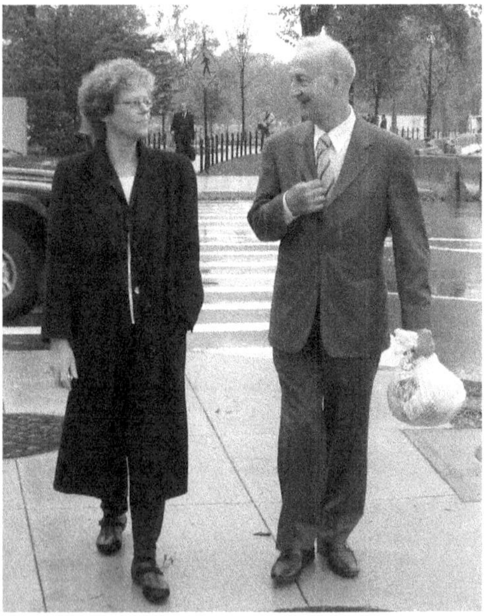

Leslie Kean and Iranian General Parviz Jafari in Washington D.C., after the landmark 2007 international press conference. Photo: Bernard Thouanel.

government unit charged with UFO investigations. The panel included, among others, two retired generals, one from Belgium and the other from Iran, a former deputy base commander from a joint American-British air base, two senior airline pilots who encountered large UFOs while in flight, the former governor of Arizona, and a retired British Ministry of Defense officer who ran the British UFO desk for several years.

One witness, a retired Commandante from the Peruvian Air Force, described how, in 1981, he had been ordered up to intercept a UFO hovering over an important military base. He vividly described a kind of dogfight in broad daylight, witnessed by personnel on the ground below, in which he fired his guns directly at the craft, to no avail. Similarly, General Parviz Jafari, then a major in the Shah's air force, was sent up in 1976 to intercept a large UFO hovering over Teheran, and he, too, became involved in a kind of aerial dogfight. Because of the UFO's evasive maneuvers he was unable to fire his missiles, but the entire episode was followed by ground- and air-based radar. When Jafari landed, he was debriefed by high ranking Iranian Air Force officials and also, surprisingly, by a colonel in the U.S. Air Force. The final U. S. Defense Intelligence Agency report on this extraordinary case, secured through the Freedom of Information Act, recounts Jafari's "dogfight" in detail, and in its conclusion states that copies were sent to the Joint Chiefs of Staff, the CIA, and the White House.

The media response to this unparalleled press conference was extensive. CNN covered the event, *Larry King Live* devoted an entire program to a panel of its witnesses, and wire services such as Reuters and Agence France-Presse sent accounts on to many of the world's newspapers. In a deliberately conservative strategy the panel speakers simply presented their personal accounts without assumptions as to the nature of the phenomenon, while at the same time inviting the U.S. Government to join in a cooperative effort to make that discovery. The hypothesis that UFOs were extraterrestrial spacecraft – based on the evidence, an eminently logical deduction – was left to the individual members of the press to ponder.

In 2008, as I write these words, disturbing UFO incidents continue to be reported, but as yet the United Sates government has publicly taken no action. However, Leslie's organization, the Coalition for Freedom of Information (CFi), has prepared a major international declaration urging the U.S. government to open an official investigation into the UFO phenomenon and to share its data with the investigatory bodies of countries such as France and the U.K. Presently the signatories to this declaration include generals (seven so far), scientists, airline pilots, and high-ranking military and civilian officials from some fourteen countries. John Podesta, whom President-Elect Obama named as head of his transition team, has been a strong supporter of Leslie's leadership with the CFi and her work with the Freedom of Information Act, so I'm hopeful that this new, international declaration will soon be considered at the very highest level of government.

Part Four: A Few Final Thoughts

Cape Cod and New York

THE TWO PLACES I'VE CALLED HOME for more than 50 years – Manhattan Island and the far end of Cape Cod – could not be more dissimilar, with rolling dunes, pine woods, and open space on the Cape, and in New York, cement, noise and excitement, and people everywhere, late and hurrying. But Manhattan, as it's been described thousands of times before by fellow refugees from the more benighted parts of the country, is a place where it's almost impossible to be bored. Even a short stroll in my teeming Chelsea neighborhood yields new and surprising sights, though when I moved here in the mid-1950s, some of these surprises were not the most welcome sort. The truth is that for decades Chelsea had been a semi-slum. Maybe not so semi.

So it was not unusual one night, many years ago, when I returned home very late after spending a grueling four hours at the Cedar Bar gassing and drinking with friends, and came upon two policemen in front of my building. The sozzled crew of a freighter berthed at a nearby pier had had a brawl, I learned the next day, and most of them had fled before the cops arrived. One sailor – the slowest of the group, perhaps – was being held prisoner in a unique way. The cops had folded each of his arms around a lamppost and then handcuffed his hands together on the other side. A clever ploy, I decided, unless the man was able to shinny up a twenty-foot lamppost. A second sailor lay on his stomach, half on the sidewalk and half in the gutter, moaning softly, and one of the cops brusquely told him to keep still or he'd be dead. I noticed, then, that a long knife was sticking out of the middle of his back.

"An ambulance is coming," the cop said, "so stop squirming."

Then the first officer turned to me – there was no one else anywhere near the scene – and told me to move along, as if I were a one-man jostling crowd. I fished out my keys and let myself into the apartment building, aware of the thin, distant siren of an approaching ambulance. Crime over, perp arrested, victim attended to, so now to bed. Chelsea, way back then.

Since that rough and tumble time the neighborhood has been gentrified, pacified, and changed into a safe but hyperactive ginza for gay life in the city. That means lots of expensive men's wear boutiques, well-attended gyms, restaurants and sidewalk cafes about six to the block, and a number of gay bars, advertised as such. (No secrecy or euphemisms necessary.) There are also, of course, a few intriguing specialty shops – porn palaces and tattoo parlors that feature body piercing. Next door to my studio there was, for years, a fetish clothing shop popular with transvestites and called the Purple Passion Flower. It was rumored to be one of the few places in Manhattan where you could get a leather-and-vinyl Little-Bo-Peep outfit in a 40 long. The shop eventually moved and was replaced by Maroons, an excellent restaurant, which unfortunately has just closed, a victim of the economic downturn. The space is now for rent.

Appearing on the streets of Chelsea, among buff men in muscle shirts who walk hand in hand, and shaved-headed, tattoo-bedecked S&M enthusiasts who troll ominously, is a surprising assortment of attractive young women. So whatever one's sexual preference, our sidewalks offer something interesting to gaze upon.

And if all of this comprises local color, the spectacle of *real* color, oil color, is available to me seven days a week: at the Metropolitan Museum and the Whitney, the Guggenheim and the Frick, Tuesdays through Sundays, while the Museum of Modern Art is now also open on Mondays. My neighborhood has also become the current center for commercial art galleries clustered near the Chelsea Piers, an escapist mecca only four or five blocks from my studio. Since moments of pure outdoor solitude are difficult to find in New York, I go to the Piers often to sit out over the water and gaze at the massive, slowly moving Hudson River. However, in my studio, located at the back of the building and away from street noises, I have all the quiet and the privacy I need to make my art, and in my visits to the Metropolitan Museum I have often found myself alone in a quiet gallery with four great Vermeers to lend me the sense of calm

I need.

On a mild afternoon I may buy some fresh-squeezed orange juice at the Chelsea Market and take it out to the end of one of the Piers where I can sit quietly, sipping the golden ichor and gazing at the contradictory currents in the Hudson, the burgeoning skyline of New Jersey, and the distant Statue of Liberty – the inspiring symbol George Bush had almost turned into a travesty. When I was first diagnosed with cancer the Chelsea Piers is where I went to contemplate what my future would bring and to memorize the glories of a river view I thought I might never get to see again.

Thinking about my New York and Cape Cod homes, I recall an ancient story about a tourist from Missouri who finds himself in a tiny, picturesque Maine village. Enchanted, he goes into a wide-porched general store, maneuvers past the cracker barrels, and approaches the elderly man behind the counter.

"Are you the proprietor?" he asks, and the man answers, "Eyah."

"Your town is wonderful," the visitor says. "A real jewel in these modern times. Have you lived here all your life?"

"Not yet," the old man answers.

I feel that way as I ponder all my years in Wellfleet and New York and hope for more.

As I write these words it is a late August morning in Wellfleet, and after a foggy start the sun has finally begun to show itself, the whitish sky becoming a sweet blue. Earlier, at about 5:00 a.m., I was awakened from a peaceful sleep by the yipping howl of a lone coyote whose cry was instantly taken up by a keening chorus of its fellow predators. The pack was close, possibly lurking in the marshy underbrush between my house and the bay, and seemed to be celebrating something – the killing of a neighbor's careless housecat, perhaps. As usual, the coyotes' dissonant yowling lasted only a minute or so and then abruptly ceased, as if an off switch had been thrown. The predawn silence resumed but I was left with the uneasy feeling that all was not right with world, certainly not the safety of small, vulnerable animals like the rabbits, squirrels, and stray dogs and cats that provide these stalkers their meager feasts.

In the gray light just before daybreak, when the coyotes began their tuneless wail, I could see that a mist had settled out over the marsh and wondered what combination of temperature and wind and sunlight the day might bring. The Cape is like that – supremely changeable. Years ago, my friend the painter Steve Pace was talking to another artist about ideal places to live. Like me, Steve was spending his summers on the Cape and the rest of the time in New York, but his friend, who had recently settled in Southern California, was urging him to move there.

"You'll love it," he said. "Southern California has a great climate."

"That's the problem," Steve replied. "I don't like climate. I like weather."

Weather is what we have on the Cape, in abundance. It's a feature of New York, too, a city that could never be described as having "a climate." Unlike some parts of the world, both Cape Cod and New York have four distinct seasons, spring, summer, autumn, and winter, instead of Southern California's blurred variations on one pleasant but uninspiring season.

Swimming conditions at the Cape's ocean and bay beaches are as unpredictable as the weather itself: bathtub-warm one day and ice-cold the next, as well as being uncomfortably shallow and malodorous during certain unusually low tides. Some ocean beaches are difficult of access because of their high, cliff-like dunes, while a few bay beaches are only a matter of yards from the main roads. Despite this range of advantages and serious obstacles, there are many blessed times when everything – tide, water temperature, and warm, abundant sunshine – comes together to make a balmy, flawless paradise. One never knows. The sun can be shining brilliantly on the Wellfleet surf while a drizzling rain is drenching the Truro beaches four miles away. But after all, it's the weather, not the climate that makes things exciting.

At various times in my life I've bathed at beautiful tropical islands with white sand and turquoise water, in warm, steady climates, and have come to think that these easy, welcoming beaches, in contrast to their counterparts on the Cape, are like lush, compliant women who yield themselves without resistance to every suntanned tourist who wanders by. On Cape Cod, however, we have to use our wiles, our sagacity, because the shoreline, beautiful as it can be, is not there to seduce us. Like determined suitors, if we plan carefully, check the tide charts and nourish our hopes, the sunning and the swimming can satisfy the soul and all the senses. The challenges and the rewards of the place provide many of the reasons we keep coming back for more.

EARLIER I'VE DESCRIBED my first summer in Provincetown, in 1956, but in her childhood, Joan Rich, my first wife, preceded me there. Toward the end of World War II she spent a month or so with the Beal family in their little summer cottage in Truro located in a dell below the high dune on which the painter Edward Hopper had built his sturdy but modest combination house and studio. One day, Joan recalled, she and her girlfriend Linda Beal decided they wanted to make paper dolls and design clothes for them, but they had no paper to work with. The nearest store was miles away, but Linda suddenly had an idea: since the old man at the top of the hill was an artist, he would surely have some spare paper around. All they would have to do would be to walk up to his house and ask for a sheet or two and he would give it to them.

Unfortunately there were two things about Edward Hopper that the little girls didn't know: that he was only a notch or two away from full hermit-hood, and that he was also notoriously tight-fisted. In their innocence Joan and Linda climbed the hill and knocked on the kitchen door. Jo Hopper, his voluble wife, opened it, and when the girls explained what they needed, she summoned the great man himself. Hopper was then well over six feet tall (it was only in his later years that he became quite bent over with a serious back problem) so he appeared to the children as a tall, scowling, intimidating presence. When Linda and Joan asked him for paper for paper dolls, he answered brusquely: "The only paper I have is watercolor paper and it costs me 75 cents a sheet and you can't have any." With that he closed the door, leaving the two disappointed and frightened children to walk back down the hill empty-handed.

Joan told me this story early in our marriage, and it stayed in my mind because it seemed so like the man and his severe, ungenerous art. If Matisse seems to be giving you the gift of his glorious, seductive color, Edward Hopper, by contrast, is content to pull you down into his stark world of loneliness and isolation, and one day, when I happened to mention him to my friends Nora Speyer and Sideo Fromboluti, they both described Hopper as "having a dead hand." He was also a rigid conservative, and Robert Motherwell once told me a depressing story about an experience with Hopper when the two were the sole jurors for a local art exhibition. At the outset, Hopper wanted to reject *all* abstract paintings from consideration, and then went on to suggest that his wife, an occasional painter in her husband's style, should be awarded first prize. Robert said that they argued fiercely until they reached some sort of armed truce about the show's selections and prizes, but he was so put off by the old man's rigidity that he vowed never again to serve on a jury with him.

And yet for many reasons I like Hopper's work, particularly his fresher, more painterly watercolors. *Nighthawks*, a desolate scene of a nearly empty diner and one of his masterpieces, has achieved a unique kind of popularity. Like the film *Casablanca* but for very different reasons, *Nighthawks* has become an icon for people of every level of sophistication, and like the film has the genuine respect of serious critics and historians as well as the general public. Again, no small feat.

Joan's story about her childhood visit to Hopper's studio was to have an awkward reprise. In 1964, we attended the Hopper retrospective at the Whitney Museum, the last major exhibition of his work before his death in 1967. We approached him as he sat among his admirers, noticing that in honor of the occasion his usually glowering face bore the merest trace of a smile. When our turn came, we greeted him to offer our congratulations, and I mentioned that Joan and I also summered in Truro in a studio not far from his. I said that she had been friends with his neighbors, the Beals, and then, fatally forgetting its outcome, I began to relate the story of her trip with Linda to his studio in search of paper doll materials.

I felt Joan give my foot a kick, but I blathered on until I suddenly remembered the denouement – that this was an insulting tale in which Hopper appeared as a cold-hearted miser.

He was watching me carefully, and as I approached the end of the story I was desperately trying to think of a way to give it a positive spin. In panic, I felt as if I was lying across the railroad tracks and an express train of my own devising was bearing down on me. At the very last moment I changed the story's ending, and told Hopper that he *gave* the girls a piece of expensive watercolor paper and that they were very grateful.

"Nope!" he said with finality. "I never gave those little girls any watercolor paper." It was as if at 83 he actually remembered a trivial incident that occurred decades before. After this denial of a charitable act I'd tried to ascribe to him, he turned to other people who were waiting to shake his hand, thus giving Joan and me a chance to wander off, relieved and astonished. Did Hopper have so few visitors that a twenty-year-old encounter with two little girls begging paper stood out vividly, or did he just know that, considering his miserliness, he would never have given his paper away, particularly to children who would waste it to make paper dolls? I'll never know, but either way his reply remained completely in character.

UNLIKE NEW YORK, the Cape is a place where moments of solitude easily shade into long minutes or even hours of contemplative peace. Though there is, as I've said, an active art world in Provincetown and a constant drizzle of cocktail parties, gallery openings, and dinners with friends, one can easily step outside these social observances and be alone, working in the studio, lolling on the beach, walking in the woods, or just lying around in a hammock, thinking.

A few days ago Leslie and I went into the Wellfleet woods for a walk and then a late-afternoon swim. Slough Pond lay smooth and mirror-like, and the sun, shining down through the dense foliage of the oaks and pines, left pools of cool shadow and brilliant golden light wherever it fell. Everything was still, and apart from our slow, quiet pace along the narrow path, these quivering, abstract patches of sunlight were the only moving things we saw. Walking beside her, I felt that Leslie's lithe, graceful body was informing me with the meditative peace of the Buddhism she once practiced, and in the powerful grasp of nature I became as contemplative and as silent as she.

After a while I decided to return to the lake and to sit for a while at the water's edge, while she continued her walk. Because Slough Pond is ringed with dense trees and underbrush, there are only a few landings, and the one I chose was sandy and very narrow. I sat with my feet at the place the water met the sand and tried to turn myself into Thoreau, meditating at Walden Pond. But since my busy mind is always churning away, helplessly absorbing trivia and everything else I see and remember, it takes an enormous effort to slow it down. For me, true meditation is almost impossible. Franz Kline once said something about half the world wanting to sit quietly by Walden Pond while the other half wants to be part of the traffic on the way to Boston. He chose to be part of the traffic, and I'm afraid his decision was also mine, a city-bred man who has spent most of his life in noisy, un-Walden-like places. After all, if Art is what Nature isn't, then, sadly, a painter can never be Thoreau.

As I sat at the edge of the pond, musing on these things, I noticed a school of tiny, almost transparent fish hovering in extremely shallow water only a few inches away from my feet. As a way of diverting my thoughts, I focused my attention on this dense little cluster and saw that they were staying within an area illuminated by bright sunlight, as if dependent upon its warmth. Since each little fish cast its own dark shadow on the sandy bottom a finger's length away, the miniature school appeared to have twice its number of members. Suddenly a bigger fish, one perhaps five or six inches long, shot from the deeper water into the center of the frantic school, scattering it wildly. In the blink of an eye the marauder rocketed off, and the miniature school instantly reassembled itself with, I assumed, one less member, for such is the violence of nature. As Annie Dillard put it, "it's rough out there and chancy is no surprise. Every live thing is a survivor on a kind of emergency bivouac."

A few minutes later, when the bigger fish made a flashing return, once more disrupting the school and retreating in an instant, I assumed that the cluster of tiny fishlets had just lost another. Within this one small pond, I guessed, teeming thousands of these miniature creatures must be successfully hatched from their eggs each year so that at least a few can survive and reproduce. This sheer, profligate waste of life permeates every aspect of creation and made me think, with an edge of anger, of the evangelicals' self-serving anti-choice slogan, "Reverence for Life" – as if they thought God would be shocked and depressed every time a big fish took the life of a smaller one.

I cheered myself up by watching a few honey bees making quick dips into the white blossoms of a dense, weedy bush next to me, while on the sandy ground between my feet two small insects flitted about passionately, one jumping on top of the other in what I took to be a buggy mating ritual. I couldn't be sure, because instead the insect might be trying to kill its rival. Nature is like that, too, entangling the faces and acts of hatred and love as confusingly as often happens in human relationships.

When I gazed back over the calm surface of the pond, I was captivated by the way an almost imperceptible breeze caused a flow of even rivulets to pass as if by magic through a vertical array of reeds, none of which wavered even an invisible inch. I was reminded of the flow of electricity moving at nearly the speed of light with no affect on its conduits. As I sat there, absorbed in this quiet panorama, I heard voices approaching. Four people, neither young nor old, were opening their beach towels and settling down in the roughly eight-foot wide sandy space just behind me. It was barely big enough for the five of us, and though I was facing away, I was uncomfortably aware of their presence.

Then one of the men spoke to me, his voice gentle and understanding. "I'm sorry we're interrupting your solitude," he said, and I appreciated the sensitivity of his concern.

"That's all right," I replied. "There's plenty of solitude here for all of us."

Soul Map

In 1993 my friend the psychohistorian Robert J. Lifton published a book entitled *The Protean Self: Human Resilience in an Age of Fragmentation*, in which he dealt with the drastic and often-confusing changes humans undergo in our multi-layered modern era. "We are becoming fluid and many-sided," he wrote. "Without quite realizing it, we have been evolving a sense of self appropriate to the restlessness and flux of our time… I have named [this mode of being] as the 'protean self' after Proteus, the Greek god of many forms." Though Lifton's definition of the protean self sounds a lot like my description of our modern collage-like existence, he stresses the radical, often sequential life changes that so many of us undergo as the result of profound cultural upheavals: "The protean self emerges from confusion, from the widespread feeling that we are losing our psychological moorings. We feel ourselves buffeted about by unmanageable historical forces and social uncertainties."

I am aware that many people may be shape-shifters like Proteus, who, in the *Odyssey* first takes "on a whiskered lion's shape,/ a serpent's then; a leopard; a great boar;/ then sousing water; then a tall green tree," one new self tumbling after and completely replacing another. But the complex, modern existence that I described in my mid-1970s article on the Collage Esthetic was more the process of continuously grafting new roles and interests upon one's already well-established, stable self, rather than a radical *swapping* of one life role for another. Unlike Proteus, one doesn't change from a serpent into a tree, but rather *adds* a new skill to one's preexisting abilities, much as learning a second language enriches and complicates but does not obliterate one's first.

Bob Lifton and I had several discussions about the differences between protean adoptions to radically new life conditions and my notion of an ever-expanding self in which little need be given up along the way. However, I was left wondering about the seemingly disparate roles I was currently occupying as painter, sculptor, UFO investigator, *de facto* therapist, writer, teacher, and all the rest. So, one summer day on the Cape I decided to examine just how the pieces fitted together.

New York City is not an easy setting for introspective thinking of any kind. Too many truck horns, fire sirens, jackhammers, too many giggling revelers, shouting waiters, and everywhere on the street, cell phoners mindlessly yakking. By comparison, the sounds of summer on Cape Cod are blessedly different: melodic birdsong, humming insects, gently rolling surf, and at home, the low, aromatic bubbling of coffee brewing in a sunlit kitchen. And so it was there, on a typical August afternoon several years ago, as I was lolling in the hammock and musing over my complex life, that I made an attempt to map my soul.

I would conjure up the various aspects of my many-sided life to see how – or if – they might present a kind of harmonious unity. In my sense of the phrase, "soul map" stands for the delineation – the process of marking out, disentangling – the various essential drives and yearnings that collectively make up one's humanity. Not surprisingly the process took quite a while. I had to leave the hammock several times on each of several days just to wander around and reflect on my inner terrain, but gradually things began to come into focus. From the beginning I realized that each element I considered had a subjective aspect – the need to express something powerful within me – *and* an objective result. It is as if each particular need was only satisfied by real-life behavior of some sort.

I began by musing about my basic moral code – essentially, the way I've treated my fellow human beings throughout my life – and it was here that I thought once more of its origin as part of my father's legacy. He had always been generous and supportive, a loving father and a noble example for me in many ways. It also struck me that my occasional anger at him, my profound disappointment at his moments of racism and anti-Semitism, had partly to do with my realization that he was violating his own otherwise admirable moral code. By exempting African-Americans and Jews and others from his usual sense of fairness and tolerance, he was temporarily condemning himself in my eyes. I was also aware that I was born of a very different time than my father and that I had benefited from an important advantage that, as a child, he had lacked: a stable, generous family environment. But at their core I had taken Dad's ethical standards, his fair and respectful treatment of (most) others, his basic honesty and sense of responsibility for his children, as my own. It's even possible that my liberalism and hatred of bigotry are in part a response to the narrow but glaring gaps in my father's tolerance of others, and are thus, in some weirdly convoluted way, another positive aspect of his legacy.

Though I am far from immune from the many petty, selfish, evasive, and irresponsible things that most of us do from time to time, a firm set of interlocking esthetic and ethical standards have long occupied a central area on my interior chart.

I've described how, as a child physically limited by the aftereffects of polio, I used my wits and imagination to entertain, to create, and to give something new to my family and friends. Because my parents and siblings were not particularly gifted in the imagination department, I could supply that kind of essential resource through my childish art and creative play. And so I thought of the paintings I was currently producing as an adult – especially the Guardians – as collectively the result of my need to *add energy* to the world, to quicken the slow, to excite the passive, to animate the melancholy. It is through my paintings that I've been able to make an independent gift of the same enlivening qualities that I was able as a child to give to my family. Thus, one of the largest territories on my soul map is the gift of energy – imaginative energy – made manifest in the art, the paintings, and sculpture I've produced throughout my life.

Since color has always been a dominant means of creating energy and a central issue in my painting, I cherish something I once read about Henri Matisse, one of the greatest colorists who ever lived. A friend of his was ill and confined to the hospital. Matisse arrived to visit him, carrying a large, glorious painting, which he propped up on a chair next to his friend's sickbed. "Here," he said,

"I'll leave this for a while to help you heal. When you are well and at home you can return it to me." Then he left and naturally his friend recovered.

From one point of view there is more than a touch of hubris in such an attitude, but to me it seems not only innocent but a quality present in most of us who truly trust our painting. So, on my inner map, beside a particular moral core at its center, the need to add to the quotient of life's vitality through my painting takes the largest place.

Next, I thought about another, very different area: my abiding curiosity, my need to *know*, to tell the false from the true. Instead of an esthetic hunger, this is more the quest of the scientist, the investigator. It is, properly, an inborn intellectual need that has been with me ever since I was a child, lying on the sunlit grass, wondering where the sky ended and what lay behind it, torturing myself with the notion of infinity. This same innate curiosity fueled my ever-deepening doubts about the existence of God, as well as my everyday interest in how things worked and what they were made of.

Though strong, this generalized inquisitiveness lay relatively dormant in me until August of 1964 when I saw that strange, maneuvering craft in the sky over Cape Cod. As I've written, my quasi-scientific curiosity suddenly focused itself and blossomed, eventually adding a major role to my life. The UFO sighting had, as it were, dumped in my lap a mass of major ontological and scientific questions that I was unable to ignore. Like it or not, I found myself using every means at my disposal to find the truth about a phenomenon already contaminated by official ridicule and mindless rumor but which also contained potentially staggering new information. In the light of all this I had to become, at least part-time, an investigator, a detective, an untrained but avid user of the scientific method.

All of this, of course, was a million miles away from my role as a painter, my sense of having a place in the rich, ongoing stream of art history. But this new quest for scientific truth delineated yet another very different area in my soul map, taking its place beside those that were already there in much the same way that acquiring skill with a word processor coexists with the ability to write gracefully with a pen. Since 1964, then, scientific curiosity and the disciplined practice of rational enquiry have occupied a third major territory.

In this context I thought of another aspect of UFO investigation, one that is entirely separate from the gathering of new information. Simple research, the accumulation of case reports, and the process of mining them for new patterns is very different from the more humane activity of working with UFO abductees to help them cope with their traumatizing experiences. This more personal interaction is, as I have said, a kind of *de facto* therapy for which there was no pre-existing method of treatment. I had had no formal training in psychotherapy, but again my childhood illnesses offered me a kind of common sense approach. My parents' reactions to my polio experience and the many ensuing months in which I was unable to walk, followed by my later serious childhood diseases, provided me with examples of how loving nurturance and understanding can keep one going. In particular, my mother's constant support and attention put a floor under me, enabling me, eventually, to recover my life and my hope for a normal future. Her nurturing behavior was built into my very bones, and so when, in my UFO work, I encountered depressed and frightened abductees, I instinctively sensed how to help them navigate a course of recovery and empowerment. Perhaps I felt I owed someone – society, perhaps – a payback for what my parents had so selflessly given me. But clearly this need to nurture and heal found its perfect outlet in the many hours over the years I've spent with abductees, trying to help them overcome the emotional scarring of their UFO experiences. This work of nurturance represents yet another territory on my soul map – again, not as a replacement for anything else, but as a fourth area, fully in harmony with the others.

Then I thought about my need to educate, to share what I've found valuable or true or amusing or important, and to make the ephemeral as clear and as precise as possible. It's this compulsion to teach that led me to publish critical articles on painting and sculpture – my own and others' – to lecture on the UFO phenomenon, the history of art, and other subjects; to write four books on UFO abductions; to make many television and radio appearances; and to teach painting at various institutions. If any of my interior territories threatened to get out of control and infect its neighbors or shade subtly over into hubris and arrogance, it has been my passionate drive to explain. It is this ambiguous asset that Gertrude Stein wittily nailed when she called the poet Ezra Pound a "village explainer," adding that this is "excellent if you are a village and if not, not."

It seems to me that the very act of writing this memoir, of trying to clarify in words my complex life, is a major example of "my need to make everything absolutely clear," as John Coplans said about my articles in *Artforum* magazine. Another time, during dinner at a Wellfleet restaurant with Leslie and her mother, Ellen Kean, I left the table for a moment, and Leslie, worried that I had been overly dominant in our conversation, asked her mother if she felt excluded or overpowered. "No," she replied after a thoughtful pause. "I think Budd just likes to impart information." This sweet, diplomatic answer, typical of Ellen's innate courtesy and affection, was a nice way of describing a village explainer who explained things a bit too incessantly.

Despite their inherent differences, it seems to me that these five different emotional/spiritual territories coexist amicably and perhaps bleed helpfully from one to another. I know that my soul map naturally contains, along with the more exotic zones I've been describing, many other, more familiar areas. Among them are the virtually universal drives, hungers, and emotions shared by most human beings, such as the love I feel for my new granddaughter, GiGi, and my daughter, Grace, and my pride at Grace's many accomplishments. There is also the affection and gratitude I have for so many friends and colleagues, and centrally the extraordinary bond I have with Leslie, my partner, my creative co-worker, and my fondest love. To sum it up, life, with all its many levels and complications, continues to be very good to me, and at my advanced age I am filled with sorrow that so little of it is left.

Unlike the Christian saints, Islamic martyrs, and Fundamentalist preachers, I do not believe in a literal afterlife, and I've seen little so far to suggest that consciousness survives death. Instead, as a humanist, I believe in a different kind of future existence. I have faith that I will survive through the many lives I've touched across so many decades; through the vital discoveries I've made in the study of extraterrestrial intelligence; and through the hundreds of works of art I've produced, which add beauty and energy to the only world any of us will ever know.

Index

www.ingramcontent.com/pod-product-compliance
Lightning Source LLC
Chambersburg PA
CBHW071246220526
45468CB00001B/20
9781933665412